William Wakefield

Our Life and Travels in India

William Wakefield

Our Life and Travels in India

ISBN/EAN: 9783337209421

Printed in Europe, USA, Canada, Australia, Japan

Cover: Foto ©Andreas Hilbeck / pixelio.de

More available books at **www.hansebooks.com**

AND

TRAVELS IN INDIA.

BY

W. WAKEFIELD, M.D.

LONDON:
SAMPSON LOW, MARSTON, SEARLE, & RIVINGTON,
CROWN BUILDINGS, FLEET STREET.

1878.

[All rights reserved.]

To

MY DEAR MOTHER,

AS A SLIGHT TOKEN OF

THE LOVING AFFECTION WITH WHICH SHE IS CHERISHED

BY ALL HER CHILDREN,

This Volume

IS AFFECTIONATELY DEDICATED

BY HER SON,

THE AUTHOR.

PREFACE.

THE following pages, descriptive of Indian scenes and character, as well as of our life in the far East for a period of two years, are written from memory, and from jottings in a diary, systematically kept by us during all our wanderings. I am indebted to the works on the principal cities of India, written by a distinguished member of the Civil Service, Mr. H. G. Keene, for much of my information with regard to the places visited. Elphinstone's *History of India*, Professor Williams's *Hinduism*, and other works of a similar character, were also consulted for accurate facts concerning the history, religions, and manners and customs of the natives.

Although originally intended merely as an extended record of our daily life in the country, as it progressed it began to assume larger proportions; and descriptions of places, people, character, religion, and other matters not immediately connected with a purely personal account of our movements, crept in. These coming under our own observation were naturally of great interest to ourselves; and on the supposition that they might prove so to others, I was tempted to

enlarge on the original plan, and enter more fully into In
topics, with which a previous extended residence, jo.
to the experience of later years, had made me fam:
Although not claiming for these pages the merit of a liter
work on Eastern matters for general publication, I ver.
to lay them before the indulgent criticism of relatives
friends as giving a faithful account of all we have seen
done during our absence, together with slight sketches'
various matters connected with the country and its inh:
tants, in the hope that they may prove interesting to th
who, although divided from us by wide seas, were ever pr
in our thoughts during the wanderings, pleasures, trials
perils which I have attempted to portray.

NORTH HILL HOUSE, PLYMOUTH,
    March, 1878.

CONTENTS.

CHAPTER I.

[Receiv]e Orders to proceed to India—Our Embarkation at Portsmouth—Her [Maje]sty's Indian Transports—Rough night at Sea—Sketch of daily life on [board]—Gibraltar—The Mediterranean—Arrival at Malta—Description of [Malta]—History of Malta—The Church of St. John—Knights of Malta—The [Pala]ce—Monastery of the Capuchins—Their mode of disposal of the Dead—[S]trada Reale—Diving propensities of the Natives—Departure from Malta—[Ill]ness on board—Passage to Port Said—Town of Port Said . *Page* 1

CHAPTER II.

[Depar]ture from Port Said—The Suez Canal—History of the Suez Canal—Suez—[Th]e Red Sea—Passage of the Israelites—Journey down the Red Sea—Island [of]Perim—Its Garrison—Outwitting the French—Aden—Its inhabitants—The [Ta]nks—Burial at Sea—The Indian Ocean—Phosphorescence of the Sea—[Ar]rival off Colaba—Lottery as to time of arrival—My illness—Arrival at [Bo]mbay 19

CHAPTER III.

[Intr]oduction—Geographical description of India—Boundaries—Divisions—Moun[t]ains — Rivers — Lakes — Desert — Early history of India — Greek Invasion —Modern history—Mahmoud of Ghuzni — Invasion of Arabs — Alexander [t]he Great — Pillage of Somnath — Ancient form of government — Origin of Mohammedan empire—House of Ghor—Pathan dynasty founded—Invasion [o]f Moguls—Baber—Mogul dynasty—Mogul Emperors—Dissolution of the empire—Rise of British power—The Portuguese—East India Company—The French in India—Clive—Warren Hastings—Title of Viceroy—Change in government — The Viceroys of India—Sepoy Revolt— End of East India Company—The Native States—The Presidencies—Mode of government—The Civil Service 37

CHAPTER IV.

Description of Bombay—The Harbour—Historical sketch—Appearance of the Town—The Fort—The commercial part—The Merchants—State of Trade—The principal buildings—The University—The Post Office—The Cathedral—Crawford Market—European shops—Population—Mohammedans—Hindus—Early history of the Hindus—Aboriginal tribes of India—Eurasians—Suburbs of Bombay—Our drive—The weather—The native town—The Bazaar—Dress of the people—Description of Bazaar—Mode of business—Malabar Hill—The Towers of Silence—The Parsees—Their history—Their religion—Their mode of Burial—Birds of Prey—Their utility—Return to Hotel—Indian Moonlight—Preparations for departure 56

CHAPTER V.

The Religions of India—The Hindu religion—Its antiquity—Its earliest form—The Vedas—Their doctrines—Doctrine of Monotheism—The god Brahma—Doctrine of Transmigration—The religious rites—The present state of the Hindu religion—Its principal doctrines—The Hindu Pantheon—Practical part of Hindu worship—The Hindu sects—Effects of the Hindu religion—The Buddhist religion—Its origin, doctrines, and ritual—The Jain religion—Its doctrines—Jain Temples—The Mohammedan religion—Its origin—The Koran—Its doctrines—Din, or practical part of Islam—The Sonnites and Shiites—Christianity in India—Its introduction and present condition—The institution of Caste—Its origin—Caste in its original form—Caste as at present practised 78

CHAPTER VI.

Departure from Bombay—Railway system in India—A railway station—Scenery on the line—Passage of the Ghauts—The Deccan—The Minerals of India—View from the Ghauts—Fortress of Asseeghur—The Forests of India—Arrival at Jubbulpur—Indian Hotels—Station of Jubbulpur—The Marble Rocks—Our expedition—Native industry—The Ryots—Indian Agriculture—The Land-tax—Irrigation of the Land—Description of the Rocks—Ancient Buddhist Temple—Stone-carving—Cave-temples of India—Their antiquity—Architecture of the Hindus—Art of Sculpture—The Buddhist Temples—The Jain Temples—The Hindu Temples—Architecture during Mohammedan ascendancy—The Saracenic school—The Hindustani school—A Monkey incident—Return to the Hotel—Evening reflections 115

CHAPTER VII.

Arrival at Allahabad—Description of Allahabad—Its history—The Station—The Fort—Pillar of Asoka—Sacred Banian tree—Departure for Cawnpore—The

Contents. ix

journey—The Railway Station—City of Cawnpore—Its history—The Cantonment—Memorial Church—Wheeler's Entrenchment—Story of the Siege—The Massacre—Slaughter Ghaut—The Civil Station—Scene of final Tragedy—Sufferings of the Victims—The Well—Inscription on Well—Memorial Garden—Motives of Nana Sahib—His history—His after-fate—Pontoon Bridge—Manufactures of Cawnpore—Tanning—Cotton-spinning—Arrival at Lucknow—Change of duty—Our daily doings—Description of an Indian Station—The Cantonments—The Barracks—The Civil Lines 144

CHAPTER VIII.

City of Lucknow—History of Lucknow—The Kings of Oudh—Modern city of Lucknow—The European Station—The Palace of the Kaisar-Bagh—Origin of the Name—The Fish Emblem—The Chattar Manzil—The Lall Baraderi—Machi Bhawan Fort—The Great Imambara—Feast of the Moharam—The Hosenabad—The Jama Musjid—The Residency—Story of the Siege—The Alam-Bagh—The Dil-Kusha—The Sikandar-Bagh—The Martiniere—Its founder Martine—Departure for Faizabad—The Journey—Its Discomfort—Arrival at Faizabad—Obtain a Bungalow—Etiquette of Visiting in India—Social law of Society—Its probable Origin, and present Condition. . . 163

CHAPTER IX.

The Seasons in India—The hot weather—Its variations and effects—The rainy weather—Its effects—The cold weather—Its variations and effects—Influence of climate on Europeans—Modes of cooling Houses—Khuskus Tatties—Thermantidotes—Punkahs—Punkah pulling—Its drawbacks—Our Bungalow—Description of Indian House—Establishment of Servants—Their number—Difference in respective Presidencies—Establishment in northern Bengal—Their expense—Difference of Creed and Caste—Its effects—Enumeration of Servants—The Khansamah—The Khitmutgar—His assistants—Their costume—The Bobberchee—An Indian Kitchen—The Bearer—The Ayah—The Bhestie—The Dhobie—The Mehtar—The Chowkedar—Theft in India—The Syce—The Gascutt—The Mahlie—The Coolies—Their duties—General character of Indian Servants 182

CHAPTER X.

Description of Faizabad—Nepaul—Faizabad native city and station—Routine of life—Our servant Esau—The Park—A Moonlight Picnic—Native Gardens—Flowers of India—Fruit and Vegetables of India—The god Rama—The Sanskrit Language—The Languages of India—Connection with Indo-European family of languages—Literature of India—Sacred and heroic Poems—The Vedas—The Institutes of Menu—The Puranas—Dramatic literature—Mode of acting—Hindu Tales and Fables—Progress of the Hindus in Geography, Logic, Astronomy, Mathematics, Medicine, and Chemistry—State of Education in India—Causes of ignorance—The evil effects of the Brahman influence—Former system of Education—Present system—Government schools—The Universities—Elementary schools—Female Education—General remarks on present state of Education—Its probable results 209

CHAPTER XI.

Approach of the Monsoon—A Dust-storm—A Thunder-storm in the Tropics—Effect of the Monsoon—The City of Ajudhya—Its history—The King Rama—The antiquity of Ajudhya—Receive orders to proceed to Gwalior—Departure from Faizabad—Destruction of Bridge at Cawnpore—Journey to Agra—Arrival at Agra—The City of Agra—The Fort—Gates of the Fortress—The Palace—The architecture of Agra—The Dewan-i-khas—The Dewan-i-am—The Zenana—The Shish-Mahal—Eastern Game of Backgammon—The Thrones—The Jasmine Tower—Description of the Palace—The Motee-Musjid, or Pearl Mosque—The Somnath gates—Their history—Mr. Simpson's denial of their authenticity—The Taj—The Begum Moomtaz-i-Mahal—History of the Taj—Its cost—Description of the Taj—The garden—The exterior—The interior—Measurements of the Taj—The Taj by moonlight . . . 239

CHAPTER XII.

The Tombs in Agra—Tomb of Itmad-ood-Dowlah—The Cheene-ka-Roza—Sikundra—Futtehpur-Sekri—Its history—Its ruins—Bhurtpur—Muttra—History of Muttra—Stone industries of Agra—Mosaic work—Jalee—Soapstone carving—Departure from Agra—The Indian Dak Gharry—The road to Gwalior—Dholepur—Indian Dak Bungalow—A Rest-house Dinner—Continue the journey—River Chumbul—Perils of the way—Arrival at Gwalior—Visit to the Fortress—Our quarters in Fortress—Description of Fortress—Gwalior—Its History—The Cantonment of Morar—Garrison of Morar—The Army in India—The Police Force—The Native Army—Its reorganization—Its loyalty—Causes that might lead to a Mutiny—Securities against a repetition of acts like those of 1857 265

CHAPTER XIII.

The Independent Natives—States of India—Their tenure of power—Their classification—The Hill Tribes—The Sikh States—The Sovereignties of Rajputana—Their history—The Rajputs—Their feudal system—The State of Marwar—The Rana of Oudipur—The State of Jaipur—Jaipur—Bhurtpur—Its history—The Central India States—The Mahrattas—Sevaji—Their rise and fall—The Peishwa—State of Gwalior—The Maharajah Scindia—His family—State of

Contents.   xi

Indore—Holkar—The Begum of Bhopal—Guzerat States—The Guicowar of Baroda—The Chiefs of Kutch and Kattywar—The Haidarabad State—The Nizam—His history—State of Mysore—Its ruler—Tippoo Sahib—His actions—The Malayalam States—Travancore—Cochin—Concluding remarks . 286

CHAPTER XIV.

Life in the Fortress—Effects of the Rains—Snakes in India—The Frogs—The Habits of Snakes—The Cobra—Unpleasant Discovery—Variety of Snakes in Fortress—Snake-bite—Indian Snake-charmers—Indian Jugglers—The Mango Trick—The Ruins in Fortress—The Palace—Jain Idols—Temples of the Jainas—Description of Jain Temple—The City of Gwalior—The Rajah's Palace—The Lushkur—Indian Music—Festivals of the Hindus—Religious Festivals—Indian Fairs—Hindu Marriages—Their Extravagance—The Marriage Ceremony—Incident at a Marriage—Condition of Married Women in India—Their Seclusion—Hindu Widows—Re-marriage of a Widow—Caste Rules relating to Remarriage—The Suttee—Its Origin—Motives of the Act—Nautch Girls—Their Dress—An Indian Nautch   313

CHAPTER XV.

Shooting expedition to the Jungle—The Spear-grass—Its effects—Our day in the Jungle—A mishap—Our return to the Fortress—Capture of supposed Nana Sahib—Probable reason for the imposture—Fate of the Impostor—Camp life in India—Start for a shooting excursion—Mahona—Jackals and Hyenas—Garra Ghaut—Arrival in Camp—Sport in India—Tiger-shooting—Fox-hunting in India—Pig-sticking—Our life in the Jungle—Our Commissariat arrangements—Peculiarities of Hindu living—Influence of caste on eating and drinking—A Brahman dinner—Food of the Hindus—Use of Rice—Use of Asafœtida—Hindu beverages—Drunkenness among natives—Hindu luxuries—The Betel-nut—Christmas-day—Chase after Leopard—Attacked with illness—Our return to the Fortress—Termination of our first year in India   343

CHAPTER XVI.

The New Year—Horse-racing in India—The Race Lottery—Commencement of the hot weather—Our Maid's Wedding—The Leave Season in India—Indian Hill stations—Their utility for the British troops—Hill stations of the Bengal Presidency—Simla—Nynee Tal—Mussoorie—Subathu—Darjeeling—Darjeeling tea—Cultivation of tea in India—Hill stations in Madras—The Neilgherry hills—Hill stations of the Bombay Presidency—The Ghauts—Mahableshwur—Increased heat of the weather—Sickness in the Fortress—Heat-apoplexy—Sunstroke—Cholera—Theory of the disease—History of Cholera in India—Causes of Cholera—Its propagation—Small-pox—Vaccination in India—Science of Medicine in India—Its practice in former days—Its condition at present . 363

CHAPTER XVII.

Departure for Kashmir—Dak to Agra—Railway journey to Lahore—Meerut—Umballa—Jullunder—The river Sutlej—City of Umritsur—Its history—The Golden Temple—Lahore—Territory of the Punjab—The Five Rivers—Description of the Punjab—Its population—The Sikhs—History of the Punjab—Rise of the Sikhs—Their origin—Religion of the Sikhs—Founder of their religion—The Guru Nanak—His life and work—His successors—Guru Govind Singh—The Sikhs and the Mohammedans—Rise of the Sikh power—Runjeet Singh—His successors—Maharajah Dhuleep Singh—Sikh wars with the English—Fall of the Sikh power—The Koh-i-noor Diamond—City of Lahore—Its buildings—Mausoleum of Jehangir—The Fort and Palace—The Civil Station—Arrival at Wuzzeerabad—Crossing the Chenab—Gujerat—Jhelum—Rawul Pindi—Arrival at Murree—Description of Murree—Start for Kashmir . . . 386

CHAPTER XVIII.

Return from Kashmir—Arrival at Gujerat—Receive Orders to Proceed to Rawul Pindi—Arrival at that Station—Rawul Pindi—Attacked by Illness—Shocks of Earthquake—Am Invalided—Departure for England—Journey to Delhi—Description of Delhi—History of Old Delhi—The line of Slave Kings of Delhi—The House of Lodi—Conquest of Delhi by Timour—The ruins of Old Delhi—The Fortifications—The Kootub Minar—The Mosque—Ancient Hindu Iron Pillar—Tomb of Altumsh—City of Seri—Juhanpura—Ruins of Toghlukabad—The Fort—Tomb of Toghluck Shah—The City of Feerozabad—The Buddhist Monolith—Tomb of the Emperor Homayoon—Capture of Rebel Princes—The Cemetery of Nizam-ud-din—His Tomb—Tomb of the Poet Khoosroo—The Bowlee, or Wellhouse—Diving Talent of the Natives—The Mosque of Keerkee—The Tomb of Sufdur Jung . . . 410

CHAPTER XIX.

The City of Shah Juhan, or New Delhi—Description of Delhi—Its modern Buildings—The Chandnee Chouk Bazaar—The Fortress—Gateways of the Fortress—The Palace—The Dewan-i-am—The Dewan-i-khas—The Peacock Throne—Private Apartments of the Emperor—The Hummam—The Ghoosul-Khana—Scenes enacted within the Palace—The Great Mosque, or Jama Musjid—Relics of the Prophet Mohamed—The Kala Musjid—History of the Siege of Delhi—Incidents during the Mutiny—General Nicholson—The Memorial Column—Departure for Allahabad—Benares—Its Temples—Province of Bengal—Its history—The City of Calcutta—Its history—Its Buildings—Our Journey to Bombay—Departure for England—Arrival in England—Conclusion 434

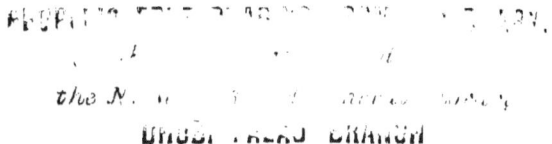

OUR LIFE AND TRAVELS IN INDIA.

CHAPTER I.

Receive orders to proceed to India—Our embarkation at Portsmouth—Her Majesty's Indian Transports—Rough night at sea—Sketch of daily life on board—Gibraltar—The Mediterranean—Arrival at Malta—Description of Malta—History of Malta—The Church of St. John—Knights of Malta—The Palace—Monastery of the Capuchins—Their mode of disposal of the dead—The Strada Reale—Diving propensities of the natives—Departure from Malta—Sickness on board—Passage to Port Said—Town of Port Said.

IN the summer of 1873, as I had received the appointment of Staff-Surgeon in the Island of Guernsey, both myself and wife not unreasonably formed hopes of a residence there for some little period. But unfortunately the uncertainty of a military life, and the laudable but unceasing activity displayed by the authorities in inaugurating the new system, termed the Unification of the Army Medical Department—which had already cost me the loss of my regiment, the Carabineers—were exemplified in our case; for, after a most pleasant tenure of my appointment for five months, a telegram received on the afternoon of the 12th December curtly told me to hold myself in readiness to embark for India with the 13th Hussars, and that the troop-ship to convey that regiment was to leave Portsmouth on the 8th of January.

Not being over anxious to go to the East, my first thought was to proceed to London, to ascertain if any change in our movements could be effected. Any hopes we had formed as to an alteration in the order received were quickly dispelled, however, shortly after my arrival at head-quarters; for an interview with the Director-General, the head of my department, made it plainly apparent that, unless I chose to resign the service, the original order must be obeyed, as the only alternative that could be offered me was to proceed to the Gold Coast, and take part in the Ashantee war, then in progress. Having no ambition to distinguish myself in that malarious region, of the two evils I chose the lesser. Our preparations for a sojourn in the sunny East were soon made; and after bidding farewell to our relatives and friends, then assembled in London, celebrating the nuptials of a member of the family, we went to Plymouth, and spent Christmas with our relations there. The 6th of January saw us *en route* to Portsmouth, the port of our departure for the land of Ind.

The morning of the 8th, the day fixed for us to leave our native country in the *Serapis*, broke dark and gloomy, and rain, accompanied with high wind, did not promise an agreeable first night at sea. On our arrival at the ship, a few hours before the time of sailing, we found the regiment to which I was attached, as well as the drafts belonging to other corps, already on board. Many of the officers we had met when stationed at Aldershot, and it was pleasant to feel that we were not utter strangers to our companions on the long voyage that lay before us.

In a short time the sound of the bell was heard, warning those on board not bound for the East to proceed on shore.

Very soon the ship was cleared, and preparations made for departure; and at four o'clock, with the band playing 'Auld lang syne,' amidst the cheers of the friends of the regiment assembled on the quay, we slowly left the shores. The first hour or two, while in Southampton Water, all was pleasant enough, and that time was occupied in putting our effects in order in our respective cabins. The *Serapis* is one of her Majesty's five Indian transports, which are employed in the conveyance of troops between the mother country and her great Eastern dominion. They are all similar in build and size, and can carry on each voyage a great number of people. We had nearly eighteen hundred souls on board, and, as may be imagined, both officers and men were rather crowded. Being built very high these transports have several decks, which enlarges greatly their passenger capacity, with the defect, however, of causing them to roll in a heavy sea, their breadth not being in the same proportion. They are fitted with every convenience for comfort, as well as with every appliance for the purpose of ventilation, so necessary in a crowded ship, especially in the warmer latitudes. Forming part of the Royal Navy, they are officered and manned entirely from that profession, the captain of the ship being supreme over all; even the commanding-officer of the troops on board, whatever his rank, being subordinate while at sea. Take them in all, they are comfortable enough, and a great blessing to the soldiers, who formerly had to make the voyage to India in crowded sailing vessels round the Cape, the discomfort and irksome monotony of which can only be realized by those who have endured it.

Directly we passed the Isle of Wight, we began to feel the

force of the wind, which was now blowing a perfect gale, and the sea, running high in proportion, caused such a pitching and rolling of the vessel, as very soon had its accustomed effect. Shortly after leaving the shelter of the land, and entering on the open Channel, nearly all on board therefore were enduring the agonies of sea-sickness. All the ladies succumbed early; and after taking my wife to her cabin, which we found already tenanted by the three ladies who shared with her its occupancy, in various stages of the malady, I descended to the lower deck to obtain, if possible, the services of one of the soldiers' wives to act as nurse, as the maid, who, as well as our little dog Fizz, followed our fortunes, was in the same prostrate condition as her mistress. Very fortunately for us an elderly female, who had followed the drum in various parts of the globe for over thirty years, and who, according to her showing, was proof against the ills that flesh is heir to at sea, volunteered her help, and a very efficient nurse she subsequently proved to be, continuing to act as stewardess to that particular cabin throughout the voyage.

Our first dinner on board was a perfect farce. Very few of our number assembled to do honour to that important meal, and every lurch of the ship caused a hurried departure of one or more of the convives. Judging from my own feelings, I should consider that, with the exception of the naval officers, none of us felt very comfortable, although some of us continued in our places with a grim calmness worthy of a better cause. The gale continued all night; and the pitching and rolling we endured in consequence were terrible. Nor were they much lessened the next day; for although the wind fell, the sea continued to run very high. This, however, gradually subsided; and on Saturday morning, as we entered the generally much-dreaded Bay of Biscay, glorious sunshine, and the almost perfect calmness of our hitherto relentless enemy, bade us hope for better things. We were not disappointed; for splendid weather followed, causing all the invalids to regain their usual health and spirits; and the ordinary routine of life at sea now fairly commenced.

'Life on the ocean wave,' however pleasant and poetical it may appear in song, is prosaic and monotonous enough in reality, so much so indeed, that a brief sketch of one day will amply suffice to give an idea of our daily doings, from the commencement until the termination of the voyage. Although breakfast is not until half-past eight, all on board are early risers; and soon after daybreak most of the gentlemen are astir, seeking their matutinal tub. To insure this with comfort, it behoves one to be prompt; for the supply of baths is limited, and the general rule of first come first served is rigidly adhered to. For those who prefer it, there are sails filled with water on deck, or a sailor is always willing to play a hose over you. Both these modes of ablution are greatly appreciated in the warmer latitudes; but at first the coldness of both air and water is sufficient to deter any but the ultra robust from availing themselves of them at such an early hour. The ladies, being few in number, and having a bathroom attached to each of the two cabins set apart for their occupation, are amply provided for, and are consequently spared the trouble experienced by the sterner sex as regards this part of the morning toilet.

After breakfast all proceed on deck, and at ten o'clock the

'assembly' sounds for the troops to fall in for inspection by their respective officers. At this hour, too, the medical officers visit the hospital, and perform all the duties appertaining to their department. At noon a light lunch is served, after which, until dinner, the time is usually passed on deck, reading, talking, or promenading up and down for the sake of exercise. At four o'clock all go below to dress for dinner, and at half-past four that meal, the great event of the day, is served. The living on board the *Serapis* was excellent; and for everything, including beer and sherry, with port and claret at dessert, each officer was charged three shillings and sixpence per day, and each lady four shillings. Other wines could also be obtained, as well as spirits, soda-water, and similar extras, all of which were supplied at most reasonable rates. Dinner over, all adjourn to the deck, where smoking and talking form the chief amusement until tea-time. At this period of the day the band usually plays, and often an impromptu dance takes place, varied occasionally by a theatrical performance, or a concert, both vocal and instrumental; plenty of amateurs, many with considerable talent, being readily found among the men of both services. After tea, which is served at eight, reading, writing, cards, or conversation in the saloon, brings up the time until ten o'clock, when all usually retire to their cabins for the night. The lights are extinguished at half-past ten, and after that hour none but the officers on duty are to be seen about.

Such is the ordinary routine of life at sea in Her Majesty's transports, varied only by arrival at and departure from any port of call, and on Sundays by divine service, conducted by the naval chaplain usually carried by these ships.

Arrival at Malta.

The weather continued fine during the whole of our passage across the Bay, and soon we approached the rocky coast of Portugal, passing very close to Cape St. Vincent and the headland of Cintra, with its large nunnery perched on a rock overlooking the ocean. Then, after running along the coast of Spain on one side, with the rugged shores of Morocco on the other, we arrived on Wednesday, the 14th, six days after leaving home, off Gibraltar. Sailing close inshore, we had a good view of that famous Rock and its fortifications. Continuing through the Straits, we entered the calm blue Mediterranean, and after passing Point de Gatta, shaping our course along the coast-line of Algeria and Tunis, on the following Monday we sighted Gozo, and at noon on the same day were anchored in the Valetta harbour of Malta.

Unfortunately it just then commenced to rain, a rather uncommon occurrence in the island, where the usual yearly rainfall is very slight; but as it was given out that we should leave early the next morning, no time was to be lost by those who wanted to see the sights of the place. Consequently, very shortly after our arrival, the greater number of us were on shore, glad enough to tread *terra firma* again, even if only for a few hours.

The island of Malta, the sky, and air, and country of which are African, while its life and civilization are European,[*] is the furthest from the main land of any of the numerous islands in the Mediterranean. Sicily, which approaches it most nearly, is sixty miles distant; the coast of Italy is

---

[*] According to Dr. Percy Badger, to whose work on the subject I am largely indebted for the historical and other facts mentioned in the following remarks.

separated from it by one hundred and ninety miles of sea; and it is fully two hundred miles from the African shore. Its circumference is about sixty miles; its greatest width twelve; and it has a total length of nearly twenty. It contains two cities, three towns, and a number of small villages. The principal city is Valetta, situated on the east side of the island; and the next in order is Citta Vecchia, located in its centre. There are numerous harbours, the principal one the Grand Harbour, whose waters wash the rocks on which the city of Valetta is built.

The climate of Malta is mild and temperate; and there is no winter, although at times it is cold, more particularly during the prevalence of the north wind. Rain falls occasionally, but snow never. The Maltese are of a light-brown complexion, strong and robust as a race, clever, vivacious, and industrious, and of a happy and contented temperament. They are Roman Catholics of a bigoted type, very much under the dominion of the priests, who flourish exceedingly, if their number, the multitude of monks and nuns constantly met with, and the religious processions so frequently passing along the streets, may be taken as any indication. For its size, the island contains a denser population than any other part of the habitable globe. The language spoken—the common Maltese—is a queer dialect, a mixture of Arabic and Italian; but among the upper classes, and for all official business, pure Italian is used, and this is now being taught in all the schools, governmental or otherwise. The inhabitants enjoy the various rights and privileges of British subjects, the direction of all public affairs being vested in the hands of a governor appointed by the home authorities, and a council of eighteen persons, eight unofficial members of whom are chosen by the people every five years.

The chief productions of the island are corn and cotton, the latter being of very fine quality. Many varieties of fruit grow in great abundance, and the Maltese oranges are well and deservedly known. Various flowers, many of a semi-tropical nature, also flourish. A curious race of dogs was at one time largely bred on the island, but is now nearly extinct. They are very diminutive in size, with long glistening white hair. In addition to other antiquities, the island abounds in caves, and to one is assigned the reputation of having been the residence of the Apostle Paul.

Every country is said to have its history, and Malta, or Melita, as it was termed by the ancients, undoubtedly possesses one of great interest. Its first inhabitants are held to have been a colony of Phœnicians, expelled by the Greeks soon after the siege of Troy, about seven hundred and fifty-five years before Christ. The Greeks remained in possession of the place until the Carthaginians, under the leadership of Hannibal, drove them out; and this illustrious general is supposed to have died and been buried on the island; for there was discovered in a sepulchral cave a stone, with an inscription on it in the Punic character, stating the cave to be the sanctuary of the sepulchre of Hannibal. Malta, thriving under the Carthaginians, attracted the cupidity of the Romans, who conquered it, and declared it a Roman municipality. They had in turn to make room for the Goths, who were succeeded in A.D. 879 by the Moors or Arabs. These remained in quiet possession for over two hundred years, but were eventually driven out by Count Roger, son of Tancred de Hauteville, who crowned himself king of Malta and Sicily. Subsequently it fell under the power of the emperors of Germany and the sovereigns of Spain, and was alternately ruled by them until 1530, when it was ceded to the powerful Order of the Knights of St. John of Jerusalem, who are its best-known rulers, and who were the founders of its cities and fortifications as they exist in the present day. The Order remained in possession until 1798, when the place was besieged by the French under Buonaparte, who expelled the Knights. This almost extinguished that ancient Order, which had risen to great power during its three centuries of rule in Malta. The French did not, however, long enjoy their victory; for in 1800 the English succeeded in gaining possession of the island; though not until after the French had sustained an obstinate blockade of two years, entailing the most fearful privations upon themselves and the wretched islanders.

By the Congress of Vienna, in 1814, the island of Malta was confirmed to the English Crown, with that of Gozo adjoining; and Malta—formerly the bulwark of Christendom against the bloody banner of Islamism and infidelity, exerting a salutary influence over the desolations of Africa, and giving decisive checks to the infamous piracies of the Barbary coast—in our own times exerts a still nobler, because a moral, influence upon the shores of the Mediterranean, and occupies, under the benign and all-powerful flag of Great Britain, a prouder position than even during her most renowned days under the sovereignty of the chivalrous Knights of St. John of Jerusalem.

On landing, we went first to the Church of St. John, which

holds the first rank among the numerous churches and convents of Malta. It was built during the reign of the Grandmaster La Cassiere, about the year 1576, and was subsequently enriched by the donations of the Grandmasters who succeeded him. The outside is not pleasing, the façade being clumsy and the ensemble quite monotonous; but the interior is magnificent. The choir is ornamented with an admirable piece of sculpture in white marble on a raised base, representing the baptism of Christ by John the Baptist, in two large figures, and the semicircular roof which covers the nave is adorned with paintings illustrative of the Baptist's life. The grand altar is very sumptuous, and attracts notice on account of the various coloured marbles and other valuable stones with which it is constructed. Under the Order this temple was richly decorated with silver ornaments and other works of art in great profusion; but these were carried off by the French, and a few paintings and pieces of sculpture, some of great beauty and value, together with two massive silver gates, closing the entrance to a chapel of the Virgin, are all that is left of the magnificent treasures which the church formerly possessed.

The pavement of the church is of high historical importance, containing the record of three centuries of glory and greatness. It is composed of sepulchral slabs, worked in mosaic, with various coloured marbles; and many of them are jewelled with jasper, agate, and other precious stones, the cost of which must have been very great. Some of these cover the graves of the Knights and other servants of the Order, the tombs of the Grandmasters being placed in a crypt. Each slab bears an appropriate epitaph, or rather a panegyric, on the virtues of the deceased.

Christians from all civilized countries being eligible to join the Order, and become Knights of Malta, as they were more generally termed, it followed naturally that adventurous spirits, from nearly all the European nations, entered the brotherhood. These were, for the sake of order and discipline, divided into parties, according to their nationality and language, each band inhabiting under its own commander separate houses or auberges, while each had assigned to it its particular post on the fortifications when attacked by their enemies. One and all, however, were subject to the Grandmaster for the time being. This division of nations was carried out even in their religious observances; for each different 'Langue' had its own chapel in the church. These chapels run parallel with the nave, forming the two aisles. They are splendidly decorated, and near each its former worshippers lie buried — Englishmen in close juxtaposition to Frenchmen, Italians, Spaniards, Germans, and others.

We proceeded next to the palace, formerly the residence of successive Grandmasters, now occupied by the Governor of the island and his staff. It is situated on the most level part of the town, which is generally very uneven, being built on the side of a hill, sloping down to the sea, with its streets and houses rising tier after tier to the summit. The exterior of the palace presents nothing striking. It is simply a pile of unadorned architecture, about three hundred feet square, surrounded by four of the principal streets, and almost enclosed on three sides with a line of open and covered balconies. It has two principal entrances in the front, which faces a spacious square called Piazza St. Giorgio, and each opens into a large court, laid out as a garden, with fountains, statuary, and flowers. The palace consists of a lower and upper story, each containing a range of apartments running round the main building, while another building transversely divides the space within into two almost equal divisions. The upper story contains numerous elegant apartments and spacious halls, embellished with views commemorative of the battles of the Order. One of the rooms, now exclusively devoted to the sittings of the Government Council, is very elegant, and entirely hung with tapestry of very superior workmanship. The drawings on these hangings represent scenes in India and Africa; and although the tapestry was brought from France about one hundred and fifty years since, the colours still look fresh and new. The rooms on the lower story are plainer, most of them being occupied as government offices. The corridors of the palace and its principal staircase are richly paved with marble in mosaic. The most interesting sight in the building is the armoury. This occupies a large saloon, extending the whole length of the structure, and contains armour and weapons belonging to the Knights of Malta, with numerous trophies of their splendid victories. Several of the suits of armour are true works of art, beautifully chased, and inlaid with gold; and the walls are covered with many curious examples of ancient warlike implements, cross-bows, maces, coats of mail, javelins, battle-axes, and other instruments of bloodshed and death, wielded in days of yore by those who long since have finished their warfare, and now sleep silently in the grave. One cannot fail to be struck with the vanity of ambition while examining these relics of the prowess of by-gone years. Is this all that remains of so much anxiety and love of power? How are the mighty fallen, and the weapons of war perished! Of the one it may be said—

> "A heap of dust alone remains of thee,
> 'Tis all thou art, and all the proud shall be;"

while the other serves for the decoration of a palace, and the momentary entertainment of a passing stranger.

From the palace we drove to the Monastery of the Capuchins, vulgarly known to visitors in Malta as the place of the 'baked monks,' from the mode of disposal of the dead members of the brotherhood. Instead of being committed to the earth, their bodies are first subjected to great heat in an oven, and then the desiccated corpses, attired in their usual garb, are set up in niches in the walls of the carneria or charnel-house of the convent, with inscriptions over their heads, setting forth their titles, names, and ages. The building itself is poor and mean, and contains nothing remarkable except a few pictures representing saintly miracles. Quickly exhausting these, we prepared to inspect the 'sight' of the place. Under the guidance of a very dirty barefooted monk, dressed in coarse brown serge, with a rope tied around his waist as a girdle, we descended a flight of steps into an extensive vault, containing that which would, I imagine, satisfy any amount of craving for the horrible. Here all the monks who had died in the convent, for many years past, were to be seen, dressed in their frocks and hoods, ranged along the walls in all stages of decay. The bones of those whose bodies were too far advanced in decomposition to allow of their standing upright in their allotted spaces, were nailed upon the walls in regular order, so as to form a kind of decoration, the skulls being placed in rows along the ceiling. A short look at this curious but disgusting spectacle was sufficient, and we speedily returned to the livelier regions above. Not, however, before our amiable guide had informed us, with sorrow in his tone, that the exhibition would shortly close, a government order having been received at the monastery directing the monks in future to discontinue this practice, and to employ the mode of burial customary in a Christian community.

We next proceeded to the Strada di Reale, the chief street, which abounds with shops. Maltese lace, in silk and cotton, for which the island is famous, divides with gold and silver filigree and cameos, most of the custom, and large quantities of each are sold to travellers. The evening, however, continuing wet and stormy, we were not sorry to gain the shelter of an hotel, and after discussing an excellent dinner, cooked in the Italian style, but modified to suit the British palate, we set out to return to our floating home. Soon after the boat had pushed off, and we were fairly in the harbour, we encountered the full force of the wind, which was blowing a gale, accompanied by sheets of driving rain, and our passage in the little craft was decidedly hazardous. However, we reached the *Serapis* without anything worse than a thorough drenching from rain and salt-water combined. The following morning brought no change in the weather, the gale continuing with great violence; and as the wind would have been dead against us if we had proceeded, the naval authorities ordered that we should remain where we were until the storm had abated. Most of our friends left the ship soon after breakfast for another day on shore, but we were unable to follow their example, as it was my turn to perform the duties of orderly medical officer, which confined me to the vessel. We were surrounded all day by numerous boats containing fruit and other articles for sale to the soldiers, none of whom were allowed to land, but who were permitted to purchase anything with the exception of intoxicating liquors. The Maltese are wonderful swimmers and divers, and many of them earn their livelihood by performing aquatic feats for the benefit of the passengers of the numerous steamers that put in at this port. The great amusement is to get a number of them in line in different boats, and, when they are all eagerly waiting, to fling into the water, at some considerable distance, a sixpence, or other small piece of silver. Directly they see it alight all plunge in and dive for the coin, which by this time has sunk to some depth; however, it is rarely lost. One by one various heads reach the surface, and soon the fortunate captor emerges from the depths, holding aloft in triumph the coveted prize, which he immediately transfers for safety to his mouth. A few strokes enable him to reach his boat, and then he and his companions are again ready and willing to repeat the performance.

The evening was so wet that we did not attend, as had been our intention, a state performance at the opera, followed by a ball at the palace, given by the Governor, to which we had received an invitation. Malta formerly possessed a magnificent opera-house; but this was unfortunately destroyed by fire a few years ago, and up to the present time it has not been rebuilt. The old theatre is now used for the purpose; but it is a small, mean building, a great contrast to the one destroyed, which was one of the most perfect of its kind in Europe.

The following morning, Wednesday, the 21st, saw us again

under weigh. As soon as we cleared the smooth water of the harbour, we experienced the effects of the gale. Although the sky was clear and fine, with very little wind, the sea had not subsided, and it was very rough, causing in many cases a return of the malady from which all for some time had been exempt. We ourselves did not individually suffer, but we were very glad when, after the lapse of forty-eight hours, it became smooth; for one gets tired of being tossed about day and night, and having to assist locomotion by catching at everything within reach to steady the feet. Nothing of any consequence occurred to vary the usual routine, with the exception of a great increase in the number of the sick among the soldiers, chiefly from pleuro-pneumonia, or inflammation of the lungs and investing membrane. We had already had a number of cases of this disease, soon after crossing the Bay, and it had been attributed to the dampness of the decks, consequent on the heavy weather we experienced for the first few days after leaving Portsmouth. Leaving, however, all these cases in the Military Hospital at Malta, we had congratulated ourselves upon having got quit of this troublesome complaint, and we saw it with sorrow again making inroads on our charge; for a few days after leaving the island we had our hospital full of men, many of them in a serious, if not dangerous, condition.

On Monday, the 26th, we arrived at Port Said, which stands on a narrow stretch of sand, immediately at the entrance of the Suez Canal. The town of Port Said itself is not very important, having originated only since the opening of the Canal. It is the great coaling station for ships either proceeding to or returning from the East, and large quantities of coal are stored here to meet the exigencies of the traffic. It is an irregularly-built straggling place, the houses chiefly of wood, but boasts of an hotel, and a number of drinking saloons, or gambling dens; while its inhabitants, with the exception of a few English officials, are composed chiefly of Jews, Arabs, and Greeks, without a shred of good character amongst them, and all equally ready to plunder, or even murder, the unwary sailors of the numerous vessels that touch here. None of us were permitted to land, on account of an epidemic of small-pox, then raging in the town. Few regretted this curtailment of liberty; for there was nothing to tempt us, even had there been no risk of bringing contagion on board, which would have produced fearful consequences in a crowded transport, a contingency all were willing to evade by any means.

CHAPTER II.

Departure from Port Said—The Suez Canal—History of the Suez Canal—Suez—The Red Sea—Passage of the Israelites—Journey down the Red Sea—Island of Perim—Its garrison—Outwitting the French—Aden—Its inhabitants—The Tanks—Burial at sea—The Indian Ocean—Phosphorescence of the sea—Arrival off Colaba—Lottery as to time of arrival—My illness—Arrival at Bombay.

LEAVING Port Said the following morning, we entered at once upon the passage of the Canal, on our way to Suez. As this was the first occasion that either of us had seen this stupendous engineering work of modern days (it was not completed at the time of my former voyages to and from the East), we surveyed the scene with great interest, being curious to watch the progress of such an immense vessel as the *Serapis* through such a narrow strip of water. The Canal extends in a fairly straight line from the Mediterranean to the Red Sea, cutting through the Isthmus of Suez; and the project, when first mooted by that distinguished French engineer, M. Victor de Lesseps, met with a poor reception in our own country, the principal engineers of Great Britain holding that it was utterly impracticable. Hence, although of the utmost importance to our country as the most expeditious route to our possessions in the East, the originators failed to induce our government to assist them in the idea of making it a national undertaking, for the most deeply interested of all European powers in the success of a plan so advantageous to the welfare of our Indian empire. England's blindness to its merits or feasibility was justly punished by the humiliation that must have been experienced, in seeing this great work successfully carried out by the talent and energy of foreigners, as a commercial speculation.

Marvellous are the events which fill the rapidly revolving cycle of time! Again does a 'silent highway' run through the land of Egypt, uniting the seas of Europe and Africa. What existed in that dark and mysterious land centuries ago is now reproduced, and Egypt, no longer shrouded in mystery, only needs a better form of government to rise to an eminent position amongst other nations. The idea of a canal through the Isthmus was considered practicable, and the excavation actually commenced, upwards of two thousand five hundred years ago; and in the reign of Ptolemy Philadelphus, king of Egypt, two hundred and seventy-three years before the Christian era, the union of the two seas was perfected. This canal passed very nearly along the same track as its modern successor, entering the Red Sea near the site of the present town of Suez, and was of sufficient breadth and depth to allow of the passage of galleys of considerable size. Moreover, it is an historical fact that, in the year 31 B.C., Cleopatra, after the battle of Actium, seeing that the forces of Egypt were unable to resist those of Rome, attempted to take her fleet through it into the Red Sea, with the view of escaping into a distant land — a project which failed in consequence of the hostility of the Arabs inhabiting that part of the country the canal passed through. The channel existed for several centuries after Cleopatra's time, but became gradually blocked up and obliterated by the then unconquerable sand. And thus it was left for M. de Lesseps to reproduce, nearly in the same spot, the wonder of the ancients, with all the improvements suggested by modern science.

Standing on the deck of a large ship while passing through the Canal, one cannot fail to be struck with the contrast between its size and that of the small body of water on which it floats. From a seat in the centre of the deck, with the bulwarks obstructing the view, no water is to be discerned on either side; and as the movement of the vessel is very slow and even, you can hardly realise the fact that it is on its proper element, as it appears to be gliding over the sand, which is everywhere presented to the eye. The Canal banks are composed entirely of sand, and being of a shifting nature, a constant system of dredging is necessary to keep the passage of a proper depth. This depth is very considerable, sufficient to meet the requirements of the largest steam-vessel. The breadth is not so satisfactory, and only one ship can pass at a time; but in order to meet the requirements of ships coming in opposite directions, the Canal is divided throughout its whole length into stations, at regular intervals, connected with each other by the telegraph. A widening out of one bank at each of these places, forms a siding, into which one ship is shunted to allow another ship coming from the opposite direction to pass. The block system appears to be rigidly adhered to; for on arrival at each station, unless the signal points the way clear, you are not allowed to proceed, but are detained in the siding until the signal is all right. Detention is often caused by mishaps. A ship may run its bow on to the bank, and take the ground, and it often requires some considerable time to extricate a vessel so placed. Frequently part of the cargo has to be unloaded, and one of the steam-tugs always kept at certain places sent to assist in pulling it out of its difficulty. This is a class of accident of common occurrence; for the Canal is so narrow that the slightest deviation from the proper course is sufficient to cause it. Very good steering is therefore requisite, and this is performed by a special body of French pilots trained to the work. The rate of progress through the Canal is very slow. Ships are not permitted to proceed after dark, and although the entire length of the Canal is only a hundred miles, it is considered expeditious to make the passage in between thirty-eight to forty-five hours. The only part where the speed can be increased is on the lakes through which the Canal passes, one or two of which are of great size. Originally depressions in the land surface, they materially assisted the work of forming the Canal, and saved a great deal of cutting, as on the admission of water through the artificially-formed passages at either end, they rapidly filled up, and became small inland seas.

The whole of the country traversed by the Canal is most uninteresting. No towns, no villages, no trees even, are to be seen; nothing but sand—a desert waste—meets the eye, its level monotony broken only by occasional sand hillocks, though towards the Suez end a range of mountains is seen in the distance, shrouded in the fiery mist which rises from the glaring, glittering sand, between them and the spectator. With the exception of the officials at the different stations, and at the town of Ismailia, nothing animate is to be seen, besides a few flamingoes or other birds, and occasionally an

Arab caravan, with its long string of camels, passing over the waste. All is dreary, dead, and desolate, as if a curse had been laid upon the land, and never been removed. The only bright or verdant spot in this abode of desolation is Ismailia, now rapidly growing in importance. It is on the Bitter Lake, the largest and deepest of all the bodies of water formed by the union of the two seas, originally a broad and deep depression in the midst of a wide area of low-lying land, all of which became inundated on the admission of the water. This same depression is currently reported to have been excavated in the removal of clay and other materials to assist in the erection of the great Pyramids of Egypt!

We passed two nights in the Canal, made fast by hawsers to the banks on each side, which kept us motionless until the approach of daylight allowed us to proceed further on our way. Soon after dark it became bitterly cold, and we experienced palpable proof of how a rainless country derives its moisture; for the dew that fell from sunset to sunrise was very heavy—sufficient in quantity, and so thoroughly wetting, as to have satisfied the most thirsty land. We arrived at Suez early in the afternoon of the third day following our departure from Port Said, and it was with a feeling of great satisfaction that we welcomed a change of scene; for the dreary monotony of the last few days had depressed the spirits of all on board. The town of Suez stands on the shores of the Red Sea, at the upper end of that part of its waters known as the Gulf of Suez. It is a pretty large compactly-built town, and has greatly increased in size and importance since the opening of the Canal. Large docks have also been built, and everything provided calculated to be of service to the numerous ships of all nations that now proceed by this route to the East. Not very far from the town is the place where it is supposed the Israelites crossed in their flight out of Egypt. Sceptics who doubt the miracles contained in the Bible, point triumphantly to the fact that at this particular spot a reef of rocks stretches from shore to shore, which, in their opinion, justifies the belief that the passage was effected in a different manner to that described in the fourteenth chapter of Exodus.

The Red Sea of the maps has the appearance of a narrow stretch of water, closely confined by land on both sides; but although it certainly is not very broad—only one hundred and ninety-two miles at its greatest breadth, when no coast is visible—it resembles in fact a small ocean, particularly if the weather is stormy. The navigation of this sea is always difficult. The whole of its surface is studded with numerous little islands, chiefly of volcanic origin; whilst concealed by the water there are numberless coral reefs, rendering the voyage highly dangerous if the greatest caution is not observed. The heat supposed to be experienced by travellers through this region is a subject familiar to all. It is undoubtedly very great, particularly during certain months of the year. Indeed, it could hardly fail to be otherwise; for the Red Sea is, as it were, a kind of funnel placed between two scorching tracts of land, upon whose sandy desert wastes the tropical sun pours down its burning rays. The country in sight on either side of the Red Sea is not very interesting. On the one hand are perceived, following in order, the elevated territories of Egypt, Nubia, and Abyssinia; and on the other, throughout its whole length, lies the high table-land of Arabia. The general appearance of the whole Arabian coast is that of a solitary waste belt of sand, ending in a range of high barren hills, stretching away peak after peak until they are lost in the hazy distance. The only inhabitants are a few wandering Arabs, wild and savage enough to rob and murder those who are so unfortunate as to fall into their clutches.

We had a delightful passage, and the eight days we spent in this generally-dreaded furnace were pleasant enough. The heat, although great, was not distressingly so, and we were well protected from the sun during the day by a large thick awning covering the entire deck. The evenings were devoted to music, dancing, and other amusements; and those who had any leaning towards astronomy were well able to gratify their taste, for in this part of the world the stars are wonderfully magnificent, the various constellations being much more brilliant and distinct than when we viewed them at home.

On Tuesday, February 3rd, we passed the island of Perim, and knew we should now soon arrive at Aden, where we intended to call, in order to take on board a few men, who had volunteered from the regiment stationed there, for service in India. Perim is a desolate and solitary rock commanding the entrance of the Straits of Bab-el-Mandeb, and would effectually prevent, if required, the passage of vessels from the Red Sea into the Indian Ocean, or *vice versa*. With this strategical object in view, we now keep a small garrison on the spot, and some guns are mounted in a little rude fort on the summit of one of its rocky sides. A few European as well as some native troops from Aden, under the command of a British subaltern, are told off for this duty, being relieved and their places taken by others every three months. This time, although it may appear short, is found quite long enough for those whose duty leads them to such an exile, more particularly as experienced by the young commanding officer, who is alone in all his glory, martial etiquette not permitting him to associate with the rank and file under his command. It is said that at one time it came to the ears of the general at head-quarters, that a certain officer on this post had been on very intimate social terms with the senior non-commissioned officer of his detachment, a very intelligent well-read sergeant. When taken to task for this offence, and asked what explanation he had to offer for this serious breach of military discipline, the unhappy subaltern replied that he really was in no way responsible; and whilst admitting the truth of the general tenor of the accusation, begged most respectfully to urge in his defence that he had had no option in the matter. During his residence on the island, two courses had been open to him—one to completely isolate himself from his fellows, which in his case would have produced that form of insanity known as melancholia; the other, to mix with the best society the place afforded. To preserve his wits, therefore, he had chosen the latter.

It is only of late years that we have had any association with this island, taking possession of it in 1865. There is a very good anecdote told of the cause which led to its annexation, which may not be generally known. Towards the end of 1865, the British settlement of Aden was honoured by the arrival, early one morning, of two vessels of war belonging to the French navy. The officer in command landed to pay his respects to the Governor, and, as is usual, was asked, together with his companions, to dine that evening with his excellency;

an invitation frankly accepted. Conjectures as to the motive of the visit were rife all day in the minds of the English officials; but it was not until after the gubernatorial dinner that the mystery was explained. One of the guests, in a moment of confidence, then imparted the fact that they were on their way to take possession of Perim in the name of the French Government. The importance of this communication was instantly seen by the Governor, as Perim, in the hands of the French, would, in the event of war between the two nations, nullify the strategical position for the command of the Red Sea, which we had taken up in Aden. The wily politician immediately formed his plan, and while with a smiling face he complimented his guests on the acuteness of their nation, and wished them success in the enterprise, found means to despatch an armed gunboat with some troops to the coveted island. The astonishment of the Frenchmen may well be imagined when, on their arrival the following day, they found the British flag raised triumphantly aloft, and the place garrisoned by the soldiers of our ubiquitous nation.

At 7 a.m. on the following morning (Feb. 4) we arrived off Aden, and soon after breakfast, as our stay was to be very short, we prepared to go ashore, a distance of about half a mile from the ship, which was now moored in the excellent harbour. The sun was very hot, compelling the use of helmets, puggeries, and umbrellas. Landing from the steam-launch, we proceeded to a species of square, where are to be found the one or two hotels the place boasts, as well as the shops, all of which are kept by Parsees, who come from Bombay for that purpose. Motley crowds of semi-nude Arabs and Somali Africans surround you immediately on your arrival, and never cease importuning you to purchase ostrich feathers, coral, and trifling articles of native workmanship. Aden is famous for its ostrich feathers, which are brought from the opposite coast of Africa. But one has to be wary in bargaining; for the native traders in this commodity are arrant cheats. They keep a set, which they term 'travellers' feathers,' for the benefit of those who are only passing through. And these are generally valueless; for it is not uncommon to find, on close examination, a large and apparently valuable feather to be made up of small and useless feathers, most artistically joined together. If the buyer is acquainted with their tricks, and makes them produce the other set, usually retained by them for sale to residents, good feathers can undoubtedly be obtained, and at prices extremely moderate as compared with the value placed upon them in England and elsewhere. There is not much to be seen here. The place is dreary and dull, exactly like the crater of an extinct volcano, with neither a blade of grass nor a tree to break the monotony of its cindery appearance.

Aden itself is built on a small flat, probably the bottom of the crater, surrounded by precipitous rocks, on the east side of a peninsula, between two fine bays. " It is a strongly-fortified rocky promontory, strikingly like Gibraltar, and unquestionably one of our strongest and most important stations, opening up Arabia to our forces, and commanding the entrance to the Red Sea. It has been in British occupancy since the year 1839, and many unavailing attempts have been made by the fierce tribes in the vicinity to regain its possession. The houses of the Governor, or Resident, as he is termed, and of the various other officials, along with those of the few

European inhabitants, are built close to the sea; and the greater portion of the considerable number of troops always in garrison are located at a place called the Camp, about three miles distant. With the exception of the official and military European element, the population is composed of Parsees, Arabs, and Somalis. The last-named are the aborigines of the opposite coast of Africa, and perform all the labour of the place. They are an intelligent, lively race of Africans, black as ebony, with long curly hair, which they usually arrange in ringlets, and dye of a red colour. This gives them a most fantastic appearance. It is also not their custom to lavish much of their hard-earned money in raiment, contenting themselves with pretty nearly the garb attributed to Adam before the Fall. At first sight this strikes the stranger as being peculiar, to say the least; but the eye soon gets accustomed to it, and their skins being black, the glaring impropriety of their appearance, in a civilized sense, is in a measure toned down. Although at the present time Aden may be termed only a fortified rock, with little or no trade, yet at one period it was of the utmost commercial importance. Ages ago it was the chief, or rather the only, commercial town in this part of the world, where the commodities of Asia were exchanged for those of the West. On the site of this now barren rock there stood then a flourishing city, the 'Emporium of the East,' where traders from Europe and India jostled each other in the race for wealth. Nothing remains of all this prosperity, with the exception of a few ruins, notably those now partially restored, and known as the Aden Tanks. These receptacles for the storage of water are well worthy of attention, and few visitors, I imagine, quit the place without inspecting them. They are three miles from the harbour, and can be easily reached in the manner we did, by engaging one of the carriages always to be found on hire at the landing-place.

The road to the tanks passes through the native city or town proper of Aden, and also near to the barracks and other buildings of the camp. Within a few yards of the nearest tank is a small garden, with trees and plants, kept up with great trouble by the officers. This is the only verdant spot in the whole place—a veritable oasis in the midst of a howling wilderness. The tanks are a succession of deep excavations hewn out of the solid rock, communicating with each other, quite gigantic in design, capable of containing an enormous quantity of water, and were only discovered, and cleared of the accumulated rubbish of ages that concealed them, a few years ago. They were evidently built for the reception of the rain which falls even here occasionally, and their size warrants the belief that they were intended to meet the requirements of a large town; but it has not been decided who were the original conceptors and designers of the great work, so necessary in this arid land. To the Phœnicians, who are said to have been the earliest colonists of Aden, the credit is given by many authorities; while others again ascribe it to the Arabs of later times. And from certain features in the workmanship, and the descriptions of works of similar design said to exist in other parts of Arabia, I incline towards the latter opinion, and am tempted to attribute to that once powerful race the construction of what even at present would be considered a splendid system of water-works, confirming in its magnitude all that is said of the former prosperity of Aden.

To the European, Aden does not present the appearance of a desirable place of residence. The climate is hot, but healthy; and as very little rain falls, the changes of seasons are not well marked. Living is expensive, nothing being produced in the settlement. Even such necessary articles as firewood and vegetables have to be brought in from the interior by the Arabs, and often the supply of these is small, or fails altogether. Water is very scarce and dear, and in times of great drought only obtained by the condensation of sea-water. The very appearance of the place is depressing; and although it has been imagined to be the site of the garden of Eden, nothing like Paradise is left; and it can be truly said that if this residence of our common ancestors formerly existed here, since their time Aden has considerably altered for the worse. The idea is of course a popular fallacy, originating perhaps in an ironical contrast between Aden as it is and Eden as it was, founded on the similarity in the names, identical if the fifth letter of our alphabet is substituted for the first. There is, however, an old legend current among the Arabs which may have been the origin of Aden being considered the site of a place of paradise, confounded in later years with the garden of Eden, which runs as follows: "The tribe of Ad, one of the most famous tribes among the ancient Arabians, were descended from Ad, the son of Aws, the son of Aram, the son of Shem, the son of Noah, who, after the confusion of tongues, settled in Al Ahkaf, or 'the winding sands,' in the province of Hadramaut, where his posterity greatly multiplied. Their first king was Shedad, the son of Ad, of whom the Eastern writers deliver many fabulous things, particularly that he finished the magnificent city his father had begun, wherein he built a fine palace, adorned with delicious gardens, to embellish which he spared neither cost nor labour, proposing thereby to create in his subjects a superstitious veneration of himself as a god. This garden or paradise was called the garden of Irem, and is mentioned in the Koran, and often alluded to by the Oriental writers. The city, they tell us, is still standing in the deserts of Aden, being preserved by Providence as a monument of divine justice, though it be invisible, unless very rarely, when God permits it to be seen."

On our departure from this port, we found ourselves fairly on the Indian Ocean, about eight days' sail from Bombay, and with no land visible until we reached our destination. The weather was fine, and the sea calm, and life flowed on in its usual peaceful manner. The ordinary routine of a soldier's duty followed day after day, varied occasionally by a fire-parade, very frequently carried out in transport ships, since it is absolutely necessary that in the event of fire occurring all on board should, in their allotted stations, fulfil their part in the preservation of order and discipline, and assist in endeavouring to subdue the conflagration. Immediately the fire-bell rings out the alarm, no matter what time of the day or night, or what occupation is in hand, all rush to their respective posts. The ladies and children are collected in the saloon and locked in, and the wives and families of the soldiers in the forward part of the ship are similarly treated. The engines are stopped, and all ports closed; while the soldiers assemble at the several pumps and hoses, to which they have been appointed under certain officers soon after their arrival on board. These 'squads' assist the sailors in keeping up a continuous supply of water. Another party of troops, with fixed bayonets, take possession of the boats to prevent their forcible abduction. They also guard the approaches to the various store-rooms; no one being permitted to pass except the head steward and his assistants, whose business it is to pack up and transport to the boats provisions and necessaries of all kinds. The captain of the ship, with the commanding officer of the troops and his staff, are the only persons allowed on the quarter-deck, from which commanding position they issue the several orders considered necessary. The duty assigned to the medical officers of both services is to proceed at once to their respective hospitals, and make arrangements for the removal of the sick and helpless. The chaplain, paymasters, and quartermasters have no particular active employment assigned them, but are not idle, their mission being the charge of the ladies and children in the saloon, and to assist each other in allaying the natural fears of the softer sex. Thus every one has his place, and understands what he is called upon to do, so that in case of actual need no flurrying or obstruction shall take place in the endeavours to extinguish the flames, each man performing his duty calmly and deliberately, made perfect by the practice of these frequent fire-parades.

A few days after leaving Aden, we lost by death, much to the regret of all on board, four of our men, who had been suffering for some time from our old enemy pleuro-pneumonia, which, despite all our efforts for its removal, still stuck to the ship. As there is an uncomfortable feeling engendered by the presence of a corpse on board, very little time elapses between death and the disposal of the remains in the solemn and impressive manner peculiar to burial at sea. The unusual stillness prevailing—all machinery and other sources of noise being stopped—broken only by the mournful tolling of the ship's bell, heightens the feeling of awe always felt in presence of the dead, but more particularly in a small closely-packed community, to nearly all of whom perhaps the departed one was well known. And it is a relief to all when, after the words, 'We therefore commit his body to the deep,' the heavily-weighted hammock-cloth in which the corpse is sewn up slides off the gangway, and disappears beneath the wave, to await that time of glorious resurrection when sea and earth shall both give up their dead.

The weather continued fine for our voyage, and the Indian Ocean, which is rough enough at times, particularly during the prevalence of the monsoon, was calm and pleasant. We witnessed for three nights in succession a very peculiar appearance of the air and water, differing from anything ever observed before by any person on board, although the same phenomenon has been noticed by others in the same latitudes; and that distinguished American navigator Maury mentions it in his *Physical Geography of the Seas*. His description exactly tallies with what we ourselves saw. The whole sea, as far as the eye could reach, was of a milky-white colour, plentifully sprinkled with bright flashes of phosphorescent light, with here and there great black floating patches. Every now and then a snake-like body twisted about, emitting in its various undulations flashes of blue and crimson fire. The appearance of the sky was also remarkable; intensely black, as if a severe storm was brewing, and not one of the stars, usually so bright in this region, visible in the whole of the

Arrival at Bombay.

firmament. The whole scene was so grim and weird that one felt awe-stricken, and at first could only gaze in silence. But on trying to solve the mystery, examination of the water showed it to be full of animalculæ; the dark floating masses proved to be spawn, while sea-snakes and jelly-fish innumerable added their quota to produce this marvellous phosphorescence, due to the excessive presence of marine life.

As our voyage now approached its termination, and we anticipated shortly to sight Colaba Light, at the entrance of Bombay harbour, some little excitement was manifested as to the exact time we should come abreast of this beacon. On that depended the fate of a lottery of thirty pounds, formed by a sweepstakes of sixty subscribers, each of whom had drawn from a set of numbers of one up to sixty, thus covering the entire number of minutes in an hour. The vessel arrived at the appointed goal between fourteen and fifteen minutes to ten o'clock, and the stakes therefore fell to our share, these numbers having been allotted to us. We shortly afterwards arrived in the harbour, and soon all were busy in preparations for departure, and in bidding farewell to the officers of the ship, and those whose destination lay in another direction. As I had most unfortunately a few days before been attacked with the disease to which so many of our men had fallen victims, I was not able to accompany the regiment to the depôt of Deolali, *en route* to Lucknow, being directed instead to remain at Bombay until my health was re-established. A country or native boat from the number surrounding us was quickly hailed; with the good wishes for our future welfare of the friends with whom we had associated, we left the ship; and after a short row across the harbour, our party, including the dog, nearly mad with delight at his release from the close confinement he had endured, were again on *terra firma*, after a pleasant voyage of thirty-five days. We took a carriage at the landing-place, and soon found ourselves comfortably housed in the new Esplanade Hotel of Bombay, where we intended to remain until sufficiently recruited to proceed on the land journey which now lay before us.

CHAPTER III.

Introduction—Geographical description of India—Boundaries—Divisions—Mountains—Rivers—Lakes—Desert—Early history of India—Greek Invasion—Modern history—Mahmoud of Ghuzni—Invasion of Arabs—Alexander the Great—Pillage of Somnath—Ancient form of government—Origin of Mohammedan empire—House of Ghor—Pathan dynasty founded—Invasion of Moguls—Baber—Mogul dynasty—Mogul Emperors—Dissolution of the empire—Rise of British power—The Portuguese—East India Company—The French in India—Clive—Warren Hastings—Title of Viceroy—Change in government—The Viceroys of India—Sepoy revolt—End of East India Company—The Native States—The Presidencies—Mode of government—The Civil Service.

OUR voyage being now concluded, and the shores of India safely gained, it will, I think, be advisable, before proceeding with the personal portion of my narrative, to give a sketch of this great country, to render more intelligible the scenes and incidents hereafter to be described. Hindustan itself, that part of Asia in which England is acknowledged as paramount, may be compared in extent and population to the continent of Europe without Russia. It is the central great peninsula of Southern Asia, and approaches in form to a triangle, with the Himalayas for its base, and for its apex Cape Comorin in the Indian Ocean. Its extreme length north and south is one thousand nine hundred miles, and its greatest breadth one thousand five hundred miles, narrowing southward, while the estimated total area of the whole is 1,558,254 square miles. Geographically this large region is divided into two grand divisions. Hindustan proper, which lies between the Himalaya and the Vindhyan mountains, includes the Punjab and Sinde; Peninsular India, forming the second division, and subdivided into the Deccan and India south of the Krishna river, extends to Cape Comorin, comprising also the greater part of the British Presidency of Madras.

The great mountain systems of Hindustan are the Himalayas, the East and West Ghauts, and the Vindhyan range. The Himalayas, as is well known, are the most gigantic mountains in the world, having an average height of sixteen thousand feet, while their loftiest summits attain an altitude of upwards of twenty-eight thousand feet. The East Ghauts separate the Carnatic from the table-land of the Deccan, and have an average height of three thousand feet. The West Ghauts extend from Cape Comorin to the river Taptee, parallel to the western coast, and reach from five thousand to six thousand feet above the sea level. The Vindhyan mountains run east and west across the central part of India, a base to the triangle of which the East and West Ghauts form the other two sides. Their average height does not in many places exceed three thousand feet.

The rivers of Hindustan, like its mountains, are on the most magnificent scale. The Indus rises in Thibet, and, after a course of one thousand six hundred miles, falls by several mouths into the Indian Ocean. The sacred Ganges, although not the largest, is the most important of the Indian rivers, alike from the fertility its waters diffuse, and the facilities it affords for internal communication. It has a course of about one thousand four hundred miles from its origin in the Himalayas, terminating by numerous mouths in the Bay of Bengal.

Rivers and Lakes of India.

The Brahmapootra exceeds the Ganges in size, and probably in the length of its course; but its source is imperfectly known, although its main stream has been traced to Upper Assam. It discharges itself into the Bay of Bengal. Among the other rivers of note, the Jumna, Chumbul, Sone, Goggra, are all tributary to the Ganges. The five rivers of the Punjab—the Sutlej, Bees, Ravee, Chenab, and the Jhelum—are affluents of the Indus. And Peninsular India has the Nerbudda and Taptee flowing westward; and the Krishna, Godavery, and Mahanuddy entering the sea on the east.

In remarkable contrast to its mountains and rivers, the lakes of Hindustan are few in number, shallow, and comparatively small in size. The scarcity of these natural reservoirs is, however, in some measure, obviated by the numberless tanks or artificial collections of water scattered all over the country. Their construction is due largely to the piety of the natives, it being considered a highly meritorious action on the part of the followers of Brahmanism to employ their wealth for this purpose. There is one great desert, the Indus, or Sandy Desert, which stretches five hundred miles from the south-east confines of the Punjab to the Run of Cutch, and 'embraces nearly the whole of the delta of the Indus. Across that river it is continuous with the desert of Beluchistan, and with that wide band of sterility which spreads from Central Africa, north-east, over the whole centre of the Asiatic continent.

Ancient India has no connected history of its own, and although we can gather from the Hindu sacred books a vivid picture of the religious and social condition of India a thousand years before the origin of the Buddhist religion, B.C. 543, and the invasion of the Greeks, B.C. 327, they afford scarcely a suggestion of its political relations. The Greek account of the invasion of Alexander may therefore be termed the first landmark of Indian history. Even the later works of the Hindus, composed during the revival of Brahmanism, between the decline of Buddhism and the coming of the Mohammedans, treat principally of mythology and doctrine, and only of history as it may be made subservient to magnify the antiquity and glory of Brahmanism.

From what we can gather in the misty pages of the Vedas and other sacred books, it would appear that, about two thousand years before Christ, the Aryans, a Sanskrit-speaking race, whose Hindu descendants still number three-fourths of the inhabitants of the country, descended from the plains of Central Asia and settled in the Punjab. They were a pastoral and agricultural people; their form of government was patriarchal, and the offices of prince and priest were united in one person. After remaining some centuries in the Punjab they advanced southward to the valley of the Ganges, where their internal dissensions and their wars with the original inhabitants of those parts can be clearly traced. Later on, having completely subdued Oudh and Bengal, they effected the conquest of Southern India, and afterwards that of Ceylon. By this time, however, a great change had come over the Aryans themselves. Their primitive simplicity had disappeared; patriarchs had become luxurious princes, and had deputed their sacerdotal duties to the Brahmans, who at length succeeded in establishing themselves as the superior and principal caste among the people.

In the seventh century before Christ a new religion arose,

Early History of India.

called Buddhism. This was in effect a social reform, a revolt against the pride of caste and exclusiveness of the Brahman priesthood, and became, during several centuries, almost supreme. No authentic information can be gleaned as to the reigning sovereigns of the country throughout this time. The claim to universal sovereignty in India during these dark ages has been advanced by princes of many dynasties, but apparently on very insufficient grounds. It is more likely that the country at that time was divided into many portions; for we read of the kings of Delhi, Canouj, Bengal, Malwa, Guzerat, and other places, who all probably considered themselves lords paramount. Very little of their deeds or exploits has however been preserved, and of the earlier confused assemblage of dynasties nothing is known with the exception of a few purely mythological legends. And although our first definite knowledge of India dates from Alexander's invasion, yet the Greek historians give only a fragmentary narrative. Nor could it well be otherwise; the Greeks penetrated but a short distance into the country, and most of their knowledge must have been obtained from native sources as vague and incomprehensible as the sacred writings themselves. The modern history of Hindustan may be said to have commenced A.D. 1000, when Mahmoud of Ghuzni, a Mohammedan sovereign belonging to the tribe of Turks, one of the three great nations whom we include under the name of Tartars, made the first of his many successful expeditions into the country. This prince, however, was not the first leader of Mohammedans into India; for in 664 the Arabs, then in the height of their power as a nation, after the conquest of Persia penetrated into the country at the mouth of the Indus, and advanced as far as Mooltan.

They never, however, obtained any permanent footing, and were in 750 finally expelled. All their conquests were restored to the Hindus, who retained possession until the next inroad of the followers of the Prophet, which took place about two hundred and fifty years after the expulsion of the Arabs. This invasion was the first of any extent that India had endured; for all accounts agree that a very small portion of the land was entered by the Greeks under Alexander, who went no further than the Indus, and scarcely saw the skirts of Hindustan proper.

Mahmoud of Ghuzni was therefore the first invader of India who advanced any distance into the country. This monarch, whose original dominions extended from the Indian Ocean to the Caspian Sea, in thirteen successive expeditions conquered and made subservient to his rule the northern part of India, including the Punjab. Sinde, Bundelcund, and Guzerat, all large and extensive provinces, fell also to his arms; and after each victory he returned laden with slaves and treasure, the pillage of the celebrated temple of Somnath, in Guzerat, yielding alone a fabulous amount of gold and precious stones. He was of course opposed by the reigning native princes; but in most cases their resistance was feeble. This was probably due to a want of unanimity; for at that period the whole country was divided into a number of independent governments. As many even as one hundred and eighteen are said to have existed at one time. Many of these must have been very inconsiderable; but Canouj, Delhi, Ajmir, and Guzerat were great kingdoms. Most of the territories were under Hindu rajahs, whilst petty chiefs held independent towns or villages; and as most of these various governments had divergent interests, and were generally at feud with each other, the progress of the invader was made comparatively easy, as one power after the other succumbed to his arms. Mahmoud does not appear to have retained any of the ravaged territory until 1023, when, on his eleventh expedition, being opposed on his march to Canouj, he annexed the province of Lahore. Here was planted the first permanent Mohammedan garrison on the east of the Indus, and the foundation laid of the future Mohammedan empire in India, which endured under his successors for nearly two centuries, until, in the year 1174, the Ghaznevide dynasty was overturned by Ala-ud-din of Ghor.

The origin of the house of Ghor is not known with certainty; but the prevalent, and apparently the correct, opinion is, that both they and their subjects were Afghans, who always look upon the mountains of Ghor, situated in the northern portion of the tract included in the branches of the Hindu-Koosh, as their earliest seat.

This race, whose descendants still exist as an independent people in Afghanistan, have altered little since their first invasion of Hindustan, and are as strong, turbulent, and warlike as ever. In appearance they differ widely from the Hindus, and are burly muscular men of a fair complexion. Many have a decidedly Jewish cast of countenance, easily accounted for if their history can be believed, since the earliest and constant traditions of all the Afghan historians show that, styling themselves the Bani Israel, they claim descent in a direct line from Saul, or Malik Twalut. Saul, it is said, had two sons, Barakiah and Iramia (Jeremiah); and the latter a son named Afghana. When Bakt-u-nasr (Nebuchadnezzar) took the children of Israel into captivity, the tribe of Afghana, on account of their obstinacy in maintaining the Jewish religion, were driven into the mountains about Herat. Rapidly increasing, they extended their migrations eastward into the Cabul Valley, and along the right bank of the Indus to the confines of Sinde and Beluchistan. Living among idolaters, many of their tribe fell into idolatry; and in the ninth year after the announcement by Mohammed of his mission, and more than fifteen hundred years after the time of Solomon, the Afghans for the first time heard of the advent of a new prophet, through a fellow-Israelite who, having been convinced at Medina of the truth of the new religion, sent a message to his countrymen at Herat and Cabul to come and examine the doctrines of Mohammed for themselves. They accordingly sent six of their chief men, under a leader called Kish, to Medina. These at once embraced the new religion, and returned to Afghanistan to proselytise their fellow-countrymen. In the course of a few years a large proportion of the Afghans became Mohammedans; but many resisted to the last, and there is a tradition still current among the Afghans that the Kyber Hills were inhabited, until a comparatively recent period, by a colony of Jews. The term Pukhtun, corrupted into Pathan, is said to have been conferred on Kish by Mohammed himself. It has been adopted by the Afghans as a national designation, and is the name under which they are generally known by the natives of India. Indeed, in Afghanistan the term Afghan is now applied only to the direct descendants of Kish. But the tribes whom the Afghans reject as not of the same lineage as themselves, because they cannot prove their register in the

The Pathan Sovereignty.

same genealogy, are nevertheless allowed to be of the same stock as the predominant race; and these tribes call themselves Afghans or Pathans indifferently. The true explanation, however, of the nominal distinction between Afghans and Pathans is probably this: that in the time before the appearance of Mohammed, the entire nation derived their descent and title from Afghana, the grandson of Saul; while, as soon as the new religion became known, the first converts, who were of the family of Kish, reserved to themselves the proud designation of Afghans, and ignored altogether the tribes inhabiting the eastern boundary of the country, who did not adopt Mohammedanism for many years after it had been embraced by the tribes about Cabul and Herat.

The family of Ghor remained in possession, and even extended their conquests in Hindustan, until the death of Shahab-ud-din, the last of that dynasty, which occurred in 1206, when the house of Ghor became extinct. The kingdom then broke at once into separate states; and India, under the government of Kutb-ud-din, who, originally a Turkish slave, had been raised by Shahab-ud-din to the rank and power of viceroy, became an independent kingdom, and, after the disturbance caused by the dissolution of the Ghor empire had subsided, ceased to have any connection with the countries beyond the Indus. Thus Kutb-ud-din founded the Pathan or Afghan sovereignty, which had its seat at Delhi.

This dynasty had a very disturbed tenure of power for three centuries, during which all Hindustan, some isolated portions excepted, was brought to acknowledge the supremacy of the government of Delhi; but its subjection varied from entire control to very imperfect dependence. During the reigns of the kings of this line many important cities were founded besides Delhi, and various tombs and other buildings still bear witness to their magnificence and power. The progress of improvement was, however, much retarded by internal dissensions, and by the inroads of an enemy as yet fresh to India—the Moguls.

The famous Mogul leader Chengiz Khan, originally only a petty Tartar chief, having subdued the other nations of Tartary, and swollen his band with their united hordes, burst on the Mohammedan kingdoms of India with an army never equalled in numbers before or since. After laying waste Central and Western Asia, the Moguls turned their attention to India; and although at first they did not obtain any permanent footing, they left behind them fell marks of their visits. These irruptions under Chengiz Khan were unqualified calamities. He had no religion to teach, and no seeds of improvement to sow; nor did he offer an alternative of conversion or tribute. His only objects were rapine and slaughter, and the only traces he left were to be found in the devastation and ruin of every country he visited.

Although Timour, or Tamerlane, was the first Tartar chief who ravaged India to any extent (commencing in 1398), and the first who, after a series of conquests, proclaimed himself emperor over the country, the entire conquest of India was not effected until 1525, when Baber, his descendant, possessed himself of a great part of the country, established the seat of his government at Agra, and there founded the Mogul dynasty. Under the Mogul emperors Hindustan enjoyed a comparatively firm and settled government, first rose to any eminence among nations, and made that rapid progress in civilization which is testified to by the magnificence of their cities and great works, even as seen in the present day.

Those who wish to familiarize themselves in detail with the history of this great dynasty cannot do better than consult the valuable work of Mr. H. G. Keene, of Agra.* As frequent references to Mogul monarchs will be found in my narrative, I must, however, give a slight sketch of their history. The Mogul empire of Hindustan, then, dates only from the time of our Henry VIII., when Agra was taken from the Afghan house of Lodi, on the 10th May, 1526, by Baber, prince of the small but fertile district now called Khokhand. He was the sixth in descent on the father's side from Tamerlane; but his mother was a Mogul lady, descended from Chengiz Khan. Baber's early life was a succession of surprising vicissitudes and romantic adventures. When only fifteen he conducted his own government in Khokhand, and soon afterwards attempted the conquest of Samarcand. A series of revolts, however, compelled Baber to leave Samarcand after a siege, during which he lost his own hereditary domains through the rebellion of his subjects. He then spent nearly two years in the utmost poverty and distress; sometimes in the mountains, but oftener in the camp of his uncle, a Mogul leader. A little later, having collected a few followers, he effected the conquest of Cabul, over which he reigned for twenty-two years, and which was retained by his descendants till the end of the seventeenth century. Having now regained a position of power, he annexed the country around his capital, and began those enterprises which resulted in the conquest of

* To this work—*History of the Mogul Empire*—I am much indebted.

India, and the establishment of the Mogul line. He was essentially a man of war, a great Tartar general, but one in whom the usual cruel nature of those times was wanting. He was humane and considerate to his foes; and even after the trials of a long and adventurous life retained the same kind and affectionate heart, and the same easy and sociable temper, with which he set out on his career, while the possession of power and grandeur had neither blunted the delicacy of his taste, nor diminished his sensibility to the enjoyments of nature and imagination.

Baber died at Agra in 1530, ruler-in-chief of all the territories of Hindustan and Cabul, from the Hindu-Koosh to the borders of Bengal. His son and successor, Hoomayon, quarrelled with his brothers, became involved with the Afghan settlers, was finally driven out of Agra by a chief of the former line of rulers, and fled to Sinde, and subsequently to Persia. However, after many wanderings, he ultimately recovered Hindustan, quite as much by luck as by management. He died by a fall from a building, still standing in a part of Old Delhi, in 1556, and was succeeded by his son Akber, the offspring of Hoomayon's marriage while in exile with a Persian lady, Hameeda Begum. This prince, then only fourteen years old, ascended the throne under the auspices of Bairam Khan, a powerful minister, from whose dictation he was only able to get free by the most strenuous exertions. These exertions, however, hardened and developed his character, and to them, and to the general circumstances under which he gradually established his power, he was indebted for the ultimate prosperity of his reign. With the fall of Bairam Khan in 1560 commenced the era, short but grand, of the Mogul empire in its palmy state. Akber was the first to see that if he would rule the Hindus he must not treat the Moslems as favoured foreigners, but blend all his subjects into a common nationality, with common rights and privileges. He advocated strongly the intermarriage of members of the different creeds; and himself set the example by an alliance with the ancient native house of Amber (Jaipur). For several years after the commencement of his reign he was occupied in campaigns against various enemies of the new regime, both Hindu and Mohammedan, and subdued Bengal and the Deccan. During the intervals of peace he found time to build the fort at Agra, Futtepur Sekri, and a mausoleum to his father Hoomayon, as well as many other fine buildings. Like most despots, he was wilful and freakish; but, unlike most despots, he showed no disposition to indulge his whims at the expense of others. Rebels against his government were treated with firmness, but a door of conciliation was kept open as long as possible. Next to his civil administration was religious reform dear to his heart; but his scheme of a new national religion, formed of a mixture of the Hindu and the Mohammedan beliefs, never obtained any hold upon the people, and died a natural death soon after his decease. At his best Akber was far in advance, not only of the average of Eastern rulers, but of the average of rulers in any time or place. Justice was administered fairly to all his subjects, and he relieved the burdens of the cultivating class by an impartial landed settlement, and of the people generally by abolishing many taxes and fees.

This great monarch died in the year 1605, his last moments embittered by the quarrels of his children, and was succeeded by Jehangir, his eldest son. Of Jehangir little need be said. He was intemperate and cruel. In his first year his son Khoosroo rebelled; and when the rebellion was repressed sixteen hundred of the prince's adherents were impaled and set up in a double row, and through this avenue Khoosroo was conducted to receive his father's forgiveness. In 1607, the second year of his reign, Jehangir married the widow of Sher Ufgun, daughter of Itmad-ood-Dowlah, whom he had long loved. He raised her to the throne matrimonial by the title of Noor-Juhan, and also deferred to her advice and opinion in all matters. In his reign Sir T. Roe, the first English ambassador to India, was sent thither by James I. He found the Mogul court still very splendid, though the administration of the provinces had declined from the regularity that obtained under Akber.

On Jehangir's death, at Rajori, in 1627, Shah Juhan his son ascended the throne, and at once displayed that turn for graceful sumptuousness that was to mark his era. He celebrated his accession with great pomp; and soon after his return from the war in the Deccan, where he had the misfortune to lose his wife, he commenced the magnificent Taj at Agra, of which more anon. In 1637 the Court moved to Delhi, thenceforth the capital of the Mogul empire. In 1658 Shah Juhan's four sons began to fight for the succession; and the heir-apparent, Dara, being defeated by his younger and more energetic brother Aurungzebe, the latter immediately deposed his father, who was however allowed to live in regal state at Agra, until his death in 1666.

Aurungzebe was a cold and crafty zealot, well versed in affairs both civil and military, but his character and policy were

Decline of the Moguls.

the reverse of those of his predecessors. Fruitless campaigns against the Mahrattas, and injudicious oppression of his Hindu subjects, together with vexatious reforms and fanatical regulations, marked the greater part of his long reign, and by estranging all his people undermined the great Mogul empire. When he died, in 1707, this once formidable power commenced the downward course, from which it never rallied.

His son, Prince Moazzim, who succeeded under the title of Bahadur Shah, engaged in endless fights with his brothers and with the Mahrattas and the growing power of the Sikhs, and after a short and inglorious reign died at Lahore in 1712. His death was followed by the usual struggle among his sons. The eldest, Jehander Shah, reached the throne after slaying all his brothers, but was himself put to death in the following year by his nephew, who, under the title of Farokshir, ascended the peacock throne. He adopted the inane policy of his predecessor, and was murdered in his turn, in 1719, by the Seiads, a race of powerful Mohammedan nobles, who raised an obscure prince of the blood to the throne, under the title of Mohammed Shah. Under his rule the monarchy declined even more rapidly than before. The Jats took possession of Agra, and the Mahrattas under Sivaji regaining their independence, became in their turn the aggressors, and threatened even Delhi. But the most fatal blow was the terrible invasion of Nadir Shah of Persia, who in 1739 plundered Delhi, after murdering nearly all the inhabitants. The power of the Moguls thus came to an end; their viceroys broke up their dominions into numerous small independent kingdoms; and although, after the death of Mohammed Shah, we read of other Moguls—Ahmed Shah, Alamgir, and

Shah Alum—they possessed but a shred of power. The Mogul empire had ceased to be a power, although it did not become utterly extinct; for that king of Delhi who joined with the mutineers in 1857 was the last representative of the Great Moguls.

Let us now turn to that part of the history of India which may be termed its European connection. The discovery of the route to the East by the Cape of Good Hope, by Vasco de Gama, in 1498, gave to Portugal, as long as she retained her naval superiority, the monopoly of the Indian trade. In a very short time the Portuguese had possessed themselves of Goa, Diu, and other places on the coast. Here they founded large cities, which they retain even now, but shorn of their former glory, and mostly in ruins. The Portuguese were followed by the Dutch, who obtained no permanent settlement in the country, and a few years later by the English, the French, and the Danes.

The first English East India Company was incorporated by Queen Elizabeth in 1600; and in 1615 Sir Thomas Roe, the first ambassador from England, was sent to the court of Jehangir. Within seventy years from the establishment of the Company's first factory at Surat, the town of Madras was founded, and Bombay and Calcutta, then insignificant cities, ceded to its power. The French were for a long time successful in their endeavours to oppose the growth of the Company. Both were assisted in their numerous engagements by various native princes, with whom they formed alliances; but in 1751 the genius of Clive gave the French their first check. Subsequent reverses completed the ruin of their cause; twenty years later as a power in India the French had ceased to exist; and the great victory of Plassey laid at the feet of Clive the rich provinces of Bengal and Behar. After putting the military and civil services of the Company on a satisfactory footing, Clive returned to England in 1767, leaving Warren Hastings administrator of affairs at Calcutta, with the title of President, which was exchanged a few years later for that of Governor-General. Hitherto affairs in India had been managed solely by the Company; but the regulating act of 1773, which created the first Governor-General, created also his council, and was the first that recognized the Company as a ruling body. Eleven years later came Pitt's India Bill. This, although nominally leaving the government to the Court of Directors, virtually transferred it to a Board of Control, whose president became Secretary of State for India. The first Governor-General was opposed throughout by a hostile council, but nevertheless succeeded in consolidating the power of the Company; and his energetic repulse of the formidable alliance of the Nizam, the Mahrattas, and Hyder Ali, in 1780, probably saved British India.

Warren Hastings was succeeded by Lord Cornwallis, who ruled from 1786 to 1793. He effected the complete reform of the civil service, and introduced the permanent settlement of the land revenue of Bengal.

Under his successor, Lord Wellesley (1798 to 1805), the Mysore war was concluded by the capture of Seringapatam, and death of Tippoo Sultan; the Mahratta confederacy was broken up; and the brilliant campaigns of Lord Lake and General Wellesley against Scindia and Holkar, added to the strength and extent of the Company's dominions.

In the administration of Lord Minto (1807 to 1813) nothing remarkable occurred, and the terms of office of the three succeeding viceroys—Lord Hastings, Lord Amherst, and Lord Bentinck—which bring us to the year 1835, were periods of peaceful progress, with the exception of the first Burmese war.

Lord Auckland, who came next, by his resolution to support Shah Shuja against Dost Mohammed, brought on the Afghan expedition (1839 to 1842), the disasters attending which it was left for his successor, Lord Ellenborough, to retrieve. This administration also saw the conquest of Sinde, under Sir C. Napier. Under Lord Hardinge (1844 to 1847), the first Punjab war broke out. The second destroyed the power of the Sikhs. Their country was annexed by Lord Dalhousie, who followed Lord Hardinge, and whose able reign of eight years was marked by the annexation of Tanjore, Nagpur, and Oudh. He left India in bad health in 1856; and in 1857, exactly one century later than Plassey, the victory that first led to the onward progress of the British power, occurred the Sepoy revolt, which cut short the career of the East India Company, and led to the assumption of the direct government of India by the Crown. Thus England is now the unquestioned ruler and paramount power in all India, with the exception of the states of Nepaul and Bhootan, which alone maintain their absolute independence. The other native states are all more or less dependent, and have relinquished political relations with each other, or with any but the paramount British power. British India, with its two hundred and forty millions of inhabitants, is now divided into nine provinces, each under its own civil government, and each independent of the others, but subordinate to the supreme government.

The old division of the country into three large presidencies is, however, still in a measure observed; for we find the Bengal Presidency more directly under the control of the Viceroy; and the Madras and Bombay Presidencies, each with its own Governor and Commander-in-Chief; but in grave matters all are subordinate to the supreme government at Calcutta. This again is largely controlled in its actions by the Secretary of State and the Indian Council at home.

The Bengal Presidency being very much the largest of the three, is subdivided into seven provinces—Bengal, the North-western Provinces, the Punjab, Oudh, the Central Provinces, British Burmah, and Assam. These, with the presidencies of Madras and Bombay, make up the total of nine.

The three first of the seven provinces of Bengal are, from their extent and importance, placed under the administration of officials termed Lieutenant-Governors. The remaining four are ruled by Chief Commissioners; and all are, in a measure, controlled by the Viceroy, who is aided by a council of five members and the Commander-in-Chief in India. The duties of these several governments are all carried out by members of the Indian Civil Service and military officers in civil employ; and it is to the talent and energy of the various secretaries, judges, magistrates, collectors, and commissioners, forming this body, that India enjoys at the present time the just rule and the accompanying prosperity, which present so marked a contrast to her condition under the sway of the native sovereigns.

CHAPTER IV.

Description of Bombay—The Harbour—Historical sketch—Appearance of the town—The Fort—The commercial part—The Merchants—State of trade—The principal buildings—The University—The Post Office—The Cathedral—Crawford Market—European shops—Population—Mohammedans—Hindus—Early history of the Hindus—Aboriginal tribes of India—Eurasians—Suburbs of Bombay—Our drive—The weather—The native town—The Bazaar—Dress of the people—Description of Bazaar—Mode of business—Malabar Hill—The Towers of Silence—The Parsees—Their history—Their religion—Their mode of burial—Birds of prey—Their utility—Return to hotel—Indian moonlight—Preparations for departure.

FOR the first week after our arrival in Bombay we remained quietly in the hotel. During that time I quite recovered from the effects of my illness, with the exception of a little weakness, and was able to go out and visit the places of interest in the town. Since my former visit Bombay had increased greatly in size, and many fine buildings had also been erected. I was curious to note the changed aspect of the place; and my wife also was anxious to form a nearer acquaintance with the novel scenes of Eastern life and character, now for the first time presented to her view.

Bombay, the most important commercial city of India, possesses one of the most perfect natural harbours in the world. It is a large, wide, land-locked expanse of water, enclosed by a number of small islands very close to each other, between which and the mainland there is a large channel most effectually protected on both sides, and of sufficient breadth and depth to allow almost any number of ships, of the largest size and tonnage, to anchor within easy distance from the shore. The town of Bombay itself is really situated on a cluster of small islands, connected with each other by causeways; but at the present time these islands have become so mixed up with each other that the casual observer would take them for only one, divided from the mainland by a narrow creek. Bombay was given, in 1662, by the Portuguese, to our Charles II., as a part of the dowry of their Princess, Katharine of Braganza. A few years later it was handed over to the East India Company, already established at Surat and at Fort St. George, now known as the town of Madras. The advantages of Bombay as a trading port were fully appreciated by the Company, and the gradual rise of their power soon converted the small fishing village into a town, which, increasing yearly in size and importance, is at the present day second to none in the empire. The city, particularly as viewed from the deck of a ship on entering the harbour, is very picturesque. It is irregularly built, with a background of hills clothed nearly to their summits with cocoa-nut trees and waving palms. These afford shelter to numerous white bungalows, the abodes of the more affluent Europeans, which, gleaming here and there amidst the dark foliage, lend life and novelty to the scene. The whole forms a perfect tropical landscape, particularly striking to those who make acquaintance for the first time with any part of our Indian possessions. In former days the town was encircled by a wall, and a large fort and other defences guarded it against foreign foes: but more peaceful times have dawned upon the city; no trace is left of its fortifications; and the ground upon which they stood is at the present time covered with buildings and noisy with the busy hum of men. This part of the town is what may be termed the European portion; and although it still retains its former name, and is termed the Fort, no signs of its warlike nature are left. The so-called 'Fort' is separated from the native town by the Esplanade, and a large 'maidan' or piece of common land. It is entirely devoted to the purposes of commerce. It is in fact the business part of the town, both official and private; for the various government offices are to be found here, as well as the Exchange, the Banks, and the offices of the merchants, to whose energy and perseverance the present high commercial status enjoyed by Bombay is due.

The merchants of Bombay include Europeans and natives of the country, with that curious race the Parsees, who have likewise a large share in its commercial prosperity. The opening of the Suez Canal much increased its foreign trade, and has rendered this town the chief depôt of Indian commerce. A great number of factories have also of late years been erected; and it is considered probable that in the matter of the weaving and dyeing of fabrics India will be rendered comparatively independent of England, and that Bombay will be able to supply to other parts of the Indian empire those articles which hitherto have had to be purchased elsewhere.

The principal buildings in this locality, all of recent construction, are the Government Secretariat and Municipal Offices, very large palatial edifices; the University, a small structure, but perfect of its kind, standing in a prominent position on the Esplanade, facing the sea; and, close to it, the Law Offices, a building in somewhat the same style of architecture. The new Post-office is a fine commodious structure, with ample room to carry on the great amount of work thrown on the department here, as Bombay is the port of arrival and departure of all foreign mails, and the whole yearly correspondence of India probably reaches sixty-five millions of letters, besides newspapers. Many of the banks and places of business of the different merchants are fine structures, and European in style and character. The only building of any antiquity in this neighbourhood is the Cathedral, an unpretending edifice, which, erected at the time when all the principal part of the town was contained within the walls of the Fort, now appears somewhat out of place in the centre of this busy haunt of commerce.

There remains to be mentioned the Crawford Market, the mart where everything required for the table may be bought—the Covent Garden of Bombay—which in the early morning presents quite an attractive sight. There is also a Dockyard. Here likewise are all the shops for the sale of European goods. They are just like those at home, only, as the keepers are anxious to realize a fortune quickly, they put such an exorbitant price on their goods that it is no wonder new-comers are alarmed; for it also astonishes the old residents, who for a long time have been painfully aware of the fact that two shillings in India are not nearly equal in value to one at home.

In walking through this part of the town, or, in fact, any portion of Bombay, one cannot fail to be struck with the great number of people about. The whole of the streets appear to be filled with human life; nor is this strange, when one considers that this by no means very extensive town contains, after Calcutta, the greatest number of inhabitants of any city in the Indian empire, its population at the last census being six hundred and fifty thousand. Many of these are Europeans; but the greater number are, of course, natives, Hindus and Mohammedans, and it is calculated that the Parsees reach fifty thousand.

The inhabitants of Hindustan have been estimated to number upwards of two hundred and forty millions. Most of these by far are Hindus, who are said to be in the proportion of more than three to one, as compared with the Mohammedans—one hundred and fifty millions to forty millions. The remainder of the population comprises Europeans, Parsees, Eurasians or half-castes, and the Aboriginal or hill tribes. The Mohammedans, who form about one-sixth of the entire population of India, are of Afghan, Persian, Turk, Beluch, and Arabic origin, being the descendants of the numerous invaders who have entered Hindustan from the north-west since the commencement of the eleventh century. They are a fine well-proportioned race, approaching in colour a dark brown, with regular features indicative of their origin. Some are met with in whom these peculiarities are wanting, and who approach more closely to the type of the great mass of the population. These most probably are the descendants of Hindus, who either embraced the religion of their conquerors of their own accord, or were converted to that faith by the forcible means generally employed towards the vanquished by the victorious followers of the Prophet.

The Hindus are well-formed, and in some parts of India,

as the Deccan and the upper plain of the Ganges, are even robust, energetic, and hardy; but their chief bodily characteristic is extreme suppleness and flexibility of the animal fibre, rendering them the best runners, climbers, leapers, and wrestlers in Asia, though incapable of maintaining exertion or resisting fatigue for any lengthened period. The face of the Hindu is oval, with dark-brown eyes, having a tinge of yellow in the white, and the hair is long, black, coarse, and straight. The upper classes, especially in Hindustan proper, and particularly towards the north-west, are nearly as light in colour as the natives of South and Central Europe, and they are also far more handsome and tall than the lower classes. As we proceed towards the southern extremity of the peninsula, the hue of the skin is observed to darken by degrees, until in the lower castes it assumes almost the blackness of the negro. This, however, depends very much on the position in society of the inhabitants; for although the natives of the more southern Madras Presidency are usually dark, still the upper classes, and many of the females of that part of India, are not darker than the majority elsewhere. It is difficult to speak in general terms of the character of the inhabitants of a country which shows so much diversity in class and nationality, and where so many varieties of race, creed, and even climate exert their influence on the habits and feelings of the people. Again, Englishmen in India have less opportunity than might be expected of forming opinions of the native character. Even in England, few know much of people beyond their own class; and what they do know, they learn mainly from newspapers and publications, of a description which does not exist in India. In India also differences of religion and manners put bars to our intimacy with the natives. We know nothing of the interior arrangements of families but by report, and have no share in those numerous occurrences of life in which the amiable traits of character are most exhibited.

These considerations should make us distrust our own impressions, when unfavourable, but cannot blind us to the fact that the Hindus have in reality some great defects of character. These defects, no doubt, arise chiefly from moral causes; but they are also to be ascribed in part to their physical constitution, and in part to the soil and climate. Some races are certainly less vigorous than others, and all must degenerate if placed in an enervating atmosphere. In India a warm temperature is accompanied by a fertile soil, which renders severe labour unnecessary, producing a state of listless inactivity, which may be taken as a characteristic of the whole people. Akin to their indolence is their timidity, which arises more from the dread of being involved in trouble and difficulty than from want of physical courage. From these two radical influences almost all their vices are derived. The most prominent vice of the Hindus is want of veracity, in which they outdo even most Eastern nations. Perjury, which is only an aggravated species of falsehood, is naturally common. These failings, however, are usually only brought under notice through dealings with the lower orders, for the merchants and bankers are generally strict observers of their engagements. Hindus are also cunning and well fitted by nature for intrigue. Penetrating the views of a person with whom they have to deal, they will present things in such a form as best suits their own designs, and contrive by indirect manœuvres to make others unwittingly contribute to the accomplishment of their own ends. Like all people who are slow to actual conflict, they are very litigious, and much addicted to verbal altercation, while their public spirit is confined to their caste or village. Great national spirit has indeed at times been shown in war, especially where religion is concerned; but in most affairs of life they display an utter want of manliness. Yet this censure, although true of the Hindus generally as compared with other nations, by no means applies to all classes, or to any at all times. The Hindus of the more northern parts of India are hardy and brave, even to desperation, while great part of the labouring people are industrious and persevering. And Hindus generally agree in this, that at all ages they are very sharp and intelligent, fond of conversation and amusement; while their contempt of death is indeed an extraordinary concomitant to their timidity when exposed to lesser evils.

It is generally accepted that the Hindus are not the aboriginal inhabitants of India, but that, having arrived from the north-west, they first occupied that part of the country north of the Nerbudda, called emphatically Hindustan, and subsequently crossed that river into the Deccan, or south of the land, where they dispossessed the natives, as before. No reliable information exists, however, to prove this fact, and the relation of the original Hindu tribes to the other Indo-European nations, and to the aboriginal inhabitants of India, can only be surmised; as with the exception of the misty pages of the earliest Brahmanical sacred writings, nothing is afforded to elucidate the mystery. Most historians admit the fact of a connection between the original Sanskrit-speaking tribes and the other nations of Western Asia and Europe, as proved by the common origin of their respective languages; for undoubtedly Sanskrit, Zend, Greek, Latin, Slavonic, and the Celtic languages, must have all sprung from one common source. They are sisters, though Sanskrit may be considered the eldest, as it generally preserves the earliest form, and its structure is the most transparent for philological purposes. It is perhaps going too far to assert that the connection thus proved is one of race. That is more a question belonging to physical science than to history, as it is enough for our purpose if it is granted that in some remote pre-historic time the ancestors of these various tribes were living in close political relations to each other; and the similarity which we find in their languages must undoubtedly prove this, even although the question of race should remain as unsettled a problem as before. It is a subject beset with difficulties, although it is surmised that at some period in the past, and in some limited region of Europe or Asia, there lived a tribe from whose imperfect dialect all the rich and cultivated tongues now spoken and written by the teeming millions of Europe, and of some of the fairest parts of Asia, have descended. To know when and where this tribe lived and formed its language is unfortunately beyond our power. It is indeed often assumed and asserted that the original Indo-European home was in the north-eastern part of the Iranian plateau, near the Hindu-Koosh mountains; but so definite a determination possesses not the slightest shadow of authority or value. We really know next to nothing of the last movements which have brought any branch of the family into its present place of abode, for even these lie beyond the reach of the very hoariest traditions which have come down to us.

The daylight of recorded history dawns first upon the easternmost—the Indo-Persian or Aryan branch; for, probably not far from two thousand years before the Christian era, we see the Sanskrit-speaking tribes just across the threshold of India, and working their way towards the great fertile territory of the Ganges, of which they were soon to become the masters; and we know that India at least was not the first home of the family. This epoch however, early as it appears to us, is far from the beginning of Indo-European migrations, and who can say which of them has wandered widest in the search after a permanent dwelling-place? We know, or at least have good grounds for surmising, that most of the European nations are of Asiatic origin, and the researches of the learned are daily adding to an accumulation of evidence which tends to prove that the aborigines of Great Britain sprang from the nations of the East. This hypothesis of Asiatic colonization is based chiefly on the information afforded in the study of the early religion of the Aryan tribes, and of that of the primitive inhabitants of our own island. We find at the outset that the emigration of bodies of people in every age has been attended with one universally accompanying circumstance—the importation of their religious opinions and rites into the country of their adoption; and that there is a striking similarity between the religious rites of the Druids and those of the Eastern nations, none acquainted with the testimony of ancient authors on the subject will venture to question. Druidism, like the Brahmanical superstition, was but a modification of the same thing—the original worship of the elements, which at one time prevailed in Asia. Among other things, both the Druids and the Brahmans cultivated astronomy, doubtless in connection with astrology, which so largely entered into their religious rites. But the most remarkable point of similarity is the belief in the transmigration of souls, held by both Druids and Brahmans, which is still a fundamental part of the religion of the Hindus at the present day. Various other traces and traditions bearing on the subject might be quoted, but, without attempting to pursue the enquiry further, it may be remarked that strong evidence exists to prove that an aboriginal people, whose manners and religion indicated an Asiatic origin, in remote times occupied the south-western peninsula of England. And beyond this, the similarity of customs points to the fact that it is to the branch of the race which peopled India we are indebted for our ancestors, and that the Hindu is to our own countrymen, not only a man, but a veritable brother, if these theories as to our common descent from the Aryan branch of the human race can be believed. And certainly there may be some grounds for the assertion; for, throwing aside all suppositions or evidences as to manners, language, or religion, it is a well-known fact that a tribe of men called the Kafres, to the number of about one million souls, inhabit at the present day their original home on the slopes of the Hindu-Koosh mountains, west of the Chitral Valley, down to the Cabul river. Their language has no affinity with the Persian or Arabic, but with the Sanskrit, and their religion, although grossly idolatrous, is closely allied to Hinduism, facts which have caused them to be considered by many the remains of the primitive Aryan family; while their fair complexions, blue eyes, the strength and courage of their men, and the beauty of their women, have pointed them out as the possible progenitors of the English race, who have still preserved the same appearance, while the Hindus, sprung from the same stock, on forsaking their more northern home for the plains of India, have deteriorated both in size and complexion, their dusky hue and other differences being attributable to climatic influences from which our race has been exempt.

The aboriginal native tribes of the country, although dispossessed by the arrival of the Hindus, were by no means exterminated; and under the various names of Bheels, Coles, Gonds, Dufflas, and Looshais, still exist in the peninsula to the number of several millions. They are mostly dark in colour, of small and active frame, and with a peculiarly quick and restless eye, totally uncivilized, or owning only a few importations of Hindu superstition or civilization. They have little clothing, and few arms beyond bows and arrows. Their ordinary food consists of wild berries and game; but they have no repugnance to the killing and eating of oxen, and they bury their dead instead of burning them. These tribes chiefly inhabit the fastnesses of the Vindhya and Satpura mountain ranges, and their offsets and continuations as far east as the hills of Bhaugulpur in Bengal. They also exist on the eastern frontiers of Bengal, and in considerable numbers in Candeish, Guzerat, and along the West Ghauts. There is, in fact, scarcely any considerable mountain or hill region in India where some of them are not to be found; and the districts they inhabit are the wildest portions of the whole peninsula, many of them remaining still unexplored.

The Eurasians, or half-castes, the result of the union of the European and native races, exist in considerable numbers all over India, and are of all shades of colour, from black to nearly pure white. In feature they resemble more nearly their European progenitors, but in size and development they show unmistakably their native origin; they are, as a class, poor, weak, effeminate creatures. Some are strong, well-educated men, holding positions of trust; but these are rare. Most of them are unfit for laborious work, and are generally found employed as clerks, or in other similar subordinate offices. In the city of Bombay, and in various other parts of that presidency, a considerable number of Eurasians are found who are termed Portuguese, being the descendants of mixed marriages of men of that nation, the earliest settlers in the country. This race is similar in every respect to the other half-castes, and they profess, like the majority of the others, the Roman Catholic religion, but perhaps in a more bigoted form, as handed down from their ancestors, in whose time the despotic sway of the Inquisition flourished at Goa, Damaun, and other places on the Bombay coast.

The European officials and merchants of Bombay do not reside in the Fort. They only retain their offices and warehouses in that quarter of the town, and their bungalows are situated in what may be termed the suburbs. The principal resort of the more wealthy classes is Malabar Hill, a considerable elevation overlooking the sea, and distant four miles from the commercial part of the town, from which it is divided by the native town and the Breach Candy road. This separates also Kamballa Hill, Byculla, and Mazagon, the remaining suburban quarters on this side of the town. On the other side of the Fort is Colaba, a narrow neck of land jutting into the sea, and terminating in a point on which stands the lighthouse, the first object seen on entering the harbour. Here are the barracks for the European soldiers, and it is a favourite place of residence of the mercantile classes.

We had a delightful drive one afternoon around the greater part of the environs of Bombay, which gave us a very good idea of the place and of the mode of living of its inhabitants, both European and native. We left the hotel about three o'clock, an earlier hour than usual for the evening drive; but although the direct rays of the sun are hot, the air at this period of the year (February) is only just pleasantly warm. There is never any great variation in the temperature at Bombay; it does not experience the great alternations of heat and cold which obtain in the more northern parts of India; and between eighty and eighty-five degrees is the usual range of the thermometer. Although this is a trying heat to endure always, yet it is not inimical to the constitution. Bombay is reckoned one of the healthiest towns in the country for foreigners; and undoubtedly a good deal of the immunity they enjoy from the effects of an unaccustomed high degree of temperature is due to the sea-breeze, that delicious panacea for tropical heat, which, commencing about sunset, blows steadily all night, rendering the greater part of the twenty-four hours comparatively cool.

Our road led us first through the native town, which, like all resorts of the indigenous inhabitants of the East, is neither clean nor savoury, despite the efforts of the municipal authorities. Still it affords a marked contrast to many Indian towns in the matter of cleanliness, particularly to those under native rule, where dirt and abominations of all kinds so abound that one ceases to wonder that cholera, the scourge of Asia, has taken up its permanent abode in this country. A native city, although not pleasant to the smell, is, however, very interesting and amusing, particularly to a new comer; and the Hindu quarter of Bombay forms no exception to this rule. The narrow streets, with their curious little shops in the bazaar portion crowding on to the footway, were thronged with people. The majority were clothed in flowing garments of all shapes and colours; but the coolies and other low castes were not overburdened with raiment. A scanty loin cloth, or even less in some cases, constitutes their sole attire, certainly affording no hindrance to the play of their limbs in the pursuit of their occupations, but offering a more complete exposition of the human form divine than is compatible with Western ideas. The women, however, make up in their dress for the deficiencies of their husbands and brothers. Seldom does one meet with a woman, either in town or village, who is not covered from head to foot with a long flowing garment called a saree, folded round the body in various turns, with a long loose portion at the back, pulled over the head to form a veil if necessary. Among the poorer classes these robes are made of cotton, dyed various colours, but they are worn of silk by the richer; and the gay tints of the sarees lend plenty of life and colour to an Indian crowd. The women of India wear nothing more than this, with the exception of the Mohammedan females, who have in addition a pair of loose trousers. Neither Hindus nor Mohammedans wear stays or any such artificial supports, yet their figures, particularly when young, are most graceful, undulating with every movement. Their

An Indian Bazaar.

features are regular, and the majority may be termed decidedly pretty; but they age very rapidly, becoming fat and plain, and in extreme life are veritable witches in appearance, possessing none of the charms of old age which in so many cases render the females of a European community so interesting in declining years.

Bazaars in England and in India materially differ. In the East a bazaar is a street in a native city, containing the shops and the abodes of the different retail traders; and in large towns there are several streets or bazaars, each more particularly devoted to some special line of business. Thus the manufacturers of brass articles will be found all congregated together. The same practice obtains among the silver and gold workers, the cloth merchants, the dealers in provisions, wood, and oil. All are close to each other, saving the intending purchaser endless trouble, as the vendors of the particular article of which he is in search are all to be found in one special locality. The shops themselves, to be sure, are merely open, dark, dirty raised sheds, opening from the dwelling-houses on to the narrow street, crowded with the commodities in which the proprietor deals. A clear space is left in the centre, in which, in the intervals of business, the shopkeeper and his assistants are to be seen squatted in indolent enjoyment of their leisure. Perfectly motionless, and with eyes half closed, they appear like sleepy spiders waiting for their prey. No sooner does this approach in the person of a customer than an instantaneous change takes place. They spring back to life at once, their listlessness is exchanged for bustle, and they plunge forthwith into the noisy argumentative discussion, which apparently is necessary to the completion of all matters of sale or purchase in the East. The smallest article cannot be bought without a haggling as to the price, and a tenth part of the original value set on it is generally accepted. This result is attained by a good half-hour's abuse of each other and the article in question, between the shopkeeper and the would-be buyer, assisted generally by a chorus of sympathizing bystanders. As all talk together in the shrillest of voices, with the utmost power of their lungs, the din produced in a bazaar, when business is brisk, is something indescribable, causing the visitor to beat a hasty retreat, with the opinion that what with the uproar, and what with the perfume (decidedly not of 'Araby the blest'), an inspection of an Indian bazaar may be an amusing, but is certainly not a pleasant, undertaking.

After passing through the native town we came on the broad and level road leading from Byculla to Malabar Hill, and surmounting the steep ascent soon found ourselves on the summit, with a perfect view of the whole of Bombay and its adjacent coast. This hill is certainly a most charming part to reside in, and that it is so appreciated is evident from the numerous bungalows already erected. These are for the most part large handsome houses, with fine compounds, or gardens. The rent of these residences is, however, very high; more than a thousand a year being generally demanded. Hence only the higher officials and the more opulent merchants live here. The Hill is not confined to Europeans; for of late years rich Parsees and other native traders have settled on it, and in their style of living vie with, or even exceed, their neighbours.

The Parsees.

On our return home we passed the 'Dokkma,' or 'Tower of Silence,' of the Parsees, who here dispose of their dead in the manner handed down to them from remote ages. These people claim to be the descendants of the ancient Persian race, driven out of Iran after the Mohammedan conquest of Persia, who were allowed to settle in Bombay by its then inhabitants, on the condition that they venerated the Hindu religion, so far as not to offend in any way the scruples of its devotees, and also that they never carried arms nor mixed in the political affairs of their adopted country. These conditions were complied with, and being a conservative race they preserve them to this day; for no other occupation is followed by them than the peaceful pursuit of commerce. They have also preserved intact their religious observances, and still continue the worship of fire in the same manner as the first followers of Zoroaster two thousand five hundred years ago, although at the present day, from their residence in Hindustan, it has lost something of its purity from mixture with various Hindu forms and observances. The Parsees believe in God, the creator, ruler, and preserver of the universe, without form, and invisible; a great Light, from whom all glory, bounty, and goodness flow. Thus regarded, his most perfect form is seen in the splendour of the sun; but he is usually worshipped under the symbol of fire, a flame of which is never allowed to become extinct in their sacred temples, but is constantly fed with pieces of perfumed wood at the hands of the priests attached to the building. They also believe in the independent existence of an evil principle or author of evil, and in the immortality of souls. They possess very many copious rituals, among which may be mentioned the purification of physical and moral impurities by cleansing with holy water, and by numerous prayers. [Eating anything cooked by a person of another religion is contrary to their faith, and they object to beef and pork, especially to ham. Marriages can only be contracted with persons of their own caste or creed, and polygamy is forbidden.] A very serious schism has lately broken out in the Parsee community. One party, having become more liberal in their ideas, wish to make sundry innovations in their religion and mode of life, and are stoutly resisted by the conservative section. However, there is little doubt that as their intercourse with Europeans becomes closer, the more advanced party will be successful.

These Towers of Silence, or burial-places of the Parsees, are walled enclosures, containing one or more square towers built of grey stone. In the top of these towers is a spacious grating, upon which the naked corpse is placed, and left to be devoured by the crows and vultures and other birds of prey, who are in consequence attracted to this locality, and are always to be seen, in various stages of repletion, on the branches of the trees surrounding the cemetery. A very short time suffices for these ravenous creatures to entomb the fleshy parts in their capacious maws, and the bones either fall, or are pushed through the grating, to join the other relics of mortality in the vault below.

It is said to be the custom for the mourning relatives and friends of the deceased to watch most anxiously the dispersion of the remains, to enable them to foretell, according to the order in which the several parts are disposed of, the future state of the soul, now escaped from its earthly tenement. Great is the delight of the mourners, if they observe that the right eye is consumed before its fellow, as this is the best augury for complete happiness in the next world. This mode of disposal of the dead is, to my mind, a revolting custom, discreditable alike to the enlightened ideas of the Parsees, and to the government that permits it. But owing to the policy we have hitherto pursued in India, never to interfere in any way with the religious observances of the inhabitants, no check has been placed upon the practice. Consequently this filthy and unsanitary method of disposal continues to be employed, not only in Bombay, but in every locality where Parsees are present in any number. It would become an intolerable nuisance, were it not for the presence of birds innumerable, who perform their part in the proceeding so expeditiously, that the sense of sight only is offended.

It is not only in large towns, or near these Towers, that such birds congregate. All over the country, whether in inhabited districts, or in the desolate jungle, there are to be seen innumerable varieties of the feathered tribes, more especially birds of prey, vultures, hawks, crows, and similar species. At first one cannot help wondering for what purpose such numbers exist. A very short residence in the East, however, is sufficient to point out their utility. They are the natural scavengers of India, and without them one could scarcely live. Sanitary rules are unknown to the natives. They consider the proper place for filth, offal, or refuse of any description to be anywhere, as it is thrown down. They trust to Providence to remove it, and they certainly do not trust in vain; for a very short exposure of anything consumable is sufficient to bring a flock of birds, who cause its rapid disappearance. The birds are often assisted in this by jackals, wolves, and other unclean feeding animals, which also exist in large numbers, and in many places make 'night hideous' with their din. They too are simply a necessary evil to obviate the sanitary apathy and ignorance of the inhabitants, which no amount of teaching can reform. The invariable answer of a native to any suggestion as to improvement in the mode of living or otherwise is, that his ancestors lived in the same manner, and that if good enough for them, it must be equally so for himself and his family.

By the time we got back to the hotel it was quite dark; for there is no twilight in this country. Directly the sun sinks below the horizon, a transition from bright light to an ashen-grey colouring takes place. This is rapidly succeeded by the darkness of night, and the simultaneous appearance of the stars; while, if at the proper lunar period, the whole scene is momentarily bathed in delicious floods of moonlight, the silvery rays causing surrounding objects to be as discernible as at midday. An Indian moon must be seen to be appreciated. The clear atmosphere enables moon and stars alike to shine forth in the fullest strength and beauty, making a scene of heavenly splendour so brilliant, yet so soft and exquisite, that the most indifferent observer of nature must be moved at the magnificence of such a testimony to the power and prescience of the Creator.

The few succeeding days we spent in quietly inspecting various objects of interest, finishing each evening with a walk on the Esplanade, close to the sea, before our return to the hotel for dinner. And so, having completed a stay of a week in Bombay, we began to think of making preparation for our departure, and of endeavouring to rejoin the regiment before it arrived at its destination. Obtaining the necessary leave, and documents to frank our party on the journey, we therefore packed up our belongings, and were ready on the evening of the 18th to continue our travels the following morning.

CHAPTER V.

The religions of India—The Hindu religion—Its antiquity—Its earliest form—The Vedas—Their doctrines—Doctrine of Monotheism—The god Brahma—Doctrine of Transmigration —The religious rites—The present state of the Hindu religion—Its principal doctrines—The Hindu Pantheon—Practical part of Hindu worship—The Hindu sects—Effects of the Hindu religion—The Buddhist religion—Its origin, doctrines, and ritual—The Jain religion—Its doctrines—Jain Temples—The Mohammedan religion—Its origin—The Koran—Its doctrines—Din, or practical part of Islam—The Sonnites and Shiites—Christianity in India—Its introduction and present condition—The institution of Caste—Its origin—Caste in its original form—Caste as at present practised.

IN the preceding chapter I have attempted to describe the native inhabitants of India, their character, dress, and other peculiarities; but no reference has yet been made to those very important features in their life, religion and caste. These are, however, so constantly brought under the notice of the sojourner in India, and affect so thoroughly the whole structure of native society in the country, that I purpose a' brief description of the various religions followed throughout this large continent, concluding with a slight sketch of the vexed subject of caste. Not only are the religions of India matters of deep interest in themselves, but they force themselves upon the attention of every visitor to that country, and make some sort of acquaintance with them a necessity. Hence, I trust my readers will pardon this rather long digression from my more personal narrative.

Hinduism is the most ancient, indeed it may almost be called the original, religion of India, and even at the present day it is professed by nearly two-thirds of the inhabitants. That with other forms of religious observance it enters largely into the life of the natives, is patent to the traveller very shortly after his arrival. For, to quote the words of Elphinstone*—"There is indeed no country where religion is so constantly brought before the eye as in India. Every town has temples of all descriptions, from a shrine which barely holds the idol, to a pagoda with lofty towers, and spacious courts and colonnades. To all these votaries are constantly repairing, to hang the image with garlands, and to present it with fruit and flowers. The banks of the river, or artificial sheet of water (for there is no town that is not built on one or other), have often noble flights of steps leading down to the water, which are covered in the early part of the day with persons performing their ablutions, and going through their devotions as they stand in the stream. In the day the attention is drawn by the song, or by the graceful figures and flowing drapery, of groups of women as they bear their offerings to a temple. Parties of Brahmans and others pass on similar occasions, and frequently numerous processions move on with drums and music to perform the ceremony of some particular holiday. They carry with them images borne aloft on stages; representations of temples, chariots, and other objects, which, though of cheap and flimsy materials, are made with skill and taste, and present a gay appearance.

"At a distance from towns, temples are always found in

* *History of India*, a work to which I am much indebted for the facts in this chapter.

inhabited places, and frequently rise among the trees on the banks of rivers, in the heart of deep groves, or on the summit of hills. Even in the wildest forest a shrine covered with vermilion, with a garland hung on to a tree above it, or a small flag fastened among the branches, apprizes the traveller of the sanctity of the spot. Troops of pilgrims and religious mendicants are often met on the road; the mendicants are distinguished by the dress of their order, and the pilgrims by bearing some symbol of the god to whose shrine they are going, and shouting out his name or watchword whenever they meet with other passengers. Frequent religious meetings on days sacred to particular gods, called 'melas' or fairs, are common, and are chiefly intended for the humbler classes, who crowd to them with delight, even from distant quarters. And though the religion presented in so many striking forms does not enter in reality into all the scenes to which it gives rise, yet it still exercises a prodigious influence over the people, and has little if at all declined in that respect since the first period of its institution."

The followers of Brahma, holding the original belief of the country, the Mohammedan religion being of much later date, naturally exist in much greater numbers than the adherents of Islam, and their worship, thus mixed up with temples, shrines, and religious processions, is obtruded far more on the public gaze. It is to them the remarks above more fitly apply. For although the followers of the Prophet have their mosques, these edifices are not generally found, save in large towns; neither does one meet with any large number of that persuasion, except in cities, where they celebrate their days of festival, and not in country towns or small villages.

The Vedas.

It is impossible to speak with any certainty regarding the antiquity of the Hindu religion. The earliest sacred writings of the Hindus are without known date. If the Rig-Veda, the oldest of the works called the Vedas, which together form the original Hindu Bible, and which is probably the oldest literary document in existence, coincided with the beginning of Hindu civilization, the popular creed of the early Hindus, as depicted in some of its hymns, would reveal not only the original creed of the nation, but throw a strong light upon the early creed of humanity; and we are indeed able to gather from the Institutes of Menu, a work composed by an author of that name, who is supposed to have flourished about nine centuries before the Christian era, that the early religion of the Hindus was as pure and simple as that of the present day is gross and superstitious. For although this early collection of sacred writings has been handed down through successive generations of Brahmans or priests, and is studied by them and explained to the worshippers of Brahma to-day, much in the same manner as was performed by the priests centuries before the land of Ind was known to Europeans, the true faith, as inculcated by the Vedas, has been almost entirely lost sight of, and though nowhere entirely forgotten is never steadily thought of except by philosophers and divines. Its place has been taken by an idolatrous, superstitious, form of worship, which has either been forced on the country by the priests from motives of policy, in order to retain their power with the ignorant, credulous, natives; or has been the result of the degeneration of the powers of a people who, although civilized at an early date in the world's history, failed to retain their position. Never since the Western world became acquainted with them have they shown the cultivation and intellectuality that must have obtained among them in former days.

Between the Hindu religion of the past and that of the present there are many points of variance. The religion of the early days of Hinduism was derived from the Vedas, to which scriptures very frequent reference is made. There are four Vedas, consisting of hymns and prayers, with precepts which inculcate religious duties, and arguments relating to theology. They are not however single works. Each is the production of various authors, who probably wrote at different periods; and of their antiquity there can be no doubt, since each is written in an ancient form of the Sanskrit, so different from that now in use, that none but the more learned of the Brahmans themselves can understand them. For the first Veda is claimed an antiquity of over two thousand years before Christ, and without going so far as to admit this as a certainty, it is extremely probable, for it is now generally agreed by Oriental scholars that the works were completed in their present form in the fourteenth century before Christ.

The primary doctrine of the Vedas is the Unity of God. "There is in truth," say repeated texts, "but one Deity, the Supreme Spirit, the Lord of the Universe, whose work is the Universe." This doctrine of monotheism was at first universal, it being declared that "of all duties the principal is to obtain a true knowledge of one Supreme Brahm or God. For he created the heavens and the earth, and having willed to produce various beings from his own divine substance, first, with a thought, created the waters, and placed in them a productive seed. From this seed sprung the mundane egg, in which the Supreme Being was himself born in the form of Brahma. By similar mythological processes he, under the form of Brahma, produced the heavens and the earth and the human soul; and to all creatures he gave distinct names, and distinct occupations. He likewise created the deities, with divine attributes and pure souls, and inferior genii exquisitely delicate. The whole creation is only to endure for a certain period; when that expires, the divine energy is withdrawn, Brahma is absorbed in the supreme essence, and the whole system fades away. Man is said to be endowed with two internal spirits—the vital soul, which gives motion to the body, and the rational, which is the seat of passions, and good and bad qualities; and both these souls, though independent existences, are connected with the divine essence which pervades all beings." That the doctrine of the transmigration of souls was believed by the Hindus at an early date, we find in the following passage: "It is the vital soul which expiates the sins of the man. It is subjected to torments for periods proportioned to its offences, and is then sent to migrate through men and animals, and even plants—the mansion being the lower the greater has been its guilt—until at length, having been purified by suffering and humiliation, it is again united to its more pure associates, and again commences a career which may lead to eternal bliss." This triple order of the passage of the soul through the highest, middle, and lowest stages of existence, as declared by Menu, results from good or bad acts, words, and thoughts. For sins of act, a man takes a vegetable or mineral form; for sins of word, the form of a bird or beast; for sins of thought, that of a man of the lowest caste. A triple self-command in thought, word, and deed, leads to emancipation from all births, and final beatitude.

Regarding the practical part of this religion, prayers and penances were enjoined on all true believers, as well as frequent ablutions, and the performance of sacrifices by oblations to the manes, and to fire in honour of the deities. For it was considered that among the creatures of the Supreme Being many were superior to man, who should be adored, and from whom protection and favours might be obtained through prayer. The most frequently mentioned of these are the gods of the elements, the stars, and the planets; but other personified powers and virtues likewise appear. The three principal manifestations of the Divinity (Brahma, Vishnu, and Siva), with other personified attributes and energies, and most of the other gods of Hindu mythology, are indeed mentioned or at least indicated, but the worship of deified heroes was no part of the system. Moreover, even Brahma, Vishnu, and Siva are rarely named, enjoy no pre-eminence, are never objects of special adoration; and lastly, there seem to have been no idols or images, and no visible types of the objects of worship.

Such is a brief outline of the original Hindu religion, which may be considered a comparatively pure and simple form of the worship of God in the earlier stages of this world's history. Of the exact time of its duration we cannot speak with certainty; but we know it was in full force nine centuries before Christ; that in the year 543 B.C. the new religion of Buddhism arose, which, supplanting the original Hinduism, became the popular belief of the country; and that on the decline of Buddhism, in the sixth century of the Christian era, it was followed by a revival of Brahmanism, much modified, however, and with none of its original purity. This degraded form of Hinduism was accepted by the people of the country, and is followed by them at the present day.

The principal changes in the Hindu religion since its revival, and as at present practised, are:

The neglect of the principle of monotheism. The neglect of some gods, and the introduction of others. The worship of deified mortals. The introduction, or at least the great increase, of sects, and the attempt to exalt individual gods at the expense of others. The doctrine that faith in a particular god is more efficacious than contemplation, ceremonial observance, or good works. The use of a new ritual instead of the Vedas. And, lastly, the introduction of idols and symbols, to whom actual homage and prayer is offered.

The scriptures of this new religion are the Puranas, which contain philosophical speculations, instructions for religious ceremonies, fragments of history, and innumerable legends relating to the actions of gods and heroes, all more or less corrupted by sectarian fables; so that they do not form a consistent whole, and were never intended to be combined in one general system of belief.

The Hindus seem to be still aware of the existence of a Supreme Being, as inculcated by the Vedas, from whom all others derive their existence, or rather of whose substance they are composed; for, according to the modern belief, the universe and the Deity are one and the same. But their devotion is now directed to a variety of gods and goddesses, of whom it is impossible to fix the number. Some accounts, with the usual Hindu extravagance, make the deities amount to three hundred and thirty millions; but most of these are ministering angels in the different heavens, or spirits who have no individual name or character.

The following seventeen are the principal and perhaps the only ones universally recognized, as exercising distinct and divine functions, and therefore entitled to worship:

1. Brahma, the creating principle; 2. Vishnu, the preserving principle; 3. Siva, the destroying principle: with their corresponding female divinities, who are mythologically regarded as their wives, but metaphysically as the active powers which develop the principle represented by each member of the triad—namely, 4. Saraswati; 5. Lakshmi; 6. Parvati, called also Devi, Bhavani, or Durga. 7. Indra, god of the air and the heavens. 8. Varuna, god of the waters. 9. Pavana, god of the wind. 10. Agni, god of fire. 11. Tama, god of the infernal regions, and judge of the dead. 12. Cuvera, god of wealth. 13. Cratikeya, god of war. 14. Cama, god of love. 15. Suurya, the sun. 16. Soma, the moon. 17. Ganesa, who is the remover of all difficulties, and as such presides over the entrances to all edifices, and is invoked at the commencement of all undertakings.

To these may be added the planets and many sacred rivers, especially the Ganges, which is personified as a female divinity, and honoured with every sort of worship and reverence. Many animals and birds are also held in reverence, more especially the bull and cow. These sacred animals are forbidden to be slain or used for food, and are to many, especially those belonging to certain temples, living objects of great veneration and adoration.

Brahma, Vishnu, and Siva form the celebrated Hindu triad,

Hindu Deities.

whose separate characters are sufficiently apparent, but whose supposed unity may perhaps be resolved into the general maxim of orthodox Hindus, that all the deities are only various forms of one Supreme Being.

Brahma, though he seems once to have had some degree of pre-eminence, and is the only one of the three mentioned by Menu, was never much worshipped. He has now but one temple in India, and, though invoked in the daily service, his separate worship is almost entirely neglected. It is far different with Vishnu and Siva. They and their incarnations attract almost all the religious veneration of the Hindus. The relative importance of each is eagerly supported by numerous votaries, and there are heterodox sects of great extent, which maintain the supreme divinity of either to the entire exclusion of his rival. All these various gods have their own particular temples in various places, and are represented by images carved out of stone, at whose feet the prayers of the devotees are offered. Most of the Hindu gods, though supposed to be endued with human passions, are usually depicted with something monstrous in their appearance. They are of various colours—red, yellow, and blue; some have twelve heads, and most have four hands. Certain of the female divinities are fearful to look upon; notably Devi, who is represented with a black skin, and a' hideous and terrible countenance, her head encircled by snakes, and streaming with blood, like a fury rather than a goddess. There are, however, exceptions to this rule; for Vishnu is represented as a comely and placid young man dressed like a king of ancient days; while the deified mortals, the principal of whom are Rama and Krishna, retain the natural form they held when living. These are at the present day objects of great adoration, Krishna more especially; for his followers comprise all the opulent and luxurious, almost all the women, and a very large proportion of all ranks of Indian society.

As to the practical part of their religion, the Hindus are enjoined to listen to and obey the Brahmans or priests, and to offer daily prayers to their own particular divinity, with all the sacraments alluded to as existing at the time the faith was in its purer form. But there is also a new form of worship never alluded to by Menu, which now forms the principal duty of every Hindu. This is the worship of images, before whom many prostrations and other acts of adoration must be performed, frequently accompanied with secret orgies that tend much to bring disgrace on the present Hinduism. It is undeniable that a strain of licentiousness and sensuality mixes with the Hindu mythology, both in their books and songs and in their acts of devotion in certain temples and at certain festivals. The most singular anomaly in this religion is the idea of the power of religious austerities; and of sacrifices, sometimes of life itself, as was formerly the case in the suttee, when the living widow was burnt on the same pile as the corpse of her husband, or when the devotees, prostrating themselves on the ground, allowed the heavy wheels of the sacred car of Juggernauth to pass over them, whereby they were either killed or severely injured. For it was supposed to be possible, by self-inflicted tortures, or austerities of every description, or by leading the ascetic life followed by the numerous fakirs or holy men, to acquire such an ascendancy over the gods as to render them the passive instruments of man's ambition, and even force them to submit their heavens and themselves to man's sovereignty. Of late years, however, this has rather become merely the tradition of former days; for the new principle is that the same objects, which were formerly to be extorted in this manner, are now to be won by faith.

As to a future state, the Hindus still hold the original belief in the transmigration of souls; but believe that between their different stages of existence, they will, according to their merits, enjoy thousands of years of happiness in some of their numerous heavens, or suffer torments of similar duration in some of their still more numerous hells. Hope, however, seems to be denied to none; the most wicked man, after being purged of his crimes by ages of suffering and by repeated transmigrations, may ascend in the scale of being until he may enter into heaven, and even attain the highest reward of all the good, which is incorporation in the essence of God.

There are three principal Hindu sects; namely, the Saivas (followers of Siva), the Vaishnavas (followers of Vishnu), and the Saktas (followers of some one of the Saktis—the female associates or active powers of the members of the triad). Each of these sects branches into various subordinate forms. Besides the three great sects, too, there are smaller ones; and the Sikhs have founded one involving such great innovations that it may almost be regarded as a new religion. It must not be supposed, however, that every Hindu belongs to one or other of these sects, though probably all have a bias. The admission to a sect is easy, the chief part consisting in the whispering of a short and secret form of words by the 'guru,' or religious instructor, and the painting on the man's forehead of a peculiar mark. This, although the most singular peculiarity of the Hindu appearance, fails to convey any information to the uninitiated, and indeed is generally taken by strangers as a sign of the caste, and not of the sect of the wearer.

Finally, it may be remarked, in the words of the author from whose work many of the above remarks are derived: "That in the Hindu religion, although the rewards and punishments are often well apportioned to the moral merits and demerits of the deceased, they no doubt exercise considerable influence over the conduct of the living; but, on the other hand, the efficacy ascribed to faith and to the observance of the forms of devotion, and the facility of expiating crimes by penance, are unfortunately prevailing characteristics of this religion, and have a strong tendency to weaken its effect in supporting the principles of morality. Its indirect effect on its votaries is even more injurious than these defects. Its gross superstition debases and debilitates the mind, and its exclusive view to repose in this world and absorption hereafter, destroys the great stimulants to virtue afforded by love of enterprise and of posthumous fame. Its usurpations over the provinces of law and science tend to keep knowledge fixed at the point to which it had attained at the time of the pretended revelation by the divinity, and its interference in the minutiæ of private manners extirpates every habit and feeling of free agency, and reduces life to a mechanical routine. When individuals are left free, improvements take place as they are required, and a nation is entirely changed in the course of a few generations, without an effort on the part of any of its members; but when religion has interposed, it requires as much boldness to take the smallest step as to pass over the innovations of a century at a stride. And in India a man must be equally prepared to renounce his faith and the communion of his friends, whether he merely makes a change in his diet, or embraces a whole body of doctrines, religious and political, at variance with those established among his countrymen."

There are two other religions which, although distinct from the Hindu, appear to belong to the same stock, and shared with it in the veneration of the people of India before the introduction of an entirely foreign faith by the Mohammedans. These are the religions of the Buddhists, or worshippers of Buddha, and of the Jainas. They both resemble Brahmanism in their character of quietism, their tenderness of animal life, their doctrine of repeated transmigrations, and their belief of various hells for the purification of the wicked, and many heavens for the solace of the good. The great object of all three is the ultimate attainment of a state of perfect apathy, which in our eyes seems little different from annihilation; and the means employed in all are the practice of mortification, and of abstraction from the cares and feelings of humanity.

The differences of these two religions from the Hindu belief are, however, no less striking than their points of resemblance, especially in Buddhism, so called from the title of the 'Buddha,' meaning the 'Wise' or 'Enlightened,' acquired by its founder. Buddhism has now existed for two thousand four hundred years, and is the prevailing religion of the world; for although in Hindustan, the land of its birth, it has now little hold except among the Nepaulese, and some other northern tribes, it bears full sway in Ceylon, and over the whole Eastern Peninsula, and claims two-thirds of the immense population of China. It is found also in Japan, and north of the Himalayas it is the religion of Tibet, and of the Mongolian population of Central Asia, and extends to the very north of Siberia, and even into Swedish Lapland. Its adherents are estimated at four hundred millions,—more than a third of the human race. According to the Buddhist books, this religion had its origin in the sixth century before Christ. Its founder was Sakya or Gautama, a prince of a family located somewhere on the confines of Oudh and Nepaul, who, finding the doctrines of the Brahmans unsatisfactory, began the life of a religious mendicant. After some years' meditation, he commenced to preach his new religion, and for forty years traversed the greater part of India under the title of the Buddha, making numerous converts. After his death, his principal followers reduced his teachings to writing, the result being their Tripitika or canonical scriptures, and the Buddhist faith, early manifesting a zealous missionary spirit, became the religion of India to the exclusion for a time of Hinduism, spreading thence to other countries. Buddhism is based on the same views of human existence, and the same philosophy of things in general, that prevailed among the Brahmans. It accepts without questioning, and in its most exaggerated form, the doctrine of the transmigration of souls; for, according to Buddhist belief, when a man dies, he is immediately born again, or appears in a new shape, which shape may be, according to his merit or demerit, any of the innumerable orders of being composing the Buddhist universe, from a clod to a divinity.

Contrary to the opinion once confidently and generally

held, that a nation of atheists never existed, it is no longer to be disputed that the Buddhist nations are essentially atheistic; for most of their sects entirely deny the being of God, and even those who admit His existence, refuse to acknowledge Him as the creator or ruler of the universe. According to this belief, nothing exists but matter, which is eternal. The power of organization is inherent in matter; and although the universe perishes from time to time, this quality restores it after a period, and carries it on towards new decay and regeneration, without the guidance of any external agent. They further know no beings with greater supernatural power than any man is supposed capable of attaining by virtue, austerity, and science; and a remarkable indication of this startling fact is to be seen in the circumstance, that the present Buddhist nations have no word in their languages to express the notion of God. Another basis of Buddhism is the assumption that human existence is on the whole miserable, and a curse rather than a blessing. This notion, or rather feeling, is, like transmigration, common to Buddhism and Brahmanism, but is more prominent in the new than in the old Hindu faith." This is well exemplified in Eastern countries. A Hindu sets little value upon his life; but in China and other Buddhist countries, a man sets no value on his life at all. Even the punishment of death has little or no terror for them, and is sometimes coveted as an honour. For in addition to the little value the Buddhists set on their present existence, they have the most undoubting assurance that the soul, if dislodged from its present tenement, will forthwith find another, with a chance at least of its being a better one.

The ritual or worship of Buddhism, unlike the Hindu, is very simple in its character. There are no priests or clergy, properly so called, only an order of religious mendicants or monks; but they have no sacraments to administer, or rites to perform for the people, every Buddhist being his own priest. They live in monasteries, and subsist partly by endowments, but mostly by charity; and the only thing like a clerical function they discharge is, to read the scriptures or discourses of Buddha in stated assemblies of the people held for that purpose, and to act as educational instructors to the young. The adoration of the statues of Buddha—who is generally represented seated, cross-legged, erect, but in an attitude of deep meditation—and of his relics, is the chief external ceremony of the religion. This, with prayer and the repetition of sacred formulas, constitutes the ritual. Flowers, fruit, and incense are also daily offered in the same manner as in Hinduism. Both, however, in its morality and religious observances, Buddhism is far simpler than the faith it overthrew. It was, in fact, a reaction against the exclusiveness and formalism of Brahmanism, and the irksome restrictions of caste; for although Buddhism did not expressly abolish this ancient institution, it declared that all followers of Buddha were released from its restrictions. Buddhism was, in fact, an attempt to render religion more catholic, and to throw off its intolerable burden of ceremonies, and was thus eagerly welcomed by a people smarting under the heavy yoke of the enormous power of the Brahman priesthood. It is surprising therefore that the Hindus should have voluntarily returned to the faith they had found so oppressive. But that they did so is seen in the fact that in the fifth century after Christ

The Jain Faith.

persecution of the Buddhists commenced, a modified and idolatrous form of Hinduism arose, and Buddhism languished, until it finally became extinct. Now nothing is left of its presence in India except a few ruined temples.

The followers of the Jain religion, or the Jainas, hold an intermediate place between the followers of Buddha and Brahma. This heterodox sect derives its name from Jaina, the denomination of its deified saints, and is supposed to have had its origin about the sixth or seventh century of our era (although its followers claim for it a much greater antiquity, and even state that it was supplanted by Buddhism), to have become conspicuous between the eighth and ninth centuries, and two centuries later to have gradually declined. Numerous adherents, however, are still found in every part of Hindustan, particularly in the cities along the Ganges and in Calcutta; but more especially to the westward, the provinces of Mewar and Marwar being apparently the cradle of the sect. They are also numerous in Guzerat, in the upper part of the Malabar coast, and may be said to be generally scattered throughout the Indian peninsula, forming a large and, from their wealth and influence, an important division of the population. The tenets of the Jainas are, in several respects, analogous to those of the Buddhists, so much so that they are considered by many to be merely offsets of the followers of Buddha, when his religion was extirpated in Hindustan; but they resemble in others those of the Brahmanical Hindus. With the Buddhists they share in the denial of the divine origin and authority of the Vedas, and in the worship of certain saints, whom they consider superior to the other beings of their pantheon. They differ indeed from them in regard to the history of these personages; but the original notion which prevails in their worship is the same. They also deny the existence, or at least the activity and providence of God, and believe, like the Buddhists, in the eternity of matter. They show the same scrupulous care of animal life, being so particular in this respect that they carry a brush with them on all occasions, with which they carefully sweep every place before they sit down, lest they should inadvertently crush any living creature. Like the Buddhist priests, too, the devout Jainas do not eat or drink after dark, for fear of swallowing minute insects. With the Brahmanical Hindus, on the other hand, they agree in admitting the institution of caste, in performing similar ceremonies, and in admitting the whole of the Hindu gods, worshipping some of them, although they consider them as entirely subordinate to their own saints, who are therefore the proper objects of adoration.

By the Jainas all objects, material or abstract, are arranged under nine categories, of which we need only notice the last — the liberation of the vital spirit from the bonds of action, or final emancipation. This final emancipation is only to be obtained while in possession of five senses; while possessing a body capable of voluntary motion in a condition of possibility; while possessing a mind; and chiefly through the sacrament of the highest asceticism, in that path of rectitude in which there is no retrogression; also in the practice of abstinence. And, although believing in the doctrine of transmigration in a minor degree, they hold that those who through devoutness and austerities attain to final liberation while in the state of man (and not in that of a demon or brute), do not return to a worldly state, and have no interruption to their bliss. The chief objects of their worship are a limited number of saints, who have raised themselves by austerities to a superiority over the gods, and who somewhat resemble those of the Buddhists in appearance and general character, but are entirely distinct from them in their names and individual histories. They are called Tirthankaras, and there are twenty-four for the present age; but twenty-four also for the past; and twenty-four for the future. All bear a fabulous character in their dimensions and length of life, some being depicted of enormous height and size; while all remain alike in the usual state of apathetic beatitude, and take no share in the government of the world. The Jainas have no veneration for relics, no monastic establishments, no hereditary priesthood, their religious instructors being taken from all castes of the people. The Jain temples of the present day are generally large handsome buildings, somewhat resembling Hindu temples, often circular and surrounded by colossal statues of the Tirthankaras. The walls are painted with their peculiar legends, and they have frequently marble altars, with the figures of saints in relief. They are not so profusely carved and decorated as were the temples of ancient days, many of which still remain, although mostly in a ruinous condition.

We next come to the Mohammedan religion, which, although not indigenous, but introduced and forced upon the inhabitants by a foreign foe, must now be regarded as one of the beliefs of India. Its adherents probably number more than fifty millions, scattered all over the Indian continent. As far as we are aware, it was first introduced into the country in 664 by the Arab invaders, who forced the inhabitants of those parts of the country that fell into their power, either to embrace the faith of Islam or suffer death. But as these inroads into Hindustan were not of very great extent, the masses of the population were unaffected, and the new faith, unless by compulsion, made no converts until it received a fresh impetus in the invasion of Mahmoud of Ghuzni in 1001. As he was followed by rulers belonging to various dynasties, but of the same faith, culminating in the rule of the Mogul Emperors, whose sway extended over the greater portion of the continent, the work of conversion to Islamism, either voluntarily or forcibly, naturally made rapid progress. And we owe it only to the sound sense of the greatest and wisest of the Delhi royal line, who always showed a certain amount of religious toleration, that our extensive empire in the East is not purely and entirely Mohammedan, instead of divided into various religions antagonistic to each other; the greatest safeguard against general rebellion that one could have among a conquered but powerful and treacherous nation.

Mohammedanism is also called Islam, which signifies resignation, entire submission, to the will and precepts of God.* In its exclusively dogmatical or theoretical part it is 'iman,' faith; in its practical, 'din,' religion. The fundamental principles of the former are contained in the two articles of belief, 'There is no god but God, and Mohammed is God's apostle.' The Mohammedan doctrine of God's nature and attributes coincides with the Christian, so far as He is taught by both to be the Creator of all things in heaven and earth, who rules and preserves all things—without beginning, omnipotent, omniscient, omnipresent, and full of mercy. Yet, according

* I am indebted for my sketch of Mohammedanism mainly to Sale's *Koran*.

to the Mohammedan belief, He has no offspring, He begetteth not, nor is He begotten; nor is Jesus called anything but a prophet and apostle, although His birth is said to have been due to a miraculous divine operation; and as the Koran superseded the Gospel, so did Mohammed Christ. The crucifixion is said to have been executed upon another person, Christ having been taken up to God before the decree was carried out. He will come again upon the earth to establish everywhere the Moslem religion, and to be a sign of the coming of the day of judgment. Next to the belief in God, that in angels forms a prominent dogma. Created of fire, and endowed with a kind of incorporeal body, they stand between God and man, adoring or waiting upon the former, or interceding for and guarding the latter. The belief in the resurrection and the final judgment is the next article of faith. The day of judgment will call up all angels, men, and animals. The trial over, the righteous will enter paradise to the right hand, and the wicked will pass to the left into hell; both, however, have first to go over the bridge Al Sirat, laid over the midst of hell, finer than a hair, and sharper than the edge of a sword. The righteous will proceed on their path with ease and swiftness, but the wicked will fall down headlong to hell below. The blessed destined for the abodes of eternal delight will be met by angels, who, according to their degree of righteousness, will procure for them the corresponding degree of happiness. A separate abode for women will also be reserved; but there is considerable doubt as to the manner of their admission and enjoyment. The last of the precepts of pure faith taught by Mohammedanism is the full and unconditional submission to God's decree, and the predestination of good and evil, which is found from the beginning inscribed on a preserved table. Not only a man's fortunes, but his deeds, and consequently his future reward or punishment, are irrevocably and thus unavoidably pre-ordained (fate), a doctrine which has no doubt contributed largely to the success of Islam, by inspiring its champions with the greatest indifference and contempt for the dangers of warfare, their destiny being immutably fixed under any circumstances.

The 'din' or practical part of the religion inculcates as the chief duties, prayer, almsgiving, fasting, and pilgrimage. Every Mohammedan is obliged to pray five times in the space of twenty-four hours; the prayers consisting of verses from the Koran, accompanied by a certain number of inclinations of head and knees and prostrations; the head of the worshipper being always turned in the direction of Mecca. The duties of almsgiving and fasting are strictly enjoined, and at their great religious festivals the latter is strictly carried out, more particularly at the feast of Ramadan, when the Moslem is commanded to abstain from eating, drinking, smoking, bathing, and every unnecessary indulgence in worldly pleasure, from daybreak until sunset.

The fourth paramount duty of the Mohammedan, namely, the pilgrimage to Mecca, is so well known that no description is needed except to mention that this pilgrimage to the temple at Mecca—the birthplace of the Prophet, and not, as is often stated, to the spot of his interment, which is at Medina, also in Arabia—is emphatically urged upon everyone, and that every male or female whose means and health permit is bound to perform this rite once while in life, as otherwise he or she might as well die a Jew or a Christian. Those who return successfully, after the performance of this arduous duty, are considered certain of salvation, and are allowed to prefix the proud title of Hadji to their name. There are in this, as in all religions, several sects, with points of difference between them. The great schism, that of the Sonnites and Shiites, or partizans of Ali, is maintained on either side with implacable hatred and furious zeal. Though the difference arose at first on a political occasion, it has, notwithstanding, been so well improved by additional circumstances and the spirit of contradiction, that each party detests and anathematizes the other as abominable heretics, and further from the truth than either the Christians or the Jews. The chief points wherein they differ, are: That the Shiites or Shias reject the three first Khalifs as usurpers and intruders, whereas the Sonnites or Sonnis acknowledge and respect them. Secondly, the Shiites prefer Ali, another prophet, to Mohammed, or at least esteem them both equal; but the Sonnites admit neither Ali nor any of the prophets to be equal to Mohammed. The Sonnites also charge the Shiites with corrupting the Koran and neglecting its precepts, and the latter retort the same charge on the former. And to these disputes, 'and some others of less moment, is principally owing the antipathy which has long reigned between the Turks, who are Sonnites, and the Persians, who are of the sect of Ali. This in a minor degree prevails in India, society being divided into two portions, each side vehemently opposing the other, which sometimes, particularly on feast-days, leads to riot and bloodshed.

The subject of Christianity in India is one upon which I need not dwell at length, as correct means of information in this respect are afforded by the yearly reports of the various

Missionary Societies. There is no doubt that India was one of the earliest fields of Christian missions; for we find a Syrian church planted in Malabar, which undoubtedly had a very early origin. The Jesuit missionaries, from the middle of the sixteenth century, met with much success. On their first arrival in India, to disarm prejudice, they had recourse to the pious fraud of introducing themselves to the people, not as foreigners, but as white Brahmans. By fostering the native system of caste, and admitting a large amount of compromise in the way of religious observance, they induced great numbers to receive the outward form of Christian baptism, and the number of natives professing Roman Catholicism now is considerable, more particularly in the Madras Presidency, and other parts of Southern India—the scene of the earliest efforts of the Jesuits.

The zeal and activity of the priests continue to this day, and there are few parts of India where their presence is not felt. Their efforts are crowned with more success than those of the missionaries of other Christian denominations; for, sparing no time or trouble in the work of conversion, they are in addition largely assisted by the very nature of their religion, which, admitting outward forms and observances, appeals more directly to the senses of a people who take extreme delight in processions and shows of pomp; and the appeal to God for mercy through a palpable mediator, such as a picture or statue, is readily understood, as being more akin to their former faith, than the extreme and beautiful simplicity of a purer and more spiritual worship.

The earliest Protestant missionaries in India came from Holland and Denmark; and England's first missionary effort was put forward by the Society for the Propagation of the Gospel, and by the Christian Knowledge Society, which commenced in the beginning of the eighteenth century by aiding the Danish mission already established in Southern India. Subsequently the East India Company adopted the policy of excluding missionaries altogether from their territories; but since the beginning of this century, when these restrictions were withdrawn, a great work has been entered upon, in which all denominations are represented. Progress is, however, necessarily slow; for the natives are as yet as a nation ignorant, utterly conservative in their notions, and disinclined to make any change, unless it materially affects their comfort in life. Moreover many, particularly in the northern parts of Hindustan, where missionary work is of later date, seem to entertain the notion that by becoming converts, they become at the same time perpetual recipients of charity. These people, probably under the idea that they should be paid, or at least reap some substantial advantage, for resigning the creed of their fathers, utterly neglect their work, and become mere hangers-on of the missions, to the serious detriment of their funds. Many too, in adopting the religion of their white rulers, and becoming free from the restrictions of caste, or the public opinion of their countrymen, consider it necessary to adopt the manners and customs and mode of living, in use among their new co-religionists. Against this there is nothing to be said, were the changes effected gradually and in moderation; but unfortunately they rush to the other extreme. A large number only copy the worst vices of the Europeans; and becoming a lazy, drunken, and generally dissolute set of men, are abhorrent to the white community, who, as a rule, on this account do not favour the engagement of native Christians as servants or in other offices. Mere mockeries of the title of Christians, they are equally scouted by their own countrymen as outcasts, and have then no other alternative than to swell the number of those supported by the funds of the different missions. These remarks, however, do not apply to the greater portion of Madras, or other parts where Christianity has been long established. There nearly all the servants in the employ of Europeans, and many others occupying various positions of trust and importance, belong to the Christian faith. Nearly all, however, are Roman Catholics, and cannot strictly be styled converts, as they only follow the faith of their forefathers for several generations, in which they were born and bred. Caste is one of the chief causes of the slow spread of Christianity; and although this faith has been classed among the religions of India, it can hardly as yet be termed either popular or extensive, or with any deep root in the country. Still we are justified in hoping for the best; for we have signs, year by year, that education is making progress, and among many of the better informed natives caste rules are becoming an intolerable burden.

Caste has existed among the Hindus from time immemorial, and has so far withstood all attempts to break it down. To a European it appears a curious perverseness in the character of an otherwise intelligent nation; and it is undoubtedly a source of trouble to their rulers, as well as a bar to the progress of Western ideas. It might almost be inferred, from the influence exerted by caste rules on the daily life of the Hindus, that the whole of their religion was centred in caste observances, and that Hinduism and caste were convertible terms. And, in point of fact, strictness in the maintenance of caste is the only real religious test exacted by the Brahmans of the present day; for in matters of mere faith Hinduism is all-tolerant and all-receptive. No person who is not born to fulfil priestly offices can ever become a priest; but any one can be admitted into the lower ranks of Hinduism who will acknowledge the supremacy of the Brahmans, and obey the rules of caste. So long as he keeps to his own particular caste, he can hold any opinions he likes; in some cases, it has been said, even to accepting the doctrines of Christianity. That the peculiar Hindu rules of caste are of very ancient origin we have proof in the work of Menu, before quoted, which gives a good picture of the state of Indian society about a thousand years before Christ. In this description the whole of the Hindus, the only people then inhabiting the country, who followed one common religion, are divided into four classes, in accordance with the theory that the Deity created distinct kinds of men as he created varieties of animals, and that the members of the separate divisions were born, and must remain from birth to death, distinct from each other. These four classes of society were as follows:

1. The Brahmans, or sacerdotal class, who were looked upon as the chief of all created beings, and whom even kings were compelled to treat with the most profound respect. Hence the Brahman became the most important personage in society; his life and person were protected by the severest laws in this world, and the most tremendous denunciations for the next. His own offences were treated with singular lenity, but all offences against him with terrible severity. He was forbidden

to live by service, but on alms; and it was incumbent upon virtuous men and kings to support him with liberality, while all ceremonies of religion involved feasts and presents to him. The Brahmans were also the sole exponents of religion, the only educated class in the community who could read and explain the Vedas, or other sacred writings. Hence they wielded a power before which even kings submitted. And although at the present day this class, the only original one that has survived, is shorn of a good deal of its dignity, and its sacred character as a caste is no longer held in the same veneration as formerly (for many follow other occupations than the priesthood), there still exists a superstitious reverence of the Brahmans, more particularly shown towards those who continue to follow their original avocation.

2. The Kshatryas, or military class, who, although far from being placed on an equality with the Brahmans, were still treated with honour, it being acknowledged that the sacerdotal order could not prosper without the military, or the military without the sacerdotal, and that the prosperity of both in this world and the next depended on their cordial union. The military class enjoyed, in a lesser degree, the same inequality in criminal law that the Brahmans possessed in respect to the classes below. The kings and princes belonged to this class, as well as all ordinary ministers. The command of armies, and of military divisions, in short, the whole military profession—and in strictness all situations of government—were theirs by birthright. It is, indeed, very observable that, even in the code drawn up by themselves, with the exception of the interpretation of the law, no interference in the executive government is ever allowed to Brahmans.

3. The Veisyas, or mercantile class, come next; and that their rank was not high, is shown in the order that where a Brahman is enjoined to show hospitality to strangers, he is directed to show benevolence even to a merchant, and to give him food at the same time with his domestics. The practical knowledge required from a member of this caste was more general than that of the other classes; for, besides a full knowledge of the means of breeding cattle, and a thorough acquaintance with all commodities, and all soils, he had to understand the productions and wants of other countries, and, in addition to keeping herds of cattle, to carry on trade, to lend at interest, and to cultivate the land.

4. The Sudras, or servile class, come last, and their duty is briefly stated to be to serve the other superior castes, more especially the Brahmans. Their condition was never to be improved, neither were they allowed by any means to approach the dignity of the higher classes or to accumulate property. They were permitted, if other employments failed, to subsist by handicrafts, especially joinery and masonry; but they were not regular artisans in the strict sense of the word. No mention is made of handicraftsmen in Menu, a circumstance which affords ground for surmise that the divisions into castes took place while arts were in too simple a state to require separate workmen for each. When the necessity arose, these functions in the community were filled by the mixed classes, which arose to supply the want, and which are in existence at the present day, most of them having been formed by intermarriages of the four original castes. And although at that time mixtures of castes, though not absolutely forbidden, and even carried into effect, entailed disadvantages

on the children, and the offspring of a Brahman woman and a Sudra became a Chandala or outcast; it is also worthy of notice, that though the classes do not seem to have associated at their meals at the earliest period of their history, there was no actual prohibition against eating with other castes, or partaking of food cooked by them (which is now the great occasion of loss of caste), except in the case of Sudras, and even then the offence was to be expiated by very slight penalties.

Such, omitting the minute and childish laws and formalities, many hundreds in number, by which it was proposed to carry the principles of caste into the pettiest affairs of life, is a brief outline of the institution as existing in India in its earliest days, when the Hindus were, comparatively speaking, only a small community, and it was possible to keep up such divisions in society, and relegate every individual to his proper station and duty. But as civilization increased, bringing with it a knowledge of arts and other matters previously unknown, and the numbers of the community received their natural augmentation, great changes took place, although the Hindus have preserved their customs more intact than any other people.

At the present day the four great classes no longer exist; for, with the exception of the Brahmans, the pure castes have disappeared, and out of the intermixture of the others have sprung innumerable classes, many unauthorized except by the people themselves. And although the Rajputs still loudly assert the purity of their descent from the Kshatryas, and some of the industrious classes claim the same relation to the Veisyas, it is generally understood that these castes, as well as the Sudras, are extinct, and that the Brahmans only have preserved their lineage undisputed. The Brahmans have been successful in excluding the other castes from access to the Vedas, and in confining learning to their own body; but they too have departed, in a great measure, from the rules and practice of their predecessors. In some particulars they are more strict than formerly, but in most respects their practice is greatly relaxed. They do not now all confine their attention to priestly offices, nor subsist on alms; for they enter into service, and are to be found in all trades and professions, while the proportion supported by charity, according to the original system, is quite insignificant. It is common to see them as husbandmen, and still more so as soldiers, and even of those trades which are expressly forbidden to them under severe penalties, they only scruple to exercise the most degraded, and in some places not even those. Their peculiar secular occupations are those connected with writing and public business.

The modern castes maintain their divisions with greater strictness than the ancient classes, neither eating together, nor intermarrying, nor partaking in common rites. Many of these are mixed castes, some even of great antiquity, resulting from the permissible intermarriage of the pure castes with each other, or with the classes formed from such unions. This was allowed in the time of Menu, who mentions such divisions of society as being then in existence, in addition to the four great and principal grades. The greater number, however, in India at the present day (and new ones are being constantly created,) are what may be called trade castes. They partake rather of the nature of associations for mutual support of familiar intercourse, and are dependent on a man's trade, occupation, or profession, which differs in degrees of honour. Thus soldiers, agriculturists, workers in metal, &c., are considered high caste, while fishermen, curriers, or dealers in animals and liquor, are considered low caste. Burners of the dead, or executioners, are looked upon as Pariahs, or outcasts, and are shunned by all. But the most curious anomaly in this strange institution remains in the fact, that numbers of Hindus, following out the destiny which their descent has marked out for them, become illustrious as Thugs—thieves or assassins—without thereby losing consideration or respect from their countrymen, or forfeiting their rights to the privilege of caste. Many of the trades unions resemble the guilds of artizans once common in Europe, and have numerous sub-castes under them. Each society keeps aloof from the other, and shuts itself up in its own independence. And yet within each caste, individual independence is impossible, because no individual can act alone, but only in conjunction with his caste-fellows.

Although it is understood that purity of caste is incapable of acquisition, yet, contrary to opinions commonly entertained, there is no obstacle to a change of caste; there is nothing to prevent the son of a potter becoming a worker in metals, or joining any class equally held in honour to the original one in which he was born; only he cannot aspire to enter one considered purer or more honourable. But this question rarely arises. Averse to change, the Hindus are content to accept tranquilly the fact that occupations depend on hereditary descent, and to plod on in the manner of their forefathers, although they well know that caste at the present day does not tie a man down to follow his father's business, nor obstruct the enterprise of individuals, since all castes have risen to power in India, just as in England our statesmen have sprung from every class of society. Amongst the lower classes in India, and especially among such as act as servants to Englishmen, true caste hardly exists, having degenerated merely into a fastidious tenacity of the rights and privileges of station, although, if spoken to on the subject, they would loudly assert that they strictly observe their class rules: for example, the man who sweeps your room will not take an empty cup from your hand; and your groom will not cut any grass, for that is the business of another caste. When an English servant pleads that such a thing is not his place to do, his excuse is analogous to that of the Hindu servant when he pleads his caste; and when an Englishman of birth, or of profession held to confer gentility, refuses to associate with a tradesman or mechanic, these social distinctions would present themselves to the mind of a Hindu as so many regulations of caste.

The enforcement of the rules of caste in India is still strict, though capricious; for they have multiplied almost endlessly. But however numerous and exacting, they affect, as has always been the case, a man chiefly in the four matters of marriage, food, occupation, and funeral rites. Intermarriage between different castes, allowed so far back as in the time of Menu, has been for a very long time strictly forbidden; and the prohibition of marriage, except between members of the same caste, and even sub-caste, is now strictly enforced. This rule has a tendency to lead to most objectionable results. Many of the higher castes more particularly, as existing in smaller numbers, have a greater number of males than of females. Consequently the males have to live alone, or in illicit relations with members of an inferior class. And if in any caste the reverse obtains—a preponderance of the fairer over the rougher sex, which is of rare occurrence, the only method of balancing the sexes is the awful, but to them the venial, crime of female infanticide, one, however, happily seldom perpetrated at the present day.

As to food, it is very evident that the rules are more strict than formerly, not only as to its kind, but also as to the mode of its preparation, and the persons with whom it is eaten; for the theory that food has an important effect on the preservation of blood purity is one of the most obstinate beliefs of the Hindu. The superior castes abstain wholly from animal food, and all, from the highest to the lowest, look upon the eating of the flesh of oxen as the greatest of sins. They also regard the fact of a member of a high caste partaking of food prepared by one of an inferior grade, not only as a breach of social propriety, but as an offence against religion, and some are so strict in the maintenance of this law that if even the shadow of a person of low caste, or of a European, falls on food during its preparation, the food is rendered unfit for consumption, under the idea that if eaten it will contaminate the blood, and affect the eater's character and prospects, not only in this world but also in the next.

With regard to the third point, that affecting a man's profession or occupation, it is understood that none but Brahmans are allowed free liberty to engage in the pursuits of other castes; but here Hindus are not so strict as formerly, and there is no obstacle to a man's changing his trade on the understanding that he changes his caste at the same time, and conforms to the rules and regulations of that which he then enters.

The fourth and last point, the performance of funeral rites and of 'sraddhas,' or religious acts of mourning for the dead, is a very important factor in the due maintenance of caste rules and regulations, as, according to the Hindu theory, the future prospects of the deceased depend on his relatives duly carrying out all proper observances. None but relatives can perform these rites, as it is held by them that when a man dies, and is burnt on the funeral pile, while his gross body is burned, his soul, unable to leave the body until the due acts of penance and expiation have been performed, remains near the ashes in the burning-ground as a restless, uncomfortable spirit or ghost. To lay this unquiet spirit is the object of the sraddhas, and these are celebrated on the tenth day after death, on the conclusion of the preliminary funeral rites, and then once a month for a year, and further on each anniversary. They are accompanied with much feasting and rejoicing, and costly gifts to the Brahman priests assisting at the ceremony; consolation for the expenditure, which is sometimes enormous, being felt in the fact that the soul of the departed one is thereby being pushed onwards, either through the hells or heavens, or to other births and final emancipation. Unhappy, however, is the fate of one who dies away from his kindred. The funeral ceremonies wanting, he becomes a foul wandering ghost, which takes revenge for its misery upon all living creatures by a variety of strange and malignant acts.

Regarding the loss of caste by the non-fulfilment of the various rules and regulations, although it is faintly described by saying that it is civil death, still it is not nearly so terrible as it has been represented. In most cases caste may be recovered by a frugal meal or a pecuniary offering to the members of the caste; or the outcast joins another caste, among whom he will be commonly received with the heartiness due to a new convert. The question even of the restoration of a Christian convert wishing to rejoin the Brahmanical caste, has been differently decided by his fellow caste-men in different places.

Such is the institution as at present existing; and yet, with all these fine-drawn diversities of rank and respectability, the division into superior and inferior castes is not attended in Hindustan with any feeling of humiliation on the part of the latter. Every caste or sub-division of caste forms a distinct society in the general community. Its members enjoy the sense of equality among themselves, while their position in all respects towards the other members of the general community, is determined before their birth. The divine origin of caste being universally admitted, there is no ground for personal animosity. The members of the higher castes feel no malice against, or pity for, but rather indifference towards, those of the lower; nor have the latter any envy or hatred of the former. As in the West, so in the East, caste enters into all the most ordinary relations of life, producing laws often most tyrannical and too anomalous to admit of generalization. Whilst in the West, however, good sense and Christianity have ever tended to ameliorate social differences, the feeble mind of the Hindu, and the records of his religion, have had a contrary effect.

CHAPTER VI.

Departure from Bombay—Railway system in India—A railway station—Scenery on the line—Passage of the Ghauts—The Deccan—The Minerals of India—View from the Ghauts—Fortress of Asseeghur—The Forests of India—Arrival at Jubbulpur—Indian Hotels—Station of Jubbulpur—The Marble Rocks—Our expedition—Native industry—The Ryots—Indian Agriculture—The Land-tax—Irrigation of the Land—Description of the Rocks—Ancient Buddhist Temple—Stone-carving—Cave-temples of India—Their antiquity—Architecture of the Hindus—Art of Sculpture—The Buddhist Temples—The Jain Temples—The Hindu Temples—Architecture during Mohammedan ascendancy—The Saracenic School—The Hindustani school of Architecture—A Monkey incident—Return to the hotel—Evening reflections.

WE proceeded early the next morning to the Borce Bunder Station, the terminus in Bombay of the Great Indian Peninsular Railway, by which line our journey was continued as far as Jubbulpur. During the last few years the railways have made rapid progress in India; and the three presidency towns are already connected. These large main lines have branches to every city of importance *en route*, and the line to Peshawur is approaching completion; so that in a short time complete communication will exist with every part of the empire by means of the iron road, undoubtedly the greatest pioneer of civilization ever introduced into India. The number of miles of railway at present open approaches six thousand, representing an expenditure of ninety-eight millions of pounds; while the average yearly receipts are between three and four millions. The electric telegraph runs along every line of railway, and connects all the important places in India, and a message of six words can be sent to any part of the country for one rupee. The charge between England and India is two pounds for every ten words, including the address, and four shillings for every word beyond that number.

On the Indian railways all the situations of trust and responsibility are filled by Englishmen, who also act as engine-drivers and guards. The work of the subordinate officials is performed by natives; and at the smaller and less important stations educated natives, or 'baboos,' as they are termed, fulfil the duties of station-master. The carriages are constructed with special reference to their adaptability to a hot climate, and also to afford sleeping accommodation to the traveller when on a long journey. These two ends are attained by the addition of venetian blinds to the windows, and the provision of other ventilating appliances; and by the slinging up to hooks, when required, of the stuffed backs of the seats which are hung on hinges, and afford, when suspended, two hanging couches, thus giving, with the seats below, four berths to each carriage, similar to those on board ship.

Although the carriages and officials, and even the buildings of the larger stations, are very similar to what one has been accustomed to see at home, the scene presented by the platform at the departure of a train is very different, and needs the talent of a Frith to do it justice; for it is a bewildering jumble of crowd, noise, and confusion. Railway travelling is very popular among the natives, on account of its cheapness.

Scene at a Railway Station

Hence every train is full of third-class passengers, for, with very few exceptions, they never take first-class places, and in this respect their innate love of saving has levelled all distinctions of caste and position. The rich man, or Brahman, to whom at other times personal contact with his inferiors is pollution, is content to be huddled up with people of the lowest grades of society, in a bare covered shed on wheels, rather than, to secure better accommodation, he will part with a fraction more of his beloved coin, which is dearer to him than wife, family, or even life itself. Curiosity, the besetting sin of the inhabitants of India, undoubtedly attracts considerable numbers of the crowds who throng the platforms; but the majority are composed of the intending passengers and their relatives and friends, who accompany them to witness their departure. This appears to be a necessary preliminary to travel; and as it is not uncommon for one passenger to have an escort of thirty to forty followers, all of whom have a last word to say, and say that in their usual shrill treble, some idea may be formed of the noise that prevails. To this, however, must be added the shrieks and imprecations issuing from the various ticket offices, where the native clerks are dispensing the tickets; for it is the invariable practice of their customers to attempt to cheapen the fare, or, failing in that, to put down a lesser amount, and strive to escape in the confusion. Wild and aimless runnings up and down of natives struggling under the weight of enormous bundles of personal property, which they attempt to cram into the carriages, leading to personal conflicts with the officials, who wish to place the luggage in the van, also add to the universal din.

The native police, too, the so-called guardians of order, are considerable elements of confusion, rushing from place to place to enforce a passage through the crowd for some distinguished female, who is being transported to her carriage in a covered palanquin, or for some European sahib. As their usual method of procedure to secure their ends is the unsparing use of a light, supple cane on the naked legs of their compatriots, cries of rage and pain from the victims lend a rich variety to a hubbub, which is only to be compared to Babel in its palmy days, and which is simply appalling to a nervous person, or one unaccustomed to Eastern travel. Another noticeable feature in connection with Indian railway stations, is the immense crowd always to be seen collected on the outside of the building, during the intervals of arrival and departure. This arises from the curious indifference as to time or method common to the native mind. Never do natives take the trouble to ascertain at what period the train departs for their destination; but they proceed, accompanied with troops of friends, to the station, at any hour convenient to themselves. It often occurs that they arrive a few minutes late, and have to wait until the following morning to commence their journey; this to them is a matter of pure indifference. Without any thought of leaving the vicinity of the station, they proceed to establish themselves as comfortably as circumstances admit, and eat and sleep until the doors are opened, when they rouse up into undue activity, and assist in the scene already described.

We were fortunate enough to secure a carriage entirely to ourselves. In a few minutes the train glided out of the station, and the town of Bombay was soon miles behind us.

The scenery at first was very pretty, the country being broken up into small hills, covered with cocoa-nut palms, and other trees; while the cultivated portions were fenced in with very large plants of the prickly pear, which in these parts do duty as hedges, and make a very stiff and formidable barrier for the better protection of the crops. In about six hours we reached a wilder region, one of mountains, rocks, and forests; for we were now at the foot of the Ghaut mountains, and it was necessary to ascend their precipitous sides to reach the table-land of the Deccan, along which our course lay. The Deccan is certainly the most remarkable geographical feature of Southern India. It is a central table-land—a vast plateau enclosed on all sides by lofty mountains—between which and the sea, on the east and west, are narrow strips of low, flat country, divided into several districts. From the low country on the coast to this great table-land the mountains rise abruptly in a succession of gigantic terraces or steps. Hence the name of the Ghauts, a Hindu word for steps or landing-places.

The Eastern and Western Ghauts consist chiefly of metamorphic rocks, which are continued across the country to the north of the Godavery. Between this transverse band of altered strata and the diluvial deposits of the north, a large tract of country is occupied with palæozoic rocks. Here are the principal coal-fields of India. The most important is the Ranigunj, a belt of coal-bearing strata, consisting of coal and iron beds, as well as limestone suitable for flux, and hard sandstone fitted for building purposes. The carboniferous strata lie in a basin of metamorphic rock, and cover an area of five hundred square miles, at a distance of from one hundred and twenty to one hundred and sixty miles northwest of Calcutta. The iron ores consist of 'black band' yielding thirty-nine per cent. of metal, and magnetic ironstone yielding from sixty to seventy per cent. A certain amount of coal is yearly raised; but the development of the mineral wealth of the country is yet in its infancy. Much, however, may be expected from the Geological Survey, now some years in progress. The minerals of India are abundant and varied, including, beside the coal and iron already mentioned, gold, silver, tin, copper, plumbago, lead; and in precious stones, diamonds, rubies, beryls, and many others. Gold has been found from time immemorial.

When the idea was first mooted of carrying the rail over the Ghauts, it was deemed impossible; but engineering talent has overcome the difficulty. The ascent and descent have been made practicable, by cutting out from the face of the hills zigzag tracks, wide enough to allow of the passage of a train, and each with a considerable gradient. At each of the various angles of the road a station is erected, with what is called a reversing platform, built out from the precipitous hillside. On this the train is run, after completing the passage of one of the zigzags, and the engine is removed from its former position and attached to the other end of the line of carriages. The train then proceeds again on its upward way, each extremity thus becoming alternately first and last. In descending the Ghauts, the same process is observed; while, to prevent accidents, powerful brake-vans are attached to each train.

There are numerous tunnels on the line here, and this, joined to the fact that on looking out of the window one sees below him a sheer precipitous fall of a thousand feet or more, is apt to cause alarm to nervous folk, particularly as the wheels of the carriages approach most unpleasantly near to the edge, with nothing to save their occupants from destruction in case of a mishap but a small parapet, barely three feet high. Accidents are rare, great caution being observed by all the officials; but a few years ago one entire train went over a precipice, owing to the inability of the engine-driver to stop his engine on arrival at a reversing station.

The scenery throughout the passage of the Ghauts is very grand, and amply repays one for any alarm caused by the novelty of this mode of railway travelling. The landscape is a series of rugged mountains cleft by chasms, in which, in the rainy season, torrents rage and foam. At some points dense masses of forest and long wavy grass clothe the mountains nearly to their highest ridges; while at others, solitary hills stand out bare and cheerless, some flat-topped or peaked, some even of most fantastic outline; for the chief peculiarity of these Ghauts lies in their great irregularity, the ranges of hills following no regular order, but presenting a wild eccentricity of appearance, as if scattered by an earthquake.

We reached Deolali, the military depôt for all troops proceeding from or to England, at four o'clock, and from some of the officers we saw at the station learnt that as yet the regiment had proceeded no further, but that a portion was expected to start the following morning. Three hours later we halted for dinner; and soon after resuming our journey the approach of night warned us to prepare our couches for our needed repose. Neither during the day nor night did we pass any places of great importance, with the exception of Burhanpur, an old Indian city, close to which is the celebrated hill fortress of Asseeghur, a Mahratta stronghold of vast antiquity. Deemed impregnable, it fell to our arms some years ago, but only after an obstinate siege, followed by the treachery of some of its defenders. In this part of the country there are also very extensive forests, celebrated alike for their trees and the wild beasts who obtain a shelter in their depths. The majority of the forests of Hindustan contain an immense number of large trees little known in Europe, but capable of yielding valuable timber, and distinguished by their fragrance, luxuriant growth, or adaptation for manufactures. Teak grows in many places; and other trees characteristic of Indian scenery are the banian, saul, sissoo, sappan, &c.; while in the more northern parts the oak, cypress, and poplar flourish. Bamboos also abound, and so rapidly does their growth proceed that some of these reeds have been reported to attain a height of sixty feet in six months. We had a very comfortable night in the train, and soon after daybreak were all wide awake, and ready for breakfast, which was obtained at a small station about seven o'clock. Resuming our way, we passed through very pretty scenery, the country being fairly level, and for the most part under cultivation, with here and there small ranges of hills, which assisted to vary the usual dreary, monotony of Indian scenery in the plains. Jubbulpur, our destination, was reached at noon; and we drove straight to the hotel, where a copious bath and a complete change had the effect of greatly improving our personal appearance, which a day and a night's travelling over a road covered, as is always the case in India during the dry season, with a fine white dust, had by no means improved.

The hotel was clean and comfortable, which was fortunate,

Indian Hotels.

as it was the only house of public entertainment the place could boast. India is very much behind the rest of the world in the matter of hotels. Some of the larger ones in towns like Calcutta or Bombay are fair, though expensive; but the general run of up-country inns are poor and comfortless, and if under native management, very dirty as well. They are, however, I am glad to say, improving, and great alterations have taken place within my recollection. A better class of people have lately turned their attention to hotel management, and conduct the business in a very different manner to their predecessors, who were generally natives or half-castes, with a sprinkling of Europeans, usually retired enginedrivers and soldiers, whose ideas of business were summed-up in making as much as possible out of their wretched guests, and in disposing of the profits by drinking themselves into their graves as expeditiously as they could. Very little is found for the guest in Indian hotels beyond bed and board, and this only figuratively. It is generally necessary to bring your own bedding, that usually supplied consisting only of a charpoy, or native wooden bedstead, covered with plaited thick string, with one sheet, and one pillow about a foot square, and as hard as the stone that afforded a head-rest to Jacob. A mattress is deemed a superfluous luxury; so, unless the traveller comes provided with all these necessary articles, his couch is the reverse of comfortable, extreme hardness and coolness being its only claims to favourable notice. All the meals are taken in common at specified times. They are plentiful, and that is the whole. For this accommodation the daily charge of five rupees each person is made in most of the hotels inland, while in the presidency towns eight, or even ten, rupees are often asked. This, however, includes, in the case of the hotels there, a sitting and a bedroom, both well and completely furnished. Wines, spirits, and beer are not included in this tariff, and have to be paid for at hotel prices, usually at exorbitant rates. All this, joined to the numerous extras, which being necessary are taxed accordingly, renders your hotel bills rather formidable documents; and you come to the conclusion that hotel life in India is better suited to men with 'plenty of money and no brains,' than to those who belong to the opposite condition.

Jubbulpur is both a civil and military station of considerable size and importance, the head-quarters of a division of the army, the terminus of the Great Indian Peninsular Railway, and the commencement of another line, called the Extension Branch, which proceeds from this place to Allahabad. There is no large native town in the vicinity, and it is a pretty, clean little station. The houses of the European residents are large and well built, and each possesses a considerable compound or garden. It is surrounded by low-lying hills, and the scenery is picturesque all around, particularly in the valley of the Nerbudda, a river some few miles distant. On its banks are the celebrated Marble Rocks, and to their inspection the day following our arrival was devoted.

As the rocks are about eighteen miles from the station, the usual course is to start early, and drive there and back in one day in a carriage. We formed no exception to the general rule, and a short time after daybreak saw us entering the 'gharry,' an Indian term for vehicles of all descriptions, *en route* to our destination. At that early hour, the most enjoyable time of the day in India, the air was fresh and cool. All nature seemed to be wakening into life, to revel for a brief period in its delights before the heat of the sun commenced, and we looked forward to a most enjoyable drive, trusting to reach the bungalow at the Rocks before the rays attained any great power. Our road at first led us through the station, and then along the principal bazaar of the native community, who at this place do not excel in any special manufacture. Their only occupation seemed to be cloth-weaving, and this they performed by hand in the same clumsy manner as their ancestors. But although their mode of working the material appears rude, when compared with modern machinery used for the same purpose, yet the results are often surprising; for in many places in India, notably at Dacca, extremely fine woven goods are produced by this method, which for fineness of texture have never yet been approached by any people. After passing through the bazaar we emerged on the open country, here for the most part fairly under cultivation, particularly in the vicinity of the various 'gaums' or villages, which are composed of a collection of mud huts, with thatched roofs, and crowded with natives in all stages of nudity, partial or complete, according to their ages.

These villages, which are scattered all over India, are the abodes of the cultivators of the soil, and each is a community of itself, with an elected headman, who acts in a minor magisterial capacity in the internal affairs of his own particular settlement. In all villages there are two descriptions of tenants, who either rent the land of the village landowners, or that belonging to the government, where there is no such intermediate class. These tenants are commonly called 'ryots,' and are either permanent or temporary. The permanent ryots are those who cultivate the greater proportion of the lands of the village where they reside, retain them during their lives, and transmit them to their children. The temporary tenants cultivate the remaining lands of a village to which they do not properly belong, holding them by an annual lease at a lower rate than the former class; the inferior parts falling to their share, and the better lands being in the occupation of the permanent tenants, to whom most probably they have descended from several generations of ancestors. The nature of the soil and climate makes agriculture here a very simple art. A light plough, similar to that used by his forefathers, is sufficient, with the help of two small oxen, to enable the husbandman to make a shallow furrow in the surface in which to deposit the grain. A hoe, a mattock, and a few other implements, complete all the articles necessary. Reaping is performed with a sickle, and the grain, being trodden out by cattle, is kept in large dry pits underground. The Hindus understand the rotation of crops, though the almost inexhaustible nature of their soil renders it often unnecessary. They also class the soils with great minuteness, and are well informed about the produce for which each is best suited, and the mode of cultivation which it requires.

The principal vegetable productions of Hindustan are rice, maize, wheat, barley, cotton, indigo, sugar-cane, opium, tobacco, ginger, saffron, flax, and hemp. Besides the cereals several varieties of pulse are grown, one species called 'gram' entirely taking the place of oats as food for the horse. The land affords two crops of most things annually, and they are generally good and plentiful, except in seasons of drought, caused by the absence or tardy appearance of the periodical rains. Here is the cause of those fearful famines, painfully familiar to anyone conversant with the history of this people. Although India can lay no claim to being considered a great agricultural country, it may be reckoned fairly so, growing sufficient grain for its own consumption; while the cultivation of the soil, through the exertions of the ryots, is the source of the largest item in the Imperial revenue. The land-tax contributes usually nearly a fourth of the fifty millions which are the average yearly revenue. The finances of India are also largely indebted to the tax on opium, arising from the enormous cultivation of the poppy plant in certain localities.

Simple as the Indian agriculture seems, it has peculiarities which call forth a skill and industry not required elsewhere, more particularly in the matter of irrigation. The summer crop is sufficiently watered by the rains; the greater part of the winter crop lacks this necessary moisture. The water supplies are partially afforded by rivers, brooks, and ponds, but chiefly by wells, and it is distributed over the thirsty land by manual labour. In nearly every part of the country, a well exists in every field; for by a beneficent dispensation of Providence, with very few exceptions water is to be obtained in every locality in India, at a reasonable depth below the surface. Some wells afford it of a quality fit for any purpose, but the majority supply it in a form that cannot be utilized except for irrigation. After being raised from the well, it is conveyed in channels to the fields, and received in little beds separated by low ridges of earth. Into these beds the whole area under cultivation is divided, and in the dry season they are daily flooded an hour or so before sunset. This is of course a laborious and tedious method of irrigation, and expensive to the cultivator, who has to expend money in the sinking and keeping in repair of wells, while occasionally the supply runs short and causes the destruction of the whole crop. Undoubtedly a complete system of canals would yield results almost incredible; but although the subject has been under consideration for years, I suppose it has been thought that the works would be too costly, and that the results, at least for some considerable time, would not counterbalance the immense outlay. In some places the idea has been partially carried out with the best results; but it is thought by many, that as English money would have to be employed, the funds could be better utilized in civilizing and opening up the country, by extending the system of railways. Still, although the long-debated controversy of 'canals *versus* railways' has resulted in the triumph of the latter, it is to be hoped that when the network of iron roads is complete, attention will be directed to the other and no less important work, which would materially assist the welfare of this great country.

We arrived about midday at our destination, and waited at the bungalow, which has been erected here for the accommodation of visitors, until it became cooler, for the sun was too powerful at that time of the day to render any excursion, particularly one in an open boat, either pleasant or agreeable. Soon after tiffin, when the heat had somewhat moderated, we started in a kind of punt, and after a short row on the sacred Nerbudda, the Marble Rocks burst upon our view in all their magnificence. The river, narrowing at this part, flows silently between gigantic walls of white marble, dazzling in their purity. At some places the stone is richly veined with black wavy lines, and the greater part of the surface of the rock is smooth and polished. The lower portions are more highly polished than the upper, owing to the more recent action thereon of the flowing river, which has also fashioned this part into strange shapes. Huge boulders, some almost perfectly round, are scattered on a glistening strand of fine sand and pebbles; while other large masses have been converted into arches, by the water piercing through their centres. Gloomy-looking caverns abound, and before their entrances many curious forms of detached rocks are to be seen. Very large square pieces, piled on each other, like an altar, are common; and from their regularity in shape and position, it is difficult to realize that the hand of man has had no share in carving and placing them. The course of the river through this exquisite marble gorge is about one and a half miles. Throughout it is most tortuous, and at some places so narrow, that the upper portions of the opposite cliffs, bulging forward, almost meet, particularly where the water encroaching on the lower part in years long past, has worn it away far above its present level, leaving nothing but heavy overhanging rocks on either hand. Here the channel is so narrow, that you can see nothing but the wall-like, polished, pure white cliffs, and the deep blue vault of heaven over your head; and there it widens, showing bits of the country with trees and shrubs fringing the edge; while occasionally a little island-rock of strange weird shape rears itself from the deep green water, which is so clear and calm, that it reflects

K

the picturesque forms of the towering rocks in the most striking way. It is altogether a most lovely and romantic spot, unique of its kind, and of a beauty never to be forgotten. We were charmed with it beyond expression, although we saw it by the light of the setting sun, which is said to afford a much inferior idea of its magnificence, to the glorious, clear, mellow radiance of an Indian full moon.

After our return to the bungalow, while waiting for the gharry to be prepared for our drive to the station, we strolled into the wood which surrounds the rest-house, to inspect the remains of a ruined Buddhist temple, which is considered by archæologists to be one of the most ancient, as well as most perfect, specimens of the numerous shrines formerly erected for the worship of Buddha. This particular temple is built on the top of a very steep isolated hill, and is approached by a flight of wide stone steps, over two hundred in number. The ascent is very trying, the steps being worn almost completely away by the storms of ages and the feet of former pilgrims, so that they afford but a very slippery and insecure road to the summit. However, there is an ample reward for the fatigue; for though the ruined condition of the temple at the present time affords but a slight idea of its former magnificence, this can still be gathered from the great extent of ground covered by the remains, which are surrounded by a lofty circular screen of stone, elaborately carved, in the niches whereof are numerous large figures of the same material, representing Buddha and other divinities of the Buddhist religion; while, although the screen and figures are very much mutilated, enough remains to show how elaborately the art of sculpture was carried out by the natives in former days, contrasted with similar work as at present executed. The modern sculpture is remarkable neither for design nor elegance; and the taste and talent in stonecutting and architecture displayed by the Hindus in ancient times, appears to have been utterly lost to their descendants for centuries. Their more modern attempts in this line moreover are not original. Besides the temples and monuments in those parts of the country where Buddhists still exist, there are magnificent remains of their structures elsewhere. Many are similar to that described above, and many have been converted to Brahmanical uses.

The most striking are the cave-temples found in different parts of the peninsula; and of these the most remarkable are the excavations known as the Caves of Elephanta, on the island of that name, at the furthest end of the harbour of Bombay. And although strong doubts exist as to the founders of this temple, and for what religion it was intended, the sculptures within all appertain to the Hindu pantheon. Elephanta, as well as several other temples of the same description, I had seen on one of my previous visits to India. It is carved out of the solid rock, extending some distance forward from the entrance, and is divided laterally into several chambers or vaults. Each of these contains numerous effigies of the various gods, cut out in the face of the rocky walls forming the caverns. Many of the figures are gigantic in size and weird in design, which, joined to the massive and gloomy character of the temples in which they are enshrined, creates a feeling of awe, mingled with admiration for the skill and patient labour of the people who constructed such remarkable monuments of religious zeal. Another very fine cave of this description is to be found at Carlee, about half way between Bombay and Poona, which, from its great length and height, the colonnades which run along its sides like aisles, and its vaulted and ribbed roof, strongly recalls the idea of a Gothic church. It is reckoned that there are not fewer than nine hundred of these excavations still remaining in India, nearly all of which are within the presidency of Bombay; Elephanta and Carlee are however the finest examples. The reason assigned for so many being found in this part of the country is that the Buddhists, driven by persecution from the great cities, retired among the hills of the west, and there constructed the majority of the cave-temples, which, for their number, vastness, and elaborate character, continue to excite the wonder of all who see them.

The age of these cave-temples has never been clearly ascertained; but inscriptions in a character in use at least centuries before Christ, and which has long been obsolete, would lead us to believe that many of the Buddhist caves must date from long before the Christian era, while those of similar construction which are devoted to Hindu worship, are shown almost beyond doubt, from the mythological subjects on the walls, to be much more modern. Some are even supposed to have been formed as late as the sixth or eighth century of our era.

Nearly all the great architectural efforts of the Hindus of former days were spent on structures connected with their religion; their habitations, from the palace of the sovereign to the hut of the peasant, were for the most part meanly built; and yet we find that Hindustan abounds with stupendous and highly-elaborate architectural works of a sacred character, and of great antiquity. Strictly speaking, none of these buildings possess the elegant proportions of the edifices of the ancient Greeks; rather do they exhibit the ponderous sublimity which characterizes the works of the elder Egyptians, with the addition of a great deal of sculptural representation of the deities of the Hindu Pantheon, and their reputed acts, &c. These carvings are not generally conceived or executed in good taste, or with any regard to delicacy of sentiment, according to Western ideas of decency or morality. And although many of the statues and reliefs are bold and vigorous, and the complicated groups, expressing various passions, often include very fine specimens of grace in figure and attitude, they show a complete ignorance of anatomy, gross inattention even to the obvious appearance of limbs and muscles. This, joined to a total disregard of proportion between different figures, must exclude even the best Hindu sculptures from coming into remote comparison with European works of art.

As elsewhere, so in India, the styles of art which have existed at different times have varied with the prevalent religion. The earliest faith, however, of which we have any real architectural monuments is that of Buddhism. Before its advent the Hindus, though in an advanced state of civilization, evidently did not consider it necessary to raise any elaborate temples to their gods; or if they did so, they erected buildings or monuments of an evanescent nature, for few or none now exist to tell us of the state of architecture in those early days. About two hundred and fifty years before Christ, Asoka, a powerful monarch, became a strenuous supporter and propagator of Buddhism, and it is to his zeal that the greater part of the oldest architectural remains of India are due. From his time to the present day the sequence is unbroken, and the whole history of Buddhist architecture can be most distinctly traced either in India, Ceylon, or Thibet. The Buddhist remains are, first, commemorative monuments called 'topes' or 'stupas;' and secondly, temples, 'chaityas,' and monasteries, 'viharas.'

Of the temples few built examples remain. They as well as the monasteries were usually excavated out of the solid rock; but there is little reason to doubt that many, now extant and claimed as belonging to the Hindu worship, originally owed their erection to the zeal of the Buddhists, and on the decline of that religion were seized by the followers of Hinduism, while their former occupiers were driven to construct those cave temples, some of which resemble strongly, although no doubt accidentally, a Christian basilica, with nave, aisles, and a vaulted roof, and an apse with the shrine in place of the altar. Numerous wooden ribs are attached to the vaulting of the roof. These and other portions indicate that the buildings from which the caves were copied were wooden, and may thus account for the absence of earlier-built examples. And this may also help to explain the dearth of architectural monuments dating before the time of Buddhism. For what is more reasonable than to suppose that if the earliest Buddhist places of worship were erected of wood, the buildings devoted to the religious observances of the still earlier faith of the inhabitants were also erected of similar materials? They were the same people throughout, Hindus converted from Brahmanism to Buddhism, without any foreign influence which might have tended to change their ideas as to the form of their sacred edifices. To this opinion I am inclined, chiefly for two reasons. We know that in the early days of India architectural art was most imperfectly known. The Hindus erected no stately palaces or dwelling-houses, until more Western ideas were promulgated amongst them by their Mohammedan invaders. Their kings and nobles were content with houses of mud thatched with grass, such as are seen in the present day occupied by the poorer classes; their forts and defences were probably built of the same materials, which, in a tropical climate, are not calculated to last for any great length of time. If they displayed any skill or desire to rise above their ordinary level it was directed towards their sacred edifices. Probably at first, not being competent to manipulate large blocks of stone, they employed the materials from which they formed their other buildings, supplemented largely by the use of wood for the purposes of ornament, or to give a more durable character. Even so, however, these temples could not be expected to have survived the centuries that have since elapsed; and hence we find no architectural remains of any importance in India much earlier than two or three centuries before the Christian era, when the art of building with stone and of excavating in the solid rock seems to have become known. One or other of these methods was thenceforward employed in all their sacred structures; though their residences and ordinary buildings remained as before for some considerable time.

Another fact in support of the theory of the employment of wood may be mentioned, and that is its continuous use in the more northern parts of the country for this purpose. In Kashmir I have noticed temples built entirely of deodar-wood; but to their antiquity no clue could be obtained. One or two appeared comparatively of recent date, and did not strike one as singular in a country where buildings entirely of this material prevail. Others again presented a hoary and weather-beaten aspect, and might have been set down as co-existent with the Brahmanical period, or of even earlier origin; for although no wooden structures of this description are to be met with in the plains of India, there is every reason to suppose that many of those in Kashmir may be of great antiquity, the nature of the wood employed, and the more temperate climate of that country, being conducive to their preservation; while in the more southern parts the great alternations of temperature, with other causes, tend to rapid decay. But where this wooden architecture originated must be an open question.

The 'viharas,' or monastery caves, are very numerous, for the number of Buddhist priests was enormous. The oldest and simplest examples are in Bengal; but the finest are in Western India. They consist of a central hall, with cells round three sides, and a verandah on the fourth, next the open air. Opposite the central entrance there is usually a large cell or shrine, containing an image of Buddha. The pillars are elaborately carved, and have the bracket capitals, which distinguish Indian architecture.

The other styles of Indian architecture are illustrated by the temples of the Jainas, and those of the Hindus. The former seem to have been an imitation of the Buddhist temples, without the cells for the priests. Their religious structures consist of a sanctuary, surmounted by a spire; a pillared vestibule, with a dome in front; and round the whole an arcaded enclosure, with cells containing images. The cells are also surmounted with spires, and the arcades with domes are often frequently repeated within one enclosure. The most striking feature of this style is the dome, which is constructed by horizontal jointing, not with regular arches. Domes, pillars, brackets, and capitals are all of stone, elaborately carved, and masterpieces of this art.

Ancient Hindu architecture may be divided into two styles, the northern and the southern. The finest examples are southern, and found south of Madras. The temples consist of the temple proper, or 'vimana,' in front of which are the pillared porch or 'mantopa,' the gate pyramids or 'gorpuras,' forming the entrances to the enclosure, and the pillared halls, or 'choultries.' In the south the temples are always pyramidal, and in many storeys; while in the north they are much smaller in size, the outline curved, and they do not exceed one storey. The southern examples are frequently termed pagodas. The finest is at Tanjore, and is eighty-two feet square at the base, and fourteen storeys, or about two hundred feet, in height. The pillared halls are very wonderful structures, containing sometimes as many as one thousand columns, and as these are all profusely carved with representations of men, gods, flowers, and animals, all different, the labour of their construction must have been enormous. The general arrangement of these halls sometimes produces a good effect, but with their flat roofs they cannot equal the beauty of the domed arcades of the Jainas. These buildings are of different dates, from the commencement of the Christian era down to the last century, the greater number however dating from the decline of Buddhism, and the consequent revival of a modified Brahmanism. The oldest examples are the finest, the style gradually growing more debased, until at the present day, it has become, like the religion, both absurd and obscene.

It is not until we approach more closely those parts of the country which have been most directly under Mohammedan ascendancy, that we come to the real architectural triumphs of India. Here palaces, forts, and gardens are plentifully interspersed among mausoleums and mosques of rare beauty and design. They chiefly owe their origin to the more advanced ideas of the Western invaders of Hindustan, and differ widely from the more ancient works of the original possessors of the soil, not only in form and character, but most markedly in the substances utilized in their construction. In Mohammedan edifices marble is plentifully employed, a material never used in Hindu structures, all of which have been either wrought in sandstone or granite. On the arrival of the first Mohammedans, a revival of the then decaying art of architecture took place, but greatly influenced and modified by the Saracenic ideas of the conquerors, and a new style arose which prevails to this day in the greater part of the country. The foundation of this style may be assigned to the Ghori conquerors, about the eleventh century, and the first fine work therein is the tomb of Altumsh at Old Delhi.

This monument, built about 1235, stands at the north-west corner of the great mosque attached to the Kootub Minar, and is considered, to quote the words of Keene, whose remarks on this head are of great value, 'to be one of the richest examples of Hindu art, applied to Mohammedan purposes, that Delhi has to show.' The style was, however, at its best, a mixed or eclectic style, and its origin is most probably to be found in the adaptation of the old Pathan forms and requirements to the habits of Hindu workmen. In all countries, in buildings erected by Moslems for their own use, the arch is much employed, and the ornamentation is chiefly geometric, representations of living objects being strictly forbidden by their tenets; while in buildings peculiar to the Hindus, the architraves rest usually on brackets, and the decoration freely avails itself of vegetable and animal forms, no doubt conventionalized. There is, however, ample proof that the style we are now contemplating was largely influenced by the original Hindu ideas. Many of the buildings, while retaining the graceful form and brilliant colouring of the Persian mosques and palaces, show that the eclectic architects of the new school deferred in many directions to the ideas and tastes of the artificers they had to employ. The result was natural, and most successful. In many of the buildings so constructed, the vaulted roof, and the lofty arch with voussoir and keystone, were still a necessity; but there are edifices, neither rare nor unimportant, to be found whence the arch and cupola are rigidly excluded, and where nothing exists to remind the beholder of Central Asia, except the slender column, and the occasional kiosque.

This eclectic school of architecture has had five periods; marked out from each other by the presence or absence of the influence of the unoriginative but patient craftsmen of alien blood, and pagan creed, who lent their cheap yet precious labour to the works of their Moslem masters, and who are still working out the problems suggested by that most fortunate combination. The best examples of the first period are, the tomb of Altumsh, the arches of the great mosque, and the Kootub, at Old Delhi. It is remarkable rather for a severity and gloomy appropriateness, than for the lighter graces of architectural design; but, nevertheless, does credit to the handiwork of Hindu craftsman on Mussulman designs. A century later came the second period, when the style displayed increased gloom and hardness; but showed much vigour and rude grandeur. In the buildings produced at this time, the use of the true arch is universal. Most of these buildings are in good taste; and though severely simple, do not entirely disdain the use of colour. They are more Saracenic in appearance than their predecessors, which is probably due to the fact that the Mussulmans had now become independent of Hindu aid. It is in the third period, about the year 1540, that we first find colour introduced generally and boldly, and the system of encaustic tiling, which had been in use in Persia for two centuries before this date, then came into vogue. Coloured tiles were freely employed, and the style shows the features which make it the natural precursor of existing art.

In the fourth period the Mogul school of Hindustani architecture arose, under Akber, the celebrated grandson of the conqueror Baber. This formed the basis of modern practice. It is true that the buildings about Agra and New Delhi are commonly spoken of as Saracenic (and certainly they bear some resemblance to the general characteristics of that style). But since they are separated from that style in every other respect, it is better to treat them as belonging to one which, for want of a better name, has been termed the Hindustani school. This style of building was naturalized about the middle of the sixteenth century in Hindustan proper—that part of the country in which the Mogul capitals stood. It has taken deep root, and is still flourishing actively wherever it has free play, not only in the part of the country where it originated, but in most of the provinces of the whole peninsula. The new school differs from its predecessor in two things chiefly—1. The employment of Hindu treatment, which had been accidental, capricious, and fluctuating, was undertaken on a declared system of eclecticism and amalgamation. 2. The effects of colour were much bolder than heretofore, and variegated marbles were generally used in place of encaustic tiling.

Chief among the works of this time, in order of date, are the fort at Agra, 1566; the palace at Futtehpur Sekri, 1570 to 1600; the tomb of Akber at Sikundra, 1608 to 1613; the tomb of Itmad-ud-Daulah, 1621.*

The fifth period commenced in 1627, when Shah Juhan succeeded to the throne of the Moguls, and at once began one of the most splendid series of buildings that modern times have seen. This style modified the preceding eclecticism, and adopted a softness of contour and a use of dazzling detail, and its happiest effects are unique in their charm. Persian ideas predominate, although Hindu practice is not entirely eliminated. To give a catalogue of the great works of this period would be to name nearly all the buildings which have made Indian Mussulman architecture best known in Europe; but the principal examples are the Dewan-i-khas, Agra Palace, 1637; the Jama Musjid, Agra, 1644; the Taj Mahal, Agra, 1648; the Motee Musjid, Agra, 1653; and the Jama Musjid, Delhi Palace, 1658. Within the thirty years of

* Descriptions of the principal buildings mentioned in this chapter will be found in the accounts of our visits to the various cities.

the reign of Shah Juhan, Mogul art culminated and commenced its decline. Hindu practice, divorced for a time from activity, languished awhile; but it was the active partner that was doomed to die. While the Mogul architects have sunk from the Taj and the palaces of Agra and Delhi to the stucco buildings of Lucknow, the Hindu has caught up and retained all that was best in the art of his employers, grafting it on a vitality and energy all his own. This art is still flourishing. The Indian traveller of to-day finds galleries being placed in front of modern dwellings that need not shrink from comparison with those in Venice; while the workshops of Agra continue to turn out samples of inlaying that rival in taste and finish the famous ornamentation of the Medicean Chapel. And as there is no civilized country that can at the present day claim superiority over India in the buildings it contains, few can compete with it in those it produces even now, either in grace of design or elaboration of detail, if the Hindus are left to their own devices, and not influenced by Western ideas.*

On our return to the bungalow, a ludicrous incident took place, which served my companions as an introduction to the 'langoor,' or black-faced monkey of India, a species pretty plentiful in woody or rocky places in most parts of the country. We were strolling quietly along at the side of a wall enclosing a garden, which a number of these creatures were about to scale from within. They were not aware of our presence on the outside, and did not observe us until they attained the summit, and not in time to arrest the impetus of their leap. Consequently a perfect shower of these

* From note on Hindustani Architecture in Keene's *Agra*.

mischievous rascals fell all around us, with the most comical alarm depicted on their grinning faces, which continued to express itself in shrieks and cries, heard long after they had scampered off into the adjoining forest. It is not often that one gets an opportunity of studying so closely the character and habits of the monkey in a wild state; but it was fortunate that some member of the family did not fall on either of our party, as each individual of this species is between two and three feet high, and stout in proportion, with a set of formidable teeth.

We had a most enjoyable drive back in the cool of the evening, the latter part illuminated by the rays of a splendid moon; and on our arrival at the hotel found several of our companions of the voyage sitting at a late dinner, a part of the regiment having arrived that evening. We joined the party, and after a very lively meal all adjourned to the compound, where, ensconced in bamboo or easy-chairs, with the fragrant cigar or modest pipe as accompaniments to the cheerful conversation, one and all voted themselves very comfortable, and India not such a bad place after all. Of the few pleasures enjoyed by the dweller in the tropics, none exceeds the exchange of the heat of the day, passed in a closed house, for the cool, fresh air of night, in which it seems perfect bliss to lounge away the time, until the drowsy god warns one to retire.

CHAPTER VII.

Arrival at Allahabad—Description of Allahabad—Its history—The Station—The Fort—Pillar of Asoka—Sacred Banian tree—Departure for Cawnpore—The journey—The Railway Station—City of Cawnpore—Its history—The Cantonment—Memorial Church—Wheeler's Entrenchment—Story of the Siege—The Massacre—Slaughter Ghaut—The Civil Station—Scene of final tragedy—Sufferings of the Victims—The Well—Inscription on Well—Memorial Garden—Motives of Nana Sahib—His history—His after-fate—Pontoon Bridge—Manufactures of Cawnpore—Tanning—Cotton-spinning—Arrival at Lucknow—Change of duty—Our daily doings—Description of an Indian Station—The Cantonments—The Barracks—The Civil Lines.

WE left Jubbulpur next day by train for Allahabad, and at the latter place obtained accommodation in a very good hotel in the station. This was fortunate, as the day after our arrival I received intimation not to proceed with the regiment to which I was attached, to its destination, but to report myself for duty at the rest-camp, in order to be available to accompany any other detachment of troops on the march to their allotted post. No call for duty was, however, made for a whole week, and we spent that time pleasantly, if not profitably, in visiting all that was worthy of note in the city and its environs.

Allahabad, the capital and seat of government of the North-West Provinces, consists of a large native city and an extensive civil and military station contiguous. The town is in the south-eastern extremity of the Döab, or land of two rivers, on a tongue of land formed by the confluence of the Ganges and Jumna. It is three hundred and forty feet above the level of the sea; and is distant about five hundred miles from Calcutta. Of its early history little is known, and of that little few traces are left in the Allahabad of to-day.

At one time, probably, it was a place of paramount importance in consequence of its sacred character, the union of the two river deities being regarded with reverential awe. This character Allahabad retains to the present day; for several large religious 'melas,' or fairs, are held annually on the river banks, a favourite place for those bathing pilgrimages which make Allahabad (or Prayag, its ancient name, as the Hindus call it) rank with Benares, Hurdwar, and Muttra as sacred resorts at certain appointed seasons.

The present city, which, in Heber's time, half a century ago, was small, with very poor houses and irregular streets, is a place of growing importance, having greatly improved since the introduction of a municipal system of administration. It now contains over one hundred and twenty-five thousand inhabitants, and can boast of a few fine new streets, a covered market-place, and a hospital and dispensary. The station, or European part of the town, consists of two parts: one, the new settlement of Cannington, designed since this place was made the capital of the Provinces after the Mutiny instead of Agra. It contains a number of wide roads crossing each other at right angles, like those of a city in the United States. Most of the building sites are now occupied with houses, private bungalows of the civil officials, law courts, and other public edifices, as well as numerous hotels and shops. The other portion of the station contains the college, government house, and the barracks, which are most unfortunately situated in a low, unhealthy, and in every respect ill-chosen site. There are several other notable buildings in this locality, as well as a library and museum, and the Alfred Park, or public gardens. The whole forms a very fine station, thoroughly European in character. Allahabad is considered by many to be a most desirable residence; but it has two great drawbacks—it is extremely hot and very unhealthy at certain periods of the year.

The chief object of interest here is undoubtedly the Fort, which stands exactly at the confluence of the Ganges and Jumna. The existing castle was built by the Emperor Akber about the year 1575; but from the presence of various Buddhist remains it may be inferred that the site was the centre of the old Hindu city already referred to, and these old relics of a bygone age are the most interesting features of this 'place of arms.' The Fort is comparatively modern in construction, and does not contain such gorgeous palaces and buildings as are found in the fortresses of Agra and Delhi. The place is memorable in the annals of the Mutiny for the shelter it afforded to numerous refugees, and its successful defence against the rebels by the residue of the garrison and the other Europeans. It is now always garrisoned by English soldiers, and contains the barracks and other buildings necessary for their accommodation.

In the wide space between the entrance and the gate of the Arsenal is an object of real importance to the historian or antiquary, the lofty and elegant monolith of Asoka, a stone pillar forty-two feet high, and cylindrical in form, but slightly tapering towards the summit. This pillar, which is in excel-

Sacred Banian Tree. 147

lent preservation, was first erected by King Asoka, 240 B.C., for the purpose of inscribing his edicts regarding the propagation of Buddhism in the old city of Prayag; and here it probably remained until overthrown by the idol-breaking zeal of the Mohammedans. It was re-erected by the Mogul Emperor Jehangir, to celebrate his accession to the throne in 1605; and there is every reason to believe that its original position was not far from its present site. In front of monuments of this class it is usual to find a pipal tree (*Ficus religiosa*), the descendant, it may be, of the tree of knowledge affected by the founder of Buddhism, or perhaps a survival of some old religious custom long since passed away and forgotten.* This column is similarly provided, only the tree is not now visible; for the temple in which it was placed, originally on the ground level, has, from the constant accumulations of ages been gradually earthed up until reduced to the condition of a crypt. The original tree exists only in the form of a bifurcated log in this vault, the walls of which drip with a moisture said by the Hindus to be traces of the Sarsuti, a lost sacred river, which is supposed to flow underground to this place, for the purpose of irrigating the holy tree before issuing forth to join its more ostentatious sisters. There can be little doubt that this is the original site of the holy undecaying banian tree, as it was termed, although it was really a *Ficus Indica*, or indigenous fig-tree, and is so described by a learned Chinese pilgrim who visited India in the seventh century after Christ. Whether the stump that remains is truly a part of the tree then seen cannot of course be clearly ascertained; but it matters little to the pilgrims of

* Keene's *Handbook to Allahabad*.

the present day, who come in large numbers to worship at this venerated shrine, and who accept every legend in connection therewith, not in the least doubting its truth, in the simple manner not exclusively peculiar to Hindu devotees.

On the last day of the week I received an intimation to leave on the following Monday, in charge of a number of men, for Cawnpore, from which place I was further directed to proceed to Lucknow, in order to resume duty with the regiment, which was by this time fairly settled down at that station.

We left Allahabad at six in the morning, and although only distant from Cawnpore four or five hours by ordinary train, our special was some two hours longer on the way. The country through which the line passes is flat and well cultivated, appearing like one large plain of growing crops. This arises from the peculiarity that in most parts of India the fields, although their boundaries are well defined and known to the different proprietors, are never divided by walls or fences of any description. This entails great trouble and oftentimes loss on the unfortunate ryots; for in a country like India, teeming with animal life, not only are the unprotected fields open to the ravages of the numerous fowls of the air, but to those of the various wild beasts, making it necessary for some member of a cultivator's family to be day and night constantly astir, so that his presence, with the aid of the most horrible noises of which the human voice is capable, may scare away these winged and four-footed marauders.

Immediately on our arrival, I handed over my detachment to another officer, and we were free to resume our journey; but as the train for Lucknow did not leave until the evening,

Cawnpore and the Mutiny. 149

we proposed to rest awhile at the station, and after tiffin to drive round and visit the places of interest before our departure. The railway station of Cawnpore, one of the first completed in Upper India, is a very good and convenient building, and, like all the larger ones, has a very excellent refreshment-room, with sleeping and bath-rooms, accommodating a limited number of travellers for a small charge, and thus obviating the necessity of driving about in search of an hotel—a great comfort to those whose stay in a place is only to be of short duration.

The native city of Cawnpore is by no means inconsiderable; for it is a flourishing centre of trade, and commands the navigation of the Ganges, on which river it is situated. The Ganges canal also discharges itself into the river here, after a course of four hundred miles, embracing, with its distributing channels, a waterway of over eight hundred miles. Cawnpore, by two lines of railway, is likewise connected with every town of importance in this district. The place is unknown in early history, and its first importance dates only from 1777, when it was chosen as the quarters of a British garrison, being the key of the border line which divided our frontier from the then independent province of Oudh. The city covers a wide area, and contains a population of 116,500 inhabitants, but has no buildings of any importance or merit. It is in the cantonments and civil lines that the objects of interest will be found; for it was there that those mournful events took place, which have rendered the name of Cawnpore familiar to every civilized nation, as the place where, during the Mutiny of 1857, the rebels perpetrated their most dastardly treachery and cruelty.

The cantonments are small and compact, with rows of palatial-looking barracks, affording accommodation for a considerable garrison. Passing these the first object that meets the eye is a large red-brick church with a lofty pointed belfry. This is the building that now stands as a memorial on the site of Wheeler's Entrenchment, the frail bulwark that for three weeks served as the only protection of the unhappy garrison, who took up their quarters in it after the mutiny of the native troops on the 6th June, 1857, and who, with the addition of the remaining European population, including civilians, canal and railway employés, and others, made up a total of seven hundred and fifty souls, the great majority women and children, and leaving only between two and three hundred fighting men to defend the post. This slender shelter consisted merely of two thatched barracks surrounded by a trench and a parapet of earth five feet high, enclosing an area about two hundred yards square, armed with ten field-pieces of small calibre.

At the present day no vestige of this entrenchment is to be seen, the whole having been levelled for the purpose of erecting the church and forming the garden which now mark the spot. When I visited Cawnpore for the first time, nine years after the memorable siege, it was still standing, the two buildings, and the well from which the besieged obtained their water within the enclosure, bearing the marks of the storm of shot and shell to which they had been subjected. In this exposed situation, for three dreadful weeks the feeble garrison, surrounded by their sick and dying, short of food and ammunition, were starved and bombarded in a climate under which persons of their race usually find it difficult to support life even with the aid of every comfort. At the end of that time more than half their number had succumbed and were, happily for themselves, taken from the evil that was to come. Trusting in the faith of their treacherous foe the Nana, the survivors capitulated on the condition that they should be allowed to depart down the river to Allahabad in boats provided for the purpose. What followed is too well known, for it is written on one of the saddest pages of British history. No sooner had the English embarked, and were pushing off from the shore, than a close discharge of musketry was opened on them by hitherto concealed enemies, who subsequently rushed in amongst the helpless, paralyzed, unarmed fugitives, slashing in all directions with their tulwars. When the order came to cease from slaughter very few were left, and those chiefly women and children, who were driven off and closely confined in a small house near the rebel camp. One boat alone escaped in the confusion, but grounded some little way down, and was attacked, all on board being destroyed, with the exception of four, who saved their lives by swimming down the river until all pursuit had ceased. These four were all who were left to tell the story of Cawnpore; the others who escaped the massacre at the Ghaut were disposed of in the manner described hereafter.

After inspecting this interesting site of the entrenchment which had seen the first act in the great tragedy of 1857, we proceeded to the spot where the second part took place. This was known then as the Suttee Chowrah Ghaut, or landing-place; it has now the historical appellation of 'The Slaughter Ghaut.' It is a little temple on the water's edge, from which a flight of steps leads down to the river. At the time of the tragedy there was a small village on the left, wherein the sepoys were concealed. At our visit this had disappeared, and the little temple and steps are slowly mouldering into decay. On the plaster and coping of the wall you can still see the marks of the treacherous bullets; but what a contrast did the serene calmness and solitude of the place present to us, as compared with the turmoil and devilry of which it had once been the scene!

About a mile from this spot, after crossing the canal, we came to the civil station. This contains nothing of note, with the exception of the garden which surrounds the scene of the third act in the sanguinary drama. At the close of the second, the survivors of the massacre were driven, scared and miserable, to the quarters of the Nana. On their arrival the male captives were shot, and the females and children shut up in a house near the river, not far from the well destined hereafter to be their grave. To their number was added, a few days later, a party of refugees from Futtehgurh of some fifty-five persons, consisting chiefly of women. What may have been the sufferings of these unhappy beings no one will ever know. Probably their former trials and miseries had caused the thought of the bitterness of death to pass away, a stunned apathy taking the place of any other feeling. It is, however, a relief to add, on the authority of an English official, Mr. Sherer, who held an enquiry a few days later, and whose report on the affair I have chiefly followed, that dishonour was not among the horrors endured by the delicately-nurtured females in those awful days. And whatever their sufferings, they were not long continued; for on the 14th July, six weeks after their entry into the entrenchment, and three from the time of the Ghaut episode, the steady advance of their would-be deliverers—the British troops—caused their fate to be discussed. The decision arrived at is too well known. At sundown the work of death commenced. Volleys of shot were first sent through the doors and windows; the work was completed with swords and knives; and early the next morning the corpses, and in all probability some not quite dead, were dragged out and thrown into the well. This well at that time was simply one of those narrow, deep, uncovered wells common to India. Shortly after these events it was covered in, and surmounted by a marble figure of an angel, the whole being surrounded by a beautiful circular open screen of carved stone. An inscription round the base of the pedestal tells the sad tale in burning language: "Sacred to the perpetual memory of the great company of Christian people, chiefly women and children, who near this spot were cruelly massacred by the followers of the rebel Nana Dhoondoo Punth, of Bithoor; and cast, the dying with the dead, into the well below, on the 15th day of July, 1857." The monument is encircled by cypresses, and it stands on a mound in the centre of the memorial garden, which at the time of our visit was green and filled with flowers, fit emblems of the divine hope which mitigated the despair of our foully-murdered countrywomen.

The whole story affords a marked instance of Asiatic treachery; for it was not until the very day of entrance into their entrenched position, that the General and his officers suspected that the Nana was otherwise than friendly. In that capacity they had relied on him for affording some aid against the attack of the revolted sepoys. He had even assisted at their councils, and the keeping of the treasury and magazine had been entrusted to his followers; and it was not until that fatal morning that he threw off the mask, declaring himself their bitter foe, and assuming command of their implacable enemies in person. The motive that induced this man to perform the execrable deeds that have rendered his name infamous throughout all civilized lands, has often been discussed. Whether he acted spontaneously of his own free will, can never be known with certainty. Some incline to the belief that he was a mere puppet in the hands of more unscrupulous and stronger-minded leaders of the rebellion, although the opinion that he acted on purely personal motives is in a measure supported by Mr. Sherer. "There was," he writes, "at the time of the Mutiny, residing at Bithoor," a village twelve miles up the Ganges from Cawnpore, "a Hindu of rank, named Dhoondhoo Punth, but commonly called Nana Sahib. . . . . He was the adopted son of Bajee Rao, the last Peishwa, or head of the Mahratta confederacy, and inherited his houses, landed property, and jewels. This man had a grievance which, in the usual unsympathetic way of prosperous masters, the British had wholly failed to appreciate. Adopted in 1832, he had been brought up to look upon himself as heir to the Peishwaship, a barren honour no doubt, yet preserving that character of personal distinction so flattering to all barbarians. Five years before the Mutiny old Bajee Rao died; and the government of Lord Dalhousie at once announced that the titular dignity had ceased, and that the adopted heir would only inherit the private property; the pension and salute being discontinued, and some old pieces of artillery withdrawn, which had contributed to a sort of child's play of regality in the declining years of the captive potentate. For the next four years, Dhoondhoo Punth had spared no exertions to persuade the Court of Directors to revoke this decision, and his failure constituted a deep offence." Mr. Sherer had full opportunity of being acquainted with the subject; and there is every reason to imagine that this to him apparent injustice rankled in the Nana's mind, and caused bitter thoughts against the governing nation, on members of which, as soon as opportunity offered, he wreaked a hellish revenge.

Regarding the after fate of this miscreant nothing is known. He escaped the vengeance of the soldiers at the taking of Cawnpore, and is supposed to have perished miserably in the jungles of Nepaul. Although never forgotten, his name and fate had ceased to be talked about until an event occurred at Gwalior in the winter of 1874, which brought the topic once again prominently forward. But of this more hereafter, as it took place immediately under our own observation, while we were living at Gwalior.

Our visit to the well having exhausted the sights of the place, we began to think of taking our departure for Lucknow, distant about forty-five miles, and connected with Cawnpore by the Oudh and Rohilkund Railway, the terminus of which was on the opposite side of the Ganges. We had to cross by a pontoon bridge of very rickety construction; but we noticed with satisfaction that the new bridge for trains and vehicles to connect the two lines of rail was rapidly approaching completion. Before leaving Cawnpore it may be remarked that not only is it a great commercial entrepôt, but that it also possesses manufactures, for some of which it is becoming celebrated. The town has long been known for the skill of its tanners and workers in leather; and it is astonishing what well-finished articles of saddlery, &c., can be purchased there at a very low rate. This trade has been carried on here ever since a race of men called the Chumar caste, native tanners, established their head-quarters in the city. These people are looked upon by their fellow-townsmen as the lowest of the low, and debarred from all intercourse with other castes. They are veritable Pariahs; for to flay the sacred cow and convert the holy hide into leather for the use of the unbelieving Feringhi, is the greatest sacrilege and the most impious act of which a Hindu could be capable. Our Chumar friends do not, however, seem to suffer much from the scorn of their fellow-natives; since many are well-to-do, and even wealthy. All find employment; for taking advantage of their talent the government has of late years erected a factory for tanning and converting leather into harness and other articles, for the use of the army in India. The other great industry of the place is cotton spinning, and the preparation of piece goods, twists, and cloths suitable for the use of the natives, and also for tents, for which there is an unlimited demand. At the present time there are two large mills in operation, which together possess 23,000 spindles and 250 looms, and give employment to over 1,200 men, women, and boys.

Our progress to Lucknow was slow. The train only ran about fifteen miles an hour, a very usual speed on many lines in India, where the express travels but thirty to thirty-five miles. We did not therefore arrive at Lucknow until nine o'clock, and it was half an hour later before we found ourselves installed in the cantonment hotel at that station.

The following morning, after reporting my arrival in the usual manner to the military authorities, I learned, much to our regret, that during my absence from the regiment another officer had been appointed to my post. I was in consequence directed to perform general duty in the station, being attached temporarily to an infantry regiment in the cantonments, until a vacancy arose at some post in the circle—one of the districts into which the whole of India is divided for military administrative purposes. The term circle is more usually employed to denote the area under the jurisdiction of one principal medical officer, which frequently comprises more than one division or general's command. These districts are further under the general superintendence and direction of the Surgeon-General of the British forces, who resides at Simla, the head-quarters of the Commander-in-Chief in India. As it was very uncertain how long our stay in Lucknow would be prolonged, we thought it unnecessary to rent or furnish a bungalow, and proceeded to make ourselves as comfortable, for the time, as the resources of the small hotel in which we were lodged would allow. Soon after our arrival a pony and chaise was purchased, and every afternoon was devoted to exploring the station and its environs, in which there is much to be seen; for although not of great antiquity, many of the buildings possess much historical interest, more particularly in connection with the Sepoy Mutiny. Here it was that the gallant defence of the Residency was made, which, with other brave deeds, caused the name of Lucknow to be a memorable one in the annals of that war.

The word 'station,' so frequently met with in works on Indian subjects, may need a little explanation. As everyone is aware, it is a term in hourly use among Anglo-Indians, and expressive of their particular place of residence; but many will not be thoroughly conversant with the peculiarities of what may be called the 'white towns of India,' seeing that, with the exception of the presidency great commercial capitals, they are solely confined to the use of Europeans and their immediate followers.

There are very few towns or large villages in the country wherein one or more of the dominant race do not reside, in some one or other of the numerous official capacities necessary to carry on efficiently the task of governing and directing, for its welfare, such a vast empire. To many of these posts of duty the term can hardly apply; and although many very small places of this kind are dignified with the appellation of station, I wish to convey in the following description an impression of one of the larger sort, containing the military and civil European elements in sufficient numbers really to entitle it to that designation. The usual site of a station is near to some large native town, from which it derives its name, and its size and importance is generally governed by its strategical position. In a military point of view India, gained by the sword is held by the sword, and the proper distribution of our force is a subject of the gravest anxiety, and influences greatly the choice of a locality for the formation of these necessary settlements. This being the case, it naturally follows that the greater number of the inhabitants of a station are soldiers. A large portion of the station selected is set aside for their use, and called the 'cantonments,' while the remaining part is devoted to the habitations of the members of the civil service and civilians generally, and in contradistinction is known as the 'civil lines.'

The first notable objects in a cantonment are the barracks for the occupation of the European troops. These are fine palatial-looking buildings constructed of stone, and usually with slate roofs. Many of them are double-storied, the men using the lower portion during the day, and at meals; while the upper part serves as a dormitory only. Fine buildings as the barracks in India undoubtedly are, particularly those erected in later years, it is the opinion of many that they are constructed on a wrong principle, and that comfort has been sacrificed to appearance; for, owing to the material used in their formation, as well as their style of architecture, they lack the requisite coolness so necessary to all abodes in the East. Their great size also materially adds to the high degree of temperature that obtains within them, more particularly during the hot season; for it is easy to imagine that a huge staring building composed entirely of stone and slate, and standing on a bare plain in an exposed position, attracts and retains the intense heat of the tropical sun during the daytime; and the comparative coolness of the night not being of sufficiently long duration to dissipate this, must be always uncomfortably warm. And such is the case. Most of them, more especially at certain periods of the year, and in notoriously hot stations, are neither more nor less than perfect ovens, affecting the general health of the inmates most materially. It is a moot question whether a return to the old style of mud walls and thatched roofs would not be advisable. That it would on the score of economy is undeniable; for the amount of money lavished on the new style of barracks in India has of late years been something fabulous, and it is much to be regretted that so large an outlay had not been more judiciously employed in attaining, as the first consideration, the more material comfort and well-being of the British soldier in the East. All these barracks are built in *échelon ;* each contains the greater part or the whole of a company of infantry ; each group forms the quarters of an entire regiment, and is occupied only by the men of that particular corps. The ranges of the infantry are separated from the cavalry, and again from the artillery, by a wide open space ; each arm of the service is thus kept at some distance from the others, a necessary precaution on sanitary grounds, more especially as affecting the spread of an epidemic of any nature. In rear of these buildings stand the cook-houses, latrines, and lavatories, belonging to each company ; and at some distance further off, about the centre of the range, are the quarters of the married families, similar in construction, only smaller in size.

The native troops forming part of the garrison are located a little distance away, on the flanks of the European regiments. Their quarters call for no special remark, as they live very much in their usual manner, inhabiting small mud huts arranged in long double rows.

The horses of the cavalry and artillery are not accommodated with stables. They stand in long rows in the open air in the rear of their respective lines, and are secured in the Eastern manner by heel-ropes.

There yet remains to be mentioned another great feature in a cantonment ; namely, the native bazaar. Here dwell the traders who supply the wants of the military community, as also the numerous servants and followers that accompany every regiment in the East. These bazaars often attain considerable size; and at some stations, particularly at the headquarters of a division, where a large armed force is maintained, they approach the dimensions of a small native town.

The officers of the regiments live, for the most part, in separate bungalows, situated on the sides of the various roads that intersect that part of the cantonment not occupied by the different barrack buildings. All the officers of each different corps are to be found near each other, as close to the quarters of their men as the nature of the place admits, with their messhouse as a focus from which all the other buildings radiate. The houses and offices of the general and staff are usually in the centre. Each bungalow is situated in its own compound, usually laid out as a garden; and the sides of the roads being planted with trees and turf, the general aspect of a cantonment is pretty, particularly when the flowering plants and trees are in full bloom and foliage.

The civil lines, or that part of a station inhabited by the non-military portion of the community, is usually divided from the cantonments by a wide space of unoccupied ground, but connected with it by a wide shady road, which runs through both of the divisions of the station, and is termed the mall. This road is the public promenade for the residents, and is crowded every evening with horses and carriages of every description. In its vicinity are the public gardens or park; or, failing them, the band-stand, a small tastefully laid out enclosure, with a raised platform, on which the bands of the various regiments perform once or twice weekly. These performances are the occasions for a grand muster, both of the civil and military community, the *élite* of the station collecting in large numbers for the double purpose of listening to the music and exchanging the current 'gup,' the Anglo-Indian term for small talk and scandal. The bungalows of the civilians are usually larger and finer than those occupied by the military officers, but otherwise are built pretty much in the same style, fronting the several roads, and each surrounded by its garden. The station church is commonly a prominent object, centrally situated, generally a fine commodious building, similar in style to those at home, and more pretentious than 'the cantonment church, which is erected near the barracks, and which in most localities is a quiet, unassuming edifice. The houses and shops of the large tradespeople are to be found in the civil lines. The stores for the supply of the creature comforts so necessary in this country are called 'Europe shops,' and the proprietors are usually Englishmen or Parsees. There may or may not be a native bazaar; more frequently there is not, the civil lines being usually pretty close to the native city, and thus able to dispense with what in the cantonment is a necessity. The various magistrates' offices, the treasury, and branches of the different banks, with hotels, and bungalows of regular residents, such as retired officers who make India their home, complete the list of the buildings.

Such, then, cantonment and civil lines, is an Indian station, the abode of exiles who endeavour to make their surroundings as homelike as possible. In this, in a great measure, they succeed; for the pretty houses, the well-kept gardens and roads, together with the general order and cleanliness prevailing, at once distinguish the European quarter from the native city whence it takes its name.

CHAPTER VIII.

City of Lucknow—History of Lucknow—The Kings of Oudh—Modern city of Lucknow—The European Station—The Palace of the Kaisar-Bagh—Origin of the Name—The Fish Emblem—The Chattar Manzil—The Lall Baraderi—Machi Bhawan Fort—The Great Imambara—Feast of the Moharam—The Hosenabad—The Jama Musjid—The Residency—Story of the Siege—The Alam-Bagh—The Dil-Kusha—The Sikandar-Bagh—The Martiniere—Its founder Martine—Departure for Faizabad—The Journey—Its Discomfort—Arrival at Faizabad—Obtain a Bungalow—Etiquette of Visiting in India—Social law of Society—Its probable Origin, and present Condition.

LUCKNOW is the capital of the Province of Oudh, and the residence of the Chief Commissioner who administers the province, which in extent is about half the area of England, with a total population of nearly twelve millions. Oudh is a part of the alluvial valley of the Ganges, and contains in the north large forests. The general character of the remaining soil is fertile, and the climate, although variable, moderately temperate, conducive to the growth of vegetation and to agricultural pursuits. Lucknow stands on and about a rising ground on the right bank of the river Gumti, about three hundred and sixty feet above the sea level, and contains two hundred and seventy four thousand inhabitants. Although the present city occupies the site of some ancient townships, which are said to have been absorbed in the modern city and environs, very little is known about its earlier history. Probably the first inhabitants and owners of the place were Nagas, or Ghosseins, a martial and adventurous class of one of the principal sects of Hindu devotees. With these were, most likely, allied the Brahmans from Ajudhya, a holy city of great antiquity, situated near Faizabad, at that period the principal town of the province. All we know is, that Brahman and other Hindu settlers were in possession of the place, up to the time of the first Mohammedan conquests of India, when they were subjugated by Sayad Salar, a relation of the invader Mahmoud of Ghuzni, about 1160, and their power usurped by a tribe of Sheikhs, who were known afterwards as the Shahzadas of Lucknow. Further conquests of the invaders placed the whole of the province of Oudh at their mercy, and it continued to be administered by an official termed a Nizam, as an appanage of the Mogul empire.

These Nizams succeeded each other at the will of the Emperor, until in the reign of Mohammed Shah, about the middle of the last century, Suadat Ali Khan, a Persian adventurer of enterprise and talent, was appointed to the post. He, in the decaying condition of the empire, became in a measure independent, and founded the line of the princes of Oudh; for he caused the office of 'vazirate,' or prime minister of the province, to become hereditary in his family. He was succeeded by his son Abdul Mansur Khan, whose direct heirs carried on the power. On the accession of Asaf-ud-Daulah, his grandson, in 1775, the Nawabs of Oudh, as they were termed, became of much more importance; and this ruler removing his court from Faizabad, which had been the seat of his forefathers, came to Lucknow, which he at once greatly enlarged. From that time dates the greater part of the modern city, as it stands at present. This prince, being supported by

Annexation of Oudh.

British friendship, though still nominally a provincial governor, assumed the power with virtual independence, and his grandson Ghazi-ud-din Haidar, acting on the encouragement of the English Viceroy, who thought to secure a counterpoise to the Mogul empire, declared himself an independent king or emperor. This device of Lord Hastings did not, however, succeed; for the people of India never would recognize the new dynasty. Delhi was always regarded by them as the seat of sovereignty, and the events of the Mutiny proved that the two courts, instead of possessing different interests, were as one in the object of ridding the country of British power.

The new king and his successors distinguished themselves in no particular manner except in cock-fighting, displays of fireworks, and building costly palaces, joined to a love of drinking and debauchery of all kinds. Politics, too, had ceased to interest them; for the administration of the province was virtually in the hands of the British, who became their protectors. Each successive reign produced no better results. The enormous expenditure of the monarchs on their own pleasures led to want and misery on the part of their subjects; and in the so-called reign of King Wajid Ali, in 1856, the East India Company decreed the annexation of the province, with the object of giving it a purer government.

This measure, although it bore on the face of it a spirit of rapacity on the part of the Company, and was contrary to the advice and wishes of the Governor-General (Lord Dalhousie), was duly carried out, and the nominal ruler transported to Calcutta, where he and his family still reside, surrounded by a mockery of a court, which is all that is vicious and vile. This removal of the king and annexation of the province, the only reward obtained by the Nawabs of Oudh for their long-tried fidelity, is considered by many to have been one of the chief causes that led to the terrible events of 1857.

The modern city of Lucknow possesses a threefold character. There is the native town, like unto all others, a mass of squalid houses huddled together, with small, narrow, and dirty streets. Next comes the court suburb, which was commenced by Asaf-ud-Daulah about a hundred years ago, and contains the palaces, the seraglios, and other buildings occupied by the princes and their followers. Lastly we find, to the north and west, numerous country houses belonging at one time to the royal family, and the European station.

The purely native quarter offers few attractions. It contains no buildings of any note, and its streets are only narrow crowded bazaars, devoted to commerce. It is, however, of much earlier date than the portion that contains the palaces; for it is said to have been the city founded on the site of the ancient one by Akber, in the middle of the sixteenth century. Lucknow at one time was famous for its manufactures, more especially for the excellence of the steel weapons that were made there, and for the beauty and finish of its jewellery, particularly articles of chased gold and silver. But its glory departed at the annexation. There are no longer crowds of princes and nobles to purchase such wares, and at the present day, with the exception of silver-chasing on a small scale, no particular art survives.

The first idea that would be formed of the court suburb, particularly if seen at a distance, would be that of a magnificent city of palaces, whose gilded domes and lofty minarets,

Description of Lucknow. 167

surrounded by palms and other trees, make up a most beautiful Oriental picture. And undoubtedly the distant aspect of the place is more than pretty, but the greater part of its charm is dispelled on a closer acquaintance; for, unlike the old cities of Agra, Delhi, and others, which contain solid and magnificent buildings of a distinct Eastern type, Lucknow, although possessing some very large, and in some cases graceful, structures, will not bear comparison with the other great cities of India. The time at which it was built had some influence on this result; for Hindustani architecture had then fallen into a deep decline. For years previously the quaint fancies and the patient labour of the Hindu artizan had passed out of use, and during the erection of the costly piles that adorn the court suburb, commencing in the year 1775, only the services of ignorant workmen could be obtained, under the direction of uneducated Europeans. Moreover, stone not being available, brick and stucco had to be used, and the result was a mixture of vulgar European and Oriental architecture, which makes this town unlike any other in India, whether of Hindu or Mohammedan origin. Nevertheless, although not possessing any great artistic merit, these large piles are not without a grotesque attractiveness. Their very number tends to create an idea of sumptuousness that is impressive; and they cannot fail to be interesting to an Englishman, from their connection with those stirring events of the Mutiny, of which Lucknow, and more particularly these buildings, was the scene.

The European station is decidedly one of the finest in the country. The roads are wide, well kept, and turf and trees abound. It possesses several beautiful gardens; the bungalows are well built, and the shops and places of business are unusually handsome. Both the civil and military portions are very extensive. Being the head quarters of a division, the cantonments are exceptionally large, occupying a space of three miles by four, and containing very commodious quarters for the large force here located.

Taking the chief buildings in detail, we will commence with the Kaisar-Bagh Palace. This, although the most modern, having been begun so lately as 1848, is the most stupendous, and at the same time the most extravagant, of the many costly piles erected by the puppet kings of Oudh; for it is said to have cost a million sterling. It was the whim of the last king, Wajid Ali, who still survives, and was built for the seclusion of the countless inmates of his harem, who were lodged in fantastic buildings around a great square court-yard. The whole, in style, reminds one of a stucco theatrical structure, pseudo-Italian in character, the stagy effect of which is heightened by the entire group being plentifully bedaubed with gilding, ochre, and whitewash. Besides the great central quadrangle, there are numerous detached buildings, and before the downfall of the monarchy the effect of the whole, although grotesque, must have been somewhat impressive; for all the central places were laid out as gardens full of fountains and flowers, and the rooms were crowded with costly furniture. The whole of this luxury was destroyed in the Mutiny; for the palace was most obstinately defended by the rebels, in opposition to the advance both of Havelock and Sir Colin Campbell, in the endeavour to relieve the Residency, which place it covered.

The name of the Kaisar-Bagh can hardly fail to strike one

as possessing somewhat of a European character. The origin of the term is curious, as showing to what lengths the inordinate vanity of an Oriental can attain. These effete monarchs, who at their best barely possessed a shadow of real power, to add to their dignity called into requisition a title apparently borrowed from Western civilization, and styled themselves the Kaisars or Cæsars of the East. This dignified appellation was engraved on the royal seal, and prefixed to all their state documents.

The word kaisar, although it smacks of German origin, is however an old Arabic and Persian word, and has been used, both in writing and speaking, by the natives for many centuries to designate a supreme ruler, which these Oudh monarchs certainly were not. It was only their vanity that led them to usurp such a title—a title which, while these pages are being written, has been most fittingly revived in the person of our most gracious sovereign; for the appellation by which she is now to be known in India, namely, Kaisar-i-Hind, signifying Empress of India, is one easily understood by her Eastern subjects, and literally expresses her dignity, in the native tongue, as a supreme ruler over the whole of the country.

The heraldic emblem of these Oudh monarchs, a large fish, was also plentifully employed to denote their sovereignty; for there are few buildings of any note in Lucknow, or in the province generally, that are not graced by this device, which is usually to be found carved in stone on the arches of the gateways of the buildings.

This emblem denotes their high Mohammedan connection; for the 'mahee muratib,' literally 'the fish of dignities,' was a standard or imperial ensign of honour conferred by the

Mogul Emperors only on the chiefs of the highest rank, and it was equivalent to the three horse-tails of the Turkish Empire.

At a short distance from the Kaisar-Bagh we come to a very curious building called the Chattar Manzil, erected about the year 1830, by Nasir-ud-din, as a seraglio. It is a large fantastic pile, dazzlingly white, with every pinnacle and protection covered with gilt ornament. Surmounting each tower and minaret is a model of a large open umbrella in metal, profusely gilded. It is from these that it derives its name, 'chattar' being the Hindustani word for these useful articles. At one time it was surrounded by a high wall, for the better seclusion of its inmates. Now that is pulled down, and it stands open to the road facing the river; the rooms, properly fitted up, being used as a club-house and library by the European inhabitants of the station. Surrounding this edifice are numerous detached buildings, now utilized as law courts. They call for no special notice with the exception of the Lall Baraderi, a handsome structure possessing some of the dignity that stamps most of the Mogul buildings at Delhi, although somewhat marred by being smeared over with red ochre in order to give it the appearance of having been built with sandstone of that colour, a favourite material, and one generally employed in the construction of the lordly piles at the Mohammedan seat of empire. The building was originally the 'dewan-i-am' or 'hall of audience,' to the palace which formerly stood here, but is not to be seen now, having been levelled after the Mutiny. Within it all the business of state was transacted. In its day it has witnessed some stormy scenes, and it is still used as a durbar room for the reception of any distinguished guest of the government.

Buildings of Lucknow.

All these buildings played an important part in the Mutiny; for they were all strongly fortified, and their rebel garrisons inflicted great loss upon our soldiers, who stormed and captured them on their way to the Residency. About a mile and a half from the Chattar Manzil, following the course of the river, we come to the Machi Bhawan Fort, which was erected by the Emperor Aurungzebe on the site of the original citadel of the ancient city. During the troubled times of 1857 it was first proposed to hold this place; but after the disastrous defeat of Chinahut, where the small garrison of Lucknow attacked the rebel camp, deceived by the information they had received as to their numbers, and found them in such force that a retreat was necessary, in which severe loss was suffered, it was considered that there would not be sufficient men to defend such a large place. Our forces therefore proceeded to the smaller entrenched Residency, after having blown up the fort and its surroundings. Latterly, the Machi Bhawan has been restored and extended, and its walls now embrace what is, in my opinion, the finest building in the city, the Great Imambara, or 'patriarch's place.' This title is given by the Shiah sect of Mussulmans to a building consecrated to the 'Moharam,' or 'celebration' of the martyrdom of the sons of Ali, the immediate descendants of the Prophet, put to death by rival claimants to the headship of Islam in the fortieth year of the Hejira (A.D. 666). This celebration lasts ten days, and is shared by all classes of the followers of this religion. The ceremony begins with the exhibition of frames of wood-work gaudily decorated with gold and silver paper, which are supposed to represent the tomb of Hosen in Turkish Arabia.

These are paraded about for ten days, which are held as a period of fast and lamentation. Upon the tenth day a funeral procession takes place, and crowds of men and mourners, accompanied by native bands playing barbaric music, follow to the spot of the symbolical sepulture of the tazias. Often they are thrown into a river; a few are buried in the earth; but of late the greater number, after being carried round the streets, are, in a spirit of economy, preserved with the view of their serving again the year following. During the whole time the Imambaras are illuminated, hymns chanted there in honour of the martyrs, and great religious enthusiasm prevails.

This Imambara was built in 1784 by the Nawab Asaf-ud-Daulah, as a relief work in a time of scarcity, and he is buried in the middle of the central room. The dimensions of this hall are one hundred and sixty-seven feet by fifty-two. The total height is about sixty-three feet. The fabric is built throughout of solid masonry, no particle of wood entering into its construction, and affords a fine example of constructive skill. Not far from the Great there is a building styled the Lesser Imambara, or Hosenabad, which was the work of the last king but two, Mohammed Ali, and forms the tomb of its founder. It is surrounded by an enclosure or garden, within which is the Jama Musjid, or chief mosque, and also a small model of the Taj at Agra. Most of these buildings are coloured in distemper, in the glaring fashion that spoils so many of the Lucknow edifices; but they present a grand sight when illuminated on a night of festival during the Moharam.

About half-way between the Machi Bhawan Fort and the

The Residency.

Chattar Manzil stand the ruins of the Residency, the place which in all Lucknow possesses to Englishmen the deepest historic interest. Here it was that a handful of our brave countrymen for months kept at bay whole hordes of rebels, who, despite their efforts, never succeeded in gaining possession of the place; and here the remnant of the brave garrison, after enduring every privation and suffering, were finally relieved by Lord Clyde, after a feat of arms that will ever live in history, and which did more to prove to the natives of India the stuff their white rulers were made of, than any other episode in the war.

The Residency was originally a magnificent mansion, built about the end of the last century for the use of the Political Resident at the court of Oudh. It stood in its own grounds, and surrounding the chief building were the houses of the officials connected with the Agency. At that time the native town extended to within a short distance of the spot. This added much to the losses of the besieged, the enemy being able to approach very near under the shelter of the houses, which stood close to the line of the outer defence. An entrenched square, including the grounds and all the buildings of the Residency, defended by a few hastily constructed batteries, was the only bulwark of the garrison against the ceaseless onslaught of the infuriated savages, who were said at one time to have exceeded a hundred thousand in number. This marvellous siege began on the first of July; for although the city of Lucknow and its neighbourhood had been kept in order hitherto by the firm measures of Sir Henry Lawrence, it was with great difficulty, for the annexation of the province was fresh in the minds of its inhabitants, who had also a further deep cause for sympathy with the rebels, since few families had not some relation serving in their ranks—Oudh having for years been the great recruiting ground for sepoys belonging to the Company's service. The disaster at Chinahut, on the 29th June, hastened the event; for the survivors of that affair, and the rest of the garrison, amounting in all to nine hundred and twenty-seven Europeans, and seven hundred and sixty-five native troops, chiefly Sikhs, had barely time to blow up the fort, before they found themselves strictly invested in the Residency, which had been prepared for defence in anticipation of the coming storm.

The siege then began in earnest, and in this frail enclosure some thousands of persons, combatant and non-combatant, men, women, and children, were penned up and rained upon with shot and shell for fifteen weeks, with wounds and disease thinning their ranks daily, for cholera and small-pox were epidemic, and this, joined to the numbers slain by the fire of the foe, greatly reduced their strength. On the first relief by Havelock on the 26th of September, the garrison had lost five hundred of their number, while an equal number in proportion of the women and children had been killed, or had succumbed to their privations. Many more perished before the final relief by Lord Clyde on the 17th November, when the remnants of the original defenders, and of the first relief thrown in by Sir H. Havelock and Outram, who, although not in sufficient numbers to raise the siege, contributed materially to preserve the post, were escorted by the victorious troops to the head quarters of the army at the Dil-Kusha, and the Residency and grounds silently evacuated, after witnessing a siege of a kind unparalleled in history, where despair was unknown, and where the bravery and general endurance of all deservedly received the admiration of the whole civilized world.

Such is in outline the story of Lucknow—the bare facts only; for the most skilful pen would fail to convey fully all that they imply, and for the visitor of the present day it is difficult to realize the terrors and tumultuous feelings of those awful months. The scene now presented to the view is peaceful. The whole place is laid out as a charming garden, containing the ruins of the houses and batteries, all of which bear witness to the frightful ordeal through which they have passed. In the centre of the grounds are the ruins of the Residency proper, which, being on higher ground than the other buildings, formed a prominent mark for the enemy's fire, and was early in the siege reduced to the shattered condition in which it remains. Yet in the 'tykhana' or cellars of this house were harboured during the whole time the European women and children. The upper rooms formed an imperfect shelter for a portion of the officers; many of them were killed within its walls, including the great and good Sir H. Lawrence, the Civil Commissioner, who, wounded by a cannon-shot a few days after the commencement of the siege, died shortly afterwards, and now lies buried in the cemetery close by, with the simple epitaph below his name, 'He tried to do his duty.'

There are various other ruins to be seen as well as other sites of interest, and all these spots are easily found, being marked by stone tablets, while a further idea of the former state of the city may be formed by the aid of a model, which is in the museum outside the Bailie Guard entrance.

In various parts of the country, for some miles surrounding Lucknow, are numerous tombs and pleasure gardens. These do not call for special notice with the exception of the Alam-Bagh, an enclosure containing a large pavilion, intended by the king as an occasional residence for a favourite wife, and which is interesting as having been the base of the British operations, and as containing also the grave of that Christian soldier Havelock.

The Dil-Kusha, or 'Heart's Delight,' is a somewhat similar country residence, now falling into decay; but it was a handsome and commodious villa when it formed the head-quarters of the British army, and received within its walls the rescued garrison of the Residency. North of this building will be found a large walled enclosure called the Sikandar-Bagh. This became notorious in the Mutiny as the scene of the slaughter of more than two thousand rebels—all trained soldiers belonging, strange to say, chiefly to Oudh regiments of the revolted Bengal army. These men obstinately defended themselves for some time; but the 93rd Highlanders, with other detachments of British and Sikh infantry, entered by a breach and bayoneted the whole number.

Turning to the north-west, not very far from the Dil-Kusha, stands a building sufficiently striking from its possessing a little of every known order of architecture, while its bizarre effect is heightened by the summits of the battlements and pavilions being crowded with statues in brickwork and plaster. High above all too rises a large central tower, with a belvidere and flagstaff, supported by flying buttresses. From the top of this an excellent view of Lucknow is to be obtained. This curious and extensive building was erected by Claude Martine, a French adventurer, who, entering the Company's service about 1745, became eventually a Major-General, and was for many years at the Court of Oudh in a semi-official capacity. Here he amassed an enormous fortune, part of which he laid out in building this place as a residence for himself. He called it Constantia, although at the present time it is better known as the Martiniere, after its founder. Martine bequeathed the property for the use of a school for European children, and seeing that the king of Oudh coveted its possession, ordered that his body should be interred in a vaulted chamber of the basement, which was duly carried into effect. This was a clever expedient to prevent the place being seized after his death, for Martine thought that although a Mussulman ruler might violate the rights of property, he would probably respect a tomb.

The inspection of these buildings and other places of interest employed our time here most pleasantly. During our stay too we had formed several acquaintances among the residents, whom we met constantly at private parties or in the public gardens on band-nights. Altogether therefore we were most comfortable; the only drawback being our unsettled condition, which forced us to linger on at the hotel. This, as no attention was paid to home comforts, was becoming unbearable, particularly at the beginning of April, when the weather began to show unmistakable signs that the hot season was approaching, a time of year when a well-appointed and well-kept bungalow is a desideratum. Fortunately our discomfort soon came to an end, as on the twelfth of the month I received an order to proceed to Faizabad for duty. The summons was quickly obeyed; for two days later we started for that city, after a sojourn of six weeks in the interesting station of Lucknow.

We left the hotel at an early hour, and drove to the railway station to catch the morning train to take us to our destination, a journey of seven hours, Faizabad being distant about eighty-nine miles from Lucknow. It was a very trying morning; and the hot wind, blowing with great force, added greatly to our discomfort, as we were obliged to close every window and aperture in the carriage to prevent its ingress. Many methods have been tried to cool the carriages, and lower the temperature experienced by the traveller by rail, during the prevalence of these winds, but nothing as yet has been devised of a perfectly satisfactory nature, and one has to be content to endure, throughout a journey in the daytime, a period of close confinement in a dark and shut-up box, in which the thermometer stands at anything between ninety and one hundred degrees Fahrenheit. This condition of things is very injurious to Europeans, and often attended with fatal results, passengers being attacked with heat apoplexy, and dying before assistance or means to relieve them can be obtained. Even if no untoward results occur, the intense unalleviated heat affects more or less the healthiest constitution, and towards the end of the journey one usually feels an excessive fulness in the head, joined to a general sense of weariness and exhaustion. Hence very few people travel by rail during the hot weather, or if obliged to do so they usually select the hours of night for their journey; but it occurs sometimes that there is only one train to the desired station in the twenty-four hours, and that leaving during the most trying part of the day. In these cases there is no choice, and one must endure in the best manner possible that which cannot be obviated, trusting to good fortune that there will be no worse result than great bodily discomfort. Unfortunately for ourselves the only train to Faizabad left at nine a.m., and from that hour until the time of our arrival, five p.m., our misery was intense. We were in a half comatose condition when we arrived at our destination, and were released from our darkened chamber of horror.

Awaiting our arrival on the platform was the officer whom I had come to relieve, to enable him to take up an appointment at a hill station. He kindly invited us to dine with his family that evening, to enable us to inspect his bungalow, which, with the furniture, he was prepared to make over at a fair valuation. This offer we gladly accepted, as we were very anxious to possess a house for ourselves, and quickly, after a bath and a change of clothing at the hotel in which we had secured rooms, we were on our way to our entertainer's abode. This with its contents we found admirably adapted to our requirements. We entered into possession the following day, and thus for the first time since our arrival in India we had a home of our own. It soon presented a cheerful appearance; and in a few days we were quite prepared to receive in our drawing-room the return calls of the residents of the station.

One great peculiarity of Indian life concerns the etiquette of visiting. It is the custom in this country for the newcomer in a station, immediately on arrival, and after reporting himself to the officer commanding and the other authorities, to call, accompanied by his wife if married, either on all the military and civil officials in the place, or at least on those holding the higher positions, with as many more as he is desirous of knowing. These visits, after the lapse of a few days, are returned, and this formality over you are supposed to be mutually acquainted. The social law on this subject is very strict, and occasionally carried to extremes; for in the case of two families arriving at a place much about the same time, the difference of a few hours only entitles the first on the spot to be regarded in the light of residents of the station by the second, who will have to call on them accordingly. It is curious that this method of forming acquaintanceship should have been held so long in favour by Anglo-Indians, as it is exactly the opposite to the custom that obtains in the mother country. It probably first originated when the number of Europeans in India was very small, consisting entirely of members of the military or civil services. Both these services holding an equally good social position, there was no likelihood of ineligible persons seeking admission within the charmed circle; while at the same time the practice afforded an opportunity to those who, from want of means or disinclination for society, did not care to enter into the friendly gaieties that served to beguile the leisure of their fellow-exiles, thus to intimate their desire. As a strong feeling of conservatism usually pervades all ranks of society in India, the custom has been preserved intact even to the present day; and although the number of Europeans in the country has of late years largely increased, and a great many of them, following the pursuits of trade or other occupations, can lay no claim to be admitted within the ranks of the *élite*, no untoward results have followed. Two distinct classes of society have been formed in India, possessing different interests and tastes, never clashing and each mutually respecting the other; and thus the current of English society ripples onwards as smoothly and as pleasantly as it usually does at home.

The ordinary time of day for paying and receiving calls is between noon and two o'clock, in the cold weather, and in the other seasons of the year any time during the cool of the evening. The latter was the period when we underwent the ordeal; for the hot winds during the daytime effectually prevented any exposure to the heat from eight a.m. to sunset, unless such as was absolutely compulsory.

CHAPTER IX.

The Seasons in India—The hot weather—Its variations and effects—The rainy weather—Its effects—The cold weather—Its variations and effects—Influence of climate on Europeans—Modes of cooling Houses—Khuskus Tatties—Thermantidotes—Punkahs—Punkah pulling—Its drawbacks—Our Bungalow—Description of Indian House—Establishment of Servants—Their number—Difference in respective Presidencies—Establishment in northern Bengal—Their expense—Difference of Creed and Caste—Its effects—Enumeration of Servants—The Khansamah—The Khitmutgar—His assistants—Their costume—The Bobberchee—An Indian Kitchen—The Bearer—The Ayah—The Bhestie—The Dhobie—The Mehtar—The Chowkedar—Theft in India—The Syce—The Gasscut—The Mahlie—The Coolies—Their duties—General character of Indian Servants.

THE seasons possess a deep interest to the dweller in India, as their periodical changes greatly affect one's occupation and material comfort in a land where the characteristic of the climate, contrasted with that of Europe, is heat. In so vast a country, varying in height from the level of the sea to the summits of the Himalayas, a wide range of heat and cold must of course be experienced in different localities. While some places enjoy a comparatively temperate climate, others have earned an unenviable notoriety for the intense heat prevailing there during the greater part of the year, rendering them anything but desirable places of abode to the stranger, who, compelled either by duty or self-interest, has to fix his residence there, and endure as best he may a climate most trying and inimical in every way to the European constitution.

The Hot Season.

There are three distinct changes of season during the year in India—the hot season, the rainy weather or monsoon, and the cold, or rather the temperate, period.

The hot season, which in most places is the shortest, may be said to commence about the middle of March, continuing on to the end of June, the usual time for the monsoon to make its appearance. During this season, over the greater part of the country the sun is scorching, and the heat intense; even the wind is hot. The land becomes brown and parched, dust flies in whirlwinds, and brooks and rivers become dry or are reduced to narrow channels of very moderate dimensions. The variations in height of temperature in various places during this period are considerable, being much influenced by proximity to the sea coast, or to mountain ranges, or by height above the sea level. It is not uncommon to observe two stations, only a few miles apart, show a very marked difference, according to their height above the sea. The climate is also in a measure determined by the proximity of waste lands, or jungles, or notably of sandy deserts, such as exist in Sinde, where the radiation of heat from the sand is intense, and the inhabitants dwell for the greater part of the year in a dry and scorching condition of the air, which possesses also a very high degree of temperature.

The agent that influences most powerfully the heat of the various localities is undoubtedly water, more particularly large areas, such as the sea. This is well exemplified in the case of the three presidency towns, and other places on the coast, where the variation of the seasons is not so marked as further inland, and where, although during the hot weather a higher degree of temperature is attained, it is slight as compared with other less favoured localities. Such places, too, do not suffer from the hot wind, and the nights are always cool and pleasant, through the agency of the sea breeze. On the other hand, so little variation in the climate is both monotonous and trying; for, with the exception of a short cold season, when a slight coolness in the air is discernible in the early morning or evening, the inhabitants of Calcutta, Bombay, and Madras exist in a mean annual temperature of eighty to eighty-five degrees, the condition of the air in the rainy season being particularly moist, hot, and oppressive.

The geographical positions of the three divisions of the country also affect materially the condition of the climate, more particularly during the hot and cold seasons. The stations of the Bombay and Madras Presidencies enjoy for the most part much more temperate conditions than the stations of Bengal, notably those of the North-West Provinces and the Punjab. The two minor Presidencies, being smaller in size, are probably more amenable to the influence of the sea, which more or less surrounds them, and which to many of the stations not too far inland affords the blessing of comparative coolness, and exemption from the hot winds. These, although found to be prevailing in many of the localities in Bombay and Madras, are not of such intense heat as in the middle and upper portions of Bengal, where the climate of India is undeniably at its worst. There the hot wind blows with great force during the day, very often continuing all night as well, and it is not an uncommon thing to experience a temperature of a hundred degrees or even more within the house.

Apart from the disagreeable personal feelings caused by

The Rainy Season.

living in so heated a condition of atmosphere, the hot season of the year is not unhealthy; and, provided always that there is no undue exposure to the sun, or excess in the matter of diet, it is generally found that there is less sickness among Europeans during the hot weather than in any other period of the twelve months.

The next peculiarity in the climate of India is the periodical rainy season. This commences usually about the latter end of June and lasts until the middle of October, although variations as to commencement and duration continually occur. The rains are brought from the Indian Ocean by a south-west wind, or monsoon as it is termed, and are pretty well distributed over the whole area of the country; being heaviest, however, if anything, near the sea, especially in low countries, unless in situations protected by mountains. The amount of the rainfall is so great that it can scarcely be conceived of in Europe, for, although it is confined to four months, and many days of every month and many hours of every day are fair, the total rainfall in this time is considerably more than double that which is distributed over the whole twelve months in England. The arrival or setting in of the rains is anxiously looked for by those who for the previous three months have been enduring the dry heat of the hot weather. All nature, too, rejoices in the change, for a few days suffice to convert the dusty, bare, and parched land, into fields of rich verdure. Vegetation of every description springs into life, the trees and shrubs put forth their blossoms and fruits, and the eye is again gladdened by the sight of variegated flowers and rich green grass, doubly acceptable when for so long a period it has rested on nothing but a dried-up brown soil and withered trees, shrouded by clouds of burning and blinding dust. There is also a sensible diminution in the temperature, more particularly during the fall of rain, continuing for some time after its cessation; and the hot wind makes its final exit from the scene, withdrawing one great source of heat; but the sun is still very powerful, and during what is called the 'break,' when the cool wind drops and no rain falls for several days, it shines forth from between the clouds, producing, together with the saturated condition of the earth and air, a most oppressive moist heat, causing one to perspire freely on the slightest exertion, and making life almost unendurable away from the artificial breeze produced by the punkah.

This condition of the climate during the rainy season is experienced with slight variations over the greater part of India, including the presidency towns or stations near the sea, but on the mountain ranges a great difference is observed. There the hot season, which is never oppressive, the climate approaching that of a particularly warm summer at home, gives place to a period of cold and fog. The rainfall in these regions is excessive, and their altitude decreasing the sun's power, there is thus created a season both cold and damp, often attended with serious results to many who seek these resorts for their health's sake. Nor is it only in the hill stations that the change in the weather is felt, for in the plains a general unhealthiness may be said to prevail during the monsoon, and cases of sunstroke frequently occur, through incautious exposure to the sun's rays when obscured by the clouds and portending no danger. The oppressive close-heated condition of the atmosphere is the cause of numerous cases of heat-apoplexy, more particularly amongst those who observe no caution in their mode of living. And to end our catalogue of woes, towards the end of this season, when the profuse vegetation to which it has given life commences the process of decay, malarious fevers are rife, and the scourge of India, the cholera, makes its unwelcome appearance.

We now come to the cold season. This, the only really enjoyable time of year, may be said to last a good deal longer, fortunately for us, than either of the other two. The climate begins to undergo a change in the beginning of October. The nights and early mornings become sensibly cooler, and this increases until at the end of the month the coolness has longer duration, the sun loses a considerable amount of power, and the cold or temperate weather sets fairly in and lasts until the middle of March. Then another period of grilling begins, a thought ever present in the minds of all our countrymen, even in the midst of the enjoyments of this most delightful time, which is rendered doubly precious by the previous discomfort of the purgatory through which they have passed.

The degree of cold varies very much all over India during this winter. In some places, as I have before remarked, particularly in the presidency towns, or in portions of Lower Bengal, or stations on the coast, very little change, except during the night, is felt. In all parts of the country at a low level, if towards the south, the greatest cold experienced is only what may be termed moderate heat, and, on an average of the whole of India, is not much more than that marked temperate on our thermometers; while the hottest time of the day, even at that period, rises but just above our summer heat at home. The cold, however, is much more sensibly felt than would be supposed, especially in the night and early morning. In many places, in parts which are much elevated above the sea, slight frost sometimes takes place for an hour or two about sunrise. Far north, as in the Punjab, the cold weather is longer in duration, much more intense, and with the exception of snow, which rarely falls except on the hills, approaches rather the character of an English winter; while in stations on the mountain ranges the climate is nearly one of Canadian severity.

This season, especially in localities where the change is well marked, and the air becomes cold and bracing, is not only acceptable to the fevered residents, but exerts a favourable influence on the health of the community. The strong are now able to enjoy more exercise in the open air, and approximate their lives to what they had been accustomed to when at home, and in a short time their ruddy and fresh appearance testifies to the benefit afforded by the variation in temperature. The weakly and delicate gradually recover from the ill effects caused by the unwholesome rainy season; and although some debilitated constitutions are not able to endure so extreme a difference without some suffering, and there is a prevalence in many places of malaria, a legacy from the preceding season, this time of the year may be considered favourable to health, as well as the only period of real enjoyment during the twelve months.

With all the advantages of the cold season, however, it cannot be denied that the climate of India is most trying to Europeans; one foreign to their nature and habits, and prejudicial to their health. Few remain under its influence long without suffering in some mode or other from its ill effects; while in the case of young children it either proves fatal in a short time or necessitates their removal to another climate. To bring them up in the East is rarely attended with beneficial results, either to their health, intellect, or morality. The enervating climate destroys the first, and weakens the second; while the native associations of their youth corrupt the third.

As one may well imagine, although it is impossible to ward off the effects of the heat in the open air during the hot and rainy seasons, various means have been invented and adopted to lessen at least the temperature within the dwelling-house. This is performed most satisfactorily during the prevalence of the hot winds by closing all the doors and windows at an early hour, soon after sunrise, leaving only open those that face the west, from which direction the wind blows, and filling up these spaces by screens made of the roots of a sweet-smelling grass stretched over a bamboo framework, called 'khuskhus tatties.' These fit in tightly, and are constantly kept wet with water through the agency of a native coolie stationed outside in the verandah. Thus the fiery wind in passing through the interstices of wet grass loses a considerable amount of its heat by evaporation, and is rendered comparatively cool before its admission to the apartment. Another mode of cooling the air is by the aid of a machine called a 'thermantidote.' This is a large wooden box fitted into an opening, admitting the cooled air through 'khuskhus' curtains at the sides, and then sending it circulating through the room with some degree of force by the aid of a hand wheel, with fans or paddles within the apparatus, which is worked from the outside. This method, however, is not in such general use as the former. The cost of the machine prevents its adoption by many, while the apparatus is also apt to get broken or come to a sudden standstill, an event that cannot occur to the more simple 'tatties.'

These processes are of course only applicable during the presence of the hot wind, which usually commences to blow about eight a.m. and subsides at sunset, although it frequently continues through the hours of night. After its cessation, and in places where it does not occur, as well as during the whole prevalence of the rains, one depends solely, as an aid to coolness, on that well-known article of Indian furniture the 'punkah.' This necessary adjunct to every chamber is merely a large heavy wooden fan, terminated by a fringe of cloth, suspended loosely from the ceiling, and swung backwards and forwards by means of a rope fastened to its centre, and passed through a hole in the wall into the hands of a coolie without, who pulls and tugs at the swaying machine for a spell of four hours without cessation, when he is relieved by another who continues the work for a similar period. Many ingenious mechanical means have been devised at various times to cause an even and continuous swinging of the punkah, but none succeed in performing the work so satisfactorily as the manual labour of experienced native punkah-wallas or coolies; although the temper is sorely tried by their somniferous propensities at night, when the sway of the punkah frequently declines by degrees until it ceases altogether, and its stoppage has the effect of awakening the sleeper, and bringing him back from the land of dreams to the very earthly fact that he is suffering extreme bodily discomfort in a condition of simmering heat, and a prey to

An Indian Bungalow.

numerous mosquitoes hitherto kept at bay by the strong current of air. The process of rousing the sleeping attendant has then to be performed by the aid of various missiles always kept at hand, or by shouting 'kincho! kincho!' 'pull! pull!' This usually after a time galvanizes him into fresh life, testified at first by various spasmodic and erratic jerks at the rope, causing the heavy board above one's head to swing about in an alarming manner. That however subsides as the coolie more fully realizes his position, and soon the even swaying, bringing comfort to his master, is resumed; alas, too often only for a time! Ere long the same scene is repeated, and hence the hot season nights of the resident in India, instead of periods of sweet repose, are very commonly a mixture of broken sleep, discomfort, indignation, and rage.

Undoubtedly, without these aids to coolness, the European in India would suffer much more than he does from the heat; and although one feels grateful for them at the time, it is with a sigh of satisfaction that their removal is witnessed; for the tatties are damp, and unless very fresh water is used, unpleasant, and the never-ceasing swing of the punkah is trying to the nerves, while the backslidings of the coolies ruffle the temper. But, chiefest of all facts, their removal heralds the approach of the cold weather, and in its delights all soon forget the miseries that accompany these necessary evils.

The bungalow in which we found ourselves now fairly established at our new station, was one of the ordinary type common to the country—a large one-storied building, built of bricks, and plastered with chunam. This is a substance made from sea-shells, which, applied wet, and beaten flat with smooth pieces of wood, quickly dries, and hardens into a firm white concrete, admirably adapted for the surface of both walls and floors. The house (like others) was raised a few feet above the level of the earth, and approached by steps leading up to the large covered-in verandah, which always surrounds the whole or the greater part of a bungalow. It is erected on the sides more especially exposed to the sun, against whose power it affords a welcome protection. This is further increased by closing in the spaces between the pillars of the verandah with suspended 'purdahs,' or curtains of matting, which can be raised or lowered at pleasure. The roof of a bungalow is generally high, and sloping down towards the top of the verandah. In former days it was invariably formed of a thatch of grass; but at the present time tile roofs are usually employed. Although better in many respects, they tend, however, to increase the heat within. The tiles become intensely hot from exposure to the direct rays of the sun, and there can be no doubt that the 'pucka-built' houses of brick of the present day, although more imposing and durable, as well as superior in many ways, do not contrast favourably as regards coolness with the 'cutcha-built' domiciles of the earlier period, when mud, wood, and grass, were the only materials used in their construction.

Usually one large room is formed out of the entire centre of the house, with an entrance both in front and back. This apartment is generally divided by a cloth or rep purdah into two parts, the front being the drawing-room, while the back serves as a dining-room. On each side of the large centre room are smaller ones, entered both from the main apartments and from the verandah. These all have bath-rooms attached, and are the sleeping chambers. With the exception of a few small glazed frames in the upper part of the walls near the roof, which serve for the purpose of ventilation when open, there are as a rule no windows to be found in an Indian bungalow. Numerous doors, the upper portions of which are composed of glass, take their place, all opening into the verandah, and placed opposite to each other in various parts of the rooms to insure a free and thorough passage of air; as a draught, which in England is carefully avoided, is in this country a necessity, and a principal point in the construction of every dwelling.

The kitchen and other offices are never attached to the house, but form, with the huts of the servants and the stables, a little colony in the compound, some distance from the main building, from which they are usually separated by a part of the ground laid out as a garden, if the occupier possesses horticultural tastes.

Being now fairly settled down in our own home, the first consideration in connection with the important subject of housekeeping was the formation of a proper staff of servants, indispensable to one's comfort and well-being in a country where the services of others are required far more than in any other part of the world. It is the generally accepted opinion of those not conversant with Eastern life, that the European in India usually entertains a preposterous number of native servants. A very short experience of the country is, however, sufficient to dispel this idea, and to show the fallacy of applying to all the residents of this vast peninsula the practice of a custom that obtains only among a few, inhabiting a small portion of the land; for the number and variety of attendants retained in the service of families differ greatly, and to a large extent depend on one's position in society, or in the official world. To the married, the absence or presence of children creates a difference; while the unmarried, or temporary widower whose wife is in England, can dispense with the services of many attendants, since the military officer has his mess, where everything is provided by the regimental servants, and the civilian either shares with one or two others the comforts of a home, or obtains it at the club, with which every large station is now provided. Another matter of importance affecting one's retinue, is the place of residence. In the Bombay and Madras Presidencies, the domestic servant can and does apply his hand to every department, consequently fewer are necessary in the household; moreover, their complete indifference to caste or religious rules, joined to the fact that their ranks are recruited largely from among the native Christians and the half-caste descendants of the Portuguese, enables them to perform various duties impossible to the more orthodox Bengali, and hence they individually receive a much higher rate of pay than that granted to their fellows in the larger Presidency. But this paucity of servants creates results far from satisfactory; for the Oriental, ever slow in his movements, seldom or never performs two or more several duties of an opposite character in an efficient manner, and a family household in Bombay and Madras usually contrasts unfavourably with one in the Bengal Presidency, particularly in the stations of Northern India.

A well-organized establishment in this part of the country numbers on its muster-roll some eighteen or twenty servants, more or less, according to one's position or mode of living.

Perfection of the Bengal System.

To each man severally is appointed his respective duty, for which he is ever present, and at which, however inexperienced at first, he soon becomes an adept. Thus the household machinery goes on without let or hindrance, in a manner unsurpassed in any other part of the world. I can unhesitatingly assert that the system is perfection, and that in no mansion in England can any *ménage* in every detail be better conducted in style and finish than in the principal stations of Bengal, particularly when the master has the means and takes pride in his establishment. It is easy to understand that with a well-trained retinue of servants, each performing only his individual work, everything goes on smoothly, especially when it is remembered that, with few exceptions, each attendant thoroughly understands what is required of him, and possesses the Oriental good qualities of temperance, cleanliness, quietness, and civility. This multiplicity of domestics by no means necessitates a proportionate expense; for the actual cost of twenty servants in the North will not exceed the cost of a quarter of the number in Bombay and Madras, and although the staff may appear excessive, it is absolutely necessary, as one very soon finds out for himself after a short experience. In this part of India natives of the class from which servants are drawn are less robust and more indolent than their countrymen in the other Presidencies, and more or less under the dominion of the rules of religion and also of caste, which here exerts its most powerful influence.

Religious scruples make it necessary to obtain the services of domestics holding different tenets. Thus while Mohammedans are employed solely in all culinary matters and every detail connected with the table, Hindus discharge all duties appertaining to the domestic arrangements in the house, and the labour of the stable and garden. Caste, too, increases the number of servants materially. A Hindu, according to his caste, which often means simply following the occupation of his forefathers, cannot or will not perform more than one especial duty. One man will draw water from the well and fill a bath, but will not empty or clean it after use, and this has to be done by another. The bearer or valet again will brush your clothes and boots, but considers it a degradation to be asked, and most probably will flatly refuse, to remove a plate or any article containing food from the table. And while it is often necessary to keep one servant to dust the furniture and perform the ordinary functions of a housemaid, it is obligatory to retain another to do what is usually termed the dirty work of a house, as this can only be performed without offence to native prejudices by one of the lowest of the low, who is regarded as a pariah or outcast by his fellows.

Enough has been said to show the reason why the European is forced to surround himself with such a large following; and much as one regrets to see so large a portion of one's income taken up in engaging the services of natives, yet so it must be. Without them there would be no comfort in life; and it will be compulsory on one and all to continue to keep house in this fashion, until caste—that great barrier of European progress in India—is abolished, once and for ever. Unfortunately there are no very distinct signs at present of any mitigation of this evil. It is the cherished institution of a country, the inhabitants of which are averse to change, and although education, bringing more advanced ideas, has already tended towards its abolition amongst the higher class of natives, I incline to the opinion that it will be a long time before much progress in its removal is made among the Hindus of a lower grade, especially those who fulfil the duties of domestic servants. These men are not only ignorant, but content to remain in their ignorance; and being naturally lazy, caste affords them a convenient shelter for their refusal to fulfil, for their monthly pay, more than the one office permitted to them. The wily native, under this plea of caste, undoubtedly chuckles over the fact that he does very little for his money, and that it also insures the engagement and prosperity of numbers of his fellow-countrymen. The Mohammedan natives are however equally indolent; and although they have not caste as an excuse, they adhere most religiously to the idea of giving as little value in work as possible for their wages, and act as valuable auxiliaries to the Hindus in their disinclination to perform more than is enjoined on them in their particular service. Let us now pass in review the staff of servants to be found in an ordinary European household, the establishment of one who lives comfortably and well, but whose rate of pay, and more humble grade in the official world, exempt him from the style of living expected in his more fortunate brethren, whose large salary and high position render it obligatory upon them to fulfil a duty to society, by becoming its leaders in matters of entertainments and lavish expenditure generally. In India it holds good to the letter, that 'to whomsoever much is given, of him shall be much required;' really a matter of necessity in a country where rank is always associated with ideas of pomp and show; and any magnate evading this duty through parsimony, ceases to be a credit to his order, and loses the respect of Europeans and natives alike.

The 'khansamah,' or butler, as he is termed in Bombay and Madras, is one of the principal domestics in the establishment in connection with the table, and is frequently made the head servant in the family, exercising authority, not only over those more immediately in his own department, but held responsible for the good behaviour and thorough performance of their various duties by all the others who comprise the household. In Bengal it is usual for a Mohammedan to fill this post, but it is not uncommon to find native Christians, or even unorthodox Hindus, thus employed. These, however, have generally migrated to this part of the country from Bombay or Madras, and are not indigenous to the place. To this household executive officer, the highest rate of pay is given, averaging usually from twelve to sixteen rupees, or even more, per mensem. With this he finds himself in everything in the matter of living and clothing. Indeed, nothing beyond wages is expected by any domestic from his employer, although it is usual to grant them some little assistance towards their wardrobe, especially when it is desired that all the house-servants should be neatly and uniformly dressed. The pay of the khansamah is, however, largely supplemented by a percentage on every article he buys. This 'dustoorie,' as it is termed, is a custom of the country allowed by all, and either so much per cent. is paid him on all dealings by the tradesman, or he draws it by means of charging his employers a trifle on each account above the bazaar prices. The latter arrangement is easily effected, for the khansamah has far more varied duties than a butler at home. To him is entrusted the entire control of the table, and he not only directs the cook and is responsible for the edibles, but provides what he best can; for, although the mistress plans and arranges her meals for the day, it frequently happens that one or more of the things desired cannot be obtained, and it is left to his discretion to supply the want. In India no marketing is ever performed by Europeans, the bazaar being no place for ladies; and it is usual for the trade to be carried on in the early hours of the morning, when the bazaar may be seen thronged with these gentry, most of whom have received their instructions as to what they are, if possible, to procure, the morning or the evening before.

At breakfast the khansamah usually makes his appearance, but only directs. He does not condescend to lay the cloth, for this is the special function of his assistant, who has likewise entire charge of the plate, glass, and crockery. After this meal a consultation with his mistress takes place, his accounts are gone into and balanced, and then for some hours he disappears. He occasionally attends at tiffin, but is seldom seen again until near dinner-time, when he emerges in all his pomp. He is particularly grand if there are guests, for he and his brothers in the station are jealous rivals. From the fact of their always attending their employers when they dine out, each has become tolerably well acquainted with the other's skill in the gastronomic art; and it is a point of honour with them to outdo their fellows and provide a more *recherché* dinner for the friends, than that offered a few days before to the present hosts. It will thus be seen that the duties of a khansamah are both onerous and important, and one may consider himself very fortunate in securing a good specimen of the class, as the comfort of a family depends greatly on their exertions. There are of course exceptions, but they are as a general rule honest, willing, and industrious, much superior in every respect to the other servants, and in a measure educated. Nearly all can read and write their own language, possessing in addition sufficient knowledge of English to facilitate their intercourse with their employers—a great boon to many, particularly to newcomers or 'griffs,' to whom the native tongue is as yet a sealed book.

We now come to the khansamah's assistants, chief among whom is the 'khitmutgar' or table-attendant. His duty is to wait at the different meals, to lay the cloth and arrange the silver and glass, &c. All the table-ware is in his charge, and he is responsible for its cleanliness and well-being. The khitmutgar receives the monthly stipend of eight rupees, and if the family is large or entertain greatly, one or more in addition have to be hired to assist him, but being held inferior in rank receive a smaller amount of pay.

The khansamah and khitmutgar dress alike; their attire consisting of snowy muslin in summer, and dark cloth in the cold weather, neatly edged with some more brilliant colour or gold lace. The turban is not a shapeless mass of cloth bound around the head in the manner common to the other servants, but a stiff, elaborately-plaited concern, across which is stretched a coloured band whereon glitters the crest of the family in silver. Around the waist is girt a long twist of bi-coloured cloth, the same colours being given to all the family domestics clothed in livery. A khitmutgar, particularly in Bengal, is usually of the Mohammedan persuasion, and his

The Bobberchee.

chief object and ambition in life is to attain to the dignity of a khansamah.

Following this individual is the 'malsalchie,' or embryo khitmutgar, who acts in the character of scullery-maid, his duty being to wash up and make himself generally useful. His rate of pay is low, usually four rupees per month, but this is increased in time; for from observation he soon becomes proficient in the khitmutgar's art, and then seeks a situation in that improved capacity.

The 'bobberchee,' or cook, is an important character in every household. He is usually an elderly man, with wages averaging from eight to fifteen rupees a month, according to his talent. This is often surprising, and it is really wonderful to see the perfection to which he brings the art of cooking, considering the means at his disposal. Unlike an English cook, he has no well-arranged kitchen, with ovens, fire, and pots and pans of every description. Instead of these we find only a dark shed, containing at one end a raised platform of brickwork, with several circular holes or shallow wells. In these depressions are placed the handfuls of wood or charcoal which serve for firing. The only cooking vessels, called 'decshies,' consist of perhaps half a dozen round pots of copper, fitted with lids, and one frying-pan. All these utensils are thoroughly tinned at least once every two weeks. No other appliances are needed; for roasting is performed by simply hanging up the meat by a piece of string suspended to a stick, and keeping it constantly revolving by manual labour; the children of the cook, or a boy, who for a small sum acts as kitchen-assistant, performing this necessary duty. The whole cost of the utensils is but trifling; very little charcoal or wood is expended; and yet with such simple means a native can prepare a large dinner in every way equal, if not superior, to a similar one in England, which has rendered necessary the employment of a professed cook, several assistants, and the use of a large kitchen, fitted with innumerable contrivances for the roasting and boiling of the food.

Such are the servants more immediately connected with the table, and we now come to those performing the other duties connected with the house. The first and principal among them is undoubtedly the 'bearer,' who is as supreme in authority over the other house domestics as the khansamah is over those of his own department. In smaller establishments, more particularly in those of bachelors, when this latter official is not kept, the bearer is the chief and responsible officer of the household. He acts as the valet and general factotum of the wardrobe, and in addition exercises a general supervision over all the duties performed by the other house servants, being responsible for the good condition of the furniture, and the freedom from dust or the general cleanliness of all the apartments. It will thus be seen that the duties of a bearer are both varied and weighty. It is a matter of great importance to secure the services of an intelligent, honest man, the advantage of which is more particularly experienced when in camp, or on a march, or travelling, as a competent servant relieves his master of all trouble and anxiety, and subject to his approval arranges every detail connected with the ambulatory household. The wages of the bearer vary from eight to twelve rupees per month. Where there is a family it is usual to have an assistant bearer, who receives less pay, and often acts as a nurse, a duty in which he is proficient. It is not uncommon for children to prefer him to the 'ayah,' who comes next, and is the only female servant employed in the household of the European in India, with the exception of the 'matranee,' or woman-sweeper; but her duties are confined solely to the bathroom or nursery, and she never obtrudes her presence in other parts of the house.

Of the class of ayahs there are many varieties. The greater number are only fit for nurses to young children, and in this capacity they earn from five to eight rupees a month; while others again are perfect ladies'-maids, and can sew, arrange hair, and assist generally at the toilet, quite as well as one of their calling at home. These talented persons are, however, not very common, particularly in Bengal. The Madras Presidency is their principal habitat, and they ask and command very high pay in return for their services. It is not uncommon for an English-speaking Madrassi ayah to receive as much as twenty to twenty-five rupees per month— a sum paid with the greatest satisfaction by the mistress, particularly if the recipient is clever, honest, and industrious.

The 'bhestie,' or water-carrier, is a valuable member of the household, and, as may be imagined, an absolute necessity in a hot country, where the consumption of water is great. There being no cisterns or pipes within the house, every drop consumed has to be drawn and carried by the 'bhestie' from the well or tank, which may be, and frequently is, some distance away from the bungalow. His rate of pay is low, five to six rupees being thought enough remuneration for what I consider the hardest work connected with the household, since much water is daily required, and only little can be brought at one time, as the old custom of carrying the fluid in an inflated pigskin, called a 'mussack,' is still in vogue, and many must be the tramps to and fro of the bhestie before his day's work is fairly concluded.

The 'dhobie,' or washerman, is an important servant, and receives eight, ten, or even more rupees per month, according to the number in the family. For this stipend he washes and gets up all the linen, &c., in a way that leaves nothing to be desired, except in the treatment the various articles receive at his hands to effect this consummation. His mode of procedure differs materially from that employed at home; for the Indian way of washing is simply to dip or soak the articles in the waters of a tank, river, or stream, and then to beat them with force on a large smooth stone or log of wood. No doubt, this effectually cleanses the soiled clothes; but at the same time it wears them out long before their time, and the frayed edges and absence of buttons on everything included in the weekly wash testify to the vigour of his arms. Hence in most families the necessity exists of maintaining a 'dirzie,' or tailor, whose chief duty for his month's pay of six rupees consists of repairing the damage done to one's wardrobe by the over-zealous dhobie.

The 'mehtar,' or sweeper, is a very necessary official; but as his duty is not a pleasant subject to dwell upon, I will dismiss him shortly, merely observing that he performs the dirty work of the house generally, for which he receives the munificent sum of four rupees monthly, with an additional rupee or two for his wife, termed the 'matranee,' who assists him. One curious fact in connection with these last named may be noticed. They alone out of all the servants profit by their master's table. Being without caste, they can partake of all and everything, and to them are the remnants of the dishes given. Failing them, indeed, these would be thrown away, as no Hindus would touch any food other than that prepared by themselves—a feeling which is shared, although perhaps in a lesser degree, by Mohammedan servants also.

The services of a 'chowkedar,' or watchman, are often necessary in many stations, and such an individual is usually borne on the strength of the establishment, who, for the monthly sum of six or eight rupees, perambulates the premises during the night and keeps off intruders. And although Europeans sleep with every door in the house open, and their property scattered about as it was in the daytime, loss by robbery is seldom sustained, even with so numerous a body of servants as fills every private bungalow, and it is no small proof of the habitual confidence in them to see scarcely anything locked up.

This immunity from robbery is due, in a measure, to the prestige enjoyed by the white man in a land where his power and might are feared and respected; but undoubtedly its chief causes are, firstly, that the crime of theft on a large scale is confined to particular classes only; and secondly, that the hired watchmen are generally of these castes. Although by birth and training professional thieves, these men are honest, faithful, and efficient towards their employers. Their presence alone is a protection against their own class; while their skill and vigilance are equally sufficient against strangers; and although the hiring of a thief as a protection against the wickedness of his brethren is indefensible on moral grounds, nevertheless in many stations of India it is an absolute necessity, and any one declining to pay a small amount of blackmail in the shape of the monthly stipend of a chowkedar, will sooner or later be visited in his state of unguardedness by one or more of the fraternity, and will have cause to bewail his over scrupulousness.

The servants not immediately connected with the house, such as grooms and gardeners, vary with the number of horses kept and the size of the garden. It is very rare to find any European who does not possess at least one horse, and, if married, some species of carriage in addition; for in India during the greater part of the year pedestrianism is impossible, and what would be regarded as a luxury at home becomes an absolute necessity. To attend to each horse two servants are necessary: first the 'syce,' who tends and feeds the animal, cleans the carriage and harness, and performs generally the usual duties of a groom. He also acts the part of running footman in attendance on his master, if on horseback, and no matter what the distance, by the aid of short cuts and speed he is usually to be found ready to hold the horse for its owner to dismount on arrival at his destination. His wages vary from six to eight rupees a month; and although he attends the carriage in his capacity of footman, and can also act the part of driver if necessary, it is usual, if the equipage is large and with two horses, to retain in addition to the syce a 'coachwan,' or coachman, who is a superior sort of groom, and receives a trifle more pay.

A 'gasscut,' or grasscutter, is necessary to each horse. He receives the moderate stipend of four rupees, and his sole duty is to proceed to the jungle in the vicinity and gather sufficient grass for one day's consumption. In India hay is seldom or never stacked for use, but cut fresh daily by these men, who often have to go long distances in search of it. This natural hay, for it is quite dry and withered by the sun, even when growing, forms, with a certain allowance of 'gram,' a species of pulse, the only food of the noble animal in India.

The 'mahlie,' or gardener, receives five or six rupees a month. His duties need no description, being similar to those of his fraternity at home, with whom, however, his skill often contrasts most favourably. It is surprising to see his knowledge of horticulture, and the perfection to which he attains in the growth of European flowers and vegetables, together with the taste displayed in the general arrangement of the garden entrusted to his care.

In addition to the servants enumerated, it is necessary, according to the season of the year, to retain the services of a number of coolies to pull punkahs, water the tatties, etc., duties which the other domestics will not perform, and this adds considerably to the expense of an establishment; for although each individual only receives the monthly pay of four rupees, yet in a small family at least six or eight of these gentry are entertained, and their united wages help to swell greatly the grand total. It is therefore with a feeling of relief that the householder regards the advent of the cold weather, when their services are no longer required.

Although, perhaps, lazy and indolent in their manner, and lacking the wit and general intelligence which distinguish the class at home, take them as a body Indian servants are honest and willing; and although one's patience is often sorely tried by their want of capacity and frequent stupidity, it must not be forgotten that they are, as a rule, drawn from an ignorant class, possessing little or no reasoning power, and able only to act under the guidance and direction of others, to whose comfort they certainly most materially conduce. The natives of India are often accused of wanting gratitude, but it does not appear that those who make the charge have done much to inspire such a sentiment. When masters are really kind and considerate, they find as warm a return from Indian servants, as from any in the world; and there are few who have tried them in sickness, or in difficulties and dangers, who do not bear witness to their sympathy and attachment. In many cases their devotion to their master or mistress has been well exemplified in the trying times of India's history. This can arise from no other cause than gratitude; for there exists between employers and employed no caste to supply the place of clannish feeling, nor any hereditary attachment such as often influences the devotion of the family servant at home, who through good or indifferent times follows willingly the fortunes of his master.

CHAPTER X.

Description of Faizabad—Nepaul—Faizabad native city and station—Routine of life—Our servant Esau—The Park—A Moonlight Picnic—Native Gardens—Flowers of India—Fruit and Vegetables of India—The god Rama—The Sanskrit Language—The Languages of India—Connection with Indo-European family of languages—Literature of India—Sacred and heroic Poems—The Vedas—The Institutes of Menu—The Puranas—Dramatic literature—Mode of acting—Hindu Tales and Fables—Progress of the Hindus in Geography, Logic, Astronomy, Mathematics, Medicine, and Chemistry—State of Education in India—Causes of ignorance—The evil effects of the Brahman influence—Former system of Education—Present system—Government schools—The Universities—Elementary schools—Female Education—General remarks on present state of Education—Its probable results.

To return to our station and our life therein. I take up the thread of my narrative at the point which saw us fairly settled down in our new home, and with our domestic establishment in every way complete.

Faizabad is, after Lucknow, the principal town in the province, and is situated on the right bank of the Ghogra, the largest Oudh affluent of the Ganges, which is here a river of some considerable size, and a wide torrent in the rainy season. On the opposite side, at a little distance, is the well-known jungle waste, the Terai, famous for the cover it affords for various wild beasts, and reputedly the best sporting ground in India. It is much frequented by hunters at certain periods of the year, particularly during the cold weather, when the deadly fever to which it has given name lies dormant for a while. The unhealthiness of this locality is indeed notorious; and it is almost certain death for any European to visit it, except in certain specified months when it is considered comparatively healthy. Beyond this tract rise the mountains of Nepaul, a range plainly discernible from Faizabad. The sight causes a great longing to seek their cool heights and explore that little-known territory, a desire, however, which must remain ungratified. The visit of strangers to the Nepaulese state is discouraged by that power, and every obstacle is thrown in the way of the traveller, rendering it impossible to penetrate any distance within its borders. Our knowledge therefore of the Nepaulese and their habits is very meagre; and beyond the fact that their capital is a well-built interesting town, and that its inhabitants are a hardy, intelligent, industrious race, living much after the manner of their ancestors, Western ideas not having been introduced to promote a more advanced state of civilization, little is known of Nepaul to the outside world.

The native city of Faizabad is about two miles and a half in length by one in breadth, and was built by the Mohammedans chiefly of materials taken from the ruins of Ajudhya, a holy Hindu town of great antiquity not far distant. This native quarter is like unto all others, and contains no building of any importance; for Faizabad, although at first the capital of the Nawabs of Oudh, was soon deserted by them for Lucknow, which through this favour rose in importance as the other gradually declined. The European station is pretty, small and compact, separated from the native city by a long and wide avenue of tamarind trees, said to be of great antiquity. This can be readily believed; for the trunks are enormous in size and height. When in full leaf each tree is a study, and as seen *en masse* the effect is simply grand. The topmost branches on either side interlacing, thickly-clad with their delicate green leaves, form a sheltered road extending for more than a mile, and one much appreciated by the residents of the town, as well as by hordes of monkeys, which exist here in fabulous numbers, objects of veneration to the Hindu portion of the community, who feed and otherwise protect them.

The troops forming the garrison, both white and coloured, are lodged in barracks, arranged in contiguous rows on a large maidan facing the mall or principal road. On the other side of this are the bungalows of the officers, the civil officials living in another part of the station, a little down the mall, in the direction of the tamarind avenue. The English regiment in garrison was the 51st Light Infantry, of which I assumed medical charge, and our daily routine of life passed on most pleasantly. As it was the hot season, duty was carried on during the early hours of the morning; and it was very enjoyable, after rising at five, or even earlier, to take a walk or drive at that, the coolest and freshest time of the day, and then, after all hospital or other regimental work had been performed, to proceed to the shelter of the house for breakfast at half-past eight or nine. By that time it would begin to get very hot, and it was usual to cease from any out-door duty until the evening, when it was again resumed. This is always the case among the military; but the civilians follow no such rule, and attend their courts and perform their business during the daytime, for the convenience of the native suitors, throughout the year; whereas all duties connected with the soldiers in the hot and rainy seasons are—in order to avoid unnecessary exposure to the sun in their more active proceedings—carried on at the time already specified, while all marching or heavy drills are relegated to the cold season, when they can be performed up to a much later hour.

Breakfast over, we remained in the house during the rest of the day; for the hot winds were in full force, and it was necessary to close up the rooms with tatties at an early hour. And although this station enjoys the reputation of being the coolest in Oudh, it was seldom pleasant to venture out again before half-past five or six, when, as the sun began to set and lose its power, the wind died off likewise, and everyone began to stir and rouse themselves out of the dormant condition engendered by such a long confinement in a dark, close house.

During the day we amused ourselves by talking, reading, and writing, and in regulating the household affairs, which luckily worked very smoothly; for we had secured an admirable staff of servants, who, under the direction of our headman, performed all their duties in a most satisfactory manner. This khansamah—he preferred to be called butler—was a Madras Christian, rejoicing in the scriptural name of Esau, and a most perfect type of his class, thoroughly understanding all the duties appertaining to his office, and possessing a full knowledge of cookery in all its branches. He was in addition scrupulously honest in all his dealings. He had received a fair education, speaking the English language fluently, although he could neither read nor write it. He could, however, read his own tongue, and his favourite study was an Hindustani version of the Bible. He was a most devout Roman Catholic, shaping his course through life as directed by the Bible, and as advised by the priests of his faith, in whom he reposed implicit confidence. It was an expression of daily use for him to reply, when asked why he did not do a certain thing, 'that his priest had given him no order, and that there was no order for it in his Bible.' Notwithstanding this, and the supreme contempt with which he regarded the other servants and natives generally, to whom he usually applied the term of niggers (although he himself, like all the inhabitants of his part of the country, was of raven blackness), he was an excellent man, and served us faithfully during our stay in India. It is then but just to himself and the class he represents, to record the everlasting debt of gratitude both my wife and myself are under to him for his care and devotion during a trying time of sickness and sorrow.

Although the time passed thus agreeably during the hot hours of the day, we were not sorry when the evening came, and we could again go out. Our usual plan was to drive down the avenue; and after taking a complete tour of the station, continue on to the Park or Public Garden, a great place of resort for the European residents, who congregate here every evening to listen to the band, talk, or play Badminton. As the station of Faizabad is not very extensive, and the community small in number, everyone was acquainted with everybody else, which rendered society very gay and pleasant.

This park is an extensive piece of ground by the side of the river, which at this time of the year rolled sluggishly along, its calm surface unruffled, save for the frequent uprising out of its depths of the head of an alligator, a reptile common to this as to most of the rivers in India. Along the river bank, commencing at the entrance lodge to the park, at the lower end, is a wide carriage road, which continues all round the upper portion, and forms a long and pleasant drive. The centre of the park is laid out with turf, shrubs, and flower-beds. The park is kept up by a small monthly subscription, paid most willingly; for it is delightful to see one green spot amidst the general desert-like surroundings of the hot weather. Besides, the flowers were charming; for the more temperate climate enjoyed at this place favours their growth, as well as that of fruits, for the production of which Faizabad has long been famous.

The garden is much utilized by the residents for private parties, such as balls and picnics, for which it is well adapted, particularly during the hot weather, when a gathering in the fresh night air is far preferable to a similar entertainment within hot and crowded rooms. A very favourite form of entertainment is a 'moonlight picnic,' given when the moon is at her full, and her soft and silvery light sheds a subdued radiance over the scene, sufficient of itself for purposes of illumination, but usually supplemented by numerous lanthorns of variously coloured paper, suspended to the branches of the trees adjacent to the selected spot. The general effect of such a scene, with the picturesque surroundings, the glistening river, and the park-like grounds rich in tropical foliage, is one of such strange beauty as to recall the visions of fairyland in which we indulge in our youth. Among the various festivities at which we 'assisted' during our stay at Faizabad, one given by the officers of the Bengal Native Cavalry deserves more than a passing notice; for it was got up at great trouble and perfect of its kind. It was a moonlight picnic, and the part of the park selected was an open grassplot surrounded with trees, flower-beds, and sparkling fountains, close to the river, whose wide expanse of water lay spread out in full view. Although quite familiar to us in the daytime, the spot appeared to have undergone a great transformation, and was almost unrecognisable under its new aspect when we arrived on the appointed night. It was literally ablaze with light: surrounded by a high wooden framework, from which thousands of small glittering lamps were suspended; while an outer circle of illumination was formed by dismounted men of the regiment holding torches; and mounted torch bearers of the same corps formed an avenue of light leading from the entrance lodge to the enclosure. To every available branch of the surrounding trees were hung Chinese lanthorns of various colours and strange devices. Thus there was a perfect circle of fire, of illuminating power sufficient to cause a sensible diminution in the effect of the rays of the full moon, which directly overhead shone placidly down as if in contempt of all man's efforts to rival her splendour. The scene was weird and beautiful, the air cool and pleasant, while not a breath of wind in excess rose to disturb the even burning of the lamps and torches. A superb display of fireworks ushered in the proceedings, dancing was afterwards continued with unflagging energy, and it was not until the first faint streaks of pink appeared in the eastern sky, heralding the approach of another day, that the gratified guests took leave of their hospitable entertainers.

A garden or park like that described is usually found in every station. It is kept up by the European residents for their own use; for the natives of the present day take but little interest in the cultivation of flowers; and it is only members of their upper class who make any pretence of forming any description of garden or pleasure-ground around their houses. But this practice, even among the rich and powerful, is not followed so largely as in former days, when it was one of the chief native enjoyments. This is shown in the numerous 'baghs,' or gardens, found all over the country, some of considerable age, and usually containing a tomb. It was the custom of a great man to prepare a mausoleum during his lifetime, and to surround it with a carefully-laid-out pleasure-ground, which he utilized for purposes of recreation for himself and family, finding enjoyment apparently in the mingled delights of the presence of luxuriant flowers and fruit, and in contemplation of his final resting-place. These gardens, though always formal, are often pleasing, and are generally divided by broad alleys; with long and narrow ponds or canals enclosed with stone or stucco work, running up the centre; straight walks on each side, with borders of flowers in uniform beds or patterns; and surrounded with groves of orange and citron trees. What with the contrast of the dark cypresses to the trees covered with blossom, the tall and graceful palms, the golden fruits and highly-scented flowers, an Indian garden at its best is charming.

The flowers and trees of these gardens have neither been collected with the industry nor improved with the care of those in Europe; consequently we find at the present day very few indigenous plants of any merit. With the exception of some large flowering trees and scented creepers, some bearing flowers of splendid colours, and others twining among the branches of a tree with stems as thick as a man's thigh, very few varieties are met with until we come to the lower ranges of the Himalayas. Here the ridges are broken into every form of the picturesque, with rocks, mossy banks, and slopes covered with gigantic pines and other trees on the same vast scale, mixed with the rhododendrons and other beautiful flowering shrubs which have been acclimatized in this country, together with well-known ferns, orchids, and the best of our fruits in a state of nature.

Although there is such a paucity of native plants in the plains, the climate of India is favourable to the growth of European shrubs and flowers, particularly of roses, which are cultivated largely, and attain to great excellence, especially in Lucknow and other parts of the province of Oudh. Such being the case, attention of late years has been more directly applied to the production of the flowers with which we are familiar at home, and a garden in India presents much the appearance of one in England, with the exception of the presence of a few palms and other trees significant of the East. The same may be said of the fruits and vegetables. Although many varieties, common to tropical countries, such as plantains, bananas, mangoes, guavas, and custard-apples, grow in abundance with little or no care and attention, they are much improved by cultivation after the European method. This is especially the case with the mango, decidedly the best of all Indian fruits, and common everywhere, the tree which bears it being planted in orchards or singly, and thriving without any further trouble. Grown as a large shrub in a garden, and attended to in a proper manner, the mango yields surprising results, the fruit becoming large, soft, and of a delicate and luscious flavour; while those left to grow in a state of nature, are small, hard, and possess a strong and disagreeable taste of turpentine. They are, however, greatly sought after by the natives, and in the mango season, about May and June, form a staple article of their diet. The price renders these fruits accessible to the poor, and great quantities are sold annually in the bazaars, side by side with melons and water-melons, which are grown in the wide sandy beds of the rivers during the dry weather, and retailed at one farthing each, or even less, according to their abundance. Gourds and cucumbers are also very plentiful. They are sown round the huts of the poorer classes, and trailed over the roofs, so that the buildings are covered with green leaves and large yellow flowers. Of the fruits more carefully nurtured, grapes are plentiful, and also oranges, limes, and citrons. Figs are not quite so general, but are to be had in most places, and those of the Deccan are perhaps the best in the world. Pine-apples are common in some places, and peaches, nectarines, strawberries, and lechees attain excellence in more temperate localities, such as Faizabad. With the exception of oranges and similar fruits, such as the shaddock, most of the varieties named are ripe and fit for use in the hot weather. They are then most acceptable; for at that period of the year few vegetables are to be obtained, and it is not until the advent of the cold season that our hearts are gladdened with the once familiar sight of cabbages, cauliflowers, peas, marrows, and salad. These vegetables, with the exception of one or two of purely native origin, and potatoes, which are common everywhere, much engage the attention of our countrymen in India. With careful cultivation they attain to the same size as at home, but they lack in a measure delicacy of flavour, the result most probably of their rapid growth.

Situated within the Faizabad Park, on the river bank, stands an ancient Hindu temple, in an excellent state of preservation, and even at the present day much frequented by pious worshippers. For this antiquated fane, although there is nothing special in its size or magnificence to distinguish it from the multitude of others of a similar natute scattered all over the country, is held in great veneration as being erected on the spot whence the god Rama ascended into heaven, and a piece of stone is preserved within its walls on which is seen a mark which is said to be the impression left by his foot, as he made the spring to enable him to soar aloft. Rama, although one of the most venerated deities of the Hindus for centuries past, was in reality an actual living personage, a prince of the ancient Aryan invaders of India. He was born near Faizabad; but the exact date at which he flourished is not known, and the only information we have of this personage and his doings is to be found in a poem called the 'Ramayana,' which is supposed to have been written several centuries before the Christian era, and which, like other early writings, is a mixture of fact and fiction.

This poem, with the other ancient books of the Hindus, sacred or otherwise, is written in Sanskrit. There is good reason to infer that the first colonists of India used this language, which, although long since dead, is still cultivated by the learned of India, and has of late years been much studied in Europe on account of the important place it holds in the Indo-European family of languages. When it ceased to be the language of India is not correctly known, although it is supposed that for the last twenty-five centuries at least the Sanskrit has been no longer a proper vernacular language, but kept artificially in life as the sacred dialect of Brahmanism, and the cultivated tongue of literature and learning. It thus occupies a position closely analogous to that held by the Latin, since the decline of the Western empire, as the language of Roman Catholicism, and the means of communication among the learned of all Europe.

At the present time, instead of one common tongue, there are in India no less than ten principal languages, which may be divided into five northern and five southern, including the Deccan.

Of the first class we have Hindi, with its daughter Hindustani, spoken by the inhabitants of the upper plain of the Ganges and Jumna; Bengali, the dialect more particularly of Bengal proper; Punjabi, as its name denotes, the language of the most northern part of India, the Punjab; Sindi, the tongue of the province of Sinde; Guzerati, the language of Guzerat, or Gujerat, a large province in the west, the greater portion of which is included in the Guicowar's dominions. All these may be looked upon as branches of the Sanskrit, belonging to distinct divisions of the Aryan race, and may be called Indo-Aryan, altered by the mixture of local and foreign words and new inflexions, much as Italian is from Latin. The origin of the non-Sanskrit element which is found in all these northern languages has not as yet been decided; but it is generally regarded as a relic of the aboriginal tongues, which became grafted on to the pure language of the Aryan settlers.

Hindustani, or Urdu, differs from the others, and cannot be considered an Indian language proper. It is merely a corrupt form of Hindi, which grew up in the camps of the Mohammedan conquerors of India after the eleventh century, as a medium of communication between them and the subject population of Central Hindustan. It is filled with Persian and Arabic words, and being, as it were, the English of India, has enjoyed of late more literary cultivation than the other dialects. It is the *lingua franca*, the official language and means of general intercourse throughout the entire peninsula; and with various modifications, according to the several provinces, which, however, are very slight, it is understood and spoken by all excepting the totally uneducated ryot, or peasant, over the whole of India.

Of the other group of languages, Tamil and Telegu belong to the southern part of the peninsula, including many portions of the Madras Presidency, while Kanarese is a language of that part of India south of the Krishna river. These three have an origin totally distinct from the Sanskrit, and receive words from that tongue in the same manner that Latin has been engrafted on English, or Arabic on Hindi. Tamil is so much the most pure that it is sometimes thought to be the source of the other two; while Telegu, although it preserves its own structure, is much mixed with Sanskrit words. These languages have been termed Dravidian; for however they may borrow Sanskrit words in their vocabulary, they are essentially non-Sanskrit in their grammatical structure, and belong to the Scythian, not the Indo-European family. The dialects of most of the various mountain tribes in South and Central India belong to the same stock, as do most probably those of some of the mountaineers in Northern India. Thus the Dravidian tribes appear to represent the aboriginal inhabitants of India, previous to the immigration of the Sanskrit-speaking Aryans; and while the preponderating power of these invaders in the north gave that portion a language derived from their own, their influence over the ruder population of the south resulted only in filling their tongues with learned Sanskrit words, much as our own English is filled with learned Latin and Greek.

Of the remaining two southern tongues, Oriya, the language of Orissa, in the central east part of the country included in the Deccan, though probably of the Tamil family, is so much indebted to Sanskrit that it is said that if the Sanskrit vocables were excluded it could not pretend to be a language. And the same may be said of Marathi, the language of the Mahrattas, a race stretching through the western half of India, a branch of the people from beyond the Vindhya mountains. And although no guess can be made as to the period of their immigration, their language as well as the Oriya, without proofs to the contrary, may be more properly classed in the northern division.

Such are the principal languages spoken in India at the present day; but numerous dialects or patois, amounting, it is said, to at least one hundred when we include those of the aboriginal tribes, exist in various localities, some, such as the Malayalam, or language of Malabar, almost deserving a place in the list of tongues already given.

From language to literature is but a step, and a few words

will dismiss this subject. In literature the Hindus are, and always have been, far behind several neighbouring nations; and although education has of late made rapid strides among them, it has not caused any marked improvement to take place in book-writing so far, and no author of note has appeared to startle the world by his talent. It is to the earlier period of their history that we must refer for any excellence in literature; for it was many centuries ago when other nations, now risen to great eminence, were totally uncivilized, that the great Hindu authors flourished and produced those works which still continue to be held as standard authorities. Since their production there has been a long period of silence, unbroken even at the present day, if we except a few stage plays, native newspaper effusions, and controversies on the religion and habits of the country, mostly written in the worst possible taste, and in which Western ideas and sayings are plentifully interspersed amongst native, without any regard to fitness or meaning.

That an advanced state of civilization existed in India when the greater part of the world was in utter darkness, is conclusively shown by the Hindu writings, which reveal at first a civilization of great simplicity, but one that was progressive and made rapid strides. For, as Mr. Rawlinson says in his sketch of early civilization, "At first cities seem not to be mentioned, there is no organized political life, no war worthy of the name; nothing but plundering expeditions. Tribes exist under their heads, who are at once kings, priests, judges, and poets, and to whom the rest render obedience. Religion is only a worship by hymns, but scarcely yet with regular sacrifice. But as time advances, as shown in their writings later on, this extreme simplicity disappears. There are advances of various kinds. Cities are built and palaces erected, trades become numerous and luxury creeps in. The priests having come to be a separate class, introduce an elaborate ceremonial. Music is cultivated; and writing is invented, or learnt. But after all, the material progress made is not very great. Indian civilization is in the main intellectual, not material. Careless of life and action, of history, politics, artistic excellence, commerce, manufacture, the Indians concentrate their attention on the highest branches of metaphysics, ponder on themselves and their future, on the nature of the Divine essence, on their own relation to it and the prospects involved in that relationship; all of which is shown in the pages of anci .it Sanskrit literature. They also discuss and solve the most difficult questions of metaphysical science; they elaborate grammar, the science of language, they altogether occupy themselves with the inward, not with the outward, with the eternal world of mind and rest, not with the transitory and illusory world of outward seeming and incessant changefulness. Hence the triumphs of their civilization are abstract and difficult to appreciate. They lie outside the ordinary interests of mankind, and are, moreover, shrouded in a language known to few, and from which there are but few translations. It is said, however, by those whose acquaintance with the early Indian literature is the widest, that there is scarcely a problem in the sciences of ontology, psychology, metaphysics, logic, or grammar, which the Indian sages have not sounded as deeply and discussed as elaborately as the Greeks."

The most voluminous, as well as the most ancient and important portions of Hindu literature, are their sacred and epic or heroic poems. These, as well as all other works of literature, were written by the Brahmans, who, from the very earliest Indian history almost up to the present time, have been the only educated class in the community, and the sole exponents of learning in the country. Of the sacred poems it has been said that their general style is flat, diffuse, and no less deficient in ornament than abundant in repetitions, and the specimens which have been translated give no ground for questioning this decision. But however insipid, they are highly interesting, depicting manners, and customs, and incidents concerning the people among whom their authors lived. We are thus enabled to glean from them some slight historical account of the course of events during the dark period of Aryan conquest, prior to the invasion of Alexander, in the year 327 B.C.—the first landmark in Indian history.

The collections of hymns, termed the Vedas, are the most ancient and venerated of Indian sacred writings, the Bible of the Hindu faith, the doctrines of which are still observed and taught by the priests, even at the present day. They are in the earliest form of written Sanskrit, and are supposed to date from nearly two thousand years before Christ. Most of these hymns are in a language so rugged as to prove that they were written before that of the other sacred writings was completely formed, while some, though antiquated, are within the pale of polished Sanskrit. There must therefore have been a considerable interval between the composition of the greater part and the compilation of the whole; and the best authorities, as already stated, agree that their completed form dates from fourteen hundred years before the Christian era.

These books are deeply interesting to the scholar, not merely because they give an account of what manner of people the first colonists of India were, but because they are considered to be, by several centuries, the earliest documents for the history of Indo-European language, conditions, and institutions. The civil constitution, the religious rites, the mythologic fancies, the manners and customs, which they depict, have a peculiarly original and primitive aspect, seeming to exhibit a far nearer likeness to what once belonged to the whole Indo-European family than is anywhere else to be attained. And looking upon them rather as a record of the whole family than of a single branch, we are enabled to acquire some slight information regarding the race from which we ourselves, in common with other nations of Europe, are said to be descended.

The Vedas notwithstanding, the first complete picture of the conditions of Indian society is afforded by the Code or Institutes of Menu. This work not only enters into various questions of religion, but explains fully the then existing state of Indian society, describing for the first time the division of the natives into four classes or castes. The system of government, and the duties of kings and princes are fully explained, and foreign policy and war are the subject of many rules of conduct. These latter are interesting from the clear proofs they afford of the division of India, even at that early period, into many unequal and independent states, and also from the signs which they disclose of a civilized and gentle people. Revenue and taxation, law, the administration of justice and punishment of crime, are all discussed, and joined to all this are minute details of matters affecting the private life of individuals. Thus we have a very complete picture of Indian society just three thousand years ago.

Of the great Hindu heroic poems the most important is that entitled the Ramayana, which commemorates the conquest of Ceylon and the exploits generally of Rama, both as prince and as god. This work, as well as the next in order of merit, the Maha-Bharata, is of great antiquity, several centuries before Christ. Although abounding in extravagant legends, the actual heroes of both poems being made incarnations of the great god Vishnu, some of the passages show great fertility of imagination. They are, too, often spirited and poetical, and the similes short, simple, and picturesque.

The Puranas, descriptive of Hindu mythology; the Meghaduta, a sample of purely descriptive poetry; and the Gita Govinda, a collection of pastoral songs (with many others similar), are also well-known examples of Hindu poetic literature, all possessing certain merits of their own, and testifying that although at the present day backward in learning, in comparison with the progress made by other nations, India in former days had poets and other writers of no mean order.

The dramatic literature of the Hindus is however the department with which we are best acquainted, and has attained a high pitch of excellence. It is not very extensive, for although we possess plays written as early as the Christian era, and a few of the present century, the whole number extant falls short of one hundred. This is probably owing to the manner in which these dramas were at first produced, being acted once only on some particular festival, and consequently losing the popularity which plays in our times derive from repeated representations in different cities and in public theatres. Many must also have been lost in consequence of the neglect of the learned, for this species of literature fell into great disfavour, and became in fact utterly extinct. Of late years it has been resuscitated; stage plays are now popular among the educated classes, and many of the larger towns possess theatres with purely native dramatic corps. This revival has not, however, been attended with any great increase in the present stock of dramas, for as a rule the managers are content with the production of one of the old and well-known plays. These, although the plots are generally interesting and the dialogue lively, as the acts are frequently eight or ten in number, and prolonged by needless repetition, become very wearisome to any except the patient Hindu, who will sit for hours rapt in enjoyment of the spectacle presented for his delectation. Some plays indeed have been written and actually performed within the last few years, but they possess no real literary merit, and most are offensive, utterly without delicacy or sentiment, while a member of the governing class is often introduced and made to present an unfavourable comparison with his Aryan brother. Tremendous excitement was caused at Calcutta two years ago by the performance of a piece supposed to represent accurately the lives of the coolies employed by Englishmen on their indigo and other plantations. In this play the natives were depicted as being oppressed in every way by their employer, who, assisted by his white managers, was made to commit every known crime, from abduction of the wives and daughters of the coolies to actual murder. The whole performance being calculated to engender a bad feeling between the two classes, the piece was, I believe, withdrawn at the request of the government.

Of Hindu acting I can say but little; but from what I have observed, the palm must, I think, be awarded to the Parsees, who, although almost native by long residence, are still, like ourselves, strangers to the country. The Hindus seem to enter fully into the feelings of the characters they are supposed to represent, but they render the dialogue in a monotonous voice, the art of elocution not having made much progress among them. They labour, too, under great disadvantages with regard to their female characters, who are stiff and awkward, and personated by boys or young men, native prejudice not allowing the presence of any woman on the stage.

An important part of Hindu literature still remains to be noticed—their tales and fables, in both of which kinds of composition they appear to have been the instructors of the rest of mankind. The most popular fables have been found almost unchanged in their Sanskrit dress, and to them nearly all the fabulous relations of other countries have been clearly traced. Many books of European fiction have a decided Indian origin. The complicated scheme of story-telling, tale within tale, like the 'Arabian Nights,' seems also to be of their invention, and with it many well-known tales and romances. It is remarkable, however, that the taste for description seems here to have changed sides, the Hindu stories having none of those gorgeous and picturesque accompaniments which are so captivating in the Arabian and Persian tales. And the same may be said of all their literature; for although the Hindu author is imaginative enough, he descends into every detail of his subject, and presents them in a commonplace and prosaic manner; whereas the Persians, and most other Eastern writers, never enter into a long description of inanimate nature, their genius showing itself in expressions of deep feeling, fanciful and sublime conceptions, joined to highly-coloured voluptuous surroundings of the picture they attempt to portray.

Before quitting this subject, I may notice the present state and progress of education in India, which has, of course, a great influence on the renewed production of literary talent, besides affording the knowledge of various matters that, if not totally unknown, were little appreciated in former days, while essential at present to the natives of a country no longer isolated, but thrown open to the world, and holding her place among the nations. With the exception of geography, or the correct knowledge of any country outside their own, a branch of science in which they never made any progress, the early Hindu writers were not only well informed, but actually discovered facts in science which for long years remained unknown to the other countries of the world. Logic was a favourite study of the Brahmans, and it is impossible not to be struck with the identity of the topics they discussed with those which engaged the attention of the philosophers in ancient Greece, and with the similarity between the doctrines of schools subsisting in regions of the earth so remote from each other. Again, the antiquity and the originality of Indian astronomy form a subject of considerable interest. It is claimed by some that astronomical observations made two thousand years or more before Christ are still extant, and prove a considerable degree of progress already made at that period. This is still an unsettled problem; for in all enquiries on this subject we derive no aid from the early Hindu authors. The same system of priestcraft which has exercised so pernicious an influence on the Hindus in other respects has cast a veil over this science also. All astronomers, however, admit the great antiquity of the Hindu observations, and it seems indisputable that the exactness of the mean motions the Hindus have assigned to the sun and moon, could only have been attained by a comparison of modern observations with others made in remote antiquity. This branch of science has held its place to the present day, and is a favourite study with the priestly class, whom it enables to foretell eclipses of the sun and moon, and thus to work on the fears of credulous natives, who are totally ignorant of the subject.

The progress made in other branches of mathematical knowledge was still more remarkable; for a work written about the fifth or sixth century of our era, contains a system of trigonometry which not only goes far beyond anything known to the Greeks, but involves theorems undiscovered in Europe till the sixteenth century. The Brahmans are also distinguished in arithmetic by the acknowledged invention of the decimal notation, and in algebra they appear to have excelled all their contemporaries. They likewise turned their attention to other scientific subjects. Their early knowledge of medicine seems to have been very extensive, and their skill in chemistry is a fact more striking and unexpected.

Enough has been said to vindicate the claims of the natives of India to be considered, at least in their early days, highly civilized. And if during the last few centuries talent appears to have been wanting, and no progress to have been made in matters that they once excelled in, they can be excused in a manner as a nation, and the cause explained, by throwing all the responsibility of their inaction on the Brahmans. These men, in former days few in number, venerated by their countrymen, and surrounded by every privilege, were the sole students and searchers after knowledge, like the monks of Europe in later times. But the parallel holds good no further. In Europe, as civilization advanced, so did the craving for knowledge, hitherto confined to one part of the community. In a comparatively short period a totally unlettered member of the upper classes was rarely to be found; and since then, slowly but certainly, education has spread to the masses below, and mental independence has been thus achieved. Unfortunately for India, the same change did not take place there. Its inhabitants, mild and timid by nature, possessed nothing of the strength and independence of the denizens of European countries. They were accustomed to bow in submission under the tyranny of their rulers, paying the utmost reverence to the words and deeds of the priests of their religion, whose supernatural power they never dared question; and it is not surprising therefore that the Brahmans, in order to retain their standing and influence, resolutely set their faces against imparting any of their knowledge to their fellow-countrymen, in whose ignorance lay their safety. In this they were aided by the continuously disturbed state of the country, the number and constant changes of their rulers, and those who were for a time analogous to the upper classes of other countries.

For centuries India was one huge camp, with monarchs and

Evil Effects of Brahmanical Influence. 233

leaders as rude and ignorant as the population, whom they regarded in the light of serfs or slaves. These men of the sword, with no taste or time for learning, were as much under the sway of the priests as their humbler brethren; and all the offices of the state that required skill and not force were entrusted to the Brahmans, a rapidly-increasing class in point of numbers, but far inferior in every respect to their ancestors, for they appear to have lost the originality of thought and application to study which had in former days been the chief characteristic of the caste, and which alone had first raised them to the high degree of honour and veneration in which they were held by their countrymen. In this way their power increased; and as religion in their hands waxed more gross and idolatrous, it became their interest, instead of raising the standard of knowledge, to decrease it, to avoid questions, and to stand alone as a superior class, occupied solely with views for their own aggrandizement, in which they were safe so long as a general state of ignorance pervaded the masses. They continued, however, to deteriorate greatly, becoming lazy and intolerant, with no ambition save to increase the hold they possessed over the minds of the credulous natives, and to draw from them the means whereby they could sustain their selfish, indolent, and sensual existence. Thus literature languished, and became almost extinct, as these men afforded no new contributions to any branch of learning, but contented themselves with a superficial acquaintance with the works transmitted to them by their forefathers, and made no effort to increase that store.

And so it has continued to within the present century; for although under the Mohammedan rule a slightly better state of things was introduced, and the Brahman influence diminished, yet the improvement was very small. As a class the invaders were as rude and ignorant as their vanquished foes, and likewise under the dominion of their priests, who, with the exception of being able to read or recite, parrot-like, passages from the Koran, were not superior to them in general knowledge. Hence it transpired that the services of the Brahmans had again to be called into requisition. They speedily regained their former position, and became a power in the state of their foreign rulers, who behaved, as to wars and disturbances, and their treatment generally of the inhabitants of the country, just like their predecessors.

The masses of the population were compelled to remain in their ignorance, while such a state of affairs lasted, with no hope of improvement until a more enlightened and settled government arose. But better times have dawned; and whereas in former days it was considered sufficient for a native to possess a knowledge of the rudiments of his own language, imparted to him by some Brahman; and the fact of his being able to write, and read or recite chapters of the Vedas, or some similar work, caused him to take rank as a highly educated person, more enlightened ideas now prevail. We have changed all that, and instead of a few schools with priests for masters, whose principal care was not to weaken their own prestige by imparting too much from the tree of knowledge to the younger members of the community, the whole number of government and private schools at the present time in British India, excluding the native states, amounts to 53,764, giving instruction to 1,668,026 scholars; while in the states independent of our control, steady progress is being made in like manner, the rulers becoming daily more alive to the necessity of promoting education among their subjects.

In our own part of the country government schools exist in regular gradation, from those which give the humblest elementary instruction to the highest colleges, and the best pupils of one grade are able to pass through the other grades by means of scholarships. To complete the system there is a university established in each of the three presidency towns, on the model of the London University; and while writing, I hear that a large Anglo-Mohammedan college has been opened at Lahore, founded and endowed by the wealthy followers of that religion. The happiest results are expected to follow this attempt to break down the exclusiveness of this important class of the community, who have hitherto resisted all efforts to impart to the rising generation much beyond what has been taught by their mollahs, or priests. All the government institutions are intended to serve as models, to be gradually superseded by schools supported on the grant-in-aid system—a system based on the principle of perfect religious neutrality, and on regular rules adapted to the circumstances of each province; while normal schools exist all over the country for the training of masters.

The medium of education in the elementary schools for the masses, is the vernacular languages, into which the best elementary English treatises are translated. The study of the classical languages of India is still maintained, and is taught, together with our own tongue, in the Anglo-vernacular schools and colleges for the education of the upper and middle classes of society. Technical classes and colleges, for the teaching of law and medicine, also exist, and are encouraged by the government, while female education likewise receives its most cordial support. For obvious reasons, however, but slow progress is made in this latter direction, although zenana missions and similar efforts are gradually opening out a more brilliant future for the women of India.

From these remarks it will be gathered that education is making rapid strides in India, and bringing with it the happiest augury of a brilliant future for literature there, as well as the vast material benefits derived from superior knowledge. Thus and thus alone can we hope to draw closer the bonds of union between the two races; for it is no less strange than true that, notwithstanding our long connection with the country, the natives remain complete mysteries to us. Their society, their feelings, their family life, and their religious instincts, are almost as strange to us as if they lived in another planet. Slowly and surely, however, a better acquaintance will spring up; for as their minds, hitherto uncultivated, become more akin to ours, so in like manner will their thoughts and feelings. The absurdities of the prejudices connected with their religion and caste, once abated or removed—as undoubtedly must be the case in time—there will be nothing to hinder a freer intercourse between them and the dominant power, and a gradual change from their superstitious forms of religion to one of a purer description. Of the older members of the community, specially attached to idols and intolerant in their creed, and with no desire to better their condition, or to become acquainted with anything further than what they already know, but faint hopes of amendment can be entertained; it is from the younger portion of the community that we must expect these beneficial results to accrue. Already indeed they appear; for young India has taken a deep draught of the cup of knowledge, and the absurdities of his creed have forced themselves on his mental retina as he imbibed wisdom at the Calcutta College. His labours over the midnight oil have shaken his credulity in the faith of his ancestors; but the tender plant of Christianity has not as yet found in his breast a soil in which to germinate. To bring about this result time is needed; for the chief effect as yet produced by the acquisition of knowledge—as a rule—in the native scholar, has been to fill him with an overweening conceit of himself, as contrasted with his less favoured brethren, on whom he likes to impress his dignity by scattering scraps of his erudition, in a manner oftentimes ridiculous. Having studied English literature profusely, he quotes Bacon and Shakspeare, and sprinkles his discourse with sayings of Newton and Locke; harps upon philosophy, and interlards the current of his speech with the most grandiloquent expressions, gleaned from various authors, not entirely conscious that the high-sounding terms are but too often inappropriately applied, and would be absurd to any hearers except those of his own class, who not unnaturally, from his flow of language, consider him a model of culture.

There are, however, I am glad to say, exceptions to this rule, and here and there we meet with men who are quietly profiting by the new stores of knowledge opened to their view; who not only doubt their religion and other ordinances of life, but have commenced to open up a new path in which to tread, and which, although not as yet entirely separated from their original belief, is the sure road in the future to Christianity. Many again show indications of deep thought, and have fitted themselves by education for a superior position in society, with qualifications to fill responsible posts in the administration of their native land, side by side with Englishmen, but under their direction; for many years must elapse before the Hindu will be capable of exercising the power of governing or controlling, in any satisfactory manner, the various races inhabiting the land of his birth. Still every hope can be formed that in a short time a better order of things will prevail. 'Distrust between the races will, on closer acquaintance, give place to confidence. Idolatry will be banished, and education in lieu of ignorance will be the rule and not the exception, bearing in its train, among its many advantages, a probable modern revival of the literature of Ind.

CHAPTER XI.

Approach of the Monsoon—A Dust-storm—A Thunder-storm in the tropics—Effect of the Monsoon—The City of Ajudhya—Its history—The King Rama—The antiquity of Ajudhya—Receive orders to proceed to Gwalior—Departure from Faizabad—Destruction of Bridge at Cawnpore—Journey to Agra—Arrival at Agra—The City of Agra—The Fort—Gates of the Fortress—The Palace—The architecture of Agra—The Dewan-i-khas—The Dewan-i-am—The Zenana—The Shish-Mahal—Eastern Game of Backgammon—The Thrones—The Jasmine Tower—Description of the Palace—The Motee-Musjid, or Pearl Mosque—The Somnath gates—Their history—Mr. Simpson's explanation of their authenticity—The Taj—The Begum Moomtaz-i-Mahal—History of the Taj—Its cost—Description of the Taj—The garden—The exterior—The interior—Measurements of the Taj—The Taj by moonlight.

FOR nearly two months after our arrival at Faizabad the weather continued very hot; but about the end of the first week in June there were signs of the approach of the monsoon, which soon burst upon us in its characteristic manner. The approach of the monsoon is announced by vast masses of clouds rising from the Indian Ocean, which gather and thicken as they proceed over the land towards the north-east. After some days the sky assumes a threatening appearance in the evening, attended with vivid flashes of lightning. The rain is usually ushered in by violent gusts of wind, which create the unpleasant phenomenon known as a dust-storm, when clouds of dust, sand, and small stones are driven through the air with such force and in such quantity that it is dangerous, even if not almost impossible, to face the blast. If a dust-storm occurs in the day it becomes as dark as night; the wind rises so suddenly, giving scarcely any warning of its approach, that time is barely afforded to close all apertures in the house; and even then the dust finds its way in, and everyone and everything is covered with a fine white powder. Several of these storms commonly occur in the few days preceding the great thunder-storm, which may be said to be the commencement of the change of seasons; and this thunder-storm, which usually makes its appearance at night, is of alarming magnitude and severity, not to be imagined by those who have only witnessed this phenomenon in a temperate climate. For some hours lightning flashes without intermission; sometimes it merely illuminates the sky, which literally seems to open, and shows the clouds only near the horizon; at others it discovers the distant scenery, and again leaves all in darkness, when in an instant it reappears in vivid and successive forked flashes, exhibiting the nearest objects in all the brightness of day. The colours of the lightning are peculiar and varied; for while the constant flashes of the sheet-lightning are blue, and in the far distance of a rosy tint, the dangerous forked-lightning is of a dazzling whiteness, like that produced by the electric light, and, as it pursues its jagged course towards the earth, resembles a long and uneven piece of thick wire heated to a white heat. This forked-lightning is dangerous. Scarcely a storm of any magnitude takes place without injury to life and property; and I have myself a vivid remembrance of a narrow escape in Gwalior in 1868, when I was struck down by the electric fluid, which entered the ground a few inches from my standing-place, but which caused me no further hurt than rendering me insensible for a short time, followed by a temporary blindness. During all the time the lightning flashes hither and thither, the distant thunder never ceases to roll, and is only silenced by some nearer peal, which bursts on the ear with a sudden and tremendous crash that fills one with awe. After a time the thunder ceases; and though the lightning continues, nothing is heard but the continued downpour of torrents of rain, which falls in such quantities and with such force as must be seen to be believed.

Although the rain is not continuous, yet at first it is pretty constant, and there are only slight intermissions; but after the lapse of a few days the sky clears, and discloses the face of nature, changed as if by enchantment. The fields, formerly parched, are now covered with luxuriant verdure; the clear and burning sky is now varied and embellished with clouds; the dust, which formerly loaded the atmosphere, making even the sun appear dull and discoloured, has now disappeared; the burning wind, like the blast from a furnace, and the still more sultry calms, are now succeeded by a purer and cooler air, justifying, greatly to one's relief, the removal of the unsightly tatties that for the past three months have obscured the doors. Intermittent rain now falls for a month; then it descends with great violence, and about the latter part of July the monsoon may be said to be at its height. Its power diminishes about the third month, and towards the end of September the rains go as they came, amidst the accompaniment of thunder and tempest. The quantity of rain that falls during the season varies in different parts of the country. In some places it is enormous, and in Bengal it is not uncommon to experience a rainfall of fifty to eighty inches in the three months.

R

As can be readily imagined, the change of weather is agreeable to all; for although it is close and hot, particularly during the break in the rains, there is not the burning heat nor the intense glare of the sun that there was during the hot season, and one is not cooped up in the house as formerly, but can be more out of doors. Of this we gladly availed ourselves; and many and long were the walks and drives we enjoyed about the station and its environs.

The country around Faizabad is very pretty; it is undulating and park-like, and dotted all over with fine clumps of trees and large shrubs in places not under cultivation. There is however no great object of antiquity or interest to visit in the neighbourhood, with the exception of the old Hindu city of Ajudhya, which well deserves inspection and description. This city, half ruinous and of no particular importance at the present day—its sacredness as being built on the site of the original city of Ajudhya excepted—is situated about five miles from the station, and contains several very holy Brahmanical temples, but all of comparatively modern date, and without any architectural pretensions. There can be no doubt however that most of them occupy the site of more ancient temples destroyed by the Mohammedans, to whom is due the erection of the city as it exists at present. The houses and temples are filled with priests and votaries of all descriptions; for Ajudhya is to the pious Hindu the most venerated spot on earth, more holy even than the modern city of Benares, through its associations of a by-gone age, and particularly as the birthplace of Rama. Numerous pilgrims from all parts flock yearly to worship on the spot, for ever sanctified by the former presence of their best-beloved god.

The Holy City of Ajudhya.

It is only in its associations with the past that this place has any interest; for there are no high mounds of ruins covered with broken statues and sculptured pillars, such as mark the sites of other ancient cities. No traces of the original Ajudhya are to be discovered; nor is it likely that any portion of the old city should exist, since it was in the earliest days of the history of the country that it flourished. There is no information as to the time of its foundation. According to the Ramayana it was founded by Manu, the progenitor of all mankind; but no doubt exists that it was about the first city of any importance erected by the Aryan race after their arrival in India. Here the earliest Hindu kings, from whom the other princes have sprung, had their origin. From fifty to sixty generations are said to have existed here before Rama; but this statement is supported only by purely mythological legends. After these came Rama, who seems to be entitled to take his place in real history; although the earliest writings of the country attribute to him supernatural powers, such as being assisted in his victories by an army of apes headed by a monkey king, termed Sugriva, whose memory the natives still hold in remembrance, while the supposed deeds of these animals, at that time, have earned for monkeys the sacred character they enjoy to this day all over India. However, this story, when stripped of its fabulous and romantic decorations, affords the information that a prince named Rama was born at Ajudhya, and reigned over a powerful kingdom in Hindustan, with Ajudhya for a capital, and after his death was held in great veneration by his subjects, who considered him to be of a god-like nature, on account of his goodness and deeds of valour. After his decease, we hear little more of Ajudhya—excepting its destruction in the great war about B.C. 1426, after which it lay deserted—until the time of the king Vikramaditya, A.D. 78, who, being a zealous Brahmanist, restored the city, and built numerous temples on all the holy places referring to the history of Rama, his relations, and to the supposed assistant in his deeds, the monkey-god Hanamana. Hence the place became very sacred in the eyes of all Hindus, and retains that character even to the present day. This second city was destroyed by the Mohammedans, and few traces of its ancient glories can be seen amidst the half-ruinous relics of the third city erected by the conquerors. The only remains that appear to be of any great antiquity are three large earthen mounds, supposed to have been formed by the legion of monkeys when assisting Rama, and two large tombs made of brick, the occupants of which are unknown. With these exceptions there is nothing very notable in the place; the numerous temples filled with Brahmans and fakirs are, as already stated, of modern erection; and Ajudhya only interests us now from the fact that in the dark period of India's history, it was the scene of most important political and social events.

The weather continued very wet after the setting in of the monsoon, but it generally cleared towards the evening, and the social gatherings in the park were frequent and well attended. We therefore anticipated a very pleasant time, but herein were unfortunate, as at the latter end of June an order was received directing me to proceed for duty to Gwalior. This missive was not at all welcomed by us, for we liked our station, and the change was for the worse, Morar, the cantonment of Gwalior, having always enjoyed an unenviable notoriety for unpleasantness, in the shape of intense heat and frequent epidemics of sickness. With its discomforts I was well acquainted, having served there in former days for two years; and not being desirous of returning to such an undesirable locality, or of making a long journey of nearly five hundred miles at a time of year when travelling, except by railway, is difficult, every means was tried to avert the change if possible. Our efforts however met with no success; a medical officer was urgently required; no alteration in the original order could be effected; and so, making the best of the inevitable, we prepared for removal. Having sold off the greater part of our furniture at a dead loss, there being no demand at the time, we bade adieu to our numerous friends, and daybreak of the morning of the 9th July saw us with our baggage and train of servants, all of whom volunteered to accompany us, at the railway station, ready to resume our wanderings after a most pleasant but too brief sojourn in Faizabad of exactly three months.

Our train left at five a.m., and we travelled right through Lucknow on to Cawnpore, over the same road we had passed so recently. Cawnpore was reached at three p.m. without any adventure, but on leaving the station to cross over the bridge of boats to the city, we found the Ganges presenting a very different appearance to what it had on our former visit. Instead of being, as then, a comparatively narrow, sluggish stream, it was now, owing to the late rains, a wide, raging, rushing torrent, threatening each instant to sweep away the frail structure we had to traverse to reach the opposite shore. We proceeded over the bridge at a slow pace, while the creaking and swaying of its component parts raised strong doubts as to its safety, and it was with a feeling of relief that we found ourselves on the other side. Our fears of its stability were, however, fully realized; for within an hour after our passage the bridge parted, and most of it was swept away. Unfortunately the greater number of our servants, with all our baggage, were still at the terminus, detained through want of transport, which had been sent for but could not now be of any avail, as in the absence of the bridge communication from shore to shore could only be made by boat, and that there was no chance of obtaining until the following day. We did not, however, allow this mishap to detain us; but leaving instructions for our servants to bring all on to Agra, we departed for that city at an early hour by train the following morning.

The distance by rail from Cawnpore to Agra is about a hundred and sixty miles, and the line passes through no place of any importance. The country for the most part is flat and well cultivated, and does not possess any picturesque beauty. At the time of our journey the greater part, owing to the heavy rain, was under water, this being the normal condition of a considerable portion of the land in the plains of India during the monsoon. We arrived at the Toondla Junction at 11.30 p.m., and at this place, distant fourteen miles from our destination, had to change carriages, the train in which we had come so far from Cawnpore continuing its way to Delhi and Lahore, while we jogged slowly on towards Agra. We reached that station about one o'clock, and secured most comfortable rooms at the North-Western Hotel. The next day, and the one following, while awaiting the arrival of our servants and luggage, we devoted to sight-

The City of Agra. 247

seeing; for there is much that is both curious and interesting to be seen at this place, the city having for many years been of considerable importance, while it was the first seat of sovereignty of the Mogul dynasty.

Although a residence of early Indian monarchs, Agra has no history of importance previous to Akber, grandson of Baber, the founder of the Mogul empire, who in 1566 established his metropolitan palace here. The place lies on the right or west bank of the river Jumna, a hundred and thirty-nine miles south-east from Delhi, and the city walls enclose eleven square miles, about half of which area is now populated, the rest consisting of ruins, ravines, and dusty patches of desert. The population is about a hundred and fifty thousand, of whom fully two-thirds are Hindus. The native city is large and well built—a good example of an Eastern town, and being under the direction of a municipal committee, is clean and well kept. The principal European station is on the western and north-western sides of the fort and city, and consists of the usual barracks and residences for the officials, both civil and military, with the accompanying government offices. There are several churches, and for the Roman Catholics it is the seat of an episcopal see. They possess also several nunneries, besides a large Catholic Mission and Orphanage. This institution boasts of considerable antiquity, for it was founded by the Emperor Akber, a ruler very tolerant to Christians, and to whom Hindu and Moslem alike appeared as bigots. He cherished a dream of religious reform throughout the country, which never attained any great success; for although he himself had a strong leaning towards Christianity, and was even supposed to have received the rite of baptism, he made no public confession of any conversion, and died eventually in the faith of Islam. His successors were all Mohammedans of a more or less intolerant type.

The central object of Agra is the Fort, an imposing structure with vast walls and flanking defences, surmounted everywhere by beehive crenellations. It is built of red sandstone, which largely enters into the structure of nearly all the buildings in this city. In front of the principal entrance is a walled square or piazza called Tirpolya, used at present as a market-place, for which it is well adapted, being close to the railway station. On the side opposite to the gate of the Fort is the Jama Musjid, or Cathedral Mosque, a term applied to the largest and principal place of worship of the Mohammedans in every Indian city. This building stands on a raised platform eleven feet high, reached by a broad flight of steps, and is surmounted by a curious dome, in which white and red stone courses alternate in a slanting direction, the effect being very singular. An inscription over the doorway states it to have been built by Shah Juhan, in 1664, and to have taken five years to complete. The walls of the Fort are nearly seventy feet high, and about a mile and a half in circuit; and the principal entrance is the great barbican opposite the mosque, known as the Delhi Gate. This entrance is very grand and imposing, and the words of Bayard Taylor supply a good general description of the approach to Akber's Palace: "Crossing by a drawbridge over the deep moat, which surrounds the Fort, we pass through a massive gateway and up a paved ascent to the inner entrance, which shows considerable taste. It consists of two octagonal towers of red sandstone inlaid with ornamental designs in white marble.

The passage between them is covered by two domes, which seem to rise from accretions of prismatic stalactites, as in the domes of the Moorish Alhambra. This elegant portal, however, instead of opening upon the courts of the Palace ushers you into a barren waste covered with withered grass. But over the blank red walls in front you see three marble domes, glittering in the sunshine like new-fallen snow, and still further the golden pinnacles of Akber's Palace, and these objects hint that your dream of the magnificence of the Great Mogul will not be entirely dispelled."

Crossing this waste we came upon the abode of royalty, which is indeed most interesting and beautiful—interesting as a monument of the domestic life of the past, and beautiful as a specimen of pure Eastern domestic art. By many this Palace is considered even more interesting than that of Delhi; and although it does not all belong to the time of Akber, its founder, the greater part having been erected by his successors, yet it affords one of the best examples in the country of that style of architecture which is often termed Saracenic, but which may more properly be said to belong to the Hindustani school. The centre of the Palace is a great court, five hundred feet by three hundred and seventy, surrounded by arcades, and approached at opposite ends through a succession of smaller courts opening into one another. On one side of this large central space is the 'Dewan-i-khas,' or hall of public audience. In this apartment the monarch sat on his throne, raised as we still see it on an estrade, surrounded with marble inlaying. At the foot of the alcove on which the throne is placed is a slab of marble, and here, according to tradition, Akber took his stand when administering justice. This hall forms the front of the palace, behind which are two smaller courts, the one containing the 'Dewan-i-am,' or private hall of audience, the other that great feature in all Oriental surroundings, the Zenana, or harem.

The greatest care has been bestowed on the Zenana Court, which measures one hundred and seventy feet by two hundred and thirty-five. Three sides are occupied by the residences of the ladies, none of which are remarkable for size or for any great architectural beauty; but on the fourth, overhanging the river, there are three white pavilions of singular elegance. As in most Moorish palaces, the baths on one side of this court were the most elaborately and elegantly-decorated apartments; and one of the bathrooms is the most curious part of the Palace. It is called the 'Shish-Mahal,' or palace of glass, and is an apartment of some size, the chambers and passages whereof are adorned with thousands of small mirrors, disposed in the most intricate designs. The court surmounted by the Dewan-i-khas contains a curious feature of Oriental amusements in the form of a marble pavement, constructed for the game of 'pucheesee,' a kind of Eastern backgammon, in which living slave girls, who moved as directed from one square to another, took the place of the wooden or ivory draughts in ordinary use when the game is played on a smaller scale by less luxurious nations.

On the river side of these courts is an open terrace, which contains two thrones, one of white marble, the other of black slate, both very solid magnificent specimens of work. A long fissure runs through the slate throne. This, according to the popular belief, was produced in 1764, when Agra was seized by the Jats, and their celebrated leader, Sooruj Mull, seated himself upon the throne of the august Moguls, which, unable to bear such profanity, cracked with a loud report at the touch of the usurper. Near this terrace is a beautiful specimen of carved and inlaid marble, known as the 'Jasmine Tower,' formerly the boudoir of the chief Sultana; and beyond this is a square, the 'Ungooree-Bagh,' consisting of the three sides of the small court of the Zenana, which is interesting as being the place where the British officers and their families were chiefly accommodated during the terrible summer of 1857.

The whole of the parts described, comprising the Palace, are, with small exceptions, in excellent preservation, and a good idea can be formed of its appearance in the days of its glory. Those parts which have suffered from age and the effects of war, for several times in its history has the Fort been taken and retaken by Jats, Mahrattas, and English, are now being repaired by order of the government, so that in a short time this Palace, the first residence of the Great Moguls, will again justify the description of Taylor, with which I may conclude my account, the work of restoration having made such progress at the time of our visit, that his remarks are now perfectly applicable. He says, after describing the various parts, "The substructures of the Palace are of red sandstone, but nearly the whole of its corridors, chambers, and pavilions are of white marble, wrought with the most exquisite elaboration of ornament. The pavilions overhanging the river are inlaid within and without in the rich style of Florentine mosaic. They are precious caskets of marble, glittering all over with jasper, agate, carnelian, bloodstone, and lapis-lazuli, and topped with golden domes. Balustrades of marble, wrought in open patterns of such rich design, that they resemble fringes of lace when seen from beneath, extend along the edge of the battlements. The Jumna washes the walls seventy feet below, and from the balconies attached to the Zenana, or women's apartments, there are beautiful views of the gardens and palm groves on the opposite side, and that wonder of India, the Taj, shining like a palace of ivory and crystal, about a mile down the stream."

After leaving the palace we proceeded to the principal mosque of the Fort, built by Shah Juhan in 1654, which occupies a length of 142 feet by a depth of 56 feet, on the very crown of the fortified plateau, and rising far above the parapets is a conspicuous object at a distance. It is truly wonderful that it has so long escaped the shocks of war and weather. A general idea of this building may be gathered from the enthusiastic language of the author just cited, who remarks: "This is the 'Motee Musjid' or Pearl Mosque, as it is poetically and justly termed. It is in truth the pearl of all mosques, of small dimensions, but absolutely perfect in style and proportion. It is lifted on a lofty sandstone platform, and from without nothing can be seen but its three domes of white marble and gilded spires. In all distant views of the Fort, these domes are seen like silvery bubbles which have rested for a moment on its walls, and which the next breeze will sweep away. Ascending a long flight of steps, a heavy door was opened for me, and I stood in the court-yard of the mosque, on its eastern side, and the pure blue of the sky overhead. The three domes crown a corridor open towards the court, and divided into three aisles by a triple row of the most exquisitely proportioned Saracenic arches. The Motee Musjid can be compared to no other edifice that I have ever seen. To my eye it is absolutely perfect. While its architecture is the purest Saracenic, it has the severe simplicity of Doric art. It has, in fact, nothing which can be properly called ornament. It is a sanctuary so pure and stainless, revealing so exalted a spirit of worship, that I felt humbled as a Christian to think that our noble religion has never inspired its architects to surpass this temple to God and Mohammed." Much of this glowing language is undoubtedly deserved, but many consider its lines stiff and unaspiring. Its chief beauty is certainly the courtyard, where it is wholly of white marble, from the pavement to the summit of the domes; and while decidedly less ornamented than any other building of the same pretensions, the pure light and shade of the material gives the mosque such a spiritual air, that there is perhaps nothing to which it can be more aptly compared than to the evening of Wordsworth's sonnet—

"Quiet as a nun, breathless with adoration." *

Before quitting this part of the Fort, we inspected, in a room in the Palace, the notorious gates of the Ellenborough proclamation, the so-called 'Gates of Somnath.' These celebrated doors are about twelve feet high by nine in breadth, and are set in a carved frame standing about five feet higher. They have been the cause of endless controversy as to whether they are or are not the veritable gates of that most sacred temple of the Brahmans, but the idea that they are not appears to prevail. The following letter from Mr. W. Simpson, the well-known artist, appears to exhaust the subject, and as

---

* Keene's *Handbook to Agra*, from which many of the details here given have been extracted.

it explains the reason why the true identity of these gates should be established, their seizure and transportation to Agra having been perpetrated for political reasons, I am tempted to give it in full. The letter was addressed to the London *Daily News* on the death of Lord Ellenborough, who was Viceroy of India from 1842 to 1844. It will, I think, render clear and fully explain the origin and character of these disputed doors, which at one time created so intense an excitement. Such a curious instance of a myth without foundation, capable apparently of being dispelled by the simplest evidence, is not easily to be paralleled among the mistakes of history.

Mr. Simpson writes:

SIR,—In your leading article of to-day upon the late Lord Ellenborough you naturally make reference to the gates of Somnath. They were the great point of his celebrated proclamation after the Cabool war, and became the palpable evidence to the religious minds of the Hindoo, as well as the Mussulman population of India, that the avenging army had done its work, and that the Angrezzi Raj (the English rule) was still supreme. The present may be a fair opportunity for clearing up what is not generally known about these gates, and they have occupied such a very important place in our Indian history that it is right that the truth should be known. I may tell you how I first became acquainted with them. In 1860 they were in the Dewan-i-am or Public Hall of Audience in the Fort of Agra, where I suppose they still remain; but would suggest that their proper place ought to be the South Kensington Museum. I made a very careful sketch of them, including details of the ornament. As I sketched, it struck me as strange that the art contained nothing Hindoo in its design. It was all purely Mahomedan. Out of the thirty-two million of Hindoo gods there was not one of them visible. This was so strange that I began making enquiries as to whether they really were the veritable gates of Somnath. The answer always was that there should be no doubt of it, and Lord

Ellenborough's proclamation was in every case referred to. To an artist historical evidence, or even a proclamation by a Governor-General, goes for little, when there is a style of art opposed to them; so my doubts clung to me. Before leaving India I had the opportunity of putting the question to Lord Canning, a man far from indifferent to questions of this sort, but even with him Lord Ellenborough's proclamation was the infallible guide. It was only on my return to England, and in conversation with Mr. Fergusson, that I got confirmation of what I suspected. He agreed with me that the ornament was sufficient evidence that they could not possibly be the gates of Somnath; but he added, what I had not the opportunity of learning in India, that the gates in the Dewan-i-am at Agra had been inspected with a microscope, and they are of deodar pine, and not of sandal-wood. This fact, in spite of the proclamation, would command a verdict against them from any jury.

Puttun Somnath, in Goojerat, contained one of the most celebrated temples of the Brahmins. Mahmud of Ghuznee, shortly after he came to the throne in A.D. 877, made a raid into India for the double purpose of destroying idolatry and looting in that well-to-do country. The wealth of Somnath led this Mahomedan hero in that direction, and after a desperate resistance he took the place. Amongst the plunder, he carried back to Cabool the gates of the temple. They were of sandal-wood, and of great celebrity from their elaborate ornament. After Mahmud's death these gates were put on his tomb, and were treasured as evidences of Mahomedan conquest. The probability would seem to be that the original gates were destroyed by fire, and when the tomb was repaired a new set of gates were made of deodar. These gates are not new, for they bear many evident marks of age. Panels are smashed, and much of the ornament destroyed; rude repairs are done with scraps of wood and iron; and, curious link between East and West, there are a number of horse-shoes nailed upon these old portals. As they were brought from Mahmud's tomb at Ghuznee by our conquering army, they were an evidence to the Hindoo population of India that our power had no rival in the East. So far Lord Ellenborough's proclamation is correct enough; but now, as their political significance has ceased to be, it ought to be known, for historical and archæological reasons, that they are not the gates of Somnath.

WILLIAM SIMPSON.

December 23rd.

Such a letter needs no comment; and although perhaps this may appear a trivial matter to have created such a discussion, yet it is not trivial when viewed in an Eastern light. The political significance of the removal of the gates to Agra rested entirely on the belief that they were the holy gates of a temple most sacred in the memory of the Hindus, gates which were known to be in the possession of the Mohammedans in the far north, and their capture, so long desired by the Hindus, for centuries past a dream they had not the power to fulfil, could not be regarded in any other light than as a token of the invincible power of their British rulers. Of course the gates lost much of their interest, and the appreciation of British valour was much lowered, if this trophy was not the holy relic, the redemption of which lay so near the Hindu heart, but an impostor, a sham, where manufactured was not known; while discredit was also thrown on the hitherto accepted belief, that the English had made their power felt in the very heart of Afghanistan.

The Palace and mosque are the chief objects of interest in the Fort; for although there are other buildings, they do not call for special mention, being interesting only as specimens of the early Mohammedan style of architecture already described. It strikes one with surprise, that an abode so lavishly decorated and beautifully finished for its royal occupants should have been appreciated so little, for the glories of the Agra Palace must have been of short duration. Jehangir, son and successor of the founder, lived and died chiefly in northern latitudes; and in 1639 Shah Juhan, the next emperor, began the palace of Delhi, which thereafter was the capital; while the Fort at Agra became merely the citadel of a provincial town, and the residence of a Mogul governor, and was never again honoured by the presence of any member of that royal line.

We now proceeded to the famous Taj, the gem of India, the glory of Agra, the very koh-i-noor of the architecture of the world, to describe which, in the hope to convey a perfect impression of its beauty, would be folly, since words alone must fail to give any adequate idea of this magnificent and unique structure.* I will, however, essay a slight sketch of its history, together with the dry, descriptive details of its size and construction and general appearance, and the imagination of my readers must supply the rest, and fill up this meagre outline. The Taj is on the left bank of the Jumna, about three miles from Agra, and is approached by a road along the river strand, made in the famine relief operations in 1838. By the side of the road are the remains of several houses once occupied by the nobles of the Mogul court, but now fallen into ruins, leaving the Taj standing alone in all its glory amidst these relics of by-gone greatness.

This monument of marital affection was commenced by the Emperor Shah Juhan, in 1632, as a place of sepulchre and a lasting memorial for the wife of his youth, Arjumund Banoo Begum, called 'Moomtaz-i-Mahal,' or 'Exalted One of the Palace.' She was a daughter of Asaf Khan, brother of the celebrated Noor Jehan (wife of the previous Emperor

* See Frontispiece.

Jehangir), whose father, an adventurer from Persia, attained high place during his daughter's tenure of power. Banoo Begum was married to the prince about 1615, and bore him seven children, dying in childbed of the eighth, in 1629, at Boorhanpur, whither she had accompanied her husband on his campaign in the Deccan. Her body was carried to Agra and laid in a temporary vault in the garden until the mausoleum was ready for its reception. At that time it was, as already stated, a usual practice for a king or noble, who intended to provide himself a tomb, to enclose a garden, and in its centre erect a building, usually on a lofty square terrace and crowned by a dome. This, during the life of its founder, was used as a place of recreation and feasting for himself and his friends; but at his death its destination was changed; for his remains were then interred beneath the central dome, and the vaults never again resounded with festive mirth. In the present instance this was not quite the case, as Shah Juhan's queen appears to have died before the Taj was begun. In all probability the garden was already enclosed, and a favourite retreat of the deceased; and for this reason it is said, very probably with truth, that the Emperor resolved to build there a mausoleum that should surpass in splendour every building of whose existence he could learn. With this view he sent for plans and models from every quarter, and studied the designs and descriptions of all the most celebrated monuments of the kind. Finally, his choice was influenced by Eesa Mohammed Effendi, an architect sent him by the Sultan of Turkey, and the present plan adopted. The collection of the materials for building occupied some years, and when they were ready twenty thousand workmen are said to have been employed for seventeen years in the construction of this wonderful pile, which cost from first to last about two millions sterling. The native account records 9,855,426 rupees as having been given by the Rajahs and Nawabs, and out of the Emperor's private treasury 8,609,760 rupees, which would make £1,846,518 12s. or nearly the amount stated above. Most probably, nearly the whole of this vast sum was expended on the marble and jewels, for the labour was all forced, a meagre daily allowance of food being given in lieu of money. There was great distress and frightful mortality among the workmen in consequence, and the peasantry round Agra by no means worshipped the memory of the innocent Empress.* Such is the history of this beautiful structure, which we will now approach and examine more closely. No words of mine could succeed, when far abler pens have failed, in attempting to convey the true character of this 'dream in stone;' and the description of Bayard Taylor is so picturesque, and at the same time so just, that I am tempted to give it verbatim as embodying all that we remarked on the ever-memorable day of our visit. He writes:

"The Taj stands on the bank of the Jumna, rather more than a mile to the eastward of the Fort of Agra. It is approached by a handsome road cut through the mounds left by the ruins of ancient palaces. Like the tomb of Akber, it stands in a large garden enclosed by a lofty wall of red sandstone, with arched galleries around the interior, and entered by a superb gateway of sandstone, inlaid with ornaments and inscriptions from the Koran in white marble. Outside of this grand portal is a spacious quadrangle of solid masonry,

* Keene's *Agra*.

with an elegant structure intended as a caravanserai on the opposite side. Whatever may be the visitor's impatience, he cannot help pausing to notice the fine proportions of these structures, and the rich and massive style of their construction. The gate to the garden of the Taj is not so large as that of Akber's tomb, but quite as beautiful in design. Passing under the open demi-vault whose arch hangs high above, an avenue of dark Italian cypresses appears before you. Down its centre sparkles a long row of fountains, each casting up a single slender jet. On both sides the palm, the banyan, and a feathery bamboo mingle their foliage; the song of birds meets your ears, and the odour of roses and lemon flowers sweetens the air. Down such a vista, and over such a foreground, rises the Taj.

"It is an octagonal building, or rather a square with the corners truncated, and each side precisely similar. It stands upon a lofty platform or pedestal, with a minaret at each corner, and this again is lifted on a vast terrace of solid masonry. An oriental dome swelling out boldly from the base into nearly two-thirds of a sphere, and tapering at the top into a crescent-tipped spire, crowns the edifice, rising from its centre, with four similar though much smaller domes at the corners. On each side there is a grand entrance formed by a single-pointed arch rising nearly to the cornice, and two smaller arches, one placed above the other, on either hand. But no words can convey an idea of the exquisite harmony of the different parts, and the grand and glorious effect of the whole structure with its attendant minarets. The material is the purest white marble, little inferior to that of Carrara. It shines so dazzlingly in the sun that you can scarcely look at it near at hand, except in the morning and evening. Every part, even the basement, the dome, and the upper galleries of the minarets, is inlaid with ornamental designs in marble of different colours, principally a pale brown and a bluish-violet variety. Great as the dimensions of the Taj are, it is as laboriously finished as one of those Chinese caskets of ivory and ebony which are now so common in Europe. Bishop Heber truly said the Pathans (more properly the Moguls in this case) designed like Titans and finished like jewellers.

"Around all the arches of the portals, and the windows—around the cornice and the domes—on the walls, and in the passages, are inlaid chapters of the Koran, the letters being exquisitely formed of black marble. It is asserted that the whole Koran is thus inlaid in the Taj, and I can readily believe it true. The building is perfect in every part. Any dilapidations it may have suffered are so well restored, that all traces of them have disappeared. I ascended to the base of the building—a gleaming marble platform, almost on a level with the tops of the trees in the garden. Before entering the central hall, I descended to the vault where the beautiful Moomtaz-i-Mahal is buried. A sloping passage, whose walls and floor have been so polished by the hands and feet of thousands, that you must walk carefully to avoid sliding down, conducts to a spacious vaulted chamber. There is no light but what enters at the door, and this falls directly upon the tomb of the Queen in the centre. Shah Juhan, whose ashes are covered by a simpler monument, raised somewhat above hers, sleeps by her side. The vault was filled with the odours of rose, jasmine, and sandal-wood, the precious attars of which are sprinkled upon the tomb. Wreaths of beautiful flowers lay upon it, or withered around its base. These were the true tombs (and are of plain white marble), the monuments for display being placed in the grand hall above, which is a lofty rotunda (more properly octagon), lighted both from above and below by screens of marble and jasper, and ornamented with a wainscoting of sculptured tablets, representing flowers. The tombs are sarcophagi of the purest marble, exquisitely inlaid with blood-stone, agate, carnelian, lapis-lazuli, and other precious stones, and surrounded with an octagonal screen six feet high, in the open tracery of which lilies, irises, and other flowers are interwrought with the most intricate ornamental designs. It is of marble covered with precious stones."

The measurements and plan of the Taj are as follows:* The enclosure, including garden and outer court, is a parallelogram of 1,860 feet, by more than 1,000 feet. The outer court, surrounded by arcades, and adorned by four gateways, is an oblong, occupying in length the whole breadth of the enclosure, and about 450 feet deep. Beyond this are the garden and the tomb. The plinth, of white marble, is 18 feet high, and an exact square of 313 feet each way. At the four corners stand four columns or towers, each 137 feet high, and crowned with a little pavilion. The mausoleum itself occupies a space of 186 feet square, in the centre of this larger square, and each of the four corners is cut off, opposite each of the towers. The central dome is 50 feet in diameter, by 80 feet high, and the total height, from ground to spire-top, is 296 feet.

I must not omit to notice in conclusion, that in the interior of the dome there is a wonderful echo, but so quick that it catches the notes and runs them into one another so as to

* Fergusson, *Hist. Architecture*, vol. ii. p. 693.

produce a most distressing discord, unless the notes chosen be such as form a natural harmony. The chord of the seventh produces a very beautiful effect, and "floats and soars overhead in a long delicious undulation, fading away so slowly that you hear it after it is silent, as you see or seem to see a lark you have been watching after it is swallowed up in the blue vault of heaven!"

Such is a brief description of this wonderful monument; but my readers must imagine for themselves—what words cannot convey—the feelings engendered on beholding and entering this splendid mausoleum, for in the language of the author already cited, "The Taj is truly a poem. It is not only a pure architectural type, but also a creation, which satisfies the imagination because its characteristic is beauty. Did you ever build a castle in the air? Here is one brought down to earth, and fixed for the wonder of ages; yet so light it seems, so airy, and when seen from a distance so like a fabric of mist and sunbeams, with its great dome soaring up, a silvery bubble about to burst in the sun, that even after you have touched it and climbed to its summit you almost doubt its reality. While the hall, notwithstanding the precious materials of which it is built and the elaborate finish of its ornaments, has a grave and solemn effect, infusing a peaceful serenity of mind such as we feel when contemplating a happy death. Stern unimaginative persons have been known to burst suddenly into tears on entering it, and whoever can behold the Taj without feeling a thrill that sends the moisture to his eye, has no sense of beauty in his soul. And if beautiful by daylight, still more is the effect of moonlight wanting to complete the beauty of the Taj. The heavy shadows of the foliage, the deep chiaroscuro of embayed portals, the soft curve of the dome—all serve to enhance the virginal splendour of the material of the cupolas and minarets, till they appear almost transparent. The silence is unbroken except by a light breeze in the tree-tops; the blue sky is without a cloud, and the rare genius of the calm building finds its way unchallenged to the heart."

CHAPTER XII.

The Tombs in Agra—Tomb of Itmad-ood-Dowlah—The Cheene-ka-Roza—Sikundra—Futtehpur-Sekri—Its history—Its ruins—Bhurtpur—Muttra—History of Muttra—Stone industries of Agra—Mosaic work—Jalee—Soapstone carving—Departure from Agra—The Indian Dak Gharry—The road to Gwalior—Dholepur—Indian Dak Bungalow—A Rest-house Dinner—Continue the journey—River Chumbul—Perils of the way—Arrival at Gwalior—Visit to the Fortress—Our quarters in Fortress—Description of Fortress—Gwalior—Its History—The Cantonment of Morar—Garrison of Morar—The Army in India—The Police Force—The Native Army—Its reorganization—Its loyalty—Causes that might lead to a Mutiny—Securities against a repetition of acts like those of 1857.

THE tombs and monuments of the Mogul grandees are very numerous in and about Agra, and very interesting; but as it would take up too much space to mention all, I will only describe the principal, which no visitor to this city should omit to see. On the left bank of the river, not far from the town, stands the garden-tomb of Itmad-ood-Dowlah, the Persian adventurer, father of Noor-Juhan, and grandfather of Moomtaz-i-Mahal, the celebrated lady of the Taj. His daughter, the empress, first intended that the monument she raised to her father should be of silver, but was dissuaded from her purpose, and advised to use some material which, being less likely to excite the cupidity of beholders, would have a better chance of remaining unmolested. The present tomb was thereupon commenced, and was completed about the year 1628. It stands in a garden, well kept and stocked with flowers, shrubs, and cypress trees. The lower hall, which contains the tomb of the hero, is a parallelogram of white marble, inlaid with coloured stones, standing on a sandstone terrace, 149 feet square and 3·4 feet from the ground. Four bold kiosques stand at the four corners, and in the centre is a small pavilion of rich pierced-work, covered with an oblong dome, topped with two light pinnacles.

On the right bank of the river is a curious ruin, termed the Cheene-ka-Roza, which is believed to be the monument of Ufzul Khan, a literary adventurer of the seventeenth century. This tomb is chiefly remarkable for the beautiful patterns of the plaster, coloured like porcelain, by which it is still covered. From this, which is a coarse enamelling (probably in shellac) on the plaster, it derives its name of 'China tomb.'

Passing down the road by which the old Moguls used to go northward to Lahore and Kashmir, we come, about five miles from Agra, to Sikundra, the tomb of the Emperor Akber, the inscription on which sets forth that it was erected in the reign of his son and successor Jehangir, and was completed in 1613. "It stands in the midst of a large square garden, which has a lofty gateway of red sandstone in the centre of each of its sides. From these four gateways, which are upwards of seventy feet high, four grand causeways of hewn stone converge to the central platform on which the mausoleum stands. The intermediate spaces are filled with orange, mango, banana, palm, and peepul trees. In the centre of the causeways are immense tanks and fountains. The platform, of white stone, which terminates these magnificent approaches, is about four hundred feet square. The mausoleum, which is square also, measures more than three hundred feet on each side, and rises in five terraces, in a pyramidal form, to the height of one hundred feet. Around each of the terraces runs an arched gallery, surmounted by rows of cupolas resting on circles of small pillars. The material of the edifice is red sandstone, except the upper story, which is of white marble. A long descending passage leads from the main entrance to a vaulted hall in the centre of the structure, where, beneath a plain tomb, in the form of a sarcophagus, is the dust of Akber, one of the greatest men who ever wielded a sceptre, and in whom the wisdom, the power, and the glory of his illustrious line culminated." *

There are several other tombs in this neighbourhood, and on the road returning from Sikundra, but although some contain the remains of important personages they do not merit full description. Relating to the emperor Akber, however, there remains to be noticed, as an object of great interest to the visitor at Agra, the ruined city of Futtehpur-Sekri, distant about twenty-two miles from the town. This place was built by Akber, by the advice, it is said, of a fakir or holy man, called Shekh Suleem, who resided near this spot, to commemorate the birth of a son, who afterwards became the emperor Jehangir. The palaces and mosques raised in consequence of the prince's birth, are situated in a walled but not fortified enclosure, seven miles in circumference, embracing the two villages of Sekri and Futtehpur, and having in its centre a huge rock above a mile in length, running from south-west to north-east. This was formerly a noble city, and at one time the emperor intended it for his capital and seat of

* Bayard Taylor.

government, but he left it before it was well finished, driven away, so it is stated, by the unhealthiness of the site, and the badness of the water. The glories of this goodly city were thus short-lived; for in fifty years it was built and ruined. At the present time it is almost destroyed, its houses fallen, and the soil turned into fields; but many of the ruins are interesting on account of the grandeur of their style, and the elaborate finish of the workmanship. Some of the stone carvings and decorations are even at the present time in a fair state of preservation, affording a good idea of the magnificence of the buildings in the days when the Great Mogul lived here in regal state. The mosque is said to be the finest ever erected by Akber, and is approached by a magnificent gateway, the Bolund Durwaza, a splendid object in itself—perhaps the finest of its kind in India—but placed so as to dwarf the mosque to which it leads, and prevent the body of the building from having that pre-eminence which it ought to possess. At the back of this mosque is the cave which formed the original abode of the saint, to whose advice the city is said to have owed its erection. On the left is to be seen his tomb, a chamber externally of white marble, the interior consisting of that material wainscoted with red sandstone, while the screens are of the finest pierced work in marble, and at a distance resemble lace.

There are numerous remains of palaces and houses of the noblemen of the Court, similar to those already described at Agra, all more or less in a ruinous condition, but one and all testifying to their former greatness.

As it is a very usual conclusion of a visit to Futtehpur to proceed by way of Bhurtpur to Muttra, an ancient holy city,

The Holy City of Muttra.

a short account of this place and the route thither may be added; for although we did not pass that way at this time, I had traversed the road in former days, and a slight sketch of Muttra will fitly conclude my notice of Agra and its neighbourhood. Bhurtpur, distant about thirteen miles from Futtehpur-Sekri, will be fully noticed hereafter, when I have to write of native states and their rulers. From Bhurtpur to Muttra is thirty-three miles, and the road passes through the ancient towns of Koombher and Deeg, the latter containing the old fort and the palace of the original founder of the Bhurtpur dynasty—the Jat freebooter Sooruj Mull; the same whose profane touch caused the throne of the Moguls at Agra to split, as noted on a previous page. Next comes Goverdhun, famous for its large masonry tanks, surrounded by temples, tombs, and bathing ghauts; and then a drive of fourteen miles brings one to Muttra, the birthplace of the god Krishna, and the scene of his early adventures, which have caused every spot of any consequence in the locality to be held sacred. The names of towns and villages around Muttra are hence often given by devout Hindus as prænomens to their sons. Muttra, or Mathura, its ancient name, stands on the banks of the Jumna; and although the present city cannot boast of, any great antiquity, it occupies the site of one of the earliest and most important seats of religion in the country. Originally the great centre of the Hindu religion, during the prevalence of Buddhism it became a chosen spot for the followers of that sect; so much so indeed that in 634 we learn that the Buddhist monasteries there outnumbered the temples of the gods in the proportion of four to one. But whatever the changes in the national religion, the city of Mathura has preserved from remote antiquity its sacred character. Even when Buddhism prevailed, votaries were drawn from distant parts to visit its holy shrines; and when the temples of Buddha were swept away, the desecrated sites were speedily occupied in honour of the new order of divinities. Though the city was plundered of all its accumulated wealth by the first of the great Mohammedan invaders, the sacred edifices themselves survived, and for a period of seven hundred years continued to be enriched with successive donations, till Aurungzebe, the last and most fanatical of the Delhi emperors, razed every stone to the ground, and built mosques with the materials. But the humiliation was of short duration. The death of Aurungzebe and the virtual extinction of the empire, was followed first by a period of anarchy, in which neither Hindu nor Mussulman had the power to crush his neighbour, and then by the tolerant sway of Great Britain, under which both are equally protected. Thus in the present day, after the lapse of a century and a half from the period of its utter ruin, though the temples have lost the charm of antiquity, and can no longer boast of the enormous wealth which they enjoyed in the days of their former prosperity, the holy city has no lack of stately buildings, wherewith, as described of old in the Harwansa, it rises beautiful as the crescent moon over the dark stream of the Jumna, and will worthily repay the trouble of a visit from the traveller to Agra.

Before taking a final leave of this part of the country a few words should be said on the stone industries of Agra; for this city (with the neighbouring country, from Gwalior round by Jaipur to Delhi) has long been the seat of several very beautiful arts, found nowhere else in India, and which may be thus classified :—1. 'Munubbut-karee,' or Indian 'pietra dura' or mosaic work. 2. 'Jalee,' pierced screen-work in marble or sandstone. 3. Soap-stone carving—a new art.

Mosaic work appears to have originated in the East, and to have passed over to the Roman Empire in the times of its Eastern conquests, only to travel back to its native home in later times. Borrowed by the Romans, the art became what is now known by the distinctive name of 'mosaic,' that is, the mode of producing artistic designs by setting small squares of stone or glass of different colours, so as to give the effect of painting, such as is practised in Italy at the present day. The Hindustani inlaying is more properly architectural, and is not produced by tesselation, but by the insertion of large masses of jewels into blocks of white marble, so as to form geometrical patterns rather than pictorial designs—a form of art peculiar to Mogul India, and in India to this particular region, and which may more properly be termed 'pietra dura' work than mosaic. Although the period of its introduction into this neighbourhood is uncertain, the art was at its highest point about the time of Akber. On the earlier tombs and buildings in which it was employed geometric traceries only are to be found; but soon afterwards the full introduction of flower-work, as seen in the screen which surrounds the tombs in the Taj, and elsewhere, came into vogue. The traditional belief that European taste is answerable for this is not wholly unfounded, the Taj being built by a Turk of Constantinople; but however it originated, the work is now practised chiefly by the Hindus in Agra, although the legitimate application of the art is in abeyance, Europeans being too unsettled, and the wealthy natives too negligent, to allow of their dwellings being beautified by this costly method. The patient workmen have therefore turned their attention to making smaller specimens of their art, which is now chiefly confined to tables, inkstands, trays, plates, and paper-weights. As much time is required to finish even these small articles, the prices asked are not small, and to many may appear excessive; though when the value of the materials, as well as the skilled labour required, is taken into consideration, they are not really so, while the articles are certainly unique of their kind.

Jalee, the other characteristic stone industry of Agra and its neighbourhood, has been often mentioned in the descriptions of various tombs and palaces as forming the screens in these buildings, and as occurring in balustrades and parapets, where it has a good effect. It is a fine stone filagree work, made out of solid slabs of marble or sandstone, fretted into an almost endless network of geometrical combinations. The true character of Jalee can only be understood by seeing the carvings themselves, or good photographs of them; for their fineness and intricacy cannot be adequately described. Some are so minutely pierced that they actually look at a little distance like lace.

Lastly, there is the modern practice of carving in soapstone or steatite, of somewhat tough texture, and a warm grey tint. It is wrought into beautifully clean patterns, either floral or arabesque, which are worked up into boxes, card-trays, and similar articles, for drawing-room use. It is both cheap and pretty—a handsome piece of carving costing only a few rupees.[*]

[*] A full description of these arts is to be found in Keene's *Handbook to Agra*, to which I am indebted for the above sketch.

Travelling by Dak Gharry. 273

Having exhausted the sights of Agra and its neighbourhood, we departed for Gwalior, our destination, distant eighty-six miles. As there was no railway connecting the two places, although there is one in course of construction, we had to avail ourselves of the old and only rapid mode of conveyance in the country before the advent of the iron horse, the 'dak gharry,' familiar to all who have visited India, but which for the benefit of the uninitiated I may describe. Imagine a box on wheels, with no windows, but a sliding door at each side, with steps leading into the interior of the vehicle, which is raised some considerable distance from the ground. The space within contains two seats, fore and aft, with a well between; but this open space on long journeys is usually bridged over to form a flat surface, on which a mattress can be placed, affording sufficient room for two persons to recline at ease. The arrangement is very comfortable to look at, and would no doubt be comfortable in fact, were it not that the machine, which possesses four large strong wheels, is innocent of springs, and that their omission is made very plainly apparent to the traveller as he progresses on his journey. In front a small seat is stuck up for the driver, and the whole is surmounted by a flat roof, which serves for the accommodation of a reasonable amount of luggage and the insecure seat of one's native servant, who, holding manfully on by both hands, sits smiling aloft, and acts as a sort of counterpoise to keep things steady. The motive power is invariably two half-starved ponies, harnessed abreast, whose disinclination for the work expected from them is well exemplified by the time and trouble expended, as each fresh pair is attached at the posting stages, which are

T

usually eight miles apart. The whole force of the staging establishment is generally brought to bear, and in fact necessarily, to start the steeds, who evince every disposition to go sideways, or backwards, or any way but forwards. Their perverseness is usually overcome by shouts, blows, and an artistic method of holding up one of their forelegs while the wheels are turned round by the attendants. The weight of the machine being driven on to their backs, they endeavour to avoid it by springing into a gallop on the release of their legs, and the pace is stimulated and kept up by the aid of blows from the long whip with which the driver is armed, joined to his never-ceasing shouts and imprecations, until the next stage is reached, and the same process has to be gone through again.

The pace, a good sling gallop, is decidedly exhilirating, and the distance got over in a reasonable time is considerable; but this mode of travelling has its disadvantages. The cumbersome gharry sways from side to side, pursuing a serpentine course; and if the road is bordered by a precipitous descent, it appears to be the aim of the worthy coachman to see how near to its edge he can bring the wheels with safety; while the jolting and bumping over ruts and stones of the springless vehicle churns and shakes the traveller inside into a bruised and dishevelled heap of humanity. Once experienced, this is never forgotten; and a dak gharry journey is decidedly not one of the pleasantest modes of progression for the wayfarer in the East.

Two of these useful vehicles appeared at our hotel at an early hour on the morning of our departure, and being rapidly loaded with our lighter effects, (the heavy baggage having been already sent on in bullock carts, under the care of the majority of our servants,) we, shortly after breakfast, made a start; the leading gharry containing our two selves with one servant on the roof, the second serving for the conveyance of our English attendant, under the charge of the faithful Esau. It was a cloudy but fine day, and after leaving the town and entering on the broad, level Gwalior road, the rapidity of our course created a cool and refreshing current of air, very agreeable to our feelings, as the weather was otherwise hot and close. The country one passes over in this journey is most uninteresting. For hours after leaving the city, nothing was to be seen but mile after mile of flat, broken here and there by small patches of cultivation, with a few poor mud huts of the ryots. With the exception of the road, which is kept in good repair, there was an untidiness and wildness about the scene, which, affording such a marked contrast to most of the parts we had visited under British rule, told its own tale—that our methodical government had nothing to do with the administration of the province. And such is the case, for the first half of the journey passes through the native state of Dholepur, the latter half being under the Gwalior Raj. About three o'clock we arrived at the town of Dholepur, the capital and residence of the Rajah. It is a small, straggling place, containing no buildings of interest or importance, with the exception of an old stone fortress perched on a precipitous rock overhanging the river Chumbul; a place of note in its day, when the ancestors of the existing dynasty were not, as at present, petty chiefs, but warlike sovereigns, ruling over a great extent of country, including Gwalior and adjacent parts. Here we halted for dinner, and for that purpose proceeded to the rest-house, or 'dak bungalow,' as it is usually termed, which is one of the institutions of the country. These shelters have been erected by a paternal government, at intervals of ten or fifteen miles along the direct roads to or from every place of importance in India, for the accommodation of the traveller, who is charged a small sum for the use of one of the four rooms into which these buildings are divided; and which are usually furnished, that is if the presence of a dilapidated 'charpoy,' or wooden bedstead, and a couple of broken chairs, are sufficient excuse for that term to be applied. An elderly man is generally found in charge, who supplements his meagre allowance from the government by supplying and cooking articles of food, a small stock of which he keeps in store for the benefit of those wayfarers who come unprovided. The worthy custodian, on being asked if he can supply a dinner, invariably states that he has every delicacy the sahib would like to order, but this raises no hopes of recherché fare in the mind of the experienced traveller, for he knows only too well that these grand promises dwindle down at last to the offer of an attenuated 'moorghie,' or fowl, which can be either grilled or curried, plenty of rice being always at hand. As there is no choice this offer is closed with, and soon the listless demeanour of the ancient guardian vanishes, and the compound becomes the scene of ustle and activity. One of the wretched-looking fowls pecking about, regardless of their doom, has to be caught, a process usually performed by one being singled out, and chased round and round until run down and secured by the members of the family of the presiding genius, who, as his aged limbs do not allow him to enter into the chase, stands in the centre of the courtyard bawling out directions to the smaller fry, and brandishing in a manner fearful to behold a large knife, with which he decapitates the feathered victim when once secured. The united energies of the family are then brought to bear on its conversion into an article of diet, and such is the celerity of their movements that within twenty minutes of the order being given it smokes upon the board, usually in the form of a spatch-cock. This dish, from the quickness of its preparation, is universally termed in India 'sudden death,' by which name it is familiar to all whose destiny has led them to be under the necessity of relying on the resources of an Indian dak bungalow.

We partook of this delicacy, in addition to the cold viands we were provided with, and as might be expected found it, owing most probably to its preparation so soon after decease, as tough as shoe leather. Shortly after dinner we pursued our way, and after leaving the bungalow and passing down a steep defile, arrived at the river Chumbul. We crossed by means of a couple of large flat-bottomed boats, which transported the carriages and horses and their contents bodily to the opposite shore, where a steep sandy incline brought us again on to the hard high road. It was by this time getting dark, and as we were now in the state of Gwalior, where life and property are not regarded in the same manner as in the British protected parts, I gave orders for the two gharrys to keep close together, and loaded and placed my revolver ready to hand. Cases of dacoity or highway robbery are common in these parts, and it is often unsafe to travel without an escort of soldiers, provided by the respective Rajahs through whose territory the road passes. Moreover, I had a lively personal recollection of an escape experienced some few years before from assassination and plunder, at the hands of a band of these worthies, on the banks of the river we had just crossed. No such incident however occurred to arrest our journey, and we all safely arrived at the city of Gwalior between two and three in the morning of the 15th July, and were quickly housed in the dak bungalow at that place, close under the shadow of the frowning and precipitous rock on which stands the well-known fortress.

The following morning I proceeded to Morar, the cantonment of Gwalior, where the general and other heads of departments reside, and there I learned that I was required for the fortress, to take over medical charge of the artillery in the garrison, in order to allow a confrère to proceed to the hills on sick leave. Such being the case, on my return to the bungalow we decided to visit our prospective residence at once, and see for ourselves what manner of place it was, for rumour had already informed me that it was much altered as regarded its buildings, from the time when, in former days, I had been stationed within its walls with my regiment, the 103rd Royal Bombay Fusiliers, to which distinguished corps I had then the honour of belonging. On leaving the dak bungalow, we drove through part of the old native city of Gwalior (which reaches up to the base of the fort) to the principal gateway, where it was necessary to leave the carriage and follow a steep zigzag path over half a mile in length to the summit. This road is wide enough to allow of riding up or down on horseback, but the usual mode of conveyance is by 'dhoolie' or palanquin, supplies of which, with the necessary bearers in attendance, are kept just within the gateway.

The Fortress of Gwalior.

After arriving at the summit, another quarter of a mile brought us to the blocks of buildings erected as officers' quarters; and, making all necessary arrangements with the officer whom I was to relieve, we chose a set of rooms, into which we moved the following day. Our new abode consisted of two large rooms, opening into one another, with a smaller room at the end, all being on the ground-floor of a large double-storied barrack building, affording accommodation to four families, and built of stone, raised a few feet from the surface of the earth, with a wide covered verandah in front. A rent of forty rupees per mensem was duly charged each officer by the government, at whose expense these buildings were erected. Our quarters soon became habitable and comfortable; for our furniture and effects had preceded our arrival, and any article wanted to replace what we had disposed of on leaving Faizabad being obtainable in the bazaar at Morar, a few days sufficed to put our house in order, and enabled us to repeat the process of calling on and being called upon by the residents of the fortress and the station of Morar, in the manner described in a former chapter.

The fortress of Gwalior, in which we were now located, is one of those hill forts peculiar to India, and in size and importance may be said to have pre-eminence of all others. It is a lofty, isolated, precipitous rock, rising out of the plain, which is a dry sandy waste for miles around with little or no vegetation, to a height of between three and four hundred feet. In length it is about one mile and a quarter, with a breadth of a quarter of a mile at its widest part. The rock is nearly all sandstone, differently coloured, apparently by varying quantities of iron. The surface soil is scanty; but there are a few trees on the summit, some of which are of great antiquity, and numerous artificial tanks, carefully excavated in former days, serve for the storage and supply of water. The entire rock is fortified, and in a manner showing the antiquity of Gwalior, for the style of the fortifications belongs to India's earliest history. The only approach to the summit is by the steep zigzag path already mentioned, which is enfiladed at every turn, and passes in addition through several very strong gates; or by a smaller entrance on the west, similar to the former, but on a much lesser scale. Immediately below the rock is the old town of Gwalior, and its more modern part, termed the 'Lushkur,' where the Maharajah Scindia, the ruler of the Gwalior state, has his palace, surrounded by the residences of the nobles of his court, as well as the lines of his numerous soldiery. The fortress virtually belongs to the Maharajah, and his flag, a twining green serpent on a plain ochre ground, floats on the summit; but since the year 1857 the garrison has been formed entirely of Europeans, our government holding it as a guarantee of good faith on the part of the Gwalior Raj. It constitutes, in connection with the cantonment of Morar, where a large British force is assembled, a strategical position of great importance for a wide extent of country, since in the event of hostilities there is always the fort to fall back upon—a position, if defended by British troops, entirely impregnable, and from which the town, the stronghold of the Mahratta power, could be laid in ruins in the course of a few hours.

The garrison usually stationed in the fortress, consists of a wing of European infantry, and a battery of artillery, with a

History of Gwalior.

company or two of native troops. The barracks for the soldiers are situated at one extremity of the rock, and are of the modern double-storied type; while the officers' quarters, not far distant, are commodious and good of their kind. The climate upon the summit is similar to that enjoyed by the dwellers in the plain below. If there is any difference, it is a trifle hotter, which may be accounted for by the fact that one is living on an exposed solid rock, which, becoming heated by the force of the sun's rays during the daytime in the hot weather, never cools down until the advent of the rains. During the rainy season, however, the fort possesses a decided advantage, on account of its height, there being usually, at that close season of the year, a more or less constant breeze to be found on its summit, which is much appreciated, and undoubtedly renders it more salubrious. Despite its proximity to a large native city it is a healthy place, and contrasts very favourably in this respect with the cantonment of Morar.

So far as ascertained, there is no trustworthy account of the early history of this remarkable and antique fortress. Rajahs of Gwalior are mentioned in 1008, and it is on record that the fort, then long existing, was first taken from the Hindus by the Mohammedans in 1197, after a long and tedious siege. The Hindus must however have soon regained possession of the place; for it is stated that an emperor of Delhi reconquered it about forty years later. We find it in 1519 in the possession of the ruling power at Delhi, and at later dates it was constantly, according to the ascendancy of the various chiefs at that troubled time, being taken and retaken. Notwithstanding its reputation for impregnability, it therefore frequently changed masters. After the dismemberment of the Mogul empire, Gwalior came into the possession of the Rana of Gohud, from whom it was wrested by the Mahrattas in 1780, only to be a short time after successfully carried by our troops under Major Popham and restored to the Rana. This chieftain, failing in his engagements with the East India Company, was abandoned to the resentment of his former foes, who again, under Modhaji Scindia, regained possession of the coveted rock. And finally, by treaty in 1805, the fort with all the Gwalior territory was secured to Dowlat-sav-Scindia, on whose successor's behalf the fortress is at present held in trust by the British government.

The cantonment of Morar is distant four miles from the fortress, in a straight line from its principal gateway. It is a small compact station of the usual type, with the exception that the civil element is entirely wanting; for it is a purely military camp, and only soldiers and their followers, together with native tradesmen for the purpose of supply, reside within its limits. Situated in a native territory, with whose administration we have no concern, no civilian residents are of course required. It is occupied by a large garrison, and is the headquarters for a brigade, with a general and the necessary staff. The barracks are similar to those usually found in India, and with the exception of a few bungalows and double-storied ranges of quarters for the officers, it contains no other buildings save a small native bazaar. It is a comparatively healthy station, but is apt to be visited by severe epidemics of cholera, though happily these are not so frequent nor of so severe a type as formerly, a fact probably due to increased sanitation in the neighbouring city of Gwalior.

The English Force in India.

Although Morar is dull and isolated, and not looked upon as a pleasant station by either officers or men, it is a most important military post, and the garrison an unusually strong one for so small a place. This is necessary in order to command the capital of the rapidly increasing Mahratta power, as well as a great portion of the country known as Central India. The force consists of five batteries of artillery, and one entire regiment of European infantry, besides those stationed in the fortress; and there are in addition two regiments of native infantry, as well as one regiment of native cavalry.

This is a large body of men for one station, when we consider that the entire strength of the whole army in India barely amounts to a total of one hundred and ninety-four thousand men, of which the European is to the native force in the proportion of rather less than one half. For the performance of police duties and frontier service this military force is supplemented by a body of native police, all trained to arms, amounting to about one hundred and ninety thousand men, who are officered mainly by Europeans. The men composing the different native regiments are drawn from various parts of the country; and in the Bengal Presidency the Sepoys are not, as was the case before the Mutiny, divided into corps of natives chiefly from one part of the country, and all of one caste, with in many cases whole families of friends or relations serving together. We have now rather what may be termed mixed regiments, in which men of different castes, whose homes are widely distant from each other, are to be found standing side by side in the same ranks. Again, the greater portion of the Bengal regiments, especially the cavalry, are formed of men professing the Mohammedan religion; while others again are composed of Sikhs and Punjabis, men warlike in their nature, and who stood gallantly by us in the days of the Mutiny. These regiments, largely increased in number since those days, are a check on the remaining portion of the army, whom they hate and despise, differing from them in religion, caste, and feeling. And in addition to this fact, if we take into consideration the improbability of a coalition amongst the various foreign units of the mixed regiments, another Sepoy Mutiny seems not only improbable, but almost impossible. However, granting its possibility, yet if such an outbreak again occurred it would never assume such proportions as in 1857; for the European force always in India is as strong now as it was at that time lamentably weak, with all the artillery in its hands, as none but English gunners are allowed to become acquainted with the duties of the ordnance branch of the service. The stations, too, are not isolated now, but connected by railroad and telegraph; the ordinary natives are docile and contented under our rule, and would render no assistance. There is no prince or chief like the family of Delhi to inflame the passions of the people by references to their former greatness and power. And lastly, although nothing is ever certain, and a revolt of the whole or a portion of the native army might take place if England were at war with any other nation, and another power, such as Russia, our hereditary opponent in the East, should sow the seeds of rebellion, and by promises of help induce a now contented and happy body of loyal soldiers to rise and break their oath, yet I think that even then a revolt would not occur, unless the foreign power were near enough to the frontier of our possessions to be enabled to fulfil her specious promises. Indeed, in that case, even though the flame of rebellion were again to sully the name of the native army it would be but a half-hearted affair; for the memory of the retribution that followed on the attempt of their predecessors is still fresh in their minds. They fear the British power, and would distrust any others; for they have had no experience of their prowess either as friends or foes, while the valour and endurance of the former are well known. Never, as long as the empire of India lasts, will the present or future generations of its inhabitants forget that after conquering the country by dint of years of hard fighting, the Angrezi were not only able to retain what they had won, but possessed the power, although few in number as compared with their foes, to crush the first organized resistance to their rule with swift and merciless severity.

CHAPTER XIII.

The Independent Natives—States of India—Their tenure of power—Their classification—The Hill Tribes—The Sikh States—The Sovereignties of Rajputana—Their history—The Rajputs—Their feudal system—The State of Marwar—The Rana of Oudípur—The State of Jaipur—Jaipur—Bhurtpur—Its history—The Central India States—The Mahrattas—Sevaji—Their rise and fall—The Peishwa—State of Gwalior—The Maharajah Scindia—His family—State of Indore—Holkar—The Begum of Bhopal—Guzerat States—The Guicowar of Baroda—The Chiefs of Kutch and Kattywar—The Haidarabad State—The Nizam—His history—State of Mysore—Its ruler—Tippoo Sahib—His actions—The Malayalam States—Travancore—Cochin—Concluding remarks.

THE fortress of Gwalior, our present home, being situated within native territory, of which no mention has yet been made, I purpose, before proceeding further with our life upon the rock, to touch slightly upon the subject of the independent states of India and their rulers. It would not be possible to describe the whole of them within the limits of this volume, for there are an endless number in existence, the majority mere petty chieftainships, unknown to and unheard of by the ordinary visitor, and possessing no interest to any one, save to officials of that department of the government whose especial duty is to act the part of Mentor to the quasi-independent sovereignties scattered over the whole of the peninsula. I will therefore confine my remarks to a general sketch of the subject, and a fuller description of the few larger and more important states, the names of which and of their rulers will be familiar to the reader, as they often appear prominently before the public, and have lately become much better known to the outside world through the visit of the Prince of Wales to India, and the subsequent proclamation of his royal mother as empress at Delhi, the ancient capital of the Grand Moguls.

The native states of India cover an area of nearly six hundred thousand square miles, and contain a population of about fifty-five millions, while their united military forces are estimated at more than three hundred thousand men. The gross revenue of the chiefs is about sixteen millions sterling, and an annual tribute is paid by them collectively to the British government of nearly a million. As before remarked, they are, with the exception of Nepaul and Bhootan, more or less dependant, and have relinquished political relations with each other or with any but the paramount British power. Some have treaties offensive and defensive, and the right to claim protection external and internal from the British Indian government, which on its part has a right to interfere in their concerns. Others again have the same right to protection, but the management of their affairs is left to themselves; while others still are mere tributaries. The British government is however well informed as to all that transpires in these native states through the agency of officers styled Political Residents, one of whom resides at each of the various courts, and is empowered to advise the several rulers on any matter of importance, as to the line of conduct which would be most favourably received by the protecting power.

As would be expected, the states vary greatly in size and importance. Haidarabad, for instance, is as large as the kingdom of Italy, and the Nizam enjoys an enormous revenue;

whereas, on the other hand, in Kattywar and elsewhere, where family custom has led to minute subdivision, there are many chiefs of a single village; and between these two extremes there are states of every grade. Although, therefore, the number of native states in India, large and small, amounts to several hundreds, only a few are of any great importance. The whole, including petty chieftainships and aboriginal tribes of which little is known, may be classed under twelve heads.

1. The Indo-Chinese group of states, and the numerous Hill tribes of the North-East frontier.

2. The aboriginal Gond and Kole tribes in Chota, Nagpur, Orissa, and the Central Provinces.

3. The Himalayan hill states west of Nepaul, including Kashmir.

4. The numerous Afghan and Beluch tribes of the North-West frontier, inhabiting the mountains from the north of Peshawur to the base of the Suleiman range.

5. The Sikh states in the Sirhind plain, south of the Sutlej.

6. The three Mohammedan states of Khairpur in Sinde, Bhawalpur to the north-east, and Rampur.

7. The ancient sovereignties of Rajputana, lying to the south of the Punjab, and between Sinde and the North-West Provinces.

8. The states of Central India, lying to the north of the Nerbudda, and to the south and east of Rajputana.

9. Guzerat and the numerous petty chiefships of Kutch and Kattywar.

10. The southern Mahratta states.

11. Haidarabad.

The Province of Sinde.

12. The Malayalam states of Travancore and Cochin, lying together in the far south.

On the first four classes, consisting of the aboriginal tribes, and the wild inhabitants of the hills on our frontier, it will not be necessary to dwell. The knowledge we possess of them is as yet most imperfect, and most of them would be unknown or uncared for, were it not for the endless trouble they occasion on our border, by their predatory incursions into parts under our protection.

The Sikh states in the Sirhind, the remnants of that once powerful nation, are of little importance; and as the rise and progress of that important sect will be treated of hereafter, when we arrive at their natural home, the Punjab, we will pass them by. With the exception of Patiala, they are little heard of. The same applies to the states in Sinde. This latter country is now an extensive province of British India, and from the time of the defeat of the Ameers of Sinde, by Sir C. Napier, at Meanee, in 1843, has rapidly improved under its present administration. It is a large tract, uninteresting to the traveller, about three hundred and eighty miles in length by two hundred and eighty in breadth; bounded on the north by Beluchistan and the Punjab; east by Rajputana; west by Beluchistan; and south by the Arabian Sea and the Great Western Run, which separates Sinde from Cutch, which is also a small independent state. The province of Sinde is traversed throughout its whole length by the river Indus, and its chief town is Haiderabad, while next in importance is that well-known seaport, Kurrachee, the best point of departure for visitors to the country, as it is easily reached by steamer from Bombay. Another route for those in the north is down the Indus from Attock; but there is little to repay one the trouble of the journey. Great part of the province is a sandy desert, and the climate particularly sultry and dry; for being completely beyond the action of the south-west monsoon, the fall of rain during the year is inconsiderable. The population is a mixed one, consisting of Jats and Beluchis, with some few Afghans. The greater part are Mohammedans, and the remainder, who profess Hinduism, have fallen far from the strictness of observance which characterises most of its followers.

The next in order, the sovereignties of Rajputana, are very interesting, for they are undoubtedly the most ancient dynasties in India. In early days they were its most powerful monarchs, and their sway extended far and wide; for we find that at the time of the invasion of Mahmoud of Ghuzni the four great kingdoms then existing—namely, Delhi, Canouj, Mewar, and Anhulvarra, were all under the dominion of Rajput families. At all periods, indeed, the Rajputs seem to have played a conspicuous part in the history of India, and all over Hindustan there are at the present day many families who rightly or wrongly bear that name. It is a title full of honour, derived from the Sanskrit 'rajan,' king, and 'putra,' son; hence literally 'sons of kings.' The bearers of the title are naturally very proud of it, as they claim with very good reason to be descended either from the ancient royal races of India or from the Kshatriya, or warrior caste. The Rajputs have always borne the reputation of being a proud and warlike race. They offered the most obstinate resistance to the Mohammedan invaders, and were not finally conquered until the year 1527, after successfully resisting the intruders for more than

Rajputana.

five hundred years, by Sultan Baber, at the great battle of Sikri, near Agra. After that time, although they often appear on the troubled page of India's history, they were not so important a factor as before, and, shorn of most of their former extensive dominions, they withdrew to the part of the country called Rajputana, which they now occupy, and which was originally the home of their race. This province is a comparatively fertile spot, and is bounded on the north by the Punjab; east by Sinde; west by the North-West Provinces; and on the south by the dominions of Scindia and Holkar. It measures some four hundred and sixty miles from north to south; and five hundred and thirty miles in breadth; and supports a population of about eight millions. It is divided into eighteen principalities and numerous lesser chiefships, the result of the old custom prevalent among the Rajputs, which carried the principle of alienation of property to a great extent, and led to a system which it is impossible not to call feudal. With them the founder of a state, after reserving a demesne for himself, divided the rest of the country among his relations, according to the Hindu law of partition. The chief to whom each share was assigned, owed military service and general obedience to the prince, but exercised unlimited authority within his own lands. He in his turn divided his lands on similar terms among his relations, and a chain of vassal chiefs was thus established, to whom the civil government as well as the military force of the country was committed. This rule of partition was adhered to after their conquest, each chief being obliged to provide an appanage for the younger members of his father's family, and consequently Rajputana continues a land of sovereigns and nobles.

There is every reason to believe that the long-protracted opposition shown by the Rajputs to the Mohammedan invaders was chiefly owing to this peculiar system, joined to their situation as the military class in the original Hindu social scale; for the other classes in the country, though kept together as castes, were mixed up in civil society under no particular chiefs; whereas the Rajputs were born soldiers, each division having its hereditary leader, and formed clans, the members of which were bound by many ties to their chiefs, and to each other. Being also the strictest followers of the Hindu religion, the rules of caste rendered the connection still more powerful. As the chiefs of those clans stood in the same relation to the rajah that their own retainers did to them, the king, nobility, and soldiery, all made one body, united by the strongest feelings of kindred and military devotion. Their enthusiasm was also kept up by the songs of their bards, and inflamed by frequent contests for glory or for love. They treated women with a respect unusual in the East, and were guided, even towards their enemies, by rules of honour, which it was disgraceful to violate. If to these qualities we add a very strong disposition to indolence, and make allowances for the effects of a long period of depression, we have the character of the Rajputs of the present day, who bear the same resemblance to their ancestors as those did to the warriors of the earliest Indian period.

Of the chief principalities Marwar is the largest; but the most important are Oudipur and Jaipur. The Maharajah of Jodhpur is the ruler over the province of Marwar, which is in extent about 35,672 square miles, and contains a population of two millions. This potentate, also known as the Maharajah of Marwar, is of very old descent; for his family, the Rahtors, were the ancient kings of Canouj at the time of the Mohammedan invasion. After the conquest part of the family remained on the Ganges, and occasionally revolted against the Mussulmans, until they became reconciled to the yoke. But another portion, under the two grandsons of the last king, preferred their liberty; and retiring to the country between the table land and the Indus, they soon formed an extensive and powerful principality, the remains of which they enjoy at this day.

The family and tribe of the Rana of Oudipur, who rules over a state of twelve thousand square miles, with a population of little over a million, were first called Ghelot, and subsequently Sesodia, and are said to be of such great antiquity that they claim descent from Rama, the Hindu prince and god. This claim is usually conceded to them; and as Rama flourished, according to all accounts, centuries before the Christian era, we find in the reigning sovereign of this family a prince through whose veins run the bluest blood in the world; for it is a question whether any contemporary ruler, either in the East or West, would care to compare pedigrees with one who is said to be able to trace his descent from a line of ancestors whose deeds extend over a period of more than two thousand years. The present Maharana is able and intelligent, but intensely proud of his royal descent. Both he and his subjects are highly conservative in their notions, and the visitor to his capital or dominions will be better able than in any other part of the country, to acquire information by actual experience of the manners and customs of the native Hindus, before their contact with the Western invaders. In no other place in India have foreign ideas made less progress, for the people adhere to the mode of life handed down to them by their ancestors; and even at the present day, a visit to this ancient principality would almost carry one back to the state of society that existed among the Hindu nation at the time when the Institutes of Menu were composed.

The Rajahs of Amber or Jaipur have in modern times stood on an equality with the Maharana of Oudipur and the Rajah of Jodhpur, but their rise into distinction is since the accession of Akber. They were ancient feudatories of Ajmere, once the capital of the reigning sovereign of the principality of Rajputana, before its division into smaller states, and probably remained in submission to the Mohammedans after the conquest of that kingdom. They may have increased in consequence during the weakness of the neighbouring governments in the fifteenth century, for they must have been held in consideration when Akber married the Rajah's daughter, with the object of drawing closer the ties between the conquerors and the conquered. The present Maharajah rules over a province of about 15,250 square miles, supporting a population of nearly two millions, and he is an enlightened prince, prone to European ideas, and not so conservative as his fellow-sovereigns. The capital town, Jaipur, is well worthy of a visit, and easily reached from Agra by the Rajputana State Railway, which is two hundred and forty miles to Ajmere. This is distant about eighty miles from Jaipur, and the traveller once arrived there, or at the terminus, can easily make his way over the whole province, which contains much that is interesting, and affords a sight of the condition of native towns in all their integrity.

While on the subject of Rajputana, the native state of Bhurtpur may be mentioned. It is situated just within that province, although the majority of the people are of the same tribe as the bulk of the Sikhs, the famous Jat race of which so much has been said and so little verified. They have now become, in language and religion, almost identical with the Rajputs, and have lost all traces of their supposed Central Asian origin. The ruling family indeed lays claim to Rajput descent; but be this as it may, it first emerges into historical light in the person of Chooraman, a robber chief, who became powerful about the year 1720. The grand-nephew of this personage, the well-known Sooruj Mull, already mentioned in connection with various events in the history of the fort at Agra, founded the city of Bhurtpur, and ruled there about the middle of the last century. From that time till the dissolution of the Mogul empire, Sooruj Mull and his descendants continued in quasi-independence until brought into contact with the British in 1803, when the state was somewhat reduced in power and resources. Bhurtpur, which is now under British protection, is 1,974 square miles in extent, with a population of seven hundred and forty-five thousand. The capital, thirty-seven miles from Agra, is a prosperous city of sixty thousand inhabitants. It is surrounded by a mud wall, and a large ditch, now nearly dried up, with a fort at the north-east extremity, and is memorable for having for more than six weeks held at bay Lord Lake, the conqueror of Hindustan. There is a fine palace within the town, which also contains some handsome

Hindu temples, and from its proximity to Agra may be easily visited.

The next group, the states of Central India, although one-third less in extent than Rajputana, are split up into nearly four times as many provinces. Many are so small as scarcely to deserve notice, but there are two large and important sovereignties, namely, Gwalior (Maharajah Scindia) and Indore (Maharajah Holkar), which ought to be considered more fully, since between them they own more than one-half the entire area. Lastly we have Bhopal, a small and insignificant state, but which deserves notice from the fact that, for three generations, it has been under female rule, and is remarkable for its excellent administration.

The rulers of these states, as well as the greater part of their subjects, are Mahrattas, a race which have played in their time an important part in the history of India, and once appeared likely to make themselves masters of Hindustan. The wave of their onward progress was however broken by the might of English arms; the formidable confederation was destroyed, and the virtual head being removed into honourable captivity, the lesser chiefs, who even then acted independently of their so-called sovereign master, the Peishwa, withdrew to the several provinces of which they had previously made themselves the masters, and have, under the protection of the British government, increased in wealth and wisdom. Few if any of the native states of India are better managed than the principalities of Central India, and no firmer allies do we possess in the country than the sovereigns and chiefs of the Gwalior and Indore Raj.

The early Mohammedan writers do not seem to have been

The Mahrattas.

aware of the existence of the Mahrattas. We can perceive by the surnames of some chiefs whom they mention that they must have belonged to that race; but the word Mahratta first occurs in Ferishta, under the year 1485, and is not then applied in a general sense. It has been observed that in the middle of the sixteenth century the King of Bijapur adopted the Mahratta language, and enlisted a considerable number of the inhabitants of the Deccan into his army. Still they are seldom mentioned until the beginning of the seventeenth century, when they emerge into notice, and thenceforth occupy a conspicuous part in the history of the empire. They are a people of Hindu race, supposed by many to be the descendants of a Persian or North Indian people, who had been driven southward by the Mongols, and who took possession of Central India, south of the Ganges, from Gwalior to Goa, and of a portion of the Deccan. In their early days there must have been little noteworthy about them; for if they had been for any time under one great monarchy we should have heard of them, as of the other Deccan states, and, like the others so circumstanced, they would probably have had a peculiar literature and civilization of their own. They are still remarkably deficient both in native authors and in refinement; and what polish they have seems borrowed from the Mussulmans rather than formed by Hindus. In character the Mahrattas are vigorous and active, small and sturdy, well made, though not handsome, laborious, hardy, and persevering. If they have none of the pride and dignity of the Rajputs, they have none of their indolence or want of worldly wisdom. A Rajput warrior, so long as he does not dishonour his race, seems almost indifferent to the result of any contest he is engaged in. A Mahratta thinks of nothing but the result, and cares little for the means if his object can be attained. For this purpose he will strain his wits, renounce his pleasures, and hazard his person; but he has no conception of sacrificing his life, or even his interest, for a point of honour. This difference of sentiment affects the outward appearance of the two nations—there is something noble in the carriage even of an ordinary Rajput, and something vulgar in that of the most distinguished Mahratta. The Rajput is the most worthy antagonist, the Mahratta the most formidable enemy; for he will not fail in boldness and enterprise where they are indispensable, and will always support them or supply their place by stratagem, activity, and perseverance. All this applies chiefly to the soldiery; for the mere husbandmen are sober, frugal, and industrious, and though they have a dash of the national cunning, are neither turbulent nor insincere. There is one notable peculiarity in their religion—although devout worshippers of Brahma, yet, unlike other Hindus, no distinctions of caste exist among them.

The founder of the Mahratta power was Sivaji, a free-booter, or adventurer, whose father was an officer in the service of the last king of Bijapur. By policy or force he, about the year 1645, succeeded in compelling the several independent chiefs to acknowledge him as their leader, and with the large army then at his command, composed chiefly of cavalry, the Mahrattas having always been famous horsemen, overran and subdued a large portion of the Emperor of Delhi's territory. He pursued a successful career of warfare and plunder for many years, and at his death, in 1680, left the Mahrattas combined together into a powerful nation, with an immense army of born soldiers to support its authority. And although Sivaji was originally only the son of a powerful chief, and began life as a daring and artful captain of banditti, he ripened into a skilful general and an able statesman, and left a character which has never since been equalled or approached by any of his countrymen. It was his genius that kindled a zeal for religion, with a hatred for the followers of Mohammed, and thus roused a national spirit among the Mahrattas; and it was by these feelings that the government he founded was upheld after it passed into feeble hands, and was kept together, in spite of numerous internal disorders, until it had established its supremacy over the greater part of India. He was succeeded by his son Sambaji, who vigorously followed out his father's policy at first, but afterwards spent his whole time in idleness and debauchery, in which he soon dissipated the vast treasures his father had left. The troops, kept in arrears, appropriated the plunder taken on expeditions to their own use, and degenerated from the comparatively regular bands of Sivaji into the hordes of rapacious and destructive freebooters, which they have ever since remained. In the end Sambaji was defeated by the Mogul Emperor Aurungzebe, and put to death in a most barbarous manner. Although his person had been despised by the Mahrattas, his fate was pitied and resented, and the indignation and religious hatred of the nation raised to a higher pitch than ever, for it was said that his life would have been spared if he had consented to embrace the Moslem faith.

The incapacity of the rulers that succeeded him tempted the two chief officers of state, the Peishwa, or prime minister, and the Paymaster-General, to divide the empire between them. This was effected in the year 1749, when Balaji, the first named, took up his residence at Poona, a town distant about a hundred and twenty miles from Bombay, and under the name of the Peishwa established a nominal supremacy over the whole Mahratta nation; while the other made Nagpur his capital, and founded the empire of the Berar Mahrattas. This paction, of course, required the sanction of the more important among the minor chiefs and officers of state, who gave their consent on condition of receiving a share of the spoil. The ultimate result was the partition of the Mahratta kingdom into a great number of states, more or less powerful, chief among which were, besides the two already mentioned, Gwalior, ruled by Rao Scindia; Indore, by the Rao Holkar; and Baroda, by the Guicowar. At first they held together, and employed their retainers under their nominal sovereign; for in the year 1759 we find the Mahratta power at its zenith, with an immense territory, and a large force of trained soldiers. But the usual intestinal wars soon supervened, and ultimately the East India Company was compelled to interfere. The invasion of the empire of Delhi by Nadir Shah afforded these wild and warlike men an opportunity, of which they eagerly availed themselves, to wrest additional territory from the feeble grasp of the Mogul Emperor. From this time they discharged the office of arbiters in the quarrels between the emperor, his vizier, and his rebellious subjects; but the frightful defeat they sustained, in January, 1761, at the hands of Ahmed Shah Abdalli, the ruler of Afghanistan, on the field of Paniput, where they lost fifty thousand men, and all their chiefs, except Holkar, weakened their power for a while. They continued, however, to be the hired mercenaries of the Delhi Emperor until the growing influence of the British compelled them to look to their own safety; and after many long and bloody contests with the British and their allies, in which sometimes the whole, but more frequently a portion of the Mahrattas joined, they were one by one, with the exception of Scindia, reduced to a state of dependence. Scindia having raised a powerful army, officered by Frenchmen, and disciplined after the European method, continued the contest for a number of years, till his power was finally broken in 1843. The dignity of the Peishwa was finally abolished in 1818, and his territories were occupied by the British, with the exception of a portion which was made over to another Mahratta chief, the Rajah of Sattara, their faithful ally. Nagpur and Sattara subsequently reverted to the British government; but many other chiefs still possess extensive dominions under our protection.

The most important of these chiefs is undoubtedly the Maharajah Scindia, the ruler over the Gwalior state, which is an irregularly shaped province, with an area of about thirty-three thousand one hundred and nineteen square miles, and a population of nearly three millions, and is the principal fragment of the former great empire of the Peishwa. Gwalior, the capital, is not an interesting city, and contains nothing remarkable except the huge rock fortress, now our home, from the eastern side of which we looked down upon the palace of Scindia, who usually resides here for the greater portion of the year. The family of Scindia, like that of most Mahratta feudal chiefs, was of humble origin. It is said, but I do not know with what truth, that the first known name belonging to it was that of Rayaji Scindia, 'slipper-holder' about the year 1725 to the Peishwa, who took a liking to him, and promoted him to high dignity. So rapid from that date was the rise of the family, that, like the other great feudatories of the empire, Rayaji Scindia soon possessed a territory of his own, in which he was so firmly established that the British even accepted the fact, for after a long career of warfare, in common with the rest of the chiefs, on his death, his natural son Madhaji was recognized as his successor, and as an independent sovereign.

When Madhaji Scindia succeeded to his father's possessions they consisted of half the province of Malwa. He joined the Mahratta confederation, and was present at the battle of Paniput, in 1761, where he was so desperately injured as to be left for dead, but speedily recovered, and, on the retirement of the Afghans and their allies, repossessed himself of his hereditary dominions. On the death of Mulhar Rao Holkar, he became the chief of the Mahratta princes, and had the command of the Peishwa's body-guard. In 1770 the Peishwa and his two powerful feudatories, Scindia and Holkar, aided the emperor of Delhi in expelling the Sikhs from his territories, the administration of which was handed over to Scindia, who was now by far the most powerful of the Mahratta chiefs. The murder of the young Peishwa by his uncle Ragoba, and the consequent expulsion of the murderer from the throne he had seized, brought Scindia for the first time into collision with the British, who had espoused Ragoba's cause; but in the war that followed fortune distributed her favours with impartiality, and by the treaty of Salbye, in 1782, he was recognised as a sovereign prince, and confirmed in all his possessions. In 1784 he captured Gwalior, and in the following year marched on Delhi to restore his preponderance in the councils of the puppet monarch, subsequently seizing Agra, Allyghur, and nearly the whole of the Doab. The manifold advantages of European discipline had struck him forcibly during the war with the British, and with the aid of an able French officer he intoduced it into his own dominions. An army of eighteen thousand regular and six thousand irregular infantry, two thousand irregular and six hundred Persian horse, with two hundred cannon, was accordingly raised, and under the leadership of De Boigne, the officer to whom I have alluded, reduced Jodhpur, Oudipur, and Jaipur, the three largest Rajput states, and effectually humbled the pride of Holkar.

On his death in 1794, Dowbit Rao Scindia succeeded, and continued his grand-uncle's policy. During the troubles which convulsed Holkar's dominions at the commencement of the present century, he ravaged Indore and Poona, but was wholly routed by Jeswunt Rao Holkar in 1802; and having joined Bhonsla, the Rajah of Berar, in a raid on the Nizam in the following year, he brought down upon himself the vengeance of the East India Company.

The confederated Mahrattas were routed at Assaye by Sir Arthur Wellesley; the disciplined troops of Scindia were scattered irretrievably by Lord Lake at Laswari, and he only escaped total ruin by acceding to a treaty, by which all his possessions in the Doab and along the right bank of the Jumna were ceded to the British. Gwalior was, however, restored in 1805, and from this time became the capital of the state. Having been taught by his reverses a useful lesson,

Scindia declined to join the Peishwa, Holkar, and Bhonsla in their attack on the British in 1817, and thus escaped the swift destruction which was visited upon his turbulent neighbours. Syadi Rao Scindia, the present Maharajah, succeeded; and he being a mere child at the time of his accession, the Gwalior dominions soon fell into such a state of anarchy that the British were compelled to insist upon certain guarantees for the preservation of tranquillity. On these being rejected, a war followed, and the Mahrattas were routed at Maharajpur on December 29th, 1843, by Lord Gough, and on the same day at Punniar by General Grey. Gwalior fell into the hands of the British, and Scindia submitted to the conditions demanded of him, besides maintaining a contingent force of Sepoys at Morar, near his capital. In 1853 he was declared of age; and on the outbreak of the Mutiny he took the field at the head of his own army against the Gwalior contingent, which had joined the rebels. Most of his troops, however, deserted him, and he narrowly escaped by fleeing to Agra. He was subsequently reinstated by Sir Hugh Rose, and received from the British Government numerous testimonials of its grateful respect for his faithfulness as an ally. These honours Scindia richly deserves; for had he in 1857 joined the Nana Sahib when he set up at Cawnpore as Peishwa of the revived Mahratta empire, he, in his character as the first Mahratta prince, would have drawn nearly all the nation to his standard, and the consequences for that part of India would have been frightful to contemplate. But his better sense prevailed; and although he made himself unpopular with his army and the greater portion of his subjects by the step he took, he earned the gratitude of the English nation, who from that day have always regarded the Maharajah Scindia as their firm friend, fully meriting the appointment of a general in the British army, with the title of 'Sword of the Empire in India,' lately conferred on him by our gracious sovereign, on the occasion of her proclamation as empress at Delhi.

In person the Maharajah is a fine man of the pure Mahratta type, very intelligent, and his mode of ruling his state leaves nothing to be desired. He is a clever tactician, and his chief amusement is the management of the large army he is permitted to maintain. He resides for the greater part of the year at Gwalior, where he has lately erected a fine new palace; and his intercourse with the English is marked by friendliness and sincerity, as was well shown in his courteous reception of the Prince of Wales at his capital. This so affected him, that he is stated to have said, on parting, to his future emperor, "It has been much to see your face. I can hardly hope to see you again; but sometimes in England turn a kind thought towards me. All I have is yours."

The next powerful Mahratta family is that of Holkar, the members of which have at various times been formidable enemies to the British empire in Hindustan. Their sway extends over the principality of Indore, which consists of several detached tracts, some of them lying very remote from each other, and one large province, that of Malwa, famous for its opium cultivation. It possesses an aggregate area of about eight thousand three hundred and eighteen square miles, and supports a population of eight hundred thousand.

The territory, as a whole, is traversed from east to west by the river Nerbudda, and also by the Vindhya mountains—the country peculiarly of the Bheels, one of the wildest and most savage of the aboriginal tribes of India. The town of Indore, the capital, is modern, having been founded in 1767, and contains no buildings of any importance. It is distant three hundred and eighty miles from Bombay, and the same distance from Agra, and can be reached by railway from either. About seventeen miles from Indore is the station of Mhow, a favourite cantonment for British troops in the Bombay Presidency, but which is purely a military post, and contains nothing remarkable within its limits. The founder of this Mahratta family was Mulhar Rao Holkar, who was born in the Deccan in 1693, and having gained by his valour the favour of the Peishwa, obtained from him the western half of Malwa, with Indore for his capital. In 1761 he joined the great league of the princes of Hindustan formed to bar the progress of Ahmed Shah, was present at the battle of Paniput, and was the only Mahratta chief of note who returned from that dreadful slaughter. He died in 1768, and was succeeded by his niece Aylah Baee. She resigned the military power to Toghagi Holkar, who in his turn was succeeded by his son Jeswunt Rao Holkar, an able and brave man, who fought for a long time against the British, with varying success, but was compelled to conclude peace, and died insane in 1811. His son, Mulhar Rao Holkar, a minor, nine years old, succeeded, and in 1817 declared war against the British. Being totally routed at Mahedpur, he sent offers of peace, which were accepted, and an English residency was established at Indore in January, 1818. He died in 1833, and two others of the family successively ruled after him. The last of these dying without heirs, the East India Company assumed the right of nominating Mulkerji Rao Holkar, the present Maharajah, who was educated under the auspices of the British government, and who has displayed great ability since he assumed the reins of government in 1852. On the breaking out of the Mutiny in 1857, he took the field in support of the British, but the refractory behaviour of his troops prevented his rendering any effective assistance.

The small independent state of Bhopal forms part of the province of Malwa, and is in extent about eight thousand two hundred square miles, with a population of seven hundred and sixty-nine thousand. The town of Bhopal is about five hundred miles from Bombay, not very far distant from Indore, and is an old city surrounded by a stone wall, with a fort, which is also the residence of the sovereign, situated on a huge rock just outside the town. As before stated, for three generations it has been under female rule, and is a perfect model of a native state. The present ruler is her highness Nawab Shah Jehan Begum, and the female line will still be continued, for the heiress apparent is her daughter, her highness Sultan Jehan Begum, an intelligent, well-educated Hindu.

Of the next division, Guzerat and the numerous petty chiefships of Kutch and Kattywar, the Guicowar of Baroda is the only important prince, and his territory, Guzerat, a geographical division of India, contains forty-two thousand square miles, with a population of nearly three millions. Baroda, the capital, is two hundred and thirty-one miles north of Bombay, from which town it is easily reached by railway, and is a large flourishing city containing about a hundred and forty thousand inhabitants. It is the residence of the Guicowar, whose family sprang into importance about the same time as the other chieftains of the Mahratta nation, for the first of the name that we hear of is Pilaji Geikwar, who was appointed to administer the province by the Peishwa in the year 1731. None of the family have distinguished themselves in any particular way, and their rule of late years has been marked by great incompetency; so much so that, a year or two since, the British government found it necessary to remove the reigning prince (who was also accused of attempting the murder by poison of the English Political Resident), and replace him by a younger member of the family, the present prince, a mere youth, who is being carefully educated by us to fulfil in course of time the duties of his high station.

The protected principality of Kutch is in the presidency of Bombay. It is a small tract, stretching along the gulf of its own name and the Indian Ocean, between Guzerat and Sinde, and covers an area of fifteen thousand three hundred and sixty-four square miles, with a population of rather more than half a million. The territory is poor and unproductive. The ruler, styled the Rao, has under him a great number of feudatory chieftains, amounting, it is said, to as many as two hundred.

Kattywar, or Katiwar, is a term applied to a collection of districts forming part of the province of Guzerat, which collectively cover an area of twenty thousand square miles, with a population of a million and a half. Politically the country is divided among more than two hundred chiefs, some of them paying tribute to the Guicowar, and the rest to the British government, but all of them being under the protection of the latter.

Haidarabad.

We now come to the Haidarabad state, whose ruler is termed the Nizam, and whose dominions form an extensive portion of the Madras Presidency—a part of India of which but little mention has yet been made, the states already described being chiefly in Bombay and Bengal. The Nizam's dominions are extensive, comprising the part of the Deccan in the interior of Southern India, covering ninety-five thousand square miles, with a population estimated at ten millions. It is the only large independent state left, of all those that were founded by Mohammedan adventurers on the dissolution of the Mogul empire. This territory originally formed part of the kingdom of the ancient kings of Golconda, and it was by Ibrahim, the last but one of that line, that the city of Haidarabad, the present capital, was built, about the middle of the sixteenth century. This dynasty being overthrown in 1687 by Aurungzebe, the country became a province of the Mogul empire, and was ruled by an official of that court, under the title of the Viceroy of the Deccan. In this condition it remained until the year 1719, when the growing feebleness of the Delhi Raj allowed the governor, Azof Jah, to declare himself an independent sovereign, under the title of the 'Nizam-ul-Mulk,' or 'Regulator of the State.' After his death, in 1748, two claimants appeared for the throne, his son Nazir Jung, and his grandson Mirzapha Jung. A long period of strife and anarchy followed, and in the end Nizam Ali obtained the supreme power, and after some vacillation signed a treaty of alliance with the English. He aided them against Tippoo, Sultan of Mysore; and at the termination of that war, in 1799, a new treaty was formed, by which, in return for certain territorial concessions, the East India Company bound itself to maintain a subsidiary force for the defence of the Nizam's dominions. This contingent is still kept up, supplemented by a force of British soldiers at the cantonment of Secunderabad, a station not far distant from the capital. During the Mutiny the ruler of the state, Afzul-ul-Dowlah, remained faithful to the British. The royal line is still extant in the person of the present Nizam, a minor; and the management of this large state, with its turbulent Mohammedan population, has since his accession been most satisfactorily carried out by the prime minister, the well-known Sir Salar Jung, who is probably the most enlightened and talented man of the day among the natives of Hindustan.

Another large native state in the Madras Presidency, at present under the sovereignty of a Hindu prince, is that of Mysore, which lies in Southern India, not far distant from the Haidarabad state, and whose chief town, Mysore, is distant two hundred and forty-five miles from Madras. This principality covers an area of twenty-seven thousand square miles, has a population of about four millions, and contains the well-known town of Seringapatam and the pleasant station of Bangalore. The province consisting chiefly of an extensive table-land, with an average elevation of two thousand feet, the climate is for the greater portion of the year cool and healthy.

The state of Mysore was originally a Mahratta principality, but the reigning sovereign was in the year 1759 dispossessed by Hyder Ali, a Mohammedan noble, and son of the general of the Sultan's forces. He conquered several of the neighbouring states, and being in every way a most able man, soon found himself the ruler of an immense territory. He waged two wars against the British, and several against the Mahrattas, was successful in retaining his position, and died in 1782, much beloved and regretted by his people; for he was remarkable among Asiatic princes for the mildness of his character and government. His son and successor was the well-known Tippoo Sahib, who was born in 1749, and at an early age showed his predilection for the profession of arms, in which during the greater part of his life he was engaged. His government was most oppressive, and he had little time to spare for internal administration; for during his reign he was continually engaged in various contests with the British power, towards which he ever displayed an inveterate hatred. He fought with varying success against our arms; but in the year 1792, meeting with signal disaster, he was ultimately compelled to resign one half of his dominions, to pay a large indemnity, and give his two sons as hostages for his fidelity. Nevertheless his secret intrigues in India against the British were almost immediately resumed. Hostilities recommenced in 1799, and, driven from the open field and attacked in his capital of Seringapatam, he fell after an obstinate resistance, and was buried by the side of his father. Thus Mysore came under the protection of the dominant power. The Hindu dynasty displaced by Hyder Ali was restored, and still continues, represented at the present time by a young prince, who is being carefully trained under the auspices of our government in a manner befitting his rank and future position as native ruler over a large territory.

The last on our list of states, the Malayalam states of Travancore and Cochin, are comparatively unimportant, and may be dismissed in a few words. Both lie in the extreme south of India; and Travancore covers an area of four thousand seven hundred and twenty-two square miles, with a population of a million; while Cochin, equally a protected state, under the presidency of Madras, is still smaller, covering an area only of one thousand nine hundred and eighty-eight square miles, and supporting a population of a quarter of a million. This population is peculiar in its composition; for although the mass are Hindus and Mohammedans, there are also a large number of Christians and Jews, the former of which are divided between the Syrian and Romish churches, and trace their origin to the early conquest of this part of the sea-coast by the Portuguese.

For a fuller description of the native states of India, I must refer my readers to other works, as the space I can devote to them is now exhausted. The subject is very interesting, alike to the casual traveller, or to the student who seeks to gain a better knowledge of the once famous kingdoms of the continent of India, and of their rulers, whose forefathers were our most bitter enemies, but whose descendants, through time and a more extended knowledge of the benefits the English rule has conferred on their country, may without exception be reckoned as its most strenuous supporters in the East.

CHAPTER XIV.

Life in the Fortress—Effect of the Rains—Snakes in India—The Frogs—The habits of Snakes—The Cobra—Unpleasant discovery—Varieties of Snakes in Fortress—Snake-bite—Indian Snake-charmers—Indian Jugglers—The Mango Trick—Ruins in Fortress—The Palace—Jain Idols—Temples of the Jainas—Description of Jain temple—The City of Gwalior—The Rajah's Palace—The Lushkur—Indian Music—Festivals of the Hindus—Religious Festivals—Indian Fairs—Hindu Marriages—Their extravagance—The Marriage Ceremony—Incident at a Marriage—Condition of Married Women in India—Their seclusion—Hindu Widows—Remarriage of a Widow—Caste Rules relating to Remarriage—The Suttee—Its origin—Motives of the act—Nautch girls—Their Dress—An Indian Nautch.

THE weather for the first three months following our arrival in the fortress was very wet, and in the intervals of the storms it was so intensely hot that exertion of any sort was almost impossible. We therefore rarely left the summit of the rock, confining our visits to our fellow-residents, who, from the commandant down to the latest-joined subaltern, were most sociable; and numerous were the enjoyable gatherings we had together. We soon experienced the unpleasant effect that the rains in India, with their accompanying heat, have in augmenting the number and increasing the annoyance of flies and every description of insect, as well as of snakes and other reptiles. Snakes in many places are very troublesome at this period of the year, and as Gwalior fortress possessed an unenviable notoriety in this respect, one had to be very careful, if walking about after dark, to avoid treading on one of these reptiles, which as the sun set were seen meandering all over the place in search of food, since a false step on to a lively cobra would have led to unpleasant if not fatal results. Snakes are common all over India, but are specially numerous in certain localities, particularly on dry rocky places covered with old ruins, wherein they have made their undisturbed abode for many years. Unfortunately many such lurking places abounded on the plateau upon which our residence was built.

These reptiles are not often seen except in the rainy season, appearing to hibernate not only through the cold weather but also through the hot, if the same term may be applied to their condition at this latter season of the year. But a storm or two, especially if attended with heavy rain, soon causes them to appear. The general idea is that they are driven forth from their holes by the invasion of water, and this fact may tend in a measure to account for their presence on the surface of the earth at this particular time; but undoubtedly the principal motive that actuates them is the search for food after their long fast. It is only at this period of the year that frogs—their principal article of diet—exist in any number; for during the rainy season these creatures abound all over the country, entering even into the houses; and one can hardly move an article of furniture without finding several behind it, testimony to their presence being also afforded by a dismal and monotonous croaking. They appear to be a species of land frog; for water does not seem necessary to their existence, neither are they so large in size as those met with in the rivers and pools. The pursuit of these interesting creatures, as well as of the rats and mice that swarm in every habitation in the country, tempts the snakes to enter your rooms, though this does not occur so frequently as one would imagine, owing probably to the timid nature of the reptiles, which leads them rather to shun than court the abode of man. To this probably is also due the fact that more fatal cases of snake-bite do not occur; for in no case is a snake ever the aggressor; he will never use his deadly fangs unless driven to do so in self-defence, or where he has been trodden upon or otherwise caused some grievous bodily harm.

Even the formidable cobra, although stated to attack human beings, never does so, as far as I know, except when pursued and driven into a corner, whence there is no escape. In such a case he certainly is in a measure aggressive; for, rearing up to nearly half his length, the cobra darts suddenly forward with open mouth and expanded crest upon his enemy, and changes the role of the pursuer into that of the pursued, until brought low with a well-aimed blow of a long stick. But the fact remains that every member of this family is timid by nature, and makes off on the appearance of anyone; and undoubtedly the reason that Europeans are so seldom bitten is their habit of wearing boots, and causing more noise as they walk than the native, who glides about barefooted, and affords the reptile no warning of his approach. Although, as I have said, it is not common for a snake to enter into the dwelling-house of a European, yet this does occur; and soon after our arrival in our quarters we were considerably startled by the discovery one morning of a fine lively cobra coiled up behind our dressing-table, which, after an exciting chase of some minutes' duration, paid the penalty of his indiscretion by death, and subsequent immersion in spirits, with a view to preservation as a memento of the interesting event.

The chief varieties of snake found in the fortress, were the cobra, a strong and poisonous reptile, sometimes attaining the length of five feet, and whose bite is death in less than an hour; the kerait, a much smaller variety, but equally deadly; and the rock snake or boa, which, although formidable in appearance, as it often attains a considerable length and size, does not possess any poisonous fangs. The ordinary grass snake, which variety was very abundant upon the rock, is also harmless. It is a common idea among the natives that every description of snake is poisonous, and all are consequently much dreaded, although they are loth to kill these reptiles, since they are regarded as sacred. But this character given to the snakes is only a popular error; for out of the thirty-six different species known to exist in India, only six or eight varieties possess fangs poisonous enough to cause fatal results. Unfortunately, out of this comparatively small number, two varieties, the cobra and kerait, are very abundant everywhere, and it is chiefly due to them that so many natives annually perish in so miserable a manner; for despite the government reward of two annas for every deadly snake, owing to the apathy of the Hindu, or his repugnance to slay them, their number does not appear to be sensibly diminished, nor is their evil presence less felt. Last year's report on the mortality of Bengal, only a portion of the empire, records that several thousands of deaths were due to poisonous snakes alone. Although numerous experiments have been made with a view of finding some antidote to the poison secreted in the glands lying at the root of the fangs possessed by these snakes, nothing has yet been discovered which may be said to exert a beneficial effect over the deadly virus when once it is absorbed into the human system. I have myself attended several cases of snake bite, one occurring in the fortress during our stay, and have assiduously used all the remedies proposed, including excision of the part, and cauterization. The results, however, have never been satisfactory, and the opinion I formed as to this class of injury is, that the bite of a strong healthy poisonous snake is uniformly fatal, except only in the rare case of a subject gifted with a constitution so powerful (and on whom remedial measures have been employed within a few minutes of the bite,) as to be able, by the aid of ammonia and other stimulants, to retain the action of the heart, and consequently absorb and subsequently diffuse the poison over the whole system, whereby it would be rendered comparatively inert by dilution, and would be subsequently eliminated in the ordinary course of nature.

Much has been said and written about the Indian snake charmers and their supposed power of finding and securing these reptiles, after invoking their presence by the aid of music and sundry spoken charms. We of course saw many of these worthies, and one day thoroughly tested their power, but the results obtained left no doubt on our minds that their performance was a trick, although a clever one; for the snake produced, instead of being discovered on the indicated spot, was suddenly, when our attention was diverted for a moment, produced from its concealment in some part of the clothing, They do not, it is true, boast of much superfluous raiment, yet if there be only left a yard of cloth around their loins it is sufficient for their purpose. This was proved on the occasion to which I refer, when the man, having stripped with the exception of this small article of attire, and shown us that he had nothing concealed in his long hair, still asserted that he could find a snake in our verandah. Having commenced his performance, I ordered my servants to seize him and take him aside, and when in my presence he was divested of his only article of clothing, it was found to contain a snake tightly rolled up to go into a small compass, and the supposed magician stood revealed as a cheat and an impostor.

Nearly all these men are also conjurers, and some of their tricks are really wonderful, as, unlike their European brethren, they require no stage, or table, or any mechanism to assist them. They perform their deceptions entirely on the bare ground, or on the floor of your verandah, and their sleight of hand is certainly most extraordinary. One specimen of their craft, the well-known mango trick, which, as far as I know, has never been explained, so well has the secret of its performance been kept, would of itself suffice to astonish any audience at home. A seed of the mango fruit is placed in the ground in a hole prepared for the purpose and covered with earth, water is then poured over it, and it is covered with a small basket. After an interval of a few minutes this basket is removed, and the seed is observed to be broken, with a young plant just appearing above the surface of the ground. This is again covered over, and successive removals of the basket show the plant to be growing and passing through the successive stages of full leaf and flowering until finally the fruit appears; and all this in the space of fifteen minutes. The plant often attains a height of several feet, and is perfectly green and fresh and natural in every respect. When one bears in mind that all this is executed by a nearly naked individual, on the bare ground, and with no perceptible accessories other than the old basket, it cannot fail to be considered a very clever performance, and equal, if not superior, to any trick known to their European confrères.

We employed a good deal of our evening leisure in strolling about the rock, and examining the curious old ruins found in the fortress, many of which are undoubtedly of great antiquity, though unfortunately we possess no authentic history relating to the greater portion. The palace, which stands on the summit overlooking the old town, was evidently in its time a fine building, although at present a mere heap of ruins. It was of considerable size, and surrounded by the usual buildings common to Indian royal residences. Both the palace proper, as well as the zenana and other edifices, are entirely built of stone, rudely carved in many places, but lacking the elaborate finish or the ornamentation of those to be seen at Delhi, Agra, and elsewhere; and although no date can with any certainty be assigned to its erection, yet it may be justly considered to have been built several centuries earlier than the latter, at a time when the art of carving marble or inlaying stone for decorative purposes was in its infancy, for the only attempts that can be perceived of anything approaching to the work which afterwards attained to such excellence, are a few rude mosaics in blue and yellow adorning some of the walls, which to this day even retain their vivid colouring.

The most interesting objects within the fortress are the ruined temples and the large tanks built for the storage of water, as well as the statues of heathen gods carved out of the solid rock. Although there are a few carvings of Hindu divinities, most of the statues are idols appertaining to the Jain worship already noticed; and in one place in particular, in a cleft of the rock termed the 'Happy Valley,' these carvings are very abundant, and many of gigantic size. There is one indeed, a full-length figure of a Tirthankaru or god, upwards of thirty feet in height. All the temples, with the exception of one or two in use by the Hindus at present dwelling on the rock, are examples of the places of worship of the Jainas, and afford clear evidence, by their number, size, and beauty of construction, that in former days the rock of Gwalior was, like many other natural hills of similar formation, an important and holy spot of ground for the followers of that now nearly extinct religion.

One temple, which stood exactly opposite our quarters, is particularly interesting; for I question whether, with the exception of the famous relics on Mount Aboo, to the north of Guzerat, the whole of India affords a finer specimen of an antique Jain building. It is of considerable size, and evidently one of their earlier efforts in the science of architecture; for it is wholly composed of massive blocks of stone, piled on each other, and supported entirely by their own weight, no traces of wood or mortar, or any other substance, being discernible. It lessens in size from the base upwards, and is almost pyramidal in form; while from the nature of its construction it resembles at a distance an irregularly-formed heap of large blocks of stone, affording in its outside aspect little or no evidence of the marvellous ingenuity, the patient labour, and the elaborate detail, which are to be observed in its interior. It is on entering that one is struck with the beauty of this temple; for although no arches are to be seen, the arched or curved style of architecture being unknown at the date of the erection of this building, the roof is not flat, but of dome shape, artistically formed by being carved out of the blocks of stone after they had been placed *in situ*, in the manner before described.

The entrance doorway is approached by a wide flight of steps, and within the gateway or outer vestibule, the walls on either side contain a slab of stone let into the surface, and covered with an inscription in the ancient Sanskrit language. The interior consists of one large central hall, the domed roof extending to the extreme height of the building; and four smaller aisles or courts, two on each side, formed by stone pillars and cornices of the same material, ranged horizontally on their supports. Each of these smaller courts has a similar domed roof, but of lesser height, to the central hall, of which they form wings; for all open into one another, and may at first sight be taken for one large court, divided only into different spaces by the pillars required to support the roof. In this case, however, the pillars are superfluous, and have been placed only as a means of dividing the temple into its several component parts—the principal hall and its lesser courts; for as the interior is hewn out of the pile of massive stones of which the temple is formed, in a manner similar to what would have been done if its basis had been a solid rock, no pillars are needed.

The whole of the interior of this building is covered with stone carving; the entire surface of the walls, pillars, and roof being adorned with representations of men, women, and animals, wrought out in the stone.

A border of carving encircles most of the groups of figures, in which imitations of leaves and flowers predominate, and although the work cannot be said to possess the elaborate finish of the industrial stone art of later years, it is still very beautiful, and the greater part is in good preservation, considering the centuries that have elapsed since it was perfected by the hands of the industrious native followers of Jaina. Most of the figures have unfortunately undergone a certain amount of mutilation at the hands of the Mohammedans, in the times of their supremacy within the fortress, for it was the invariable custom of these furious zealots, directly they gained possession of a place, to destroy as far as possible all evidences of any other worship than their own. In this temple, as in many others that came under our observation, they had applied the chisel most industriously, for it is very seldom that a perfect figure is met with, most of them having the face chipped off, or bearing other marks of the iconoclastic propensities of the invaders.

Many other temples and relics of former days are also found on the rock, but it would be needless to describe them in detail, although they afforded us many hours of amusement in their inspection, and conjectures as to the people who had raised them, and the scenes enacted within their walls when the rock was a royal residence, and the present city of Gwalior, which lay beneath us, had no existence. Seen at a distance, the city of Gwalior is most curious and picturesque; the old town, built close under the walls of the fortress, now nearly deserted, presents the appearance in its ruinous condition of a place that had experienced a sudden earthquake, and whose inhabitants, fearing a repetition, had fled to the adjoining town, which rises at a short distance from its ruins.

Old Gwalior.

The difference between ancient and modern Gwalior is very striking, and we had a good opportunity of remarking it, as one afternoon we traversed its entire length and breadth, and further made the full circuit of the rock, on the back of an elephant. This is the best method of conveyance in inspecting a native town, and that most generally employed by Europeans in India when engaged on a similar excursion, as one is considerably elevated above the ground, and can see all things far and wide. Another reason to recommend it is, that the huge animal plods steadily on, making a way of his own through any crowd in the narrow streets, the natives giving place to his onward progress with far more celerity than they display during the passage of a horse or carriage through their midst.

But to return to our expedition. We left our quarters soon after tiffin, and after passing out of the principal gateway of the fortress, found ourselves in the main street of the old city. As Old Gwalior can boast of considerable antiquity, it of course presents all the usual incongruities of a native town in an exaggerated form. The streets are uncommonly narrow, and all the houses are mean and poor, not one possessing any claim to any architectural beauty of design. As before remarked, very few people inhabit the old city; we saw only a sparse number of half-starved squalid natives in the tumble-down houses, and it appeared to us like passing through a city of the dead. On emerging from the narrow and tortuous streets of this silent city we came upon a large open plain, which forms the division between the old and new towns of Gwalior. In the centre of this plain stands the new palace of the Maharajah, and to the right of his abode is the lushkar, or camp, of the native army belonging to this powerful chieftain. The palace, which was barely completed at the time of our visit, is a fine building of stone, covered with chunam, which gives it a white glistening appearance, resembling marble when seen at a distance. It is modern in style, and not particularly Eastern in appearance; for it is a copy, on a slightly smaller scale, of the Government House at Calcutta, the residence of the Viceroy of India. It is built in the form of a square, with open courts filled with turf, flowers, and fountains, and is surrounded by gardens, lawns, and pleasure-grounds, laid out in European fashion. In the interior are some fine rooms, notably those intended as reception and audience halls, which are fitted up most lavishly. The private apartments are small and mean in contrast, while those allotted to the zenana are still meaner, very different abodes for the fair inmates to those seen in the ancient Indian palaces, where the most costly and beautiful bowers were considered fit and necessary for the then sultanas and favourites. After leaving the precincts of the royal residence we passed through the camp, in which the army is located in mud huts, planted in long rows, in a similar manner to that in which our own Sepoys are quartered. The men composing this force are a fine body of soldiers, clothed, armed, and drilled after the European method, and no mean proficients at the military exercises, in which they are constantly practised by their ruler. Scindia is at heart a soldier, undoubtedly the best general and strategist of all the native princes; and the management and manœuvring of his forces forms his chief occupation, in which he is ably assisted by several French and Italian officers who have entered his service.

From the camp a fine gateway leads into the principal thoroughfare of the new city, which affords a remarkable contrast, with its wide streets, fine well-built houses, and multitude of inhabitants, with their bustling activity, to the silent and deserted town which it has now replaced. It contains several good buildings—temples, palaces, and residences for the sirdars and nobles of the court; and as most of the larger houses are surrounded by gardens, and trees are planted thickly on the sides of the larger streets and roads, it presents a fresh and pleasing appearance, and is as good an example of a modern Indian city as any in the country. There is of course a principal bazaar, the chief resort of the inhabitants, either for the purpose of gossiping, or buying and selling. As there is not much trade of any particular sort carried on in Gwalior, the shops only contain the articles usually met with in similar places. There are great stores of grain, sweetmeats, vegetables, and fruit, which, with tobacco and opium, are all that a native of India requires to sustain life. Judging from the number of corpulent men that one meets with in every bazaar in the country, their diet not only seems to agree with them, but brings many, especially of the richer classes, to an oily unctuous fat condition, unsurpassed in any other part of the world. This adipose state, instead of being a trial, is a sign of rejoicing to themselves, and of envy to others not so blessed with exuberance of flesh; for it carries with it, not a patent of nobility, but what to them is of much more consequence, an indication of wealth and indolence—of ample means, and time to indulge in the two chief luxuries of native life, 'eating and sleeping.' To these luxuries the rich give themselves up to such an extent, that as the chief and favourite article of diet is 'ghe,' or clarified butter, which they consume in enormous quantities, its fattening effects are soon discernible, and the contrast in appearance between them and their poorer brethren almost ludicrous; for the latter, between hard work and scanty fare, remain from childhood to old age the leanest of the lean.

On leaving the bazaar, with its motley crowd, we emerged into the open country, which is fairly cultivated to some little distance from the city, and having now exhausted all the principal sights, gave the word for home, when our ponderous steed, quickening its pace, soon brought us back to the gateway whence we had started.

Towards the end of October we ceased to employ punkahs in the house, for the cold weather was now commencing; and although the sun was powerful about midday, yet the mornings and evenings were cool and pleasant, and one could take more exercise in the open air than formerly. Our favourite amusement in the evening was to make the entire circuit of the fortress, terminating our walk at the Armstrong battery, a place from which a good view of the city could be obtained, and where we could sit down and enjoy the cool evening breeze, and at the same time watch the busy scenes of native life in the houses and streets that lay directly below. It was very seldom that our ears were not regaled with the sound of native music, denoting a wedding or the celebration of a birthday, or some other festival. Although it is said Hindu music appears to be systematic and refined, and each mode has a peculiar expression, denoting some particular sentiment or affection, I should imagine that Indian musical science, like all others, has declined; for certainly the present airs do not give to an unlearned ear the impression of any such variety or complication. They appear to be all of one sort, wailing and plaintive in character, and distinguishable at once from the melodies of any other nation; while both in the instrumental music and songs there seems to be an endless repetition of the same sounds, which to them may represent the air, but which to the uninitiated appear simply a confused discord.

The beauty of Hindu music is said to consist in the intervals, breaks, or 'sruti' between each note, the scale having three octaves of seven notes, with twenty-two different kinds of sruti to each note. But this scale has been reduced to two and a half octaves, to suit the compass of the human voice. Of this there are three modulations—the 'mandra,' or chest voice; the 'madhya,' or throat voice; and the 'tara,' or brain-and-nose voice. Of the seven notes the first, 'sa,' was imitated from the cry of a calf; 'ri,' from the bellowing of an ox; 'ga,' from the bleating of a goat; 'ma,' from the howling of a jackal; 'pa,' from the piping of a bird; 'dha,' from the croaking of a frog; and 'ni,' from the noise made by an elephant. To express the notation, only one line is used, with the initials of these notes. Other signs and harmony are not regarded, as the whole character of Hindu music is that of melody. They affirm, that to do their airs justice, they should be heard from a single voice, or accompanied merely by the 'vina,' an instrument which has been called the Indian lyre. And this statement I can endorse, so far as to say that its monotonous sound (although it would be difficult to make out any particular tune), and its accompaniment of the human voice, pitched in the shrillest of falsettos, is decidedly preferable to the music produced by a full band of instrumentalists and singers, so dear to the Hindu ear. This concerted performance is executed by a band of fiddles, or similar stringed instruments, and of tom-toms or drums, beaten with the fingers, supplemented by a few horns and trumpets, which give an occasional loud and discordant blast at intervals. To these latter no particular time or place is assigned, it being left entirely to the discretion of their possessors to throw in, when and where they please, prolonged wails, which, if not strictly musical, do serve to vary the monotony produced by two or three notes being tapped out with a muffled sound from the drums over and over again, and extracted with a squeak and a scrape from the 'strings.' The whole business is loud and unmusical, and when the instrustruments are accompanied, as is usually the case, by song, would drown the voices of the singers, if these were not exerted to a pitch fatal to all delicacy or softness. Yet, such as it is, the natives take great delight in their music, and the bands of musicians, with their following of nautch girls, are generally occupied daily, plying their avocation in the houses of the rich, at their entertainments or festivals.

These occasions are very numerous; for the Hindu loves society and to parade his wealth, and entertainments, besides occasions of rare occurrence, such as marriages, &c., are given by him on particular festivals, and sometimes to show attention to particular friends, or to do honour to a European guest or guests. Among themselves these affairs commence with a dinner, but the essential part of the entertainment is dancing and singing, sometimes diversified with the performances of jugglers and buffoons, during which time perfumes are burnt, and the guests are presented with garlands of sweet-smelling flowers. As the custom among all Eastern nations is rigidly to exclude all females from any gathering of males other than near relations, the ladies and children of the softer sex, except those of tender years, do not appear in the room devoted to the gathering, but are allowed instead to witness the dance, and listen to the song, through a species of grille or lattice-work, separating in all large houses the women's apartments from the other rooms, and behind which, unseen themselves, they are spectators of all that transpires in the guest-chamber.

It would be an endless task to enumerate all the religious festivals celebrated by the inhabitants of this country; for a glance at the Hindu calendar is sufficient to show that no nation upon earth rejoices in a longer list of holidays and festivals, qualified by feasts, vigils, and seasons of mortification. Many of these festivals are fixed for certain lunar periods, while others again are regulated by the supposed motions of the sun. Those most commonly observed may be enumerated as follows:—

The 'Makara-sankranti' is the festival of the commencement of the sun's northern course in the heavens. On this day, about the beginning of January, the sun, according to Hindu reckoning, leaves its most southern point and commences its northern course, a journey occupying that orb till the end of June. This is a festival of great rejoicing; and large melas, or religious fairs, are held at sacred spots, particularly at the confluence of the Jumna and Ganges, at Allahabad. These attract great crowds; and sale and barter, joined to religious rites, occupy the time until their termination.

The 'Siva-ratri,' a festival in honour of the god Siva, is one of great importance, particularly to the Saivites, the sect who regard this member of the Hindu triad as their chosen deity. It is held about the middle of February, and is observed as a period of strict fasting and vigil, many pilgrims flocking to the places more especially dedicated to this god.

The 'Holi,' now generally identified with the 'Dolayatra,' or swinging festival, said to be held in honour of the spring, is perhaps the chief of all holidays in the year, and is celebrated as a kind of Hindu saturnalia, or carnival, all over India. In former days this used to be one of the most revolting and brutalizing of all the idolatrous spectacles in India, when men and women under a vow, and in order to gain favour in the sight of the gods, 'took the hook,' as it was termed; that is, were suspended by hooks inserted into the various fleshy parts of their body to a beam supported on two upright posts, and swung backwards and forwards until they fell to the ground, as the various muscular portions of their persons were torn away under the strain. There are, however, no such practices permitted in the present day, and this popular festival, which is usually observed on the last three or four days of the full moon, either at the end of February or beginning of March, is carried out as a season of fun and practical joking. Men and boys dance round fires, representing the frolics of the god Krishna, singing licentious and satirical songs, and giving vent to their feelings in all sorts of ribaldry against their superiors, by whom it is always taken in good part. The great sport of the occasion, however, consists in sprinkling each other with a yellow liquid, and throwing a crimson powder over each other. All ranks engage in this sport with enthusiasm, and get more and more into the spirit of the contest till everybody is completely drenched with the liquid, and so covered with the red powder as scarcely to be recognised.

The 'Rama-navami,' or birthday of Rama, in the month of March, is kept by many as a strict fast, the temples of this god being illuminated and the idol adorned with costly gifts, while nautches and similar entertainments are kept up all night.

'Krishna-pammashtami' and 'Ganesa-caturthi' are festivals held in honour of the birthdays of those gods. The first is one of the greatest of Hindu holidays, taking place in the month of August; while the second is also popular among many, both being observed as periods of rejoicing and feasting, with adoration of the figures of the two deities.

The 'Durga-puja,' supposed to be connected with the autumnal equinox, is a festival almost solely confined to Bengal. It is held in commemoration of the victory of Durga, wife of Siva, over a buffalo-headed demon, and chiefly consists in worshipping her image for nine days, and then casting it into the water. On the same day that the Bengalis commit their images of Durga to the waters, the Hindus of other provinces celebrate the 'Rama-lila,' a dramatic representation of the carrying off of Sita, concluding with the death of Ravana, the demon king of Ceylon, of which the ninth day of the 'Durga-puja' is the anniversary.

The 'Divali,' or feast of lamps in honour of Vishnu's wife, Lakshmi, and of Siva's wife, Bhavani, is held in September, or the commencement of October, and is the prettiest of all the festivals, particularly at night, when, during the whole time of its celebration, every house and temple is illuminated with rows of little lamps along the roofs, windows, and cornices, also on bamboo frames erected for the purpose.

There are likewise festivals in honour of the Nagas, a curious race of serpents, half human half divine, supposed to exist in regions under the earth, and many others, some general and some local, upon which we need not dwell. Sufficient has been said to show that the Hindus, like other nations, have days of religious rejoicings; but all unhappily in honour of false gods, or some myth in connection with their names, and all fostered and encouraged by a debased and ignorant priesthood, to retain and rivet still further the hold they possess over the minds of their credulous countrymen.

The Mohammedans in India have also their days of festival, the same that their co-religionists observe in other parts of the world. The 'Mohurrun,' already mentioned in the description of the Imambara at Lucknow, and the 'Ramadan,' hold the first place. The latter, known as the time of fasting in honour of the month in which the Koran is said to have been sent from heaven, is universally kept by Mussulmans, and its observance consists in strict abstinence from all food or drink from sunrise to sunset during the days of its continuance, and the making up of the deficiency by feasting and rejoicing during the time the orb of day is below the horizon.

The religious festivals in honour of the various gods are celebrated by the richer classes within their houses in a manner imitated by the poorer classes, but in less sumptuous form. Generally a great hall is fitted up in honour of the deity of the day. His image, richly adorned and surrounded by gilded balustrades, occupies the centre of one end of the apartment, while the host and guests, attired in their best dresses and jewels, are arranged along one side of the room as visitors to the shrine, or attendants on the idol. The rest of the ceremony is like other entertainments, and includes music, dancing, and singing. The songs may perhaps be appropriate, but the incense, the chaplets of flowers, and other presents, are as on ordinary occasions, while the betel leaf and attar, the presentation of which to the guests forms so important a feature in all Indian entertainments, are brought from before the idol, and distributed as if from him to his visitors.

The poorest classes in India, although they do not celebrate the particular days of festival within their houses in the manner described, yet have their rejoicings also; for on these occasions they assemble in certain localities, where fairs are held to honour the event. These fairs have a strong resemblance to fairs in England, and exhibit the same whirling machines, and the same amusements and occupations. But no assemblage in other countries can give a notion of the lively effect produced by the prodigious concourse of people in white dresses and bright-coloured scarfs and turbans, so unlike the black head-dresses and dusky habits of the North and West. Their taste for gaudy processions, and the mixture of arms and flags, also give a different character to the Indian fairs; while, childlike in their nature, the Hindus enter into the amusements of these meetings with infinite relish, and show every sign of peaceful festivity and enjoyment. They may on such occasions have some religious ceremony to go through, but it does not take more than a moment, and seldom occupies a thought; and even at pilgrimages the feeling of amusement is much stronger than that of religious zeal; and many shrines and festivals are the most celebrated marts for the transfer of merchandise, and for all the purposes of fairs.

Of all occasions of rejoicing among the Hindus, a marriage in the family certainly holds the first rank. Here all classes may be said to stand on common ground, in their manner of celebrating the event according to their means, or, as often occurs, in a manner that their means does not justify. The expenditure at a marriage which is considered necessary by the natives in order to retain their position in society may be justly termed one of the curses of the country, for it is the cause of ruin to many families yearly. It seems to be a point of honour on these occasions for every one to outshine in reckless extravagance his fellow-castemen. For this purpose they will live penuriously for years before and for long years after the marriage, in order to save money, which is usually supplemented by sums borrowed at usurious interest a day or two before the ceremony, and all of which is squandered in the course of a few days in riotous feasting. The sole consolation which they derive from such a senseless proceeding, is the knowledge of the fact that they have equalled or outshone a neighbour, and that the amount spent will be the topic of conversation in the bazaar for some time to come. Naturally the rich are not so much affected by this unwritten law of the country as the poor, but the sums spent by them are sometimes really enormous, and several lacs of rupees, sufficient to enrich the happy couple for life, are often squandered by the respective fathers under the mistaken idea that it is necessary they should do so, this social custom having been handed down to them through a long line of ancestors. During the last few years, however, there has been some considerable agitation in the circles of the better educated natives on this subject, and many have resolved to show an example to their countrymen by celebrating these events in a less ostentatious form, and seconding our government in the laudable endeavour to put down a custom which to many only means ruin.

The ceremonies at a marriage are numerous, and not particularly interesting or even well-known to Europeans; for they differ according to caste, and are celebrated in the privacy of home, chiefly in the midst of near relations only, to whom the presence of a stranger would be unwelcome. The contracting parties are usually children, the bride being always under the age of puberty, while both are usually under ten. These premature marriages, instead of producing attachment, often cause early and lasting disagreements; for before the knot is tied as children, they know nothing of each other's feelings, and directly after the ceremony which has made them one, they separate and return to their respective homes until a few more years have passed over their heads, when the bride is taken to the house of her husband in a procession as showy as the parties can afford. Regarding the religious part of the ceremony I can say but little, never having been present at one; but it is generally understood that it is long and tedious, various observances having to be fulfilled under the direction of the priest or priests, the whole concluding with the joining of the hands of the bride and bridegroom, and tying them together with a blade of sacred grass or thread, after which the bride steps a certain number of paces, a particular text being repeated at each.

That this part of the ceremony is prolonged and trying to

the children, particularly to the bride, I had ample opportunity of confirming some years back, on the occasion of the marriage of the daughter of a wealthy merchant of a city, whom I had attended for severe illness which attacked her about two months before the nuptial-day. Having expressed an opinion that, although recovered, her condition was weak, and that she was unable to sustain any prolonged exertion or excitement without the risk of fainting or otherwise breaking down, I was entreated by the father, as the marriage-day could not be deferred, to attend during the time of the religious part of the ceremony, in case my surmises should prove correct, and also to see her before its commencement, and administer, if necessary, any medicine that would infuse strength to bear up against the attendant fatigue. Having consented to this arrangement, I attended accordingly, and saw my patient, a pretty little girl of ten, just before the ordeal commenced, when, thinking a moderate stimulant would be beneficial, I administered a strong dose of sal-volatile and red lavender. This compound certainly had the desired effect; for although at the termination of the ceremony, which was of several hours' duration, when I again saw her, she was in an exhausted condition, yet I heard from the proud father that while the proceedings lasted she appeared quite strong, and in fact quite lively and animated, entering into the details of the ceremony with excited interest, her sparkling eyes, which heightened her beauty, and her animation, being the theme of general admiration. This last I could well understand; for the unaccustomed stimulant, joined to the excitement of her novel position, was quite sufficient to have caused an older female to show signs of the first or lively stage of inebriation. This however I did not mention to her friends, and I reaped my reward in the shape of a handsome fee, as a testimony to the skill and the potency of the drugs of an English doctor.

I need not enter here into the condition of the married native women in India, for it is well known that, as in all Eastern nations, they are kept in seclusion, and are rarely seen by strangers, leading an uneventful life of indolence, with no occupation for the mind—education for females not being considered necessary or becoming. It will therefore I fear make but slow progress within the precincts of the zenana, though there are exceptions, and some are seeking the blessings of instruction. These remarks, however, apply rather to the females belonging to the higher castes, or of great wealth; for the women of a lower order are not kept in seclusion or indolence, but on the contrary lead a life of activity and hard work, either assisting their husbands in their daily toil, or attending to the numerous wants of their households.

The condition of married women in India has certainly improved of late years, and the hideous custom of 'suttee,' where the living widow was burned on the same pyre as her dead husband, is now fairly and entirely abolished. But there still exists a custom respecting them, one of the most cruel and unnatural of all the vexatious and absurd rules of caste— the Hindu law regarding the marriage of a widow. To show how this affects society, it is only necessary to mention that by this rule a girl of tender years, married most probably when she was nine, may, a few months after the celebration of the nuptials, by the death of the boy to whom she has been united, whom she does not know, and whom she has never seen since the day of ceremony that made them one, be converted into an Indian widow. And this is not only in name, for the unfortunate event changes the tenor of the whole life of the girl, who is brought up in a different manner to her companions, debarred from forming any ties of intimacy with members of the opposite sex, condemned to wear a distinctive dress, and to pass the rest of her life in restraints enforced on the maiden widow by the rules of caste and religion, as acts of mourning for a husband who died before she understood the full meaning of the term, and whom she in this world must never replace. For the remarriage of a widow entails all sorts of fearful consequences, loss of caste and disownment by relatives being the lesser evils in the social death incurred by such an act, which is reprobated and scorned by all orthodox Hindus, the wretched woman becoming in their eyes the vilest object of the vile, while, deserted by all, she drags on a wearying existence until death ends her sad and undeserved sufferings. It is only right to mention, that among the more advanced Hindus this law is not held in the same degree of force, and that attempts have been made to abolish it altogether; but as yet examples of marriage with a widow have been few, the general feeling of the nation being against the innovation. If, however, it were only accepted, it would be the principal means of improving the somewhat lax morality now prevailing among the female population of India, which is undoubtedly increased and in numerous instances engendered by this unnatural and inhuman law.

Before quitting this subject, some explanation must be given of the custom of suttee, formerly carried out in this country on the death of a Hindu of any note, but which at the present time, thanks to the exertions of the British government, is seldom or never put into execution. In British India it is now happily a thing of the past, and only occurs at rare intervals in the parts of the country not under our rule. The period at which this barbarous custom was introduced is uncertain. It is not mentioned by Menu, who treats of the conduct proper for faithful widows, as if there were no doubt about their surviving their husbands. It is thought by some to have been recognized in ancient authorities, particularly in the Rig Veda; but others deny the construction of the passage, for the careful editing of the Veda by European scholars has disclosed the fact that no such authority exists in the original text. The Sanskrit runs simply thus: "May these women who are not widows, who have good husbands, who are mothers, enter with unguents and clarified butter, without tears, without sorrow; let them first go up into the dwelling." It is these last words, 'arohantu yonim agre,' which have been altered into the fatal variant 'arohantu yonim agneh,' which signifies 'let them go up into the place of fire.' But there is really no authority whatever for this reading, for the verse in fact is not addressed to widows at all. And a succeeding verse in the same hymn, which was addressed to the widow at the funeral, expressly bids her 'to rise up and come to the world of living beings,' and the ceremonial Sutras direct that she is then to be taken home. That the custom is of great antiquity is clear from its mention in the works of authors who flourished several centuries before the Christian era, and, without any evidence to the contrary, the text above quoted may have been the authority for its institution, for no mention of it occurs in the histories of the earlier and most sacred gods. The motive of the act is also uncertain, but it is usually ascribed to the degraded condition to which a woman who outlived her husband was condemned, or to the fact of the relations encouraging self-immolation for the purpose of obtaining the widow's property. Still it is more probable that the hope of immediately entering on the enjoyment of heaven, and of entitling the husband to enjoy the same felicity, as well as the glory attending such a voluntary sacrifice, was sufficient to excite a few enthusiastic spirits to go through this awful trial. The sight of a widow burning is said to have been a most painful one, but it is hard to say whether the spectator was most affected by pity or admiration. In many cases there remains no doubt that the victim was stupefied with opium, and insensible to all the proceedings, dying apparently at once without any suffering; but again we have instances of women bursting from amidst the flames, and being thrust back by their relatives and friends—scenes of horror now happily banished from the country, which, like the similar self-immolation of men under the sacred car of Juggernauth, remain only as legends of the past.

In my description of Indian festivities, I mentioned that music and dancing were the principal amusements; and, as a fitting termination to the subject, a few words on the latter may be appropriate. Unlike Western nations, Eastern men never themselves indulge in saltatory performances, but sit ranged in rows instead, and watch with impassive countenances the posturings and contortions of a band of women called 'nautch girls,' who perform for their amusement the various measures that go to make up the Indian 'nautch,' or dance. These girls are usually selected for their good looks, and are trained from infancy for this employment, to which they commonly add others not quite so innocent. They usually reside together in a particular part of the bazaar, and each set is accompanied by its own band of musicians retained in its pay, an old man being generally selected as leader, on whom devolves all the arrangements, both financial and otherwise, in connection with their engagement for a performance of their talents. Among the poorer classes a nautch may consist of only two or four performers, but among the rich, and at a grand entertainment, a great number are usually engaged. This can only be done, however, by the affluent; for these girls rate their abilities at a high figure, and it is not uncommon for several hundreds of rupees to be given individually to those who stand high in the profession. Their dress is usually very handsome, and, unlike our ballet girls, they are clad in flowing drapery which conceals all their bodies, with the exception of face, arms, and feet. The latter are loaded with jewellery, massive bracelets of silver encircling both wrists and ankles, which, jingling together, keep up an accompaniment to their movements. Their performance can scarcely be called dancing; it is more properly posturing, interspersed with slow movements, with an occasional whirl round like an animated top. The band plays during the whole time, in the manner already described; the dancers keep up a continuous singing in the shrillest of voices; and to a European a little goes a long way, and a nautch once seen does not need repetition. Although the attitudes are not ungraceful, it is after all a languid and monotonous entertainment; and it is astonishing to a stranger to see the delight that all ranks of native society take in it, the lower orders in particular often standing whole nights through to witness this unvaried amusement.

CHAPTER XV.

Shooting Expedition to the Jungle—The Spear-grass—Its effects—Our day in the Jungle—A mishap—Our return to the Fortress—Capture of supposed Nana Sahib—Probable reason of the Imposture—Fate of the Impostor—Camp life in India—Start for a Shooting Excursion—Mahona—Jackals and Hyenas—Garra Ghaut—Arrival in Camp—Sport in India—Tiger-shooting—Fox-hunting in India—Pig-sticking—Our life in the Jungle—Our Commissariat arrangements—Peculiarities of Hindu living—Influence of Caste on eating and drinking—A Brahman dinner—Food of the Hindus—Use of Rice—Use of Asafœtida—Hindu Beverages—Drunkenness among Natives—Hindu Luxuries—The Betel-nut—Christmas-day—Chace after a Leopard—Attacked by illness—Our return to the Fortress—Termination of our first year in India.

THE weather was now cool enough to allow us to be out in the day. Many of our friends employed themselves in shooting and fishing, and their reports of the pleasant days they enjoyed proved so irresistible that we determined to follow their example, and go out for a day's shooting in the jungle, distant a few miles from the fortress. Jungle is a term applied in India indiscriminately to any land not under cultivation, to waste land, in fact; and it may either be forest or scrub, grass or a bare plain almost entirely devoid of vegetation. That in the vicinity of the fort was mostly a broken tract of country, sparingly watered by one or two small rivers, and covered with a large, thick, high species of grass; while dotted all over its expanse were small clumps of trees and bushes.

The spear-grass, the greatest cause of discomfort to the

sportsman in India, abounds in this as in nearly every jungle in the country, and the agony produced by its presence must be felt to be appreciated. This grass is a large, coarse species, growing to a height of five or six feet, or even more, and its stems are covered with sharp spikes, about the size and thickness of a small darning-needle, which penetrate the clothing, and stick deep into the flesh of everyone who has to force his passage through. No particular sort of attire affords any adequate protection against these points. Strong canvas has been recommended, and perhaps is the best material; but it is almost too hot for general wear, and one has to be passive under the infliction, to bear with fortitude the pain and the unpleasantness of numberless needles going deeper and deeper into the flesh with every movement, and look forward to the time when on return to camp they can be picked out like pins from a pincushion. There being no woods or large cover in this particular jungle, no big game was to be found, and we had to be content with grouse, partridges, and pea-fowl, and a species of deer called blackbuck, with the chance of meeting with a cheeta or leopard, or a few pig or wild boars.

We started about six a.m. on the morning of the 22nd October, and had a delightful drive of twelve miles to a spot near a small river, to which place we had sent a tent and some servants the day before, with instructions to have breakfast ready for us on our arrival. We left the carriage about three miles from our destination, and I walked the rest of the way, as I intended to shoot on the road to camp, while my wife followed in her 'dandy,' a contrivance of cloth and wood suspended to a pole, the ends of which are supported on the shoulders of two men, who carry it along. I shot a few partridges and snipe, and soon after passing through some very thick grass we forded the river, and arrived at our encampment, which was prettily situated on a high bank overhanging the stream. After doing justice to an excellent breakfast, finding the sun too hot for any sport, as the birds would all be lying close under shade, we employed our time in fishing. Unfortunately we did not meet with much success in this line; for although we saw plenty of fish, and some even of large size, they all had the bad taste to decline our tempting bait, much to the disappointment of my dear companion, who persevered, however, for a long time with an energy that merited a better result.

After tiffin we started again, intending to shoot in the vicinity of the camp, and then, as darkness came on, to try to intercept some of the pea-fowl that came to roost in the trees, under the shade of which our tent had been pitched. We did not, however, meet with much sport, so we made preparations for departure, and aided by the light of the moon soon reached our carriage, without any incident except the partial immersion of the dandy and its occupant in a stream of water, which proved deeper than was anticipated by the bearers, one of whom disappeared in a hole and caused the catastrophe. With the exception of the wetting no one was hurt, and we were speedily on our way home, the road being lighted up by a most glorious moon now at its full. Much to our surprise, we noticed on approaching the fortress numerous bodies of troops belonging to Scindia, while the road was patrolled by his cavalry, who, however, offered us no molestation; and although visions of another Mutiny flashed across my mind, it was fortunately nothing so serious, and the mystery of these warlike preparations was explained on our arrival at the fort.

Here we heard to our astonishment that a man professing to be the rebel Nana Sahib, of infamous memory on account of his deeds at Cawnpore, in 1857, had been captured by the Maharajah Scindia in Gwalior, and handed over to the British Resident, and previous to our arrival carefully escorted to Morar and lodged in the guard-room of the 26th Regiment. The military precautions we had observed had been taken for fear of a rescue or a riot in the city, since to many of the inhabitants of Gwalior the incarceration of the descendant of the Peishwa was not pleasing, and Scindia incurred great odium at the time among his people for giving up to justice a man who, whatever his deeds, was the representative head of the Mahrattas, and who had moreover come in his trouble to claim the protection of one who in former days owed his family allegiance. Whatever were the reasons that induced Scindia to surrender the fugitive to the British power can never be thoroughly understood, knowing, as he did, that such an act would render him unpopular with the mass of his subjects. But that he did so is now a matter of history, and that he was honest in the matter I thoroughly believe; for incidents in his early life having been recalled to his memory in the specious tale narrated by the man, he fairly thought, although he could not personally recognize him, that he was the real Nana, and immediately seized and delivered him up to justice.

That the man was a vile impostor was soon proved, and the court that tried him had evidence to satisfy themselves, that instead of being the personage he assumed to be, he was a fakir or beggar, who had previously personated the same character. His object was never clearly ascertained, but it was rumoured in Gwalior that he had acted with a view to ascertain what reception at that court the real Nana, whom many consider to be still living, would have if he claimed protection; and it was further stated that the Nana was actually concealed in the neighbourhood awaiting the result of the experiment. The result, if this rumour were true, was quite sufficient to dispel any hopes of success in seeking the protection of Scindia, in the minds of that infamous character or his adherents, who can now hope for no mercy either at our hands or even from their fellow-countrymen. Regarding this impostor it may be mentioned that, after being kept in confinement at Morar for some considerable time, he was removed to Cawnpore, and having been placed on his trial, and his imposture established, was handed over to Scindia for punishment as a rogue and vagabond. From our knowledge of Eastern justice we may rest assured that the individual in question will not give further trouble, or again cause such a needless excitement.

Nothing particular occurred to break the monotony of our life after our expedition, and the days passed rapidly and pleasantly until the week before Christmas, when we commenced to make preparations for departure to spend a fortnight's leave at a place distant some hundred miles, where it was said some good shooting could be obtained. We anticipated great pleasure from this trip to the jungle, which lay amidst some beautiful scenery, and moreover the change from a house to a tent is thoroughly appreciated by the residents in India during the cold weather. Many families even pass the whole cold season in camp, and those officials whose civil duties extend over a large district, travel, accompanied by their wives and children, from place to place on a tour of inspection, enjoying tent-life in a most luxurious fashion. Others, whose duty does not call them to do this, yet follow the same course for pleasure, and it is rare to meet with any European who has not been, during the proper season, a dweller in tents. It is a most fascinating mode of life, and most enjoyable after the close confinement to the house, so long and patiently endured; and the constant change of scene obtained by the daily shifting of the camp, joined to the amount of exercise one obtains in the open air, renders it beneficial alike to health and spirits.

Our party was to consist of ourselves and the commandant of the fortress. We were busy with our preparations for a day or two before the start, and having sent off our tents and baggage on elephants and camels to precede us, we left in the early morning of Monday, the 21st December. On that day, having posted horses at certain distances along the road, we drove about fifty miles, and arrived in the evening at a place called Mahona, where we halted for the night, putting up at the dak bungalow. This spot, which is merely a halting-place for travellers on the high road to stations in Central India, is prettily situated on the banks of a large river, surrounded by picturesque hills covered with trees and vegetation. Being in the wilds, as one may say, the jackals and similar animals were particularly numerous in the neighbourhood, and our rest was much disturbed at night by their constant howling. At one time the din was terrific, the reason being that, in addition to the usual row, a number of hyenas were having a free fight for the possession of a bone in the verandah just outside our door—a proceeding that gave great offence to our dog Fizz, who had accompanied us, and who displayed great anxiety to join in the fray. The following morning we proceeded to Garra Ghaut, distant about forty miles, where we halted again for the night, and the next day, leaving our carriage and horses to await our return, we plunged into the depths of the jungle. A journey of fifteen miles through the scrub and thick grass, which we traversed in safety and comfort on the back of an elephant, brought us to the site of our encampment, which was situated in an open spot surrounded by hills, with scenery not unlike some parts of Scotland. On our arrival, we found our tents pitched, and were soon settled down, and looking forward to the following day, when we hoped to get some good sport, as the reports of game being plentiful in the neighbourhood were very favourable.

There are certainly few places where the sportsman can enjoy better shooting than in India; nearly every species of animal dear to his heart being found in the country, in the proper localities. He can, if he aspire to big game, pursue the huge elephants, which are plentiful, particularly in the Terai, on the borders of Nepaul. The fierce bisons are to be found in the recesses of the dense forests of Central India, and if he care to brave the heat of the sun, in the months of May and June, he may be rewarded by the skins of sundry tigers. These animals are pretty generally distributed all over India, and, despite the number annually destroyed, still numerous enough in some places to be a terror to the district, on account of the depredations they commit, both on human life, and on the flocks and herds of the inhabitants. Cheetas and leopards are common, and afford good sport, while bears are numerous, especially in hilly or mountainous districts.

Of the deer tribe there are a great many varieties, generally distributed all over the country. The largest species are the 'sambhur,' an animal not unlike the red deer of Scotland, and a very plentiful variety in many places called the 'nilghi,' or blue cow. This last is a curious animal, resembling a cow in size and shape, with similar horns, but with a deer-like head and legs. But the finest deer of all is the lordly 'barra-singha,' or twelve-horned stag, a large and powerful animal, the stalking of which affords great sport to visitors in the Himalayan district. Among the smaller varieties we find the black-buck, a very pretty but common species, found nearly in every part of the country. Ravine deer, and others like the fallow deer at home, are also abundant, as are likewise numerous specimens of the gazelle tribe. The ibex and the musk deer are to be met with in the Himalayas, and there, too, are found numerous species of wild goats and sheep. And if the adventurous sportsman care to penetrate to the borders of Thibet, he will be rewarded by the spoils of the fierce 'yak' and wild horse.

Wolves, hyenas, foxes, and jackals abound all over India, as well as monkeys and apes, but the former varieties are seldom shot, being usually hunted with dogs, while the latter are rarely molested.

Among the feathered tribes chiefly sought after for purposes of sport, I may mention the bustard and 'floriken,' both of which require stalking, like deer. Pea-fowl are abundant in every place, and the cock birds, when in full plumage, are shot to obtain their tails. There are many varieties of the partridge family, and grouse and quail are exceedingly plentiful. The black and painted partridges are very beautiful, and the sand grouse is a fine bird. All these birds require to be walked up, dogs being of little use in a country where the scent does not lie. Hares are found in many places, but the rabbit is unknown, and it is necessary to take a trip to the hills in order to procure the pheasant, some varieties of which, notably the Himalayan 'monahl' and argus, are splendid birds in their brilliant colouring. Water-fowl are very numerous in every part of the country; and good sport is to be obtained in localities where 'jheels' or ponds left by the rains are plentiful, with geese and ducks of every variety, while snipe are frequently so common, that the quantity shot in one day by a single person, would appear almost incredible to those who have only met with this bird at home.

There are no game-laws in India, and no particular close time is observed, the natives killing everything all the year round—a proceeding not calculated to increase the game in the country, and which sooner or later will have to be stopped by the aid of legislation. But the cold season is the time usually selected by Europeans for shooting, except in the case of tigers, which, to be hunted successfully, must be followed during the hot months, as the grass in the jungle is too thick at any other period of the year. There are three methods of destroying these animals in a sportsmanlike way, and the first and principal means, adopted particularly in the Bengal Presidency, is to shoot them from off the back of an elephant, the tiger being beaten up and driven out of the cover by a line of elephants, or a numerous body of native beaters. In the first case, one takes his chance of getting a shot by the fact of the animal being turned up in that part of the line assigned as his station. In the second, it is usual to post the different elephants bearing the sportsmen at certain places where it is likely that the animal, driven in that direction by the beaters, will break cover. The tiger usually emerges from the cover at a slow pace, affording an excellent shot; but if only wounded by the first discharge returns to the cover, and must then be immediately followed up, or it may escape by breaking through the line of beaters, most probably injuring some of their number, and run off before it can be intercepted. If wounded severely, or brought to bay, it crouches until the elephant approaches sufficiently near, and then, if not previously disabled, it makes its charge or spring on the occupants of the howdah. Now is the critical time, and it behoves the sportsman to be cool and wary. Much, however, depends on the elephant; for it is not uncommon for that animal, especially if young and inexperienced, to take fright, and dash wildly off through the jungle—a proceeding fraught with danger for those on its back, for an elephant, when once started on its mad career, and out of the control of its mahout or driver, is a beast most difficult to check, and its riders run the risk of being jerked out of the howdah violently on to the ground, or having their heads dashed against the boughs of any trees that stand in the way. But if one is on an elephant trained and accustomed to the sport, no danger is incurred; for the huge animal makes no account of the charge of a tiger, and will receive unmoved its spring, either on its head or some other part of the body, thus affording an excellent opportunity to the occupants of the howdah to finish off the infuriated beast at close quarters.

The second mode of tiger-shooting is very generally adopted throughout the Bombay Presidency, or in cases where elephants are not obtainable, or the nature of the ground does not admit of their use. This method consists in having the jungle beaten by a line of natives, while the shooters, taking up positions in the branches of different trees at the spot where the tiger is likely to break cover, pot the animal when it passes near the place of their concealment. This is a very sure and safe proceeding, and it is not necessary to be posted very high up the tree, for tigers cannot climb; but as they can spring a height of twelve to fourteen feet, it is necessary to exceed that limit or take the chance of being pulled out of one's perch by a sudden leap. This sometimes occurs, and in 1867 was the cause of the loss to my regiment of one of its most valued officers, who, not taking the precaution of ascending the tree to a sufficient height, was dragged out and carried off by the tiger, which, although followed and destroyed in as short a time as possible, yet inflicted such injuries on our poor companion as caused his death in a few hours.

There is another way of tiger-killing to be noticed, and that is following up the animal on foot; but I need scarcely say that this is seldom done, for it is a senseless proceeding, the odds being greatly in favour of the tiger killing his pursuer, especially if that individual fails in putting him *hors de combat* at the first shot. Regarding the danger of this species of sport, I may say that, having assisted at tiger-shooting in both of the first two methods described, I have come to the conclusion that though it is certainly not child's play or utterly devoid of risk, still with ordinary precautions it may be enjoyed with comparative safety to life and limb. There is of course the chance of the elephant bolting and its attendant dangers, but this is not likely to occur if a good staunch animal is selected. And as regards the tree method of shooting no risk at all is incurred, provided one is out of reach of a spring and observes total silence, for it is a curious fact that a driven tiger rarely looks up, but keeps its eyes straight in front, and if no noise is made to attract attention will place itself directly under the tree in which its enemy is placed, without being in any way aware of it. If one is so unfortunate as to fall into the clutches of a tiger, especially of a wounded animal, the injuries inflicted by teeth and claws are usually fatal. For firstly, there is the intense shock to the nervous system, joined to the terrible injuries to the body; and secondly, there appears to be something poisonous in a tiger's bite that affects the wound caused by the teeth, rendering it liable to mortification a few hours after the infliction of the injury. Of course there are cases in which recovery has taken place, owing to the promptness with which surgical aid has been rendered; but the chances are that the patient succumbs from his injuries, and it is a matter of rejoicing that, considering the number of Europeans who annually join in this sport in India, so few serious accidents occur, thanks to the precautions observed.

The pursuit of bears, leopards, and deer must be followed on foot, except in places where elephants can travel, and this is the usual method employed when after elephant, bison, or buffalo. And although there is some attendant danger nected with the chase of each of these animals, still with nerve and good shooting there is very little risk, especially if accompanied by one or two European companions. It is utterly useless to rely too much on the assistance of your native 'shikarris,' or huntsmen; for while there are exceptions, and many are brave and trustworthy, yet their usual rule is to desert their master in the moment of peril, and leave him to extricate himself from the difficulty or danger they are afraid to share.

Although fox-hunting is carried out in India, and many stations possess a pack of hounds, which give many a good run, either after a fox, jackal, or wolf, still the sport of the country of this description is *par excellence* that of boar-hunting, or, as it is usually termed, 'pig-sticking.' No dogs are employed, but each rider carries a spear of bamboo, with a long, sharp, steel point, and the object of each hunter is to reach the boar by dint of sheer hard riding, in advance of his companions, and either transfix or wound the animal with his weapon, and thus gain the honour of the chase—'a first spear.' As this sport is now pretty well understood at home no minute description is needed; but I may venture to say that it is more exciting than fox-hunting, even in the shires. The pace is quicker, the country rough and broken up by nullahs, or ravines, making it difficult to ride, and then the additional spice of danger afforded by the probable charge of the boar, when wounded, lends zest to the sport, and makes it one of the most popular amusements of the Englishman in India. One point in connection with this subject may be briefly noticed, and that is the two different methods employed in pig-sticking, which affect not only the weapon but also the mode of using it. In the Bengal Presidency a long spear is used, the rider carrying it like a lance in rest, driving its point into the pig by the impetus afforded by the speed of the horse. In the Bombay and Madras Presidencies a much shorter spear is employed, and the rider, grasping it about two thirds up the pole, carries it with the point towards the ground, and when within distance raises the arm and jobs at the animal, a proceeding not allowed in Bengal, where the arm is not raised, and one must deliver the spear by clear riding on to the object. But the spirit of the thing and the aim of the hunters in both cases is the same. The great desideratum is to obtain first spear, and for this purpose every nerve is strained to the utmost, and the degree of emulation that is set up and the hard riding engendered thereby, must be seen or experienced, for description would fall far short of the reality.

But to return to our life in the jungle. We found the change from our quarters very pleasant, and rambled about in the day, which was moderately warm, or shot during the greater part of the time; and after dinner we either sat outside the tent smoking before a large wood fire, for the nights were cold, or kept within the larger tent, which served for our dining and sitting-room, where reading, conversation, or bezique, served to occupy us until we retired for the night.

The commissariat arrangements were well managed by the faithful Esau, and left nothing to be desired; and it was really wonderful to see the manner in which all our meals were prepared and cooked, considering that the appliances of a kitchen were wanting—a few sticks and a hole in the ground being all that seemed requisite. From the numerous little fires that we observed all around the camp about the dinner-hour, each

Food of the Hindus.

with a dark figure before it engaged in some apparently mysterious operation, we could see that our servants were also busy in the pleasant labour of preparing and discussing their evening meal, in most cases their only one in the twenty-four hours.

In the matter of eating and drinking the natives of India, that is the Hindus, are peculiar and unlike any other nation, both in the manner of the preparation and of the discussion of their food; and even the Mohammedans are slightly imbued with the same ideas, although in a much less degree, affecting chiefly their disinclination to eat or drink in the company of any but their co-religionists. But a Hindu is much more particular, and when away from his family cooks his solitary meal for himself, and finishes it without a companion, or any of the pleasures of the table but those derived from taking the necessary supply of food. In all classes the difference of caste leads to a want of sociability; for members of different castes may not eat together, neither may they employ cooking vessels that have been used by others; and the caution used against eating out of dishes, or on carpets defiled by other castes, gives rise to some curious customs. It is not uncommon at a feast, particularly at a great Brahman dinner, for the guests either to bring their own utensils or to have every different dish served in vessels made of leaves sewn together, to obviate any risk they might incur of contamination through the dishes provided by their host on ordinary occasions.

The food of the common people, both in the country and in towns, is unleavened bread, with boiled vegetables, clarified butter or oil, and spices. The bread is made from the flour of some of the different kinds of grain grown in the country, and when kneaded is fashioned into large flat cakes, called 'chupatties,' toasted or baked over the fire, and eaten hot. It is a popular idea at home that the natives of India for the most part live exclusively on rice; but this is by no means the case. Undoubtedly in some places, such as in Lower Bengal and Orissa, or some parts of Madras, all rice-growing localities, this article forms the staple component of the ordinary diet of the inhabitants. But the greater number of the natives in other parts of the country use this species of food very sparingly, and only as a luxury in the preparation of a vegetable curry of which they are very fond, contenting themselves chiefly with wheat, jowar, bajra, millet, and other sorts of grain; together with many kinds of pulse, of which latter there is a very great consumption by people of all ranks. Meat is seldom used, except by the lower classes, or by the pariahs or outcasts, and then mutton or fish are the usual articles, beef being rarely, if ever, consumed.

The inferior castes of Hindus are also less particular about eating in company with others, and care less about their vessels, and as a general rule employ only articles of metal, which can, according to their ideas, be always purified by a good scrubbing. The upper classes, or at least the Brahman section, have very little more variety in their diet than the others. If they have any it consists chiefly in the greater number of kinds of vegetables and spices they employ in the preparation of one dish, and in more careful cooking. Asafœtida is a favourite ingredient, as giving to some of their richer dishes something of the flavour of flesh. And although it may appear strange to others, the use of this odorous substance is not confined to the natives; for thin cakes, flavoured with this drug, are considered to be the proper thing to take with curry, and are usually much appreciated by Europeans, particularly by *bons-vivants*. Water is the usual beverage with all classes; very little tea or coffee is used; intoxicating drinks are taken only by the lower classes, and they rarely get completely drunk with spirits. Drunkenness is confined to damp countries, such as Bengal, the Concans, and some parts of the south of India. It prevails to a certain extent in our territories, but is so little of a national propensity that the absolute prohibition of spirits, which exists in most native states, is sufficient to keep it down. Smoking tobacco is almost the only luxury, and this is common to all classes. Some few smoke intoxicating drugs and opium, which, although it is used to great excess by some, is not touched by many, and cannot be styled a vice of the country. All but the very poorest, however, chew betel (a pungent aromatic leaf), with the hard nut of the areca palm, mixed with a sort of lime made from shells, and with various spices, according to the person's means. In conclusion it may be added that all classes of Hindus eat solely with their fingers, no forks or knives being employed, and that they scrupulously wash before and after meals.

We enjoyed some fine shooting in the environs of our camp, and one day made a good bag of teal and other duck, which we found on a jheel that lay embedded in the hills like a small highland loch. Early on the morning of Christmas-day we were very busy preparing our guns and mustering coolies, information having been brought the night before that a leopard was in a patch of jungle near by, and we being all eager to compass its destruction. Soon after breakfast we started, accompanied by a hundred coolies or so, for the hunt. On our arrival at the place indicated, a piece of jungle of very high grass immediately below a small range of hills, we separated, the commandant and myself penetrating into the cover and taking up our positions on elevated rocks, near which we expected the animal to emerge when driven out by the beaters, who commenced operations at the higher end, accompanied by my wife mounted on her favourite elephant, the sagacious old Luchmee. From her elevated position she was able to witness the proceedings, and was besides perfectly safe; for Luchmee was an old hand at this kind of game, and would have made short work of any animal that ventured to attack her. Much to our disappointment the cover was drawn blank, and we saw no signs of our quarry, which I imagine must have broken back through the line of beaters, notwithstanding their protestations to the contrary; but the excitement while the hunt lasted was most enjoyable, and appreciated by us all, although we much regretted not having secured our prey.

On reassembling we proceeded to a shady spot for tiffin, and here an incident occurred which was to mar the long anticipated pleasure of Christmas-day in the jungle, and put a sorrowful termination to our enjoyable expedition. Soon after tiffin, without any premonitory symptoms, I felt suddenly unwell, and becoming rapidly worse on my return to camp, it was speedily apparent that I was attacked with illness of a choleraic nature. Fortunately we had a small supply of medicines, for during the next thirty-six hours my symptoms were very urgent, and I was in a dangerous condition. As long as I was able I directed the means of treatment; but on the second day I became nearly unconscious, and the supply of remedies running short, our companion, who had previously sent off a runner to Morar for medical aid, started to ride to Sepri, the nearest station to us, which, although a small place, might be able to afford some assistance in replenishing the stock of drugs. Soon after he had started, my dear wife, who had throughout this trying time preserved her courage and presence of mind, suddenly devised a plan which she immediately carried into execution. This was to remove me from the cold tent, more particularly as the weather was threatening to rain, and get me conveyed to the dak bungalow at Gharra Ghaut, distant some fifteen miles, where at least the shelter of a house could be obtained, together with the warmth of a wood fire. A litter was hastily constructed, and well covered over with blankets I was slowly transported through the dense jungle, my wife directing all and following closely on Luchmee. Immediately on my arrival at the bungalow, being put into bed in a warm room, a slight improvement took place, and gradually the urgent symptoms passed off, leaving me in a feeble condition but out of danger, the whole of which was entirely owing to the happy forethought that effected the change, for I firmly believe that another night passed in the jungle with no other cover than a slight tent, would have been too much for anyone in my then condition. On the return of our friend from Sepri late that night I was much improved, and two days after was well enough to leave for Mahona in a dhooly which had been sent for my use. At that place we found a medical officer just arrived from Morar, who was glad to find his services were now not so urgently required. He accompanied us on to the next stage the following day, and then left us with Major G. to proceed home; while we, after this unfortunate termination to our pleasant holiday, travelled by slow and easy stages back to the fortress. The last day of the year saw us within one march of home, where we arrived the following day; and so concluded the months of 1874, our first year in India.

CHAPTER XVI.

The New Year—Horse-racing in India—The Race Lottery—Commencement of the Hot Weather—Our Maid's Wedding—The Leave Season in India—Indian Hill Stations—Their utility for the British troops—Hill Stations of the Bengal Presidency—Simla—Nynee Tal—Mussoorie—Subathoo—Darjeeling—Darjeeling Tea—Cultivation of Tea in India—Hill Stations in Madras—The Neilgherry Hills—Hill Stations of the Bombay Presidency—The Ghauts—Mahableshwur—Increased Heat of the Weather—Sickness in the Fortress—Heat-apoplexy—Sun-stroke—Cholera—Theory of the Disease—History of Cholera in India—Causes of Cholera—Its propagation—Small-pox—Vaccination in India—Science of Medicine in India—Its practice in former days—Its condition at present.

FOR the first week or two of the new year I was very unwell, but, slowly and gradually regaining my strength, the end of January saw me quite myself again and able to perform all the duties of my post. The weather was very cold during the months of January and February, necessitating fires in our quarters at night, but it was so far agreeable to us as it allowed of our continuing our usual long walks. Nothing particular occurred during this time. There were the usual balls and parties, which take place at this time of the year, several of which we attended, but they need no description.

About the middle of February the garrison races took place at Morar, and we were duly present the two afternoons the events came off. The meeting was a small one, and the different races not very well contested; for this station is not one of the places in India that boasts of a grand annual race meeting.

It is too far away for owners of horses to send to compete for the small amounts subscribed for the different events, consequently the station has to draw on its own resources to fill up the card. There are, however, some very good race meetings held in India, and both the horses competing and the value of the stakes they run for are equal to similar gatherings at home.

The Sonapur meeting is perhaps the largest attended of any in the Bengal Presidency, and extends over a week, drawing people from all parts of India to participate in its pleasures or profits. The Calcutta meeting also is always well attended, and one race in particular, the Derby Stakes for Arabs, calls forth a numerous entry of that class of animals, and creates among owners and trainers in India almost as much excitement as prevails among English horse racers in respect to the great Derby at Epsom. Each of the other presidency towns also has its annual meetings, and some of the larger stations follow their example; while garrison races take place in every quarter where a few troops are stationed. Some of the richer class of natives have taken to this sport immensely of late years, and many keep and train a number of horses to compete with their European fellow-subjects, who in every way show that this truly English pastime still holds a firm place in their hearts, although pursued under different surroundings.

The horses are usually ridden in the different races by our fellow-countrymen, amateur jockeys being found in every regiment in the service, while for many of the big events, and at large meetings, English professionals are engaged; but the number of natives who yearly enter the lists is on the increase, and some are no mean proficients in the art of riding. There are a good number of regular English jockeys to be met with now in India, and many make a good living, and something more, out of their skill. Some only appear in the country during the cold weather, the season when the meetings are held, returning when their services are no longer needed. The majority, however, remain for years attached to some particular stable, the horses of which they train and ride; and if engaged in that belonging to a wealthy native, as everything is left entirely to them, the appointment is apt to turn out a lucrative one. There is one great peculiarity attending horse-racing in India, in which it differs from similar sport at home, and that is in the matter of betting. There being no ring at any of the meetings, or professional layers of odds to any amount, such as are found on every course in Europe, it follows naturally that much gambling in the way of bets cannot be done, and owners or fanciers of different horses must seek other means to back their views, and win or lose according to their luck. This they are enabled to do by means of the selling lottery, held the night before, on every event on the card. There is, of course, a little mild betting between owners and others, but only for small amounts, everyone reserving his surplus cash for the lottery, the institution of the country, which I will endeavour briefly to describe.

The *modus operandi* is as follows: On the night preceding the races, it is customary for those who take an interest in the meeting to dine together at a race ordinary, prepared at the chief hotel, or club, or messroom. Immediately after dinner, the company, now swollen in numbers by the arrival of others, guests or members of the various regimental messes in the station, adjourn to the largest room available, and the business of the meeting commences. We will take, by way of illustration, a lottery, say on the 'Hunter's Plate' that figures first on the card, and for which there are six horses entered. The secretary of the meeting, who sits at the head of the table, commanding silence, reads out the names of the horses entered, and states the amount required to be subscribed to fill up the lottery. One thousand rupees at tickets of ten rupees, which gives a hundred subscribers, is a very usual amount, although there need be no limit, the only thing requisite to insure a larger sum being to raise the value of the tickets. A book, with large pages, each line in which is numbered from one to a hundred, lies before the secretary, who writes down the names of the subscribers against the respective numbers selected, until the whole have been filled in. There is no limit as to the number any one individual may take in any particular lottery, provided the stated hundred is not exceeded; or, if the bidding is brisk, the lottery may be made up to two hundred tickets, thus doubling its value, but one hundred is the usual thing, and when all are taken the lottery is said to be closed. Now commences the second and most exciting part of the proceedings. The numbers, each written on a small piece of card, are put into a hat or some such receptacle, and into another are placed pieces of folded paper, on each of which is written the name of one of the horses entered for the particular race, there being as many pieces of paper in the one hat as there are horses, and in the other, the hundred tickets. A ticket with a number is now drawn, and simultaneously one of the papers with the name of a horse, which is entered in the book against the name of the subscriber to whom the number belongs. When all the horses are drawn for, the selling part of the business begins, each name being put up to auction and knocked down to the highest bidder. Whoever purchases the name of the winner takes the lottery, the original drawer of the horse only getting for his share the amount for which it was knocked down. This is the time for owners or fanciers of certain horses to back their fancy by buying in their respective animals, and if they fear any particular horse as likely to interfere with their favourite, to purchase him as well, to make assurance doubly sure. When all the horses have been sold, the condition of the lottery is found to be materially altered, as regards its value; for not only does the purchaser of any horse pay the amount for which it was sold to the original drawer of the same, but a similar sum to the funds of the lottery. And if the bidding is brisk, the horses selling for large amounts, the total amount realized in one lottery is often very considerable, the original thousand or so of rupees subscribed being found, after the selling is over, to have risen to four or five times that sum.

As may be imagined, there is a good deal of excitement engendered at these proceedings, and the talk and noise is quite sufficient at times to render the work of the secretary no sinecure. On him devolves the entire work of keeping all the accounts, for no money passes at the time, everyone meeting the day after the conclusion of the races, and settling up everything in connection with the affair. The lottery being the only means of risking your money, and the biddings for any horse never being very high, no very large sum can be lost. Occasionally an adventurous sportsman may drop a few hundreds, particularly if in addition to 'plunging' in the lottery, he makes a few ill-advised bets, but as a general rule the winnings and losings are small, and it may fairly be said that the owners of horses in India race more for honour than profit.

The weather, unfortunately for us, soon began to grow warm, and unusually so for the time of year, for the first week of March brought with it the hot winds, and we had to prepare our punkahs and tatties to meet its approach. The early advent of the hot season caused us much regret, for we saw now an end to our walks and outdoor occupations, and looming before us the long days of close confinement to the house. And further, its premature commencement was not a happy augury of the future, as it promised an extended and trying period of heat, a foreboding which, much to our discomfort, was fully realized.

We had a little excitement to vary the monotony in the early part of April, for, on the 8th of that month, our valued friend and maid was married to the sergeant-major of the battery of Royal Artillery stationed in the fortress. And although this event was for her happiness, our joy was slightly tinged with regret, for she had been with us ever since our marriage, and we highly appreciated her always-willing services. We both attended the ceremony, which took place in our extempore church, a barrack room, wherein every alternate Sunday the clergyman or 'padre,' as ministers are termed in India, held forth to the dwellers on the rock, coming from Morar, his head quarters, for that purpose. The bride possessing no relatives in the country I stood in *loco parentis*, and gave her away at the altar in the true orthodox paternal fashion, and after the ceremony the happy couple started for their abode, amidst the best wishes and congratulations of all their friends, including our native servants, with whom she was a great favourite. Our faithful henchman, Esau, was in fact quite overcome, and felt her departure grievously, for as he talked English as well as his native tongue, he could appreciate her more fully, and he had often confided to us the tender fact that he was "very fond on the Courtis." We shall never forget his appearance at the ceremony, for being a Christian he was present in the church, where, arrayed in a gala costume of a long white garment, with a high shirt collar, and his turban off his head in deference to the sacredness of the edifice, he stood apart with a dismal expression on his black face, the most dejected-looking native it was ever our fortune to behold.

The heat increased day by day, and to do anything was an exertion; but, to keep us from utter stagnation, we got up some theatricals and tableaux, which were a great success, and much appreciated by such of the officers and ladies as were left in the fortress and Morar, while the men and their families enjoyed them immensely. As this is the time of year in India when all but the most necessary parades or duties are discontinued, a great proportion of the officers are able to obtain leave of absence, and many of our friends had taken their departure for the hills with their families. Some had proceeded to Simla, Nynee Tal, or Mussoorie, all in the Himalayas; while many had gone to Kashmir, which although a long distance off, had more inducements to offer in the way of scenery and sport, as well as in economy. Once arrived in that country the expense of living is ridiculously small, and there is no rent to pay, for tents, or at the most a rudely-constructed log hut, suffice; whereas a residence of a few months at Simla, or other hill stations, is very expensive. The rents of houses and hotel charges in these most favoured spots are high, and every necessary article of consumption can only be obtained at double the price usually given in the plains, the expense of the increased road carriage being necessarily added; consequently those who do not mind hard marching and rough living proceed now in preference to the Happy Valley. Every one who can possibly manage it goes away for some months in the hot season; for it is highly necessary for health's sake that a change to a cooler climate should be effected. Many officers and other officials send their wives and families annually to the hills for six months, and they either accompany them and remain the whole time, or join them later, according to the length of their leave. The leave season commences on the 15th April and lasts until the 15th October, when all have to be back at their posts; and it is the usual rule—as with the exception of a very few, or those on sick leave, only a certain proportion of the officers of a regiment or the civil officials of a station can absent themselves at one time—to divide the season into two equal portions, so that half of the number go away on first leave until 15th July, return on that date, and allow the remainder to enjoy a similar length of time in the second leave, which expires on the 15th October. The soldiers and their families also enjoy the like privilege, in a minor degree, a certain number being chosen from each regiment in the different garrisons and sent up to the nearest hill depôt for the six unhealthy months of the year. It is usual to make

Hill Stations.

a selection for this from among the sick and weakly, for whom a change is highly necessary; and as the number is limited the arrangement of this matter is usually left to the medical officer. Speaking from experience, I may say that to effect a satisfactory arrangement is no easy task; for the allotted number to be sent is usually only about five per cent. of the strength, and naturally nearly everyone is anxious to be amongst the favoured few.

There are in the Bengal Presidency a considerable number of hill stations for the officers proceeding on leave to select from, while many are used entirely as sanitaria for the soldiers; and others again are regular military stations, each being garrisoned by a British regiment, which, after a couple of years' residence, moves off, and makes way for another, selected from some other part of the presidency. This arrangement is undoubtedly conducive to the general health of the men of a regiment, and, in connection with the improved sanitary regulations enforced wherever troops are stationed, assists largely in maintaining the comparatively healthy condition that characterizes the British army in India at the present day. And although the climate, so unlike our native air, annually claims many victims, yet with the exception of an epidemic of cholera, or some other fatal disease attacking a station or regiment, when the death rate is naturally increased, the yearly statistics of sickness are more promising than one would imagine, and, thanks to the care and attention lavished on the soldier in every detail affecting his health, are improving year after year, affording a marked contrast to the sickness and mortality that prevailed not so many years ago, when sanitary science was in its infancy.

The question of hill stations for the British troops in India is often agitated, and is of great interest to all who are acquainted with the country. That there are many places, especially in the lower ranges of the Himalayas, which with very little outlay could afford accommodation to the whole of the army, is quite true. And undoubtedly the mere fact of living in a climate of a character to which one is accustomed would be conducive to health. But other points have to be taken into consideration, political and strategical; and as India, won by the sword, is held by the sword, it would not, in the opinion of those acquainted with the subject, be advisable to lodge the active force of our policy in isolated positions, or to remove it entirely from the vicinity of large towns, where the actual presence of the red-coated 'gora logue,' or soldier, is an evidence of the armed power of the dominant race.

The Bombay and Madras Presidencies are not so highly favoured by nature in localities of this description; and although they possess many stations, notably on the Neilgherries and on the Ghauts and on smaller hills, yet these lack the grandeur of the scenery and the vastness of range found on the Himalayan chain.

The chief of all hill stations in India is the well-known Simla, a gay and fashionable locality, the residence of the Viceroy in the hot weather, and the seat of government during that time of the year, the various offices and personnel being transferred thither from Calcutta for that purpose, while many of them, especially of the military departments, remain there all the year round. The station is a large and rapidly increasing place, situated in the Himalayas, in the Punjab,

Simla and Nynee Tal. 373

and distant about seventy miles from Umballa, a large town and military cantonment on the Sinde, Punjab, and Delhi railway, whence a carriage road allows one to proceed by dak to this favourite sanitarium. Besides a bazaar, which might almost be called a town, it contains hundreds of houses built of wood and stone in European style, dispersed amongst forests of oaks and firs along the crests of different mountain ranges. Its height is about seven thousand three hundred feet above the sea, and the summer heat has seldom been found to rise over seventy-two degrees, while the mean temperature of the year is about sixty-two degrees Fahrenheit. From its delicious climate and exquisite scenery it is deservedly a popular place among Europeans in India, who flock thither yearly from all parts, the visitors comprising nearly all the more opulent of our fellow-countrymen; for although a charming spot, possessing some excellent hotels, it is a costly place to reside in for any length of time.

Nynee Tal, in the province of Kumaon, is a very favourite spot, and can easily be reached from Bareilly, on the Oudh and Rohilkund railway. Here a horse-dak can be obtained to Rambagh, a distance of seventy-five miles. This occupies about twelve hours, and then the journey must be performed for another ten miles up the hill, either by ponies, jampans, or dandies. This sanitarium is named after the lake on the borders of which it is situated—a fine sheet of water on the top of a range of mountains, at an elevation of six thousand four hundred feet, a height which enables visitors to the place to enjoy a home-like climate and surroundings, to which the lake largely contributes.

Mussoorie, in that part of the Himalayas known as the hills

north of Deyrah, is another large and flourishing place, and I much enjoyed a residence there of several months' duration in 1869; for the scenery is exquisite, and the view of the snowy range of the Himalayas, as seen from this spot, unsurpassed by any other. It is easily reached from Saharunpur, a town on the line of rail a hundred miles from Delhi, whence a carriage road conducts one through the Doon to Deyrah and Rajpur, at the foot of the hills. Further north we find a large station at Murree, one of the starting-places for Kashmir. The smaller stations, such as Raneekhet, Chuckrata, Kussowlie, Subathoo, Dalhousie, and Darjeeling, are, the last perhaps excepted, chiefly military convalescent depôts, or quarters for a regiment, and are not much visited except by those who combine duty with pleasure.

Darjeeling, however, merits a few words; for being easy of access from Calcutta, it is much favoured by the residents of that city, who can proceed by rail to within a hundred and forty miles of the foot of the hills. It is about seven thousand four hundred feet above the sea level, in the Sikkim territory, not very far distant from the frontier of Thibet, and the view from the station overlooks mountain ranges covered with dense forests, save in a few spots where partial clearances have been made for the purposes of cultivation. No bare or grassy heights meet the eye, and were it not for the magnificence of the snow-covered mountains which form the background, the view might be termed monotonous. But with these towering snow-clad ranges, reflecting in glittering colours the rays of the sun, this opinion cannot be maintained; for such a wealth of towering peaks can rarely be seen from one spot, including, among many others, Mount

Everest, the loftiest in the whole Himalayan chain, and the highest mountain in the world, its elevation above the sea-level being no less than twenty-nine thousand feet.

The climate of Darjeeling is very moist, and the total rainfall during the year exceeds by a considerable amount that of any other hill-station in India. This great humidity, though unpleasant to the sojourner, conduces to the growth of vegetation, which is found here in great luxuriance; and it appears to suit the cultivation of the tea-plant, the tea from this part of the country being deservedly held in high esteem. This new branch of industry has only been introduced into this country of late years, and at the present time is in a flourishing condition, although just emerging from a state of great depression, mainly owing to over-speculation at the outset, and great hostility to the sale of the tea in foreign markets. The excellence of the Indian tea is however too firmly established now to meet with much opposition, and every pound produced finds a ready sale at remunerative prices out of the country, for little or none is retained for home consumption, the natives caring nothing for the infusion of the herb, and wondering at its appreciation by the Europeans. The plant is cultivated in gardens specially laid out for the purpose, and the leaf when gathered is treated in the same way as in China, the original home of this luxury. It produces a tea similar in appearance to the celestial species, though of a different flavour, harsher and rougher, but much esteemed by many, while a mixture of the two sorts—Chinese and Indian—yields a decoction of great excellence. The demand for this tea now more than equals the production, and in Darjeeling, Assam, and the Doon (a place already mentioned as being at the foot of the hills leading to Mussoorie) land is being rapidly converted into plantations for its growth. I know of no occupation in the country better suited to a man with a moderate capital, and who does not object to a somewhat monotonous and isolated existence, than that of an Indian tea-planter.

Concerning the hill stations in Madras and Bombay Presidencies little need be said, for they are few in number. There being no chain of mountains like the Himalayas, they are not on so extensive a scale; and although the scenery is in many places very beautiful, they lack the grandeur of those already mentioned. In Madras, the Neilgherry Hills take the place of the Himalayas, and on these are to be found the different stations and sanitaria utilized by the officials, both civil and military, of the 'benighted presidency,' chief among which is Ootacomund, the abode of the governor in the hot weather. This range forms a mass of mountains in South Hindustan, partly in the province of Coimbatar, at the southern extremity of the East and West Ghauts, and is, as it were, a connecting-link between them. It extends east to west thirty-four miles; north to south fifteen; and its culminating point is nine thousand nine hundred and forty-one feet high. The hills form a plateau, possessing peaks varying in height from five to eight thousand feet; and the salubrity of the climate at the different stations, as at the one already mentioned, is unsurpassed in the country. And although the higher parts are frosty even in summer, and in winter covered with snow, lower down, in the localities usually selected for the abode of man, the surface is a fine pasture, like much of our downs, the characteristics of this less-elevated portion, both in climate and vegetation, approaching those of the south of Europe.

In the Bombay Presidency the East and West Ghauts, the former bounding the table-land of the Deccan on the east, and the latter on the west, are the chief ranges that afford the elevated localities, and these are few in number and small in size. We passed over the Ghauts on our way to Jubbulpur from Bombay, and these hills were noticed in the description of that journey. Their most elevated peaks are only about six thousand feet high, and it is consequently never very cold on the summit, the usual temperature being similar to that of an English summer. Hence they afford an agreeable place of residence, as they possess in addition a great deal of beautiful and highly picturesque scenery, which is seen to perfection at Mahableshwur, a station in the Ghauts of the Concan, easily reached from Bombay, and crowded during the summer by the denizens of that flourishing city.

To return to our own doings. The other medical officer in the fortress being the senior, had consequently the first choice as regards leave, and preferring the first half, took his departure for Nynee Tal, leaving me in sole charge of the garrison, with the prospect of double work during the most trying season of the year, until his return on the 15th July, when we hoped in our turn to get away and enjoy the cooler climate of Kashmir, which we had selected for our holiday trip. We soon began to count the days to his return, as the heat became something dreadful; for although Gwalior has always had the reputation of being a hot place, this year it surpassed itself, and the thermometer often showed a temperature night after night of a hundred degrees, and even more, in the hospital and quarters, after being still higher in the daytime. To add to our misery, the hot wind often fell for days together, when tatties were of no avail. Soon the effects of this unnatural condition of things began to show itself, as daily my sick list grew heavier, and I had to chronicle with sorrow the deaths of several fine men from heat-apoplexy, while many of the children literally faded away.

Heat-apoplexy annually claims many victims in India, and is a highly dangerous disease, the prognosis being in the majority of cases decidedly unfavourable, while its approach is also most insidious. A man in perfect health at night may be found dead in his bed in the morning, without having even made a sign. Numerous deaths enumerated under this head are undoubtedly often due to sun-stroke; for this affection varies in different cases. In many instances—and probably it is the most common form—the individual, after exposure to the sun, falls down insensible, and making one or two gasps, either dies at once from syncope, or, recovering in a measure from the effects of its first onset by the remedies employed (which consist chiefly of cold douches to the head and the administration of stimulants), may either rapidly get well or die eventually from the continued fever, the partial paralysis, and the great prostration, which usually accompany the convalescence of this complaint. In other cases after exposure a man will be seen to be listless and stupid, making no complaint beyond saying that his head feels a little queer, yet in twelve hours he may be dead, and in a very few hours again even buried; for interment follows very rapidly after death in the tropics. This form of seizure usually happens towards evening, with symptoms of stupor and insensibility, succeeded by great

Heat Apoplexy.

heat of the skin, dilatation of the pupils, and great rapidity and fulness of the pulse, and the patient sinks rapidly. This apoplectic condition arises from the effects of exposure to the sun, and, although similar in its symptoms, must be distinguished from cases of heat apoplexy, the generally fatal results of which are due only to the intense heat acting as a provocative to cerebral congestion.

We were, however, spared any attacks of cholera, as this disease, though it may occur in the hot weather, usually makes its appearance during the rains. A few suspicious attacks occurred, but much to my relief they did not prove true cases of this scourge. However, it unhappily broke out in an epidemic form in the fortress during our tour in Kashmir, causing several deaths among my former charge, who were enfeebled through the causes already mentioned. This scourge of India is always present in the country at some place or other, and few of us have not been in a station during an epidemic of this dreaded disease. In former days I had served through several severe visitations of the complaint, and in the very fortress we were now inhabiting had striven in vain against the ravages it was making in the regiment to which I then belonged.

It is generally believed that epidemic cholera is of Eastern origin, and that its natural habitat is Asia; and while many affirm that India was the part of that continent where the disease originated, others again incline to the opinion that it was introduced from without into that country, further stating that this only took place at the beginning of the present century. Against this hypothesis a great deal may be said; for it is a well-known fact that the inhabitants of India have for a very long period suffered from a disease with similar symptoms, which is even referred to in some works of their earliest writers, but called by another name than that by which cholera is characterized by the natives at the present day. It may be taken into consideration in support of the theory of late introduction, that the epidemics have never been so severe, or the deaths so numerous, as in the present century. But here again, European intercourse with the inhabitants has during that time largely increased; every case that occurs in provinces under our rule is ascertained; and modern research having separated and classed the train of symptoms which in the aggregate form the special disease now termed cholera, every epidemic and every death is made known to the world. This was not so formerly, when its ravages were unchecked, and its symptoms undistinguished from any other complaint, the people, totally apathetic in all cases affecting life or health, simply calling it by any name that suited their fancy, so that what passed in former days in regard to this fatal scourge can never be ascertained with any certainty; while as no statistics were ever then compiled, it follows naturally that of late years, as shown by the carefully-prepared records, its effects have appeared to be severely felt, both among Europeans and natives. And without going so far as to say that its introduction only occurred in the present century, we may, I think, claim for this era the fact that cholera was first known and understood in India to be a separate and distinct disease, and the effects of its presence made painfully apparent to all.

According to some authors, cholera has always existed in Europe, including England; but from the description given by Sydenham, a talented physician who flourished in the seventeenth century, it may at least be doubted whether the disease he speaks of was not rather of the nature of dysentery than identical with that under consideration. There can be no doubt, however, that it existed in England, and caused frightful mortality, during the years 1831-32, 1848-49, 1853-54; and on all these occasions, whether rightly or wrongly, India has been credited as the place whence it was imported. Although not wishing to introduce a professional treatise on disease into the present volume, yet as cholera is so connected with the country which forms the subject of this work, I may be pardoned for the slight dissertation already made; and further, as it may prove interesting to some, conclude with a few words on our present knowledge of this dread disease. This may be summed up briefly in the one short sentence, 'We know little or nothing about it;' for, despite all the professional talent brought to bear on the subject, and the opportunities met with in the East for its study, it has hitherto baffled all research. The causes of cholera are still a sealed mystery, and the nature of the disease, and consequently its treatment, as yet very imperfectly understood.

The only explanation which can be given of the cause of cholera is that it is due to some *materies morbi*, some specific poison, a septic agent, the existence, increase, power, and transmission of which from place to place, are favoured by some particular state of the atmosphere, associated probably with a high temperature. Whether the cholera poison enters the blood through the skin, through the lungs, or through the alimentary canal, is a question which cannot be said to have been satisfactorily solved. According to some the theory sustained is that the poison being swallowed with the food, or drink, is reproduced in the alimentary canal, and being discharged with the excretions propagates the disease by finding access in the same way to the stomachs of others. Others again, and to this opinion I myself incline, hold that it is generated in the air under certain conditions, like the poison that produces the intermittent fevers, and is absorbed by the lungs; while many affirm that it is only an aggravated form of that well-known disease, ague. But however it originates, the action of the poison is undoubtedly encouraged by filth of all kinds, and in crowds of people under unsanitary conditions, such as so often occur in India; while, when once fairly started, it appears to be, to a certain degree, contagious: in other words, I believe that human intercourse has a share in propagating the disease, though it is not the only means of effecting its diffusion.

Another disease may be mentioned as common in India; namely, small-pox, though with the exception of the native states it is not nearly so prevalent as in former days. The natives are beginning to realize the beneficial effects of vaccination, and the prejudice against this operation is becoming rapidly lessened, although at first it was considered impious and insulting to the cow, one of the favourite Hindu deities. The country is now, however, divided into vaccination districts, and every possible means employed by the proper officials to induce the people to submit, either themselves or at least their children, to the preventive means employed by civilized nations. That this arrangement is already palpably successful can be seen in the fact that the native bazaars are not so full of men and women progressing towards recovery, who walked about most unconcernedly in the throng in the desquamative or most contagious period of the disease. However, this indifference is hardly to be wondered at when only a few years ago it was considered necessary (and means employed to create the result) that every junior member of a native household should contract this disease, in addition to its other infantile ailments.

While on this subject we may take a glance at the practice of medicine by the natives of India. We find in the first place that their acquaintance with the healing art was very extensive, even at remote periods. It is not known with any certainty when it was first studied or practised by them; but there are some medical treatises extant dating from several centuries back, and we know that two of the most celebrated Hindu physicians flourished in the eighth century, and that the writers of other countries, where this art was then in its infancy, openly acknowledged their obligations to the medical writers of India, and fully appreciated their knowledge of simples, in which they gave early lessons even to civilized Europe. India can also undoubtedly claim the honour of being the first nation in which charitable institutions for the cure of disease were inaugurated. For there is no reason to doubt the record that King Asoka, the zealous Buddhist propagandist, erected in all the large towns owning his sovereignty hospitals for the medical treatment of his subjects. And not only so, but agreeably to the tenets of the then popular religion, which enjoined strict care of all animal life, he also provided similar buildings for attending to the wants of the weakly members of the brute creation. And when we consider that this took place at least two hundred and fifty years before the Christian era, we may, I think, concede the palm of originality to our Aryan brethren in a matter which, in our own time, stands pre-eminent in every civilized nation as the greatest comfort and blessing to the sick and needy.

The Hindu use of medicines seems to have been very bold, and they were the first people who employed minerals internally; for they not only gave mercury in that manner, but arsenic and arsenious acid, which they rightly discovered to be remedies in intermittent fevers. The Hindu physicians were attentive to the pulse, and to the state of the skin, of the tongue, eyes, &c., and often formed correct prognostics from the observation of the symptoms; but the practice was entirely empirical, and then, as at the present time, they called in astrology and magic to the aid of their medicines, often accompanying them with mystical verses and charms. Their surgery was as remarkable as their medicine, especially when we recollect their ignorance of anatomy. They cut for the stone, couched for the cataract, and in their early works enumerate no less than one hundred and twenty-seven sorts of surgical instruments. But these instruments were probably always rude; and at present the native implements are so much so, that operations by their aid are often fatal. At the present day pure native science has no doubt declined; and when we do find a practitioner of strictly home growth, it will be seen that he is content to follow the practice in its entirety, as handed down to him by his forefathers, without inquiry. But it is now more generally the case, a new school having arisen since European intercourse has so much increased, that the profession of medicine in India among the purely native classes is carried on by doctors, of whom the majority have acquired their knowledge under European tutelage.

CHAPTER XVII.

Departure for Kashmir—Dak to Agra—Railway journey to Lahore—Meerut—Jullunder—The river Sutlej—City of Umritsur—Its history—The Golden Temple—Lahore—Territory of the Punjab—The Five Rivers—Description of the Punjab—Its population—The Sikhs—History of the Punjab—Rise of the Sikhs—Their origin—Religion of the Sikhs—Founder of their religion—The Guru Nanak—His life and work—His successors—Guru Govind Singh—The Sikhs and the Mohammedans—Rise of the Sikh power—Runjeet Singh—His successors—Maharajah Dhuleep Singh—Sikh wars with the English—Fall of the Sikh power—The Koh-i-noor Diamond—City of Lahore—Its buildings—Mausoleum of Jehangir—The Fort and Palace—The Civil Station—Arrival at Wuzzeerabad—Crossing the Chenab—Gujerat—Jhelum—Rawul Pindi—Arrival at Murree—Description of Murree—Start for Kashmir.

THE anxiously-awaited day at length arrived; and on the 14th of July the return of the senior medical officer to the fortress left us at liberty to take our departure *en route* for Kashmir. Our preparations had all been completed for some time, and we were quite ready for the start, which took place the same evening. We had already forwarded to Agra the greater part of our baggage, under the charge of three of our servants, which number, with Esau, formed the complement we intended to take with us. The rest of our establishment we discharged, with mutual regret; for they were all good servants, and appeared to be attached to us, but it was impossible to take the whole of them, and our return to the fortress after the expiration of our leave was uncertain.

Start for Kashmir.

One dak gharry therefore sufficed for our party, which consisted of our two selves, Esau, who went outside, and little Fizz, who completed the trio within the vehicle. We left the fortress about nine p.m. on a beautiful moonlight night, and travelled over the same road we had passed on our way from Agra, exactly one year before, having arrived at Gwalior on the 15th July in the preceding year. No adventures befell us during the night, and we slept soundly on our mattress, spread out within the carriage, waking up about daybreak on our arrival at Dholepur, where we halted for a couple of hours, and after a bath and breakfast proceeded on our way, arriving at Agra at five p.m. the same evening. We went to the same hotel as on our former visit, where we found our servants and luggage awaiting our arrival. Having already seen all the sights of this city, we made no stay, but started off on the following day for Lahore, a railway journey of twenty-four hours, the distance from Agra to the capital of the Punjab being four hundred and fifty miles.

The train left at ten a.m., and we travelled by the East Indian line as far as Ghazeeabad, which we reached at half-past five, where, pending the arrival of the train from Calcutta, in which we were to proceed, we partook of dinner, served in the excellent refreshment-room at the station. The line from Agra to this place passes through a flat but comparatively fertile country, dotted over with the usual topes of trees and mud-built villages, the ordinary characteristics of Indian scenery. No place of note is passed, with the exception of Allyghur, which city, a great mart of commerce, contains several fine gardens, and was one of the places stormed by Lord Lake in 1803, and taken from Dowlut Rao

Scindia's army, under General Perron, during our war to break the power of the Mahratta confederacy.

Shortly after leaving Ghazeeabad, on the approach of darkness, the wind fell, and the weather became intensely close and hot, such as is often felt in the country during a break in the rains. It was fortunate for us therefore that we had an entire carriage, and were enabled to don light sleeping raiment, and establish ourselves comfortably for the night, which we did soon after passing Meerut city and cantonment, the first station in which the Mutiny broke out in May, 1857. As it was dark we could not see much of the scenery we were passing through; but the loss was not great, as the whole of the country from Agra to Lahore is flat and uninteresting, although the line passes through some noteworthy towns and villages. About a hundred and forty miles from Meerut is the large cantonment of Umballa, near the city of that name, distant over one thousand miles from Calcutta, and the first town of any note we had reached after leaving the North-West Provinces to enter upon the Punjab. Another seventy miles after passing this place brings one to Loodhiana, famous for its manufacture of shawls, the well-known shawl of fine wool known as 'Rampore chuddahs' being one of the varieties here produced.

We passed Jullunder, also a large military cantonment, just as the day was breaking, and soon afterwards arrived at the Sutlej, which fine river we crossed by means of the magnificent railway bridge which spans its depths. The Sutlej is one of the five rivers of the Punjab, of which it forms the east boundary, and has its rise in the mountains of Thibet. After a course of nine hundred miles it falls into the Indus, being in its upper course a rushing, raging torrent, but expanding into a wide, steadily-flowing river further down. It is greatly swollen annually during the rains, as was the case when we passed over, and its dimensions so much enlarged thereby as to necessitate a bridge over it a mile and a half in length. Another thirty miles brought us to Umritsur, a large and flourishing city and commercial centre, well worthy of a visit from the passing traveller. It is a compactly-built town, containing nearly one hundred and fifty thousand inhabitants, and the shops and bazaars exhibit in great abundance the richest products of India, as it enjoys an extensive transit trade. Its staple articles of commerce are the shawls made in imitation of those in Kashmir, out of wool obtained from Thibet and Bokhara. Since its foundation it has been regarded as the sacred capital of the Punjab by the Sikhs, the most important race among the Punjabis, the inhabitants of this part of India. It originated when, in the year 1581, Ram Das, their fourth guru or spiritual leader, converted an ancient pool, in what was then a little village and his birthplace, into a splendid tank, and called it 'Umritsur'—'the fount of immortality,' 'the spring of nectar.' On a little island in the tank he erected a marble shrine, and to this spot the followers of the new Sikh religion and their converts came every year. The village rapidly became a town, and that town the most important city of the Punjab; for it was the centre of an organization, the desire of which was the destruction of Mohammedanism as the ruling power, but which soon grew to be political in its aim. The Golden Temple of Umritsur now stands on the spot once occupied by the shrine of Ram Das, which was destroyed during the invasion of the terrible Ahmed Shah of Cabul. It is a marble structure, square, with dome and minarets; and although considered by some to be a splendid example of the modern temple architecture of India, is by many judges termed a hybrid mixture of an idol-house and a mosque. Its roof is plated with the gilded metal from which it derives its name, and its walls are covered with erotic frescoes. It is dedicated to the god Vishnu, and is crowded with priests, the whole establishment being maintained from rich lands secured to it in former days, with which our government has not interfered. If the visitor sees it on the night of any festival it is a spectacle never to be forgotten; for the whole temple is illuminated with myriads of lamps, as are likewise the houses of the chiefs erected around the tank, the holy centre of their faith, to the shrine of which they gain access by a raised path connecting the island with the bank. The water of the tank is crowded with men and women washing off their sins, whilst multitudes who have performed this ceremony are marching round and round the sanctuary, to the accompaniments of the music, shouting, and din, which characterise religious festivals in the East.

Thirty miles from this flourishing city lies Lahore, with its military cantonment and station of Meean Meer, an arid spot, distant three miles from the capital, where we arrived at ten o'clock, tired and dusty, after a long and fatiguing journey. We drove from the terminus to the Railway Hotel, not very far distant, and right welcome were the bath and breakfast, and the rest in the cool house, after the heat and discomfort of the close and stuffy railway carriage. Towards evening we sallied forth to view the sights of the city; and as we fully exhausted these, partly on this and partly on the other occasion when we passed through Lahore, on our way home, I shall here detail what we saw.

Before, however, entering upon this topic, let us take a glance at the district of which this city is the capital, and at the religion of the Sikhs, somewhile the dominant race in the Punjab. The Punjab, which is a Persian word, signifying the Five Waters, is an extensive territory in the north-west of Hindustan, formerly under the dominion of the Sikhs, but which since 1849 has been attached to the Presidency of Bengal, and ruled over by the Viceroy, through the agency of a Lieutenant-Governor, whose residence is at Lahore. It is called the Punjab from its position amongst five great affluents of the Indus, which forms its western, as the Sutlej does its eastern, boundary. On the north are the Pir Panjal section of the Himalaya mountains, and on the west the Kyber and Soliman ranges, comprising the main stream of the Indus in that part of its course. In the extreme north it is rendered mountainous by spurs or offsets of the great Himalayan system; but with these exceptions the surface is for the most part an extensive plain, gradually sloping in the direction of the rivers by which it is so abundantly irrigated—the Jhelum, the ancient Hydaspes of the Greeks, the Chenab, the Ravee, the Beas, and the Sutlej. These streams divide the country into five districts, or 'doabs' (countries between two rivers), covering an area of over two hundred and twenty thousand square miles. The soil for the most part is far from fertile, and the vegetation scanty; large trees are scarce, and extensive tracts may be met with consisting of sand or stiff clay, producing but little in the way of crops, and nothing larger than mimosas, acacias, thorns, and other bushes. The climate is also against agricultural pursuits; for it is hot and dry, and little rain falls except in the higher country; and while in winter the cold is severe, even to a European, in summer the heat is equally excessive, and more oppressive than in any other part of India. The manufacturing industries of the Punjab are therefore more extensive and important than its agriculture; and many towns are distinguished for their silk and cotton fabrics, while it enjoys from its position an extensive trade with Cabul, Bokhara, and other parts of Central Asia.

The population, including that of the feudatory states, is estimated at over twenty-three million souls, composed of various races, partly of Afghans and Pathans, holding the Mohammedan faith, but principally of Jats and others of Hindu descent, who compose the bulk of the Punjabis; while the Sikhs proper, although at one time the dominant race, muster less than a fifth of the entire inhabitants. The Punjabis are, as a rule, in physical respects superior to any other natives of India, being fully as active as the Mahrattas, and having stout, well-rounded limbs, handsome countenances, and a graceful carriage; while the women are elegantly shaped, often very fair in complexion, and usually very attractive. The greater number of the Sikhs were originally of Jat origin; but owing to the changes operated on them by the practice of their new religion, and their life and occupations having been entirely military, they have now as distinct a national character as any of the original races. Physically they are highly endowed—finely formed, and possessed of great powers of endurance, as well as being very courageous.

The Sikhs.

They are tall and thin, darker than the generality of the Punjabis, and particularly dark for so northern a people. They are active horsemen, skilful in the use of arms, and the majority are still soldiers in the pay of our government, whose best native troops they are, or in that of the feudatory princes. A few follow the pursuits of business or agriculture; but they differ little in character from the soldiers, and are equally skilful in the use of arms. All, indeed, are still by nature warriors, but no longer fanatics; and though unpolished, unlike the other races in India they are manly, frank, and sociable, and devoted to pleasures of every description and degree, in which their freedom from caste rules allows them readily to participate.

The Punjab seems to have been a place of note in very early times, and the first portion of the continent of India made known to other nations, having been the scene of some of Alexander the Great's most arduous exploits, particularly during his expedition against Porus, one of the ancient Indian kings. With the exception of this authenticated fact, the early history of the Punjab is, like the history of the other parts of the country, wrapped in obscurity, from which it does not emerge until the first great landmark of Indian history—that made by the invasion of the Mohammedans. At the time of the great invasion in 920 it was overrun by the troops of Mahmoud of Guzni, and was the first and most lasting conquest of the invaders; for it remained in the hands of this potentate and his successors for nearly two hundred years, the city of Lahore being all the time the capital and seat of government. When the house of Ghuzni fell before the power of the house of Ghor it passed into Ghori hands; and on the accession of the line known as the slave kings of Delhi, a troubled time arose for this province; for their authority was not sufficiently established in this northern part of their dominions, and it became the scene of strife amongst the rival factions, and was ruled by a succession of turbulent and licentious chiefs, principally Afghans.

In 1519 Baber, the founder of the Mogul dynasty, conquered the country, and it became a part of the Delhi empire. It was much appreciated by several of that line, who made Lahore a place of royal residence, notably Jehangir, who lived a great part of his time in his northern possessions, and was buried in this city. During the reigns of the later Moguls, the Sikhs, who were prominent even in the time of Akber, commenced to make themselves felt, becoming a formidable enemy to the Mohammedan power they were sworn to destroy. They were, however, defeated, and little is then heard of them until after the advent of Nadir Shah of Persia, who gave the final blow to the tottering Mogul dynasty, and to whom the Punjab, with other territory, was ceded by the emperor. Nadir's return to his native country gave the opportunity for which the Sikhs had been longing, and they then commenced that series of operations which made them in time the masters of the Punjab, and formidable enemies to the growing British power.

The Sikhs, so called from a Sanskrit word meaning disciple, were originally simply a religious sect, professing the purest deism, and their faith is chiefly distinguishable from that of the Hindus, of which it is a heterodox form, by their worshipping one only and invisible God. The notion of a supreme deity, who is both creator and protector, pervades all their sacred writings; and although the existence of other Hindu deities is not denied, no divine honours are publicly paid to them. The founder of their religion is looked upon as an incorporeal supreme spirit, who had come to save the world, and who, having enjoyed personal communion with the Lord, was styled by him the 'Guru;' and being exalted himself, was invested with the power of exalting others, through conversion to the new faith. Another important distinction between the Sikhs and the other Hindus is the absence of caste, and consequently of most of the restraints inherent in that institution. The flesh of the cow is the only article of animal food prohibited by their faith, and on this head their prejudices are stronger even than those of Hindus of the orthodox Brahmanical persuasion. They do not refuse to eat or to intermarry with other Hindus, more especially with those who have become converts to their form of religion; but they do not extend the same liberality to Mohammedans, against whom they have always exhibited great national hostility.

The founder of the Sikh religion was the estimable Nanak Shah, of the caste of Kshatriyas, who was born, in 1469, in the village of Talwandi, now the town of Rajapur, in the province of Lahore. In early youth he manifested strong religious tendencies, and after travelling a good deal in Persia and Arabia, even visiting, it is said, the holy Mohammedan shrines of Medina and Mecca, he consecrated his life to religious devotion soon after his return to his native country. He entertained the idea of effecting a union between Hindus and Mohammedans by introducing simplicity of faith and purity of morals. Hence he treated both religions with respect, and laboured to remove only what was superfluous and dissonant, and to lead the people to a practical religion, to a pure worship of God and the love of mankind. The ennobling religion established by Nanak, and the benevolence of his doctrines, corresponded with the purity of his whole life, and as a governor and priest he exercised, during his stay on earth, a spiritual and temporal dominion over his disciples. At his death, in 1540, he transferred the power to a favourite disciple named Lehana, who with his successors, notably Arjun Mall, gave stability to the religion and unity to its professions, by collecting the writings of Nanak and publishing them as the 'Grunth,' or sacred book of the sect. By this time the Sikhs had entirely rejected the authority both of the Koran and the Vedas, and thus aroused the enmity of the Mohammedans, as well as of the Brahmans, who seized Arjun Mall and threw him into prison, where he died. Eager to avenge his father's death, Har Govind, the son and successor of Arjun Mall, transformed the Sikhs from a peaceful religious sect into valiant warriors, and under his reign and that of his successors a bloody contest was maintained between them and the paramount Mogul power. Notwithstanding the dissensions which broke out among themselves, they continued their animosity to the Mussulmans, and confirmed their martial habits, until the accession, in 1675, of Guru' Govind Singh, the grandson of Har Govind, and the tenth spiritual chief from Nanak, the founder. This leader first conceived the idea of forming the Sikhs into a religious and military commonwealth, and executed his design with the systematic spirit of a Grecian lawgiver, virtually becoming the founder of the future Sikh state.

The Sikh Policy.

To increase the number of his society, Govind Singh totally abolished the yet lingering distinctions of caste among its members, admitting all converts, whether Mohammedan or Hindu, Brahman or Chandala, to a perfect equality; while to preserve its unity he instituted a peculiar dress and peculiar manners, by which his followers were to be distinguished from all the rest of mankind, whilst every male was to be a vowed soldier from his birth or initiation. Their numbers were, however, inadequate to accomplish their plans of resistance; and after a long struggle, in which their bravery earned for them the title of 'Singhs,' or lions, which before had been confined to the Rajputs, as the first military order among the Hindus, Guru Govind saw his strongholds taken, his family massacred, and his followers slain, mutilated, or dispersed. He died in 1708, and with him died also the hopes of the oppressed in the Hindu provinces of India, amidst all the misery which marked the virtual fall of the Mogul empire on the death of Aurungzebe. As the Sikhs refused to appoint a successor, in accordance with the prophecy which limited the number of the Gurus to ten, he was the last and tenth head of the Sikhs in descent from the founder.

Although it is sometimes possible to crush a religion after it has taken root, this can only be done by long and steady persecution, which internal disturbances prevented the Moguls applying. The Sikhs gradually yielded to the superior power of the Mohammedans, who, in order to exterminate the hated sect, set a price upon their heads, and put every adherent they could secure to death. These severities, however, only exalted their fanaticism, and inspired a gloomy spirit of vengeance; for the remnants of the sect, escaping to the mountains, faithfully preserved the doctrines of their fathers, cherishing at the same time an unextinguishable hatred towards their persecutors. After Nadir Shah's return to Persia they ventured to leave the mountains again, and taking advantage of the confusion which reigned, they subdued Lahore, and overran the country east of the Jhelum, establishing military posts in all the districts acquired. In course of time the Sikhs became broken up into a number of independent communities, each governed by a sirdar or chief, and between these almost incessant hostilities were carried on. One of these sirdars, Maha-Singh, eventually acquired a preponderating influence among the rest; and when he died in 1792, his son, Runjeet Singh, after the expulsion of the last of the Afghan kings, Shah Shoojah, established his power over the greater part of the Punjab, including the hill states, constituting himself despotic ruler of the Sikhs, with the title of Maharajah. In 1818 this renowned chieftain stormed Mooltan, and took Peshawur, and in the following year conquered Kashmir, and the country west of the Indus, thus succeeding in establishing his power over the whole country of the Five Rivers, to which was afterwards added Ladak, or Middle Thibet, and Bultistan, or Little Thibet. His right to all the territories he thus possessed on both sides of the Indus was formally acknowledged by the British government, whose friendship he had the shrewdness to court, about a year before his death, which took place in 1839, at Lahore, the capital of his dominions.

After Runjeet Singh's decease the country fell into confusion. His eldest son, Kurruk Singh, was weak and vicious, and in a few months killed himself by his excesses. His son and successor also perished prematurely, and a natural son of the great Runjeet assumed the sovereignty, but was assassinated in September, 1843, during one of the series of outbreaks, palace revolutions, and crimes. A widow of the first Maharajah then secured the supreme power to her son Dhuleep Singh, a child of five years of age, having Herra Singh, a nephew of Ghoolab, the viceroy of Kashmir, for vizier or prime minister. Intrigues and civil disturbances now distracted the country; and from the close of 1843 to the period of its annexation to British India, the government of the Punjab was in abeyance, or what is worse, in the hands of an ignorant, bloodthirsty, rapacious, and insubordinate army. At length it became manifest that the Sikhs of the Punjab were preparing for an irruption into the territory east of the Sutlej, protected by the British; and in December, 1845, their army crossed that river and attacked our forces under the command of Sir Hugh Gough, at Moodkee. Here they were repulsed; and being further defeated, three days after, at Ferozeshah, they had to recross the river. On January 20th, 1846, having again passed over the Sutlej, they were routed, after a severe contest, at Aliwal; and the following month another great battle was fought at Sobraon, resulting in their total defeat, and the occupation of Lahore by the British.

Part of their territory was then formally ceded to the Indian government, and the remainder left to their own rule under protection, while the dominion of Kashmir and the other provinces of the Himalayas were wantonly and foolishly made over for a pecuniary consideration to the Rajah Ghoolab Singh, of Jummoo, a proceeding by which the English lost the fairest province in the whole of their Eastern possessions.

In 1848 revolts again broke out, and soon afterwards a conspiracy between several disaffected chiefs and the Afghans resulted in further hostilities, it having become impossible to doubt that the Sikhs as a nation had once more resolved on a struggle with the British power. The indecisive battle of Chillianwalla was followed by the capture of Mooltan in January, and the victory of Gujerat in February, 1849; and the Sikh power being thus completely broken, the boy Maharajah was compelled to sign away the sovereignty of the Punjab, which was then proclaimed to be a part of the British Empire in India. The Maharajah Dhuleep Singh, the last representative of Nanuk, was sent to England, and embracing Christianity soon afterwards, has ever since made our country his home, and now lives among us, an honoured noble of her Majesty's court. And as a lasting memento of our struggle with the once powerful Sikh dynasty, the Koh-i-Noor diamond, which his father Runjeet Singh had plundered from the Afghans, who had in their turn ravished it from the imperial diadem of the Great Mogul at the sack of Delhi, was sent home and presented to the Queen.

Lahore is interesting, though not so magnificent as in the days of the Moguls. Being the seat of government for the province, it is the abode of a goodly number of our countrymen. It stands on the left bank of the Ravee, is a town of considerable antiquity, and in former days was between eight and ten miles in circumference, surrounded by a brick wall about thirty feet in height, with indifferent bastions and a broad moat, part of which now remains to show that it was once fortified. There is no doubt that from its foundation it was the capital and place of residence, of the various princes and

The City of Lahore.

chiefs who have in turn governed this large province, although little is heard of it until the year 1523, when it was taken by Sultan Baber, and became for a short period the favourite seat of the Mogul empire, during which its extent and population were much greater than at present. Since that time it has been in many hands, and finally, after having been the abode of Runjeet Singh and the capital of the Sikhs, has come into ours. Although not so important a native town, perhaps, as formerly, it is still a flourishing place as regards the European population; for a large civil station, quite a town of itself, has arisen, possessing some fine government buildings and a university, while the extensive military cantonment of Mean Meer is connected with the civil lines by a road two or three miles long.

The native town does not differ from others—the streets narrow, dirty, and unpaved; the houses high, built of brick, mostly with flat roofs, and generally with a mean appearance, although this is sometimes redeemed in part by the elegant carving of the wood balconies and windows. The bazaars are numerous and animated, particularly a new one (now the chief) called the Anarkalli bazaar, which runs right into the civil station, and in which most of the articles manufactured at Lahore can be obtained. Lahore possesses some trade, though dull as regards ordinary commercial activity, and it still produces many things of pure native workmanship, the chief of which are lacquered wares and silks, more especially gorgeous shawls flowered with gold and silver thread.

Lahore contains several elegant and important buildings, and many fine mosques, Hindu temples, and tombs, mostly, however, exhibiting symptoms of decay. In the neighbourhood are large gardens filled with fruit-trees, flowering-plants, and shrubs; while extensive Mohammedan ruins testify to its former occupation by this race. The more remarkable buildings are the mosques—Padshah, Vizier Khan, the Sonara, or 'Golden Mosque,' and the Shah Dura, or mausoleum of the Emperor Jehangir. The two first mosques are built of red sandstone, with lofty minarets and cupolas; those of the Vizier Khan being entirely covered with painted and lacquered tiles, inscribed with Arabic sentences; while the third, the Sonara, has the addition of gilded minarets and domes. The mausoleum of the Emperor Jehangir and his consort, Noor Juhan, is well known for its size and magnificence, in which it rivals the similar edifices at Delhi and Agra. It stands in a large but somewhat dilapidated garden, on the opposite bank of the Ravee to the town, from which it is distant three miles; and in a corresponding garden, in line with the Emperor's tomb, is that of Azaf Khan, the wily brother of Noor Juhan. The mausoleum of the son and successor of the great Akber is built of red sandstone, adorned with a profusion of marble ornaments arranged in elegant mosaics, representing flowers and texts from the Koran, and is of quadrangular shape, with a minaret seventy feet high at each corner. It is a splendid example of the architecture of that period, and was erected by Noor Juhan, the faithful wife, after her husband's death at Rajore, when on his way to Kashmir. Here too, after some years of grief and mourning, her remains were also deposited.

The Fort and Palace of Lahore are situated on one side of the native city, facing a large, wide, open maidan or plain, and were built during the time of the Mogul ascendancy. In appearance the Fort is very similar to that at Agra, as is also the Palace, which stands on the summit, but is much smaller in size; and, although containing a few rooms ornamented with marble carvings and mosaics, does not approach in any way to the magnificence which characterizes the chief residences of this line of sovereigns. One room of the palace has been converted into an armoury, and contains a most interesting collection of arms and weapons, formerly belonging to the Sikhs; and if one cares to take the trouble to ascend a long flight of stairs to the roof of the structure, which we did, the reward will be a magnificent view of the city and surrounding country. Within the walls of this fortress, and close to the entrance, is the tomb of Runjeet Singh, the 'Lion of the Punjab,' and virtually its last native ruler. This mausoleum, built of stone, is plain and unpretending; and the only ornament the interior possesses to relieve its funereal gloom is a marble screen, sparsely ornamented, around the central vault which contains the dust of the hero.

We drove all over the civil station, with which we were much pleased, for it was the most English-looking place we had seen in India. Some of the houses of the residents are very fine, and surrounded by beautiful gardens; while the public buildings, such as the government offices, court-houses, university, and museum, are well worthy of notice, and add greatly to the importance of this part of the city.

On the morning of the 18th we left Lahore, and resumed our journey to Murree, the new state railway enabling us to get as far by its aid as Wuzzeerabad, to which place the line had already been completed, while its continuation to Rawul Pindi was being rapidly pushed on. We started at six a.m.; and although we had only sixty miles to travel, the progress of the train was so slow, and the stoppages at the stations so unreasonably long, that we did not reach our destination until nearly one o'clock. The line is a curious one, laid for the most part on one side of the high road, by which great expense was saved, and it does not pass through any place of interest. Some of the scenery, however, is rather pretty, and in the distance rise range upon range of the Himalayas. It was a very hot day, and on our arrival at Wuzzeerabad, a small native town, famous for the knives and other articles of cutlery it produces, we halted until four o'clock, when, after having sent off our baggage and servants, with the exception of Esau and Enai, in bullock-carts, with directions to make their way direct to Murree, we followed after in a dak gharry, on our way to Rawul Pindi, a hundred and ten miles distant.

Soon after leaving this city we arrived on the bank of the Chenab, now swollen by the late rains into a stream between four and five miles broad, with a rapid current. This we had to cross in order to reach Gujerat, our next stage on the opposite side, and the transit was effected by shipping the carriage and horses bodily in a large flat-bottomed boat, which was then propelled by poles, or, in places where the water was shallow, towed along by a rope, to which was attached some dozen or so of more than semi-nude coolies. To get across was a work of some difficulty, and occupied four hours; for the current was strong, and we were oftentimes carried against our wish in a direction contrary to what was intended, and the weary process of towing against the stream had to be recommenced to make up what had been lost. We, however, arrived safely on the other side, and spared no time in proceeding on our way; for it was getting late, and we wanted our dinner, the passage of the river having been more tedious than we expected. During the greater part of the year the river here is confined to its natural bed, and is crossed by a bridge of boats, which is necessarily removed during the rains. There is now, however, no necessity at any season for making a passage by the means we were compelled to employ; for a magnificent bridge, both for railway and for other traffic, now spans the entire width, and was then almost completed. This bridge is said to be the finest in the world, as it is undoubtedly the longest, being exactly two miles in length. It is built on pillars filled with concrete, sunk into the sandy bed of the river, and is a marvel of engineering skill. Since the time of which I am writing it has been formally opened for traffic by the Prince of Wales, by whom it was also christened the 'Alexandra,' after his illustrious consort. A drive of a few miles brought us to Gujerat, a place famous as the site of the battle of that name, and here we enjoyed an excellent dinner or supper, for it was now ten p.m., in the dak bungalow at the station. This dak bungalow is, without exception, the best in India, being more like a good hotel, and is much used and appreciated by the numerous travellers who pass this road, as well as by those on their way to Kashmir; Gujerat being the starting-point to reach that country by the Bhimber and Pir Punjal route.

After dinner we started again, and slept most comfortably in our carriage, arriving at daybreak at the river Jhelum, which we crossed in a similar manner to the Chenab; but as it was not so wide as the latter, the passage did not occupy so much time. On reaching the other side, we drove straight to the station of Jhelum, which is close to the river. Here we halted for the day, for it was intensely hot: a storm was brewing, and the air was very close and oppressive. Even Fizz, who generally appreciated heat, felt it rather too much, and was very quiet and dejected in consequence. Towards evening we had a thunder-storm, of short duration, and it grew cooler, enabling us to proceed with some degree of comfort on the journey of seventy miles between this place and our destination. We left at seven o'clock, and much enjoyed the drive until we fell asleep; for the scenery is very pretty, the road undulating, with ranges of hills all around, and the Himalayas in the background. A few miles from Jhelum, which is situated in a picturesque valley, the country becomes very rugged, and the road passes over numerous bridges spanning the various streams or ravines that intersect the land, here totally uncultivated and barren, and broken up into tracts of such uneven size and shape that, seen as we saw it by the light of a full moon, nothing more desolate, wild, and weird-looking could be imagined.

We arrived at Rawul Pindi at six a.m., after two consecutive nights of dak gharry travelling, a most fatiguing mode of prosecuting a journey, but which will soon be a thing of the past on this road; for all the way we could see the line rapidly approaching completion, while it is expected ere long to be further lengthened, when Peshawur, our most northern station in India, will be connected by railway with the capital towns of the three presidencies. We made but a short stay in Pindi; for having secured our tents—which had been bought for us some time previously at this station—and forwarded them on to Murree, we left for that place, which lay perched on the summit of a Himalayan range, about forty miles from the favourite station we were now leaving.

Our conveyance hence was what is known as a hill-cart, a curious vehicle, with a seat before and behind, covered with a leathern hood hung very low, and possessing two strong wheels. It is drawn by two ponies, or sometimes three, harnessed abreast, whose only pace seems to be a hand-gallop, to maintain which the whip of the driver is freely used, assisted by various shouts and imprecations, that the steeds seem fully to understand, although it may be Greek or any other language to the traveller, consisting as it does of a mixture of the Hindustani, Punjabi, and various hill dialects. The road, when fairly in the hills, is narrow and uneven, with sharp curves bordering unpleasantly close to the edge of the 'khuds' or precipices; and the shape of the cart, together with the pace, causes a lurching, bumping motion, sometimes amounting to a perfect series of jumps when passing over a particularly rough bit of ground. The occupants of the vehicle, holding on by the rails to maintain their seats, from which, however, they are perpetually being jerked, might fairly compare the situation with that of a rider on a very unpleasant rough-going horse. In both cases the exercise one acquires is, as I can speak from experience, very similar, and although unpleasant is esteemed by many a grand thing for the liver.

For the first fourteen miles, after leaving Rawul Pindi, the road is smooth and level, and leads to the foot of the hills, which rise in greater magnificence the nearer one approaches them, passing through a well-cultivated and productive country. After leaving the small village of Barracow the road begins to ascend, and as we went higher and higher the change of temperature became very apparent. Indeed, so marked was the coolness to us, accustomed so long to the heat of the plains, that we had to resort to the use of great-coats and wraps before the summit was reached. The drive certainly was very enjoyable; the pace was exhilirating, and so was the mountain air; while the scenery was exceedingly beautiful, and the green and luxuriant vegetation very refreshing to our eyes, which for so long had gazed only upon the dry, sandy, and barren land of Gwalior. The forty miles were done in four hours, which is fair work, considering the road, and that we only changed horses four times. We arrived at this favourite hill station at seven o'clock, and proceeding to what is known as Powell's Hotel, secured two very good rooms, and were soon busy in discussing our dinner, for which we were ready after our health-giving drive.

We stayed at Murree for a whole week—as we had to await the arrival of our servants and baggage, travelling by the sure but slow bullock-carts—and much did we enjoy the time; for we met very pleasant people at the hotel, and had some delightful days. We had some charming walks too; for the place abounds in beautiful scenery, with the ever-present and magnificent landscape of the gigantic mountains, towering in their lofty grandeur, range beyond range, until lost in illimitable space; and deep, broad, and extensive

Murree Station. 409

valleys, spreading out into fields of cultivation, bordered by wild forests; the whole forming as perfect a picture of the natural beauties of the Himalayas as could be seen, and which no other part of the world can match in grandeur and beauty. Since Murree was selected as a sanitarium for the Northern Punjab, some twenty years back, it has always been the summer retreat of the governor of this province, with a number of government officials, secretaries, and public officers. This tends to give the social position of this beautiful spot the importance it is so well adapted to maintain. The station is situated on a ridge, at an elevation of seven thousand two hundred to seven thousand five hundred feet, and the climate is dry and salubrious, the usual summer temperature ranging from sixty-five to seventy degrees Fahrenheit. In winter it is very cold, and snow often lies to the depth of several feet; while during the rainy season it is, like all the other hill stations, rather a wet place, and at that time of the year is rendered somewhat disagreeable by the prevalence of dense wet fogs or mists. It is a military sanitarium, and contains barracks, hospitals, and other accommodation for a number of soldiers annually, sent up for change of air from the several cantonments in the Punjab, while all the year round one entire regiment is located at this spot, or in its neighbourhood. The houses of the residents and the visitors are built somewhat after the European style, dotted about all over the sides of the hills, particularly in places whence a good view can be obtained. Pine and other trees plentifully clothe the mountains, and there is no lack of undergrowth, flowers, and ferns. That the natural beauties of Murree are well appreciated may be seen in the number of people who yearly visit the place, and who are able to find accommodation either in houses built for letting, or in the several good hotels that have lately been erected.

On the morning of the 26th July our servants and baggage duly arrived, and having already made our preparations, and laid in stores for the journey, we started the following morning with a cavalcade, consisting of ourselves, eight servants, ten mules, and their attendants, on the long march that lay between us and the Vale of Kashmir.

CHAPTER XVIII.

Return from Kashmir—Arrival at Gujerat—Receive orders to proceed to Rawul Pindi—Arrival at that station—Rawul Pindi—Attacked by illness—Shocks of Earthquake—Am invalided—Departure for England—Journey to Delhi—Description of Delhi—History of Old Delhi—The line of Slave Kings of Delhi—The House of Lodi—Conquest of Delhi by Timour—The Ruins of Old Delhi—The Fortifications—The Kootub Minar—The Mosque—Ancient Hindu Iron Pillar—Tomb of Altumsh—City of Seeri—Juhanpura—Ruins of Toghlukabad—The Fort—The Tomb of Toghluk Shah—The City of Feerozabad—Its Buddhist Monolith—Tomb of the Emperor Homayoon—Capture of rebel Princes—The Cemetery of Nizamud-din—His tomb—Tomb of the poet Khoosroo—The Bowlee, or well-house—Diving talent of the natives—The Mosque of Keerkee—The Tomb of Sufdur Jung.

THE conclusion of the last chapter having brought us to the time when we fairly started on our trip to Kashmir, I must now crave the indulgence of the reader to imagine an interval to have passed, during which we were travelling in the Happy Valley, and to take up the thread of the narrative on the 9th of October, the day we arrived at Gujerat, after having crossed the Great Pir Punjal on our return journey. I am impelled to this course by the fact that the limits of this volume would not admit of a full description of Kashmir, a country to which, however, at some future time, I hope to do ample justice in a similar work to the present, having during the course of our travels taken copious notes with that object.

We arrived at Gujerat at midday, and put up at the dak

bungalow, which we found crowded with travellers returning, like ourselves, from Kashmir, and the greater number of whom we had met during our wanderings in the Vale. Our first care was a visit to the post-office, and here we found a letter which considerably altered our plans, as it contained instructions to proceed to Rawul Pindi for duty, instead of returning to Fortress Gwalior. This was in every way a change for the better, the result of an application I had made for a transfer some little time previously, and we commenced our preparations for departure thither in a very cheerful mood. All our servants volunteered to accompany us, with the exception of Esau, who had, much to our mutual regret, to leave in order to return to his home, his father being dangerously ill and not expected to recover. Against such a wish we could, of course, urge nothing, although we were loth to part with him; for a more honest, faithful native servant never lived. We remained at Gujerat three entire days, resting after the fatigues of the mountain march; and having sent off our servants and luggage, followed them in a dak gharry, passing over the same road that we had traversed three months before on our way to Murree.

Reaching Rawul Pindi at daybreak on the morning of the 14th October, we engaged rooms at Rowbury's Hotel, where we intended to reside until we could procure a bungalow. Having called upon the authorities, both civil and military, and on such of our friends as were resident in the station, we soon settled down and again commenced our usual daily routine, the regiment to which I was attached for duty being the 60th Rifles, then in camp, and under orders to march for Meerut. Rawul Pindi is the best station in the Punjab, and we considered ourselves very fortunate in obtaining the change; for being so close to the Himalayas, situated in fact at the foot of a vast range of hills, this place enjoys a more healthy and bracing climate than the stations down country, and can boast seven months in the year of pleasant cool weather; while the remaining five are tempered by frequent refreshing breezes from the mountains. It is a large civil and military station, the head-quarters of a division of the army, and is close to a large native town of the same name, which, however, contains nothing remarkable in the way of buildings or antiquities. It is exactly one hundred miles from Peshawur, our most northern possession, a station on the borders of Afghanistan, and close to the entrance of the well-known Kyber Pass. A good road from Rawul Pindi leads to this important place, passing through Syden Bowlee, Attock, and Nowshera; all military stations in our line of defence on the frontier, of which our present abode may be considered as the base. The country around the station is fairly fertile and pretty, being very undulating, and at a short distance low ranges of hills arise, gradually merging into the higher ridges of the great Himalayas, which, although some miles distant, seem to overshadow the place. The cold weather had fairly set in when we arrived, and very cold we found it; for it soon became frosty at nights, and large fires in our rooms were necessary, and as the season advanced the climate was exactly similar to that of an English winter. We were very happy and comfortable, and looked forward to a pleasant sojourn of some considerable time in this delightful spot; but the fates willed it otherwise, for ten days after our arrival I unfortunately contracted a sunstroke (the sun being still very powerful during the middle of the day) whilst detained on duty in the camp of the regiment to which I was attached. This occurred on the 25th October, and from that time until our departure for England, in January, for it had been early decided to invalid me home, I continued very ill, for weeks in positive danger, from which I was only rescued by the care and attention of my dear wife and of my faithful friend, Mr. C. M. J. It was a time of great anxiety; for I suffered many relapses, and although recovering a little at times, and being able to go out, the good effects were only transitory, and I seemed unable to overcome the great debility after the graver symptoms had subsided. Being on the sick list the whole time we did not go about, so that there remains nothing to describe of our stay in Pindi, the latter part of which was passed in a bungalow, which we shared with our friend the brigade-major, having been removed thither from the somewhat crowded hotel during my illness.

Nothing occurred to vary the easy monotony of our days, with the exception that in the month of December we were treated to two severe shocks of earthquake, a visitation of frequent occurrence in this part of India. One that occurred on the 12th was very severe, and the sensation was far from pleasant; for it came on us in the dead of night, and the first warning we had of its approach was being awoke by the violent motion of the bed upon which we were sleeping. This was a rocking motion, nearly sufficient to jerk us out; and at the same time the house shook so violently that every instant we expected to see it fall. The walls cracked, doors and cupboards opened and slammed to again with a violent noise, and the floor beneath us appeared to undulate like the waves of the sea. This unpleasant performance lasted for the space of fully a minute; and that it was a far more severe shock than those to which the dwellers in this locality are accustomed, may be judged from the fact that considerable loss of life and property was incurred in the station and surrounding district.

The medical board met early in January; and being recommended to proceed on sick leave to England, we commenced our preparations at once, as I had somewhat recovered, and was at this time fit to travel. The morning of the 24th saw our departure in a dak gharry down the now well-known road to Lahore, which place we intended to reach by easy stages, the weather enabling us to travel in the daytime, and after leaving that city to make a detour to Delhi. This we did, partly with the view of seeing the town, and partly to avoid coming into contact with the party of the Prince of Wales, who was then visiting India, and who, after leaving the camp of exercise at Delhi, intended to proceed to Agra, where we timed ourselves to pass him and his suite, as otherwise our chance of any accommodation at the hotels, if we arrived at the same time, would be very slight. It was a long journey that lay before us, the distance to Bombay from Rawul Pindi being nearly two thousand miles; but as this, with the exception of the dak to Wuzzeerabad, could all be done by railway, the travelling was easy and pleasant. We journeyed down slowly to Wuzzeerabad, and had this time no trouble in crossing the Chenab, the river having subsided, and communication from shore to shore being easily effected by the bridge of boats. Thence we proceeded to Lahore by rail, and found the city just recovering from the excitement of the prince's visit, which had only terminated the day before our arrival. After a halt of two days we continued our journey, travelling over the line we had traversed on our way to Murree, *en route* to Kashmir, and after a night passed in the train branched off at Ghazeeabad, when an hour's run brought us to Delhi, at noon on the 29th of January.

We found the ancient capital of the Moguls full of visitors; for the camp of exercise that had been formed in honour of the Prince of Wales was just beginning to be broken up, and every house was full. We were, however, fortunate enough to secure one small room at the Northbrook Hotel, where we were fairly comfortable; and on the evening of our arrival commenced our inspection of the various sights of this interesting place.

Dehli, or Delhi, as it is now more commonly spelt, the Rome of Asia, consists at the present time of the modern city, and of ruins spreading over a district ten miles long, and averaging little less than six broad. In this area are comprised the ruins of the original Dehli, or Dilli, according to old writers, and the remains of Feerozabad, Toghlukabad, and Seeri, which, communicating with each other, formed at one time the ancient city; as well as the new city of Shah Juhan, now known as modern Delhi. Lying on the bank of the river Jumna, and in a basin receiving the drainage of the Mewat hills, the neighbourhood is well watered and sheltered from storms, and the well-chosen position embraces all the conditions necessary to the well-being of an Indian city. Although at the present day Delhi, understanding by the term the parallelogram above referred to, is, with the exception of the modern city, nothing more than a mass of ruins, it is, if less beautiful, more interesting than Agra. The very monarch who last chose it as a capital dowered the forsaken rival with a treasure, which, as it is unique in the world, is quite unapproached by anything at Delhi. But if the latter has no Taj, it offers to the visitor interested in ethnology, in history, and in architecture, a series of records relating to India from its earliest period down to the present day.*

Following the order in which the several cities that comprise the whole are enumerated, we find ourselves, on arriving at the ruined site of Old Delhi, on the scene of some of India's earliest authentic historical events. At this place, which is distant about ten miles from its modern compeer, stood, according to the best authorities, some time before the Christian era, an extensive city of the Sakas, a tribe overthrown by Vikramanditya, a prince of Malwa, about A.D. 78. After this period it ceased to be a royal residence of any of the earlier Hindu kings, although most probably it was a place of note, as the iron pillar, which will be hereafter described, is supposed to have been set up here by one of the Goopta Rajahs in 319. After this there appears to be no authentic history of this place—the original Delhi—till it was rebuilt, in the middle of the eighth century, by Anung Pal, the first king of the Tamars, a Rajput tribe. It is supposed by Cunningham that Delhi, soon after this, once more ceased to be a royal city, and fell into decay, to be again rebuilt by a Rajah of the same dynasty, and the same name, Anung Pal II., who was driven hither from Canouj, his ancestral

---

* Keene's *Delhi*, to which I am largely indebted for many of the remarks on Old and New Delhi.

metropolis. However, it is certain that this Tamar dynasty ruled at one time or other over a considerable tract of country between the Himalayas and the Vindhyan range; that their capital was in this neighbourhood, its citadel being the enclosure which now surrounds the Kootub Minar; and that they were overthrown about the middle of the twelfth century by another Rajput house, the Chouans. These latter added to the fortifications, and after a reign of about forty years were in turn overthrown by Shahab-ud-din Ghori, and his general, Kutb-ud-din, in 1193.

From this date commenced the reign of the kings of Delhi, the Pathan predecessors of the Moguls, of whose memory the neighbourhood has so many splendid monuments. Founded by Kutb-ud-din, a favourite general of Shahab-ud-din, the then reigning descendant of the house of Ghor, about the end of the twelfth century, they endured for three centuries; and the line is usually termed the Slave dynasty, in reference to the fact that these monarchs were often succeeded by favourite slaves. With them the authentic history of Delhi really begins; for little is known with regard to its earlier Hindu dynasties, although, as before mentioned, it had been a place of note for centuries before their advent. The history of Delhi and this line of sovereigns may be said also to be the history of India at that period; for, commencing as it does with the conquest of Mahmoud of Ghuzni, we can fairly trace it through that line and its successors, the house of Ghor, to the time of the accession of the founder of the Slave line, whose master may be said to have been the ruler of nearly the entire country. At his death in 1206, Shahab-ud-din held in different degrees of subjection the whole of Hindustan proper, much of which was under his own officers, and the rest under dependent, or at least tributary princes. Sinde and Bengal were either entirely subdued or in rapid course of subjection; while the distant province of Guzerat, although not entirely submissive, had lost its capital; and in Central India, Malwa and some contiguous district only remained independent. Upon his decease, although he left a nephew to succeed him, the kingdom broke up into separate states, and after a period of disturbance, occasioned by the dissolution of the empire and the extinction of the line of Ghori sovereigns, Kutb-ud-din, the before-mentioned favourite, originally a Turkish slave, who was acting as viceroy of the empire, seized the power and constituted himself king of Delhi, and first of the Pathan or Afghan line.

One of the most famous of the Slave kings after the death of their founder, which occurred four years after his accession to the throne, was Shums-ud-din Altumsh, who reigned from 1211 to 1236, and who, though of noble family, was said to have been sold like Joseph by his envious brothers. In his time the greater part of India which had before remained independent was subdued, and eventually the whole of it, with the exception of some isolated portions, acknowledged the government of Delhi, an event probably hastened by the necessity that was felt as to the unison that should prevail in the country, to enable it to withstand the irruptions of the Moguls, which commenced at this period. After his death, and a variety of short reigns of little importance, including one by a female, the Sultana Rezia, all mostly ending in the assassination of the sovereign by some profligate courtier, the throne was ascended in 1246 by Nasir-ud-din, the grandson of Altumsh. He enjoyed a comparatively tranquil reign of twenty years, and was in private life little less than a recluse or dervish, leaving the conduct of affairs generally to his ministers. To him succeeded his prime minister, Ghiyas-ud-din Balban, originally one of the band of Turki slaves, who had become enormously powerful under the weak administrations that had long prevailed. He maintained the dignity of the throne in unsurpassable splendour for twenty-two years, eventually dying of a broken heart after a defeat by the Moguls, in which action he lost his favourite son; the poet Khoosroo, his friend and constant companion, being taken prisoner at the same time. Next followed his grandson Kai Kobad, a person of dissolute habits. He was assassinated by a slave, and with him ended the direct line of Kutb-ud-din, the supreme power being seized by a military chief of the family of Khilji, the first of whom, Julal-ud-din, ascended the throne in 1289.

This monarch, a mild ruler, was murdered, in 1296, by his nephew Ala-ud-din, who succeeded him and reigned for twenty years. He was distinguished by great activity in foreign conquests, and by his taste for architecture. Upon his death in 1316, his favourite, Malik Kafoor, attempted to carry on the government, but was soon murdered; and after a period of great confusion Ghazi Mahmoud Toghluk, a successful general, grasped the sceptre, and brought in a new family to the kings of Delhi, the house of Toghluk. He was an honest and able soldier, but after five years' tenure of power, was killed by the connivance of his son Joonah, who ascended the throne in his father's fort of Toghlukabad.

This prince, known by his more popular title of the 'Bloody Lord,' was a cruel and fanatical tyrant, but was never personally molested, and died a natural death in the full exercise of the power he had so long abused, being succeeded by his cousin, Feeroz Shah, in 1350.

Feeroz Shah was one of the best men of that time, and occupied a long reign in beautifying the adjacent cities, and in creating works of usefulness, such as reservoirs for irrigation, colleges, hospitals, public baths, and bridges. In his reign Delhi consisted of the three conjoined cities connected by fortifications, with forty-seven gates, the remains of some of which can still be seen; probably at this time it reached its greatest prosperity, alike in magnificence and in the extent of its population. Feeroz Shah finally abdicated and died at the age of ninety, in 1388; and although his heirs strove to maintain the line, it was but feebly, and a period of anarchy followed, which ceased only on the occasion of the most terrible of all the Mogul incursions — that of Timour, or Tamerlane, the Tartar. It was at the end of the fourteenth century when this leader, after having conquered Persia, Tartary, Georgia, and Mesopotamia, with parts of Russia and Siberia, turned his arms without the pretext of a quarrel on the distracted empire of Hindustan. The Indian army being defeated and driven into the town, the last representative of the Toghluk family fled to Guzerat, and Delhi, surrendering under a promise of protection, was plundered and the people massacred, after which Tamerlane was proclaimed Emperor of India. On his quitting India, leaving anarchy, famine, and misery behind him, there was no kingly rule in the country, either in name or reality, for a period of nearly forty years, when the house of Lodi, following the brief dynasty of the Seiads, enjoyed a tenure of power until the advent of Baber, the founder of the Mogul empire.

During the whole of this time, from the date of the conquest of the city by Tamerlane to the invasion of Baber, his descendant, a period of a century and a quarter, the history of Delhi possesses little or no historical interest. A dim grandeur certainly hangs around the period of the Lodi dynasty, but it was soon eclipsed; and although Delhi afterwards enjoyed, for a brief period, the countenance of the first rulers of the Mogul line, who made it their place of residence, it was soon outshone by the glories of Agra, to which city the court removed. Here the great Akber ruled, while Delhi, the proper capital of India, fell into decay, unused and nearly uninhabited, until some years later his grandson, Shah Juhan, restored it in a measure to its pristine condition, by the erection in the midst of the ruins of the three ancient towns of the present beautiful city of New Delhi. The histories of the reigns of the line of kings enumerated above are very similar—wars and tumults all over India, produced by their endeavours to extend their sovereignty, and in opposing the encroachments of their terrible foes, the Moguls; and intrigues, cruelties, and oppressions at home, leading to revolts, assassinations, and frequent changes of rulers. But upon all this it will not be necessary to dwell, as the slight sketch already given will be sufficient to show the connection of these monarchs with the monuments of Pathan architecture I am about to describe, and which still remain as lasting memorials of their power and greatness.

The ruins of Old Delhi cover an area of rather more than

half that of the modern city, and although the greater portion seems to consist only of confused heaps of stone, the additions made by the Mohammedan usurpers are in much finer preservation, and are the only objects to engage the attention of the visitor; for the remains of the Hindu city, which is said to have contained numerous temples, both of the original and of the Buddhist religions, may be said to have vanished. The whole city was surrounded by fortifications, and the line of walls of Rai Pithoras, or the Red Fort, and those of the Fort of Lalkot, built in 1060, can still be distinctly traced, lofty and massive. These were the work of the original Hindu kings, and it is supposed that the first was erected to withstand the incursions of the Mussulmans, in the time of the last member of that dynasty. The principal object to strike the eye is the lofty pillar of stone, known as the Kootub Minar, the glory of Delhi, as the Taj is of Agra. This magnificent tower, the loftiest independent building of the kind in the world, is just over two hundred and thirty-eight feet high, sloping from the base from a diameter of forty-seven feet to one of scarcely nine. The shaft is divided into five storeys, of which the first and last make up one half of the total height; the second, third, and fourth, the remainder. The three lower storeys are all of red sandstone, and probably the original work of Kutb-ud-din, the founder, whose name it bears, the first of the Slave kings of Delhi, and of his successor, Altumsh, who completed it to serve as a muzeena or muezzin's station to call the faithful to prayers in the mosque close by. The fourth, and to some extent the fifth storeys, are of white marble, the work of the much-building Emperor Feeroz Shah, about the third quarter of the fourteenth century, who thus heightened and completed the tower some hundred and fifty years after its foundation. The basement story has twenty-four faces in the form of convex flutings, alternately semi-circular and rectangular; in the second storey the projections are all circular; in the third, all angular; the fourth is a plain cylinder; and the fifth is partly fluted, and partly plain. So accurate are the proportions of the three lower storeys that the lines, except where intercepted, run up in one and the same straight course. The intercepting lines are those of balconies, going all round the tower, and girdling it with a belt of rich projecting pendentives, in the purest style of the first Pathan period. The three lower storeys are also belted with bands of ornamental scroll-work, containing Arabic inscriptions—verses from the Koran, and the name and praises of the conqueror by whose orders the building was commenced. A flight of circular stairs in the interior leads to the summit; but we only ascended to the top of the first storey, a height of ninety-four feet, from the balcony of which a splendid view rewarded our efforts. The native custodian pressed us to ascend higher, urging the fact that the Prince of Wales had gone up to the summit; but we declined, as our experience of winding round and round up steep steps for nearly a hundred feet was quite sufficient for once, and we had ascertained further from our garrulous guide that, although the splendid physique of the Prince had stood him bravely in stead, many of his attendants appeared much distressed after the exertion.

Near the Kootub stands the mosque, the earliest religious Mohammedan building of this description in India, and which

The Iron Shaft.

must have been, when completed, the finest in the world. Only the walls and arches of some parts remain, together with some standing pillars, which are interesting from the fact that they are all of Hindu workmanship, and belonged to the numerous Jain and other native temples taken down to construct the fane of their Moslem conquerors. Nothing can surpass the endless variety of the sculptures on these pillars, or their sharpness and delicacy, and having been originally plastered over by their bigoted adapters, they are for the most part in good preservation, and the curious sight is presented of the ruins of a Mohammedan place of worship, consisting chiefly of remains of the former religious edifices of another faith.

In the quadrangle of the mosque, a short distance northwest of the Kootub Minar, stands the Iron Shaft, the oldest relic of the vanished Hindu city. This pillar, which may be presumed to have been erected in some conspicuous position, either within the old city or close to it, and which, probably from superstitious motives, was left undisturbed by the builders of the mosque, is in height about twenty-two feet above ground. It is believed to be of malleable iron, not cast, but built up by the welding together (by heat and hammering) of successive horizontal cylinders of metal. It slopes a little towards the top, where it is surmounted by a capital over three feet high, formed of a series of bevelled rims one above the other. Its meagre history is found recorded in an inscription of six Sanskrit lines cut upon its western face, from which we find that it is claimed as the memorial of Rajah Dava, or Bhava, supposed to have reigned in the third century of the Christian era, and an old prophecy was current in India, even so far back as the time of the first Mohammedan invasion, that the Hindu government should endure as long as the pillar stood. Its remaining inscriptions are unimportant, as are also the various tales told to travellers about its extent underground, which was found to be only three feet, on an excavation made by order of the government a few years back; but it is interesting as being, with the pillars of the mosque, a relic of the former Hindu greatness of Old Delhi.

At the north-west extremity of the mosque is the tomb of Altumsh, the successor of Kutb-ud-din, whose name occurs so frequently on the walls of these buildings as perfecting the original designs of his predecessor. He died in 1236, about forty-five years after the commencement of the building, and his tomb, supposed to be the oldest known in India, is, though small, one of the richest examples of Hindu art applied to Mohammedan purposes that Old Delhi affords, where this combination of native with foreign talent is so apparent in the earlier efforts of Pathan architecture. White marble is used to relieve the red sandstone, and one can observe the dawning of the art which afterwards led to such beautiful results in the application of inlaid colour on buildings.

Before leaving the vicinity of the Kootub, and the ruins of Old 'Dilli,' some time may be spent in examining the remains of the city of Seeri, often called Shahpur, and Juhanpuna, the remains of Mohammed Toghluck's fortification. Seeri stands to the north-east of the mighty pillar, and was founded by Sultan Ala-ud-din as an offshoot of the Old Dilli, having originally been an intrenched camp formed by that ruler to resist the advance of the Moguls, who had invaded India in the year 1303, and who were menacing the capital.

The ruins of a fort and of the palace, supposed to have been the celebrated Kasr-Hazar-Situn, or 'palace of the thousand pillars,' which Ala-ud-din built on the spot formerly occupied by his camp, are still standing, as are also the remains of the fortifications of Juhanpuna, built to protect this city and the suburbs of Old Dilli, which extended in this direction. There is no doubt that this, with Old Dilli, formed the Delhi of Tamerlane, described in the memoirs of that monarch. This is the quaint account given of the place by the invader, according to Elliott, in Dowson's *History of India*:—"When my mind was no longer occupied with the destruction of the people of Delhi, I took a ride round the cities. Seeri is a round city; its buildings are lofty, surrounded by strong fortifications of stone and brick. Old Delhi has a similar fort, but larger. From one to another, a considerable distance, runs a strong wall built of stone and cement; the part called Juhanpuna is in the centre of the inhabited area. The fortifications of the three cities have thirty gates, of which Juhanpuna has thirteen, Seeri seven, and Old Delhi ten."

Turning eastward, the fine ruins of Toghlukabad will be found about three miles from the Kootub. They are a group of buildings, gigantic in conception, built early in the fourteenth century by Toghluk Ghazi Khan, a successful military adventurer, who overthrew the house of Khilji and ascended the throne. It would appear to have been this prince's intention to have erected a new city at this spot, surrounded by a fort, but his early death put an end to the project, and with the exception of the fortifications, and a mosque, nothing else was completed, and these, together with a few ruined houses, many of which appear never to have been inhabited, are all that this unfinished city can show. The fort of Toghlukabad stands on a rocky height, is built of very massive blocks of stone, many of which must weigh several tons, and has a circuit of fortifications extending over four miles. The walls are forty feet in height, and in the citadel are the remains of a large palace. Both are built of large plainly-dressed stones, without ornament of any kind; but the vast size, the great strength, and the visible solidity of the whole, give to this fort an air of stern and massive grandeur that is very impressive. The only object of interest within the walls of the fort is the tomb of its founder, who erected for himself a mausoleum situated in the centre of a tank, not far from the principal gateway. The tomb itself is square in form, built of stone, finely ornamented with white marble, and connected with the fortress by a causeway six hundred feet long, supported on twenty-seven arches. In it are three vaults, said to contain the old king, his wife, and his son and successor. Fergusson's remarks on this grand relic of irresponsible power, will fittingly close this subject:—"When the stern old warrior Toghluck Shah (1321) founded the New Delhi, which still bears his name, he built himself a tomb, not in a garden, as was usually the case, but in a strongly-fortified citadel, in the middle of an artificial lake. The sloping walls and almost Egyptian solidity of this mausoleum, combined with the bold and massive towers of the fortifications that surround it, form a picture of a warrior's tomb unrivalled anywhere, and a singular contrast to the elegant and luxurious garden-tombs of the more settled and peaceful dynasties that succeeded."

One more ruined city remains to be noticed to conclude

the description of Old Delhi, and that is Feerozabad, or the city of Feeroz Shah, who, besides beautifying the adjacent cities, built this, and called it after his name, in accordance with the vain motives which impelled most of the Indian princes at that time to leave behind them some monument of their greatness. This city, which is situated south-east from modern Delhi, was upwards of six miles in length, and two in average breadth, and in its palmy days was said to have contained upwards of three hundred and fifty thousand inhabitants. It contains the remains of the palace of Feeroz, as also those of numerous mosques and houses; but the chief object of interest, and one which is the first attraction to visitors, is the stone monolith, called the Kotila of Feeroz Shah. This is a Buddhist relic, brought down from the sub-Himalayan country, where the contemporaries of Antiochus and Ptolemy had one of their chief seats, and consists of a single shaft of pale pinkish sandstone, over forty-two feet in length. The older inscriptions, for which the pillar was originally erected, comprise the well-known edicts of Asoka to the glorification of the Buddhist religion, and are all written in Pali, a vernacular Sanskrit of those times, dating from his reign, from two to three hundred years before the Christian era.

Having thus described the various cities which were formerly the seats of the royalty of Delhi government, we will, before approaching the modern town, examine the various tombs and other buildings in the vicinity, the work for the most part of the Mogul emperors who succeeded the Pathan line of kings.

The finest of all is undoubtedly the tomb of Homayoon,

one of the earlier Mogul emperors, who was killed by a fall from a building, and whose son and successor, Akber, completed the mausoleum, which was commenced by the deceased monarch's widow. It is near the ruins of Feerozabad, a few miles from the modern city, a little off the direct road to the Kootub, and from its height and massive proportions forms an easily distinguishable and picturesque object from many parts of the surrounding country. This costly pile is very interesting, as forming the first known example of the style of sepulchre afterwards to become so famous in the Taj of Agra, another conjugal monument, nearly a century later in date; whilst, being the earliest work of the Mogul period, it presents some of the peculiarities by which that school is distinguished. Its exterior form is that of a square of solid masonry, several feet in height, to the top of which one ascends by a flight of steps. In the centre of this square is erected a massive building, surmounted by a lofty dome, and with four side kiosques, or towers, at each corner. That it is clearly the forerunner of the Taj can be plainly seen in its dome and kiosques, its majestic portals and storeyed openings, and in its lofty plinth, with doorways exactly similar to the mausoleum at Agra, from which, however, it differs hugely in the matter of its materials. Instead of the pure and unmixed marble which renders the later edifice unique, the basement of this tomb is largely composed of ordinary stone, though white marble forms the substance of the domes and the decoration of the lower structure. In the side chambers repose the ashes of Homayoon and five of his descendants, and of eleven others, who were the councillors, generals, and friends of the kings of his line. The central hall has been rendered famous in more modern times as the place of retreat of the royal family of Delhi, after the capture of the town by the British from their rebel adherents, in September, 1857. It was into this enclosure that Major Hodson entered, attended only by a few native troopers, and arrested the sons of the ex-king, while a short time after their removal, fearing a rescue, he executed them with his own hand.

Near this tomb is the cemetery of Nizam-ud-din, an enclosure which is entered by an unimportant gateway, but which contains some fine monuments of bygone days, with the beauty of which we were much pleased. The first building is a large marble hall, with twenty-five small domes, the pillars that support them from within forming elegant groined arches, while on each of the four sides is an exquisite screen of white marble. It contains the tomb of the foster-brother of Akber, and several others of less interest. Farther on is an enclosure which surrounds the tomb of the notorious adventurer Shah Nizam-ud-din, who flourished about the end of the thirteenth century, and who is said to have been the founder of the murderous society of the Thugs, who, thanks to our government, are now almost extinct in India. His tomb has a very graceful appearance, and is surrounded by a verandah of white marble, while a pierced marble screen of beautiful workmanship encloses the sarcophagus.

There are also in this cemetery the tomb of the poet Khoosroo, who flourished five hundred years ago, whose memory is still reverently cherished by the people of India, and whose songs are yet popular; and likewise the tombs of Meerza Juhangir, the son of Akber; Juhanara Begum, daughter of Shah Juhan; and of Mohammed Shah, emperor from 1719 to 1748. These do not need description, as they are all nearly similar, and their chief interest lies in the splendid specimens of carved and pierced marble work they contain.

Hard by is Nizam-ud-din's 'bowlee,' or well-house. These well-houses were places in which the richer residents of towns, in former days, used to build rooms round the shaft of a large well, which afforded a very pleasant retreat in hot weather. Near the vicinity of this deep well are always to be found gathered a number of boys of various ages, who for a small pecuniary reward dive in, feet foremost, from a great height. Following the usual custom, we disbursed some small coins, and saw the trick performed of jumping from a height of over eighty feet into deep water, without sustaining any injury, practice having made the urchins perfect in the performance.

The mosque of Keerkee, about four miles from the Kootub, is worth inspecting, since it is architecturally most important, if not beautiful. It is an enormous structure, situated on high ground, built of dark-coloured granite, and cased all over with black chunam, which gives it a very sombre appearance. It is square in plan, supported at the four corners by towers nearly fifty feet high, has two storeys, and is crowned with eighty-nine small domes, of very plain but most solid construction.

The tomb of Sufdur Jung, an adventurer who played an important part in the politics of the Mogul empire in its decadence, and who died in 1754, is to be found on the road about half way from Delhi to the Kootub, and, though a majestic structure, is a monument of the degradation which befel Mogul architecture in the century that followed the building of the Taj. It stands in a garden, enclosed on the four sides by a wall, at the corners of which are pavilions of red sandstone. The mausoleum is on a terrace, and is surmounted by a marble dome, containing in the centre of the first floor a beautiful sarcophagus of the same material, elegantly carved and highly polished. Numerous other ruins of mosques, tombs, and small palaces are to be seen in the neighbourhood, most of them, however, falling into decay.

CHAPTER XIX.

The City of Shah Juhan, or New Delhi—Description of Delhi—Its Modern Buildings—The Chandnee Chouk Bazaar—The Fortress—Gateways of the Fortress—The Palace—The Dewan-i-am—The Dewan-i-khas—The Peacock Throne—Private Apartments of the Emperor—The Hummam—The Ghoosul-Khena—Scenes enacted within the Palace—The Great Mosque, or Jama Musjid—Relics of the Prophet Mohammed—The Kala Musjid—History of the Siege of Delhi—Incidents during the Mutiny—General Nicholson—The Memorial Column—Departure for Allahabad—Benares—Its Temples—Province of Bengal—Its History—The City of Calcutta—Its History—Its Buildings—Our Journey to Bombay—Departure for England—Arrival in England—Conclusion.

THE city of Shah Juhan, or New Delhi, was built by the Mogul emperor of that name, and must have been approaching completion in the year 1637, the date on which the court removed thereto from Agra. It is a fortified city, and the circuit of its walls is over five miles, while those of the citadel and palace make up another mile and a half. It is entered by ten gates, which pierce the fortifications at different points. It is, without exception, the most interesting of the modern cities of India, not only as affording a glimpse of what the capital of that country was in its greatest splendour and prosperity, but also as possessing the greatest historical interest in connection with our rule, so late even as 1857, when it served as the headquarters of the mutinous Sepoys, and was the very focus of the rebellion. As an Indian city, Delhi contrasts very favourably with many others in the country; its roads are wide, and the houses of the Europeans and better classes of natives are well built and handsome, while the bazaars are spacious, and kept clean and in good order, by the tact and energy displayed by an intelligent municipal council. Being almost entirely a civil station, but few troops are stationed at this place. A battery of artillery and a wing of a British regiment are located in the fort; while in a part of the town termed Durjowgunge are the lines of a native infantry regiment, as well as the houses of many European residents.

There are several noteworthy buildings of modern construction in Delhi, such as the law courts, the Queen's Serai, a huge structure for the accommodation of native and European travellers, and the Delhi Institute, the largest building in the European style of architecture in India; while a pretty drive can be had round the Queen's Gardens, which are tastefully laid out, thence passing into the famous Chandnee Chouk, or principal bazaar of the city. This bazaar is unique of its kind in India; for instead of being, as is generally the case with bazaars, a narrow place blocked up by houses and crowds of natives, it is a long and wide street, with rows of shops on either side, and has a shady walk with a double row of trees down its centre, formed by covering over the canal which in former days ran through its length. This mart of commerce has a very attractive appearance, the shops being filled with rich and showy goods displayed to the best advantage, prominent among them being the beautiful gold and silver jewellery, and the ivory paintings and carvings, for which this city is famous. One can only imagine what this bazaar must have been in the luxurious days of the Mogul empire; for although always thronged with busy crowds, the Chandnee Chouk is no longer what it was. Its glories have ceased, and it is unlikely that the scenes of gaudy pomp once enacted there will ever again meet the eye. The shops are probably as brave in outward show as ever, but the moving throng of richly-dressed nobles, riding on caparisoned horses, lounging on their elephants, or borne along in parti-coloured palankeens, have passed away never to return.

Chief of the many interesting objects to be seen in Delhi—evidences of the power and might of the old Moguls—is the Fort and Palace, the most magnificent structure of the kind in India, which was commenced by Shah Juhan in 1631, and completed, by forced labour, in the space of ten years. It is on the bank of the river Jumna, and is about a mile and a half in circuit, enclosed by an embattled wall of red sandstone nearly sixty feet high, and surrounded by a broad moat, which is separated, on the land side, from the streets of the city by a wide road or esplanade. There are two principal entrances, called the Delhi and Lahore Gates, both splendid buildings of the kind, particularly the first-named, which is probably not surpassed by any similar structure in the world. The lofty embattled walls, the stupendous towers, surmounted by elegant pavilions, the marble domes and gilded minarets, form altogether an unequalled display of taste and magnificence, and give one a high idea of the former splendour of the emperors of Delhi. The main gateway is flanked by two massive angular towers, embattled to correspond with the top of the adjacent wall, and surmounted by two elegant octagonal pavilions with marble domes. The central portion of the building is considerably raised above the towers, in the form of an elaborately-carved screen, supported on a double row of slender columns, with minarets at the ends, and over all are seven small marble domes with gilt spires. Just above the great gateway, which is somewhat concealed by the wall of the court that surrounds it, is a covered gallery, with low balustrades in front. This is entered from a room that formed, in 1857, part of the quarters of Captain Douglas, the commandant of the fortress, who was assassinated on the outbreak of the rebellion. The interior of the Palace corresponds with its noble entrance, and although of the dozen buildings originally contained within its walls some have perished, the most important still exist in good preservation, sufficient to show that, in the meridian glory of the empire, this was a place well worthy to be seen, on account of the richness of its decorations and the splendour of its court.

Mr. Keene, in his valuable work on Delhi, says that the original ground-plan of the Palace, beginning from the northward, embraced, firstly, the Poorj-i-Shumalee, a raised pavilion of white marble, containing the marble bath, inlaid with precious stones; secondly, the waterworks and garden; thirdly, the Dewan-i-khas, opening out of the private apartments reserved for the emperor's own use, all richly incrusted with patterns and inscriptions; fourthly, the block of residences called Imteeaz-Muhul, once splendid with gilding and pietra dura, enclosing a garden about three hundred feet square, with abundant fountains; and fifthly, west of this, the Dewan-i-am, still extant in much of its original beauty of red sandstone and decorated marble. This was the public façade of the palace, forming a sort of hall of justice for the disposal of business in the sight of the public. Many of these buildings and the gardens have been destroyed, or immured in British military constructions; but the principal are left. The first we enter, after passing through the great gateway of the Fort, is the Nowbutkhana, or music-house, a hall devoted to purposes of amusement, and which opened on the Dewan-i-am. This latter—for of the music-house little remains—is a large hall, open at three sides, and supported by rows of red sandstone pillars, formerly adorned with gilding and stucco. In the wall at the back is a staircase leading up to the throne, which is raised about ten feet from the ground, and is covered by a canopy, supported on four pillars of white marble, the whole being curiously inlaid with mosaic work. Behind the throne is a doorway, by which the emperor entered from his private apartments. The whole of the wall here was originally covered with mosaic paintings, in precious stones, of the most beautiful flowers, fruits, birds, and beasts of Hindustan. They were executed by Austin de Bordeaux, a French jeweller, who was in high favour with the Emperor Shah Juhan; but most of this work was destroyed, either before or during the Mutiny, and one can only form an idea of its former magnificence by the restoration in coloured lac.

Proceeding towards the left, the Dewan-i-khas, or hall of special audience, is reached, a smaller hall in *échelon* to the first, raised on a marble estrade about four feet high, with a small but beautifully-carved balustrade of perforated marble on the front side. The columns of this, the finest hall of its kind in India, were inlaid below with precious stones in floral designs, the upper sections, as well as the cornices, being very tastefully gilt; while the ceiling was plated with solid silver, which was torn down by the Mahrattas in 1760. Although the precious stones that formerly adorned this regal hall have vanished, one can still gather somewhat of its appearance in the time of its glory, from the designs and other work having been restored, but in somewhat less costly materials.

In this hall stood the famous Peacock Throne of the Great Mogul, which rested on a white marble platform. The platform still remains in its accustomed place; but of the throne nothing is now left, it having been broken up and carried away when the city was plundered by Nadir Shah in 1739. The following extract from Beresford's *Delhi* fully describes this extraordinary piece of extravagance: "The Peacock Throne was so called from having the figures of two peacocks standing behind it, their tails being expanded, and the whole so inlaid with sapphires, rubies, emeralds, pearls, and other precious stones of appropriate colours, as to represent life. The throne itself was six feet long by four feet broad. It stood on six massive feet, which, with the body, were of solid gold, inlaid with rubies, emeralds, and diamonds. It was surmounted by a canopy of gold, supported by twelve pillars, all richly emblazoned with costly gems, and a fringe of pearls ornamented the borders of the canopy. Between the two peacocks stood the figure of a parrot of ordinary size, said to have been carved out of a single emerald (?). On either side of the throne stood an umbrella, one of the oriental emblems of royalty. They were formed of crimson velvet, richly embroidered, and fringed with pearls. The handles were eight feet high, of solid gold, and studded with diamonds. The cost of this superb work of art has been variously stated at sums varying from one to six millions of pounds sterling. It was planned and executed under the supervision of Austin de Bordeaux, already mentioned as the artist who executed the mosaic work in the Dewan-i-am."

On leaving this hall and turning to the left we enter the Hummam, or Turkish Bath, once beautifully inlaid, and now very creditably restored. At the back is the royal mosque, an elegant structure of white marble, smaller than that in the Agra Palace, but more ornamental. On the opposite or south side of the Dewan-i-khas there still remain the apartments devoted to the sole use of the monarch. The Ghoosal Khana, an exquisite suite of rooms, and the Rung Mahal, all are marvels of white marble work, with floral colouring. These suffice to show the sumptuous though not extensive scale of Shah Juhan's private life.

Such then are the buildings that still remain of the gorgeous Palace of Shahjuhanabad, or New Delhi, and few that see them can refrain from pondering over the startling scenes, mostly tragic, which in the short space of its existence the Palace has witnessed. Here was seen the pomp and state of the Mogul Court during the times of Shah Juhan and his successor, Aurungzebe. Here, in 1716, the Scottish surgeon, Gabriel Hamilton, who cured the Emperor Furrokh Shah on the eve of his marriage, was rewarded by permission to establish a factory, and to maintain a territory on the banks of the Hooghly, which was the foundation of the presidency of Fort William, and all that has since sprung therefrom. Here, on the 31st March, 1739, the degenerate Mogul Mohammed Shah entered the throne-room with the ferocious Nadir Shah, of Persia, and sipped his coffee on the Peacock Throne: next day the invaders massacred the citizens before the dark and terrible eye of their leader, as he looked on from the roof of

Róshun-ud-Dowlah's mosque; the Peacock Throne was broken up, and Nadir returned to Persia with plunder reckoned at eighty millions sterling, according to the value of the day. Here, less than ten years afterwards, the Abdali chief of Cabul, Ahmud Khan, repeated the cruel lesson, and despoiled the Palace of much of its remaining wealth. Here, in 1759, the work was completed by the Mahrattas, under Sudasheo Rao, Bhao, marching to their ruin at Paniput, who tore the silver plating from the ceilings of the throne-room. Here, in 1788, the sanctity of the imperial halls was further violated by the cannon-shot of the Mussulman rebel, Gholam Kadir, who, after his defeat by the united forces of the empire, including the Mahrattas, under their chief, Sindia, then dominant master of the situation, during the troubled times of the dissolution of the Mogul Empire, rushed to Delhi to wreak his last vengeance on the unoffending person of his aged sovereign, Shah Alum. Here he lay and smoked his hookah on the faded substitute of the Peacock Throne, and here he, with his own hands, shared in the torture of the royal family and the blinding of the helpless old Emperor. Here, on the 15th September, 1803, as the sun was setting, the long cavalcade of Lake defiled into the Am-khas, where the blinded chief of the house of Timour was found seated under a small tattered canopy, the remnant of his royal state, with every external appearance of the misery of his condition. Here, in May, 1857, Bahadur Shah, the last representative of the Great Moguls, a not unwilling tool of the Company's mutinous soldiers, consented to the butchery of helpless women and children. And here finally, a few months later, the last scene of all was witnessed in the trial and condemnation to death, as a felon, of the same aged miscreant, by the British in the Dewan-i-am, the famous hall of justice of his ancestors—a sentence commuted into the no less disgraceful one of life-long penal servitude.

The great mosque of Shah Juhan, or the Jama Musjid, which stands in the city not far distant from the Fort, is the next, and after the Palace the chief object of attraction in Delhi. It was begun by Shah Juhan in 1644, and is considered to be a fine specimen of the architecture at that period, and the grandest Mohammedan fane extant in the country. It stands on a rocky eminence less than a hundred yards to the westward of the Palace gates, and has three entrances of handsome gateways of red sandstone, which are approached by magnificent flights of steps of the same material. The principal gateway is on the east, and is much larger and handsomer than those on the north and south. They all lead into a great quadrangle paved with large slabs of sandstone, in the centre of which is a marble reservoir of water. On the west of the square stands the mosque itself, oblong in form, two hundred and one feet in length and one hundred and twenty feet broad, and surmounted by three superb cupolas of white marble crowned with culices or spires of copper richly gilt. The building is partly faced with white marble, and along the cornice are compartments, each ten feet long and two and a half feet broad, which are inlaid with black marble inscriptions in the Niski character.

The interior is paved throughout with slabs of white marble three feet long by one and a half broad, each decorated with a black border. This gives it an extremely beautiful appearance. Part of the inner wall is also faced with plain white marble. Near the kibla, or that part which indicates the direction of the city of Mecca, is a handsome taq or niche, adorned with a profusion of rich frieze-work, which, though joined in several places, appears to have been cut out of a solid block of white marble four feet high and six feet in length. The mosque is flanked by two minarets one hundred and thirty feet high, composed of white marble and red sandstone, placed vertically in alternate stripes, and at about equal distances. There are also three projecting galleries crowned with light pavilions of white marble. Three sides of the terrace on which this magnificent edifice stands are enclosed by a colonnade of sandstone, and each corner is ornamented by an octagonal pavilion of white marble, the supporting columns being of red sandstone. In the quadrangle at the north-east and south-east are low pillars, on the top of which are fixed marble slabs. On one of these is engraved the Eastern hemisphere, on the other are marked certain hour lines; each has an upright iron spike or gnomon, and the shadows thrown by the sun indicate to the faithful the time of prayer. In a sort of shrine, which is opened by the attendant for a small gratuity, there are to be seen also the original Koran and the slipper of the Prophet, as well as some hairs of his beard. Whether true or false, these relics are held in extreme veneration by all true Mussulmans. There are several other fine mosques in the city deserving a visit, more particularly the Kala or Kullan Musjid, and a few temples, especially a Jain temple of recent date; but we have now described the chief objects of interest for which Delhi is renowned.

The taking of Delhi from the mutineers was, perhaps, a

greater feat of arms than many which are more talked about, and one that, without disparagement to native valour, may be truly said to have been impossible except between Europeans and Asiatics. An enceinte of more than five miles, with curtains, bastions, gates, ditch, counterscarp, and glacis, all designed and partly carried out by British engineers, with a strong arsenal and a complete park of heavy guns, was taken by a handful of men at the first serious assault.

The outbreak at Delhi commenced on the 11th May, 1857. Early in the morning the revolted troopers of the 3rd Bengal Cavalry, who had escaped chastisement at Meerut, trotted across the bridge of boats and entered the city. The whole of the garrison, being natives, joined them, and the work of villany began. The resident, and the chaplain and his daughter, were killed near the Fort, and the colonel and other officers of the native regiment were pistolled in front of their own men, standing passive. The Magazine was invested; and the Europeans—men, women, and children—chased over the walls of the city to be shot down, or driven to the temporary shelter of their rallying-point, the Flagstaff tower. The explosion of the Magazine (the remains of which are to be seen near the present post-office) by Willoughby succeeded, and during the confusion many of the defenders forded the Jumna, and, joining the main stream of fugitives, escaped with them to Meerut. Then followed for a time in Delhi a reign of the powers of evil, and no one will ever know the full extent of the horrors that ensued in the long peaceful city of the Moguls. But the day of retribution was at hand; for, on the 8th June, the small avenging column of the outraged British power arrived. Too few in number for assault, they

Siege of Delhi. 445

invested the place, remaining at their posts all through the heat of that and the following months, and, despite their losses by sickness, repulsed in that time no less than five and twenty desperate sorties of the besieged. In the beginning of September reinforcements arrived; and from the 8th to the 13th of that month English artillerymen directed the fire of fifty guns in position upon the northern walls of the city, without cessation day and night, until two breaches were made, one at the Kashmir Bastion and one at the Water Gate, and the assault was fixed for the morning of the 14th, the following day. How the Kashmir Gate was blown in by the Bengal Engineers, and the progress of the assault, is matter of military history. The saddest interest that attaches to it is connected with the fate of General Nicholson, of whom it is recorded that but for him Delhi would not have fallen. This born soldier, after leading his men over the breach by the side of the Kashmir Gate, was shot early in the day, while waving on his force, by the fire from the windows that lined the street down which they were advancing. But his spirit lived on in all ranks; for after severe and arduous fighting for five days, during which a loss of sixty-six officers and one thousand one hundred men was incurred, the whole area of the city remained in the hands of Sir Archdale Wilson and his victorious soldiers. The trial and exile of the king, and the peaceable organization of civil order, followed shortly after; and there is little now to remind the visitor of these brave days, save the monument of Nicholson, and the memorial column, one hundred and ten feet in height, which stands on a commanding point of the ridge, upon the site once occupied by one of the breaching batteries. This monument commemorates the deeds of the gallant captors of Delhi, and was erected by the subscriptions of the survivors, supplemented by aid from the government.

On the 1st of February we left Delhi, and continued our journey to Bombay, passing down the line we had previously travelled, through Toondla, the junction for Agra, Cawnpore, and Allahabad, where we halted for a couple of days. Allahabad has been already described, so nothing more need be said about it, save that it is the central point of departure for travellers, either from Calcutta or Bombay, to visit all the principal places in Hindustan. We had intended, instead of proceeding direct to our destination, to have visited both Benares and Calcutta, the only two of the principal and more interesting cities in India which we had not seen; but the time we had left at our disposal would not admit of this. Having, however, in former days, seen the most noteworthy objects, both in the 'Holy City' and in the 'City of Palaces,' I will venture, to complete this narrative, a short description of these places, and of the province of Bengal proper.

The city of Benares is about ninety miles from Allahabad, and four hundred and seventy-five miles from Calcutta, on the East Indian railway, and is approached by a short branch of that line from the junction of Mogul Serai. The Ganges here makes a sweep of about four miles long, and on the convex side of the curve stands this, the most holy city of the Hindus, believed by the natives not to belong to earth at all, but to be perched upon the top of one of the prongs of the trident of the god Siva. The city from the river presents the form of an amphitheatre, extending for three miles along the banks, here elevated some forty or fifty feet, and above which are reared a series of temples and palaces, with superb ghauts, or flights of steps. The palaces are those of Indian rajahs and chieftains, from one end of India almost to the other, every Hindu potentate being earnestly desirous to have a residence in Benares, so that he may once at least make a pilgrimage to the holy city, and when not there himself may have a resident representative in the shape of some member of his family. The more wealthy Hindus reside in large detached houses surrounded by courts, as is usual in other parts; but in many of the streets, which are exceedingly narrow, the houses are built of stone, six storeys in height, with small windows, the walls being usually daubed over with mythological representations from the Hindu pantheon, and each house containing perhaps two hundred persons. The British and other Europeans reside chiefly at Seroli, a handsome well-built station, about two miles from the city; they are few in number, consisting chiefly of officials administering the affairs of the province, which, with the city, was ceded to us by the Nawab of Oudh in 1775. The proper rajah has since then become merely a stipendiary.

Benares has long been the most celebrated seat of Brahmanical learning in India, and is still so revered at present, while it is crowded with priests and religious mendicants, who live on the alms and offerings of the numerous pilgrims that yearly flock to this place to be purified from all sin. The rajah's palace stands on the opposite side of the river. Near it is a superb temple built by Cheyt Singh, and on an elevated and conspicuous site on the city side of the stream is the mosque of the emperor Aurungzebe, erected in the 17th century—a most magnificent building. There are numerous other mosques; for although this is the head-quarters of the Hindu faith, the Mohammedan conquerors of India took care to leave indisputable signs of their power here. The temples appertaining to the original belief of the country, with which the city of Benares abounds, are, however, the chief attraction to visitors, and are far too numerous to describe. Many, such as the Monkey Temple, are fine buildings, but the majority are small, some being even stuck like shrines in the angles of the streets, and under the shadow of the lofty houses. They are usually covered over with beautiful and elaborate carvings. Fakirs' houses, as they are called, adorned with idols, occur at every turn, while religious mendicants, with self-distorted limbs, and in most hideous attitudes of penance, literally line the chief streets on both sides. Sacred bulls wander about undisturbed, an unceasing tinkling of discordant music prevails everywhere, and the visitor, becoming weary of the crowd, noise, and dirt, is soon glad to beat a hasty retreat from the tortuous streets of the holy city, carrying away with him the impression that the theory one forms of this pagan worship, is as nothing compared to its practice, when seen in its hideous reality.

Leaving Benares, the line passes through the station of Dinapur, the well-known city of Patna, and several other places of lesser note, until it terminates at Calcutta. The latter portion of this journey lies through the province of Bengal proper, a flat and moist country, chiefly remarkable for the weak and puny condition of its inhabitants—the Bengali being inferior in every respect to his more northern brother—and for its being the principal seat of the rice and indigo cultivation.

The City of Palaces.

In former days Bengal was a province of note, enjoying independent sovereignty, and its kings were powerful and long resisted the inroads of the Mohammedan and other invaders of India. Since the year 1758, when Meer Jaffir granted a free tenure of Calcutta to the Company, the power of the Nawabs of Bengal has, however, gradually grown less, and the present representative is nothing more than a pensioner of the British government. The city of Calcutta, the seat of the supreme government of British India, is situated on the left or east bank of the river Hooghly, a branch of the Ganges, about one hundred miles from the sea, and as the river is deep enough for the largest ships to proceed to the town itself, Calcutta is consequently a large and important maritime port. It is about five miles in length, by one and three quarters in its widest part, and is divided into two distinct portions, the northern occupied by natives, the southern by Europeans. In the former, the streets are narrow and the houses mean, presenting in fact the usual characteristics of a native city; but in the latter the streets are spacious, the roads wide, and most of the houses detached, large, and handsome, built of brick and stuccoed. This gives them the appearance of marble structures, and has earned for Calcutta the title of the 'City of Palaces,' which it at present enjoys. The suburbs of Calcutta are extensive. That part known as Garden Reach is the most striking in architectural and park-like features; the houses are inhabited chiefly by Europeans, and possess large and extensive gardens, laid out with fine trees, and gay parterres of tropical and other plants. The city was founded in 1600, but little was done until forty years later, when the East India Company obtained permission to establish their first factory on the Hooghly. Before arriving at its present magnitude, Calcutta had various vicissitudes of fortune, and many were the times that its earliest foreign settlers were driven out by the Nawab of Bengal and other foes.

In 1757 the town extended about half a mile above and below the old fort, called Fort William, which was erected on the site of the village of Kalleeghatta, and thus gave rise to the present nan.e being bestowed on the settlement protected by its walls. In this year the city was plundered by the Nawab Sooraj-oo-Dowlah, and after a spirited defence many of our brave countrymen were taken prisoners, and died of suffocation in a prison at the fort, called the Black Hole, where they had been placed for safe custody. The city was, however, recaptured a few weeks afterwards by Clive. He effectually routed the Nawab, who then signed a treaty that it should be held by the English, and the following year his successor granted it in free tenure. From this date Calcutta became virtually the seat of an independent power, and becoming the capital of British India, increased year by year until it has attained the size and magnificence of the present day. There are many interesting buildings here, chief among them the present Fort William, one of the largest and most regular fortresses in all India, which was constructed by Lord Clive after the battle of Plassey in 1757. It mounts six hundred and twenty guns, and will hold over fifteen thousand men, and is usually garrisoned by an English regiment, one or two native regiments, and a battery of artillery. On the north side of what is termed the Esplanade is Government House, the palace of the Viceroy, a magnificent pile, built by the Marquis of Wellesley. It is a building of stone, and has four wings, with a stupendous dome in the centre, and is surrounded by a colonnade of Ionic pillars. After the Government House, the principal edifices worth noticing are the Town Hall, the Supreme Court, Government Treasury, the Metcalfe Hall, the Hindu College, the Medical College, as well as many churches and monuments, erected to the memory of men illustrious in Indian annals.

We remained at Allahabad for a couple of days, and then went on direct to Bombay. No particular incident occurred during the long railway journey, and we arrived safe and well in that city on the morning of the 6th of February, thirteen days following our departure from Rawul Pindi. The medical board met a few days after our arrival, and I was directed to proceed home by the troopship *Euphrates*, which was to sail on the 23rd of the month. We spent the interval at the Adelphi Hotel, at Byculla, and on the afternoon of the 22nd duly went on board, and settled ourselves in the cabin, which, owing to the fact of my being an invalid, had been granted us for our sole use and benefit. The anchor was weighed at daybreak the following morning; and after a voyage home essentially the same in character as our voyage out, we arrived at Portsmouth on the 27th March, and disembarked at the same spot that had witnessed our embarkation two years previously. Eventful years they had been to us; for we had travelled many thousands of miles, and seen many strange and interesting sights. And having attempted to give a brief record of what we had seen and done from the day of our departure to the day of our return, I will conclude with the earnest wish that my friends and readers will derive some interest and pleasure from following us through the various scenes of Oriental life and travel depicted in these pages, descriptive of our residence in the East.

W. Brendon and Son, Printers, Plymouth.

www.ingramcontent.com/pod-product-compliance
Lightning Source LLC
Chambersburg PA
CBHW022115300426
44117CB00007B/717